The DICTIONARY *of* *Irish Family Names*

The DICTIONARY *of* *Irish Family Names*

Ida Grehan

Roberts Rinehart Publishers

Published in the United States by Roberts Rinehart Publishers,
5455 Spine Road, Boulder, Colorado 80301

Distributed by Publishers Group West

Published in Ireland by Roberts Rinehart Publishers,
Trinity House, Charleston Road, Ranelagh, Dublin 6

ISBN 1-57098-137-X

Library of Congress Catalog Card Number 96-72313

Typesetting:
Red Barn Publishing, Skeagh, Skibbereen, Co. Cork, Ireland

Printed in the United States of America

Foreword

"... This soft land quietly
Engulfed them like the Saxon and the Dane—
But kept the jutted brow, the slitted eye;
Only the faces and the names remain."

—Donagh MacDonagh, *Warning to Conquerors*

The genealogical trail can be a tortuous one that leads the explorer a merry dance through government offices, archives, libraries and newspaper files. On the trail there are many experts and expert sources to be consulted – professional genealogists, historians, historical geographers, passport offices, military records, graves and memorials, death certificates and wills. You need good shoes and a stout heart as you turn detective, storyteller, archaeologist, digging, seeking and ultimately transforming ghosts into ancestors. But however long and winding the search it all begins with a name.

The faces and names of MacDonagh's poem remain but today have been scattered around the globe. It is estimated that the Irish diaspora contains some 70 million people in three continents. Each year Ireland witnesses an influx of visitors as a small portion of that great mass return home – to holiday, to reunite with family and friends and increasingly to claim through research a piece of their past through their roots. In recent times this search for who we are and where we come from has not been confined to the returning exile or visitor. The last decade has seen an unprecedented rise in interest on the part of Irish people living in Ireland in their own personal histories. More and more adult education programmes are springing up in response to this interest and there is now a choice of extra-mural programmes on genealogy and third level diploma courses on local studies and family history.

The first step on the journey of discovery for all should be this generous reference book – the *Dictionary of Irish Family Names.* Irish names are as complex and variant as Irish personalities and Ida Grehan gently guides the reader through the etymology, variant spellings, and geographical distribution of more than five hundred and fifty names. This is a book for family bookshelf and library stack – for the genealogist, local historian, researcher, and for all who have an interest in or curiosity about who is who and where they belong in the great Irish family. Expert, concise and enlightening, this book will answer immediate queries quickly, but I wager that you will find yourself caught up in the author's enthusiasm for her subject and will be quickly tempted to further investigation and deeper study.

Each entry has, along with the standard information about the name and its related forms, fascinating vignettes from Irish history – tempting the reader down leafy byways and historical alleys to seek out more and more information about our famous and infamous sons and daughters. It is these skilfully-drawn pen sketches of key figures in Irish life, both historical and contemporary, which gives this book its distinctive character and which will lure the reader back again and again to dip into this well of information.

Dr. Patricia Donlon
Chief Herald of Ireland

Introduction

The great High King of Ireland, Brian Boru, is said to have invented surnames. He died in battle in 1014, leaving a lasting legacy to Ireland—the name O Brien—a most distinguished one in Irish history. Only in comparatively recent times has the spelling of Irish names been standardized. However, prior to this, they were also anglicized, a process which frequently obscured the original name. Would you, for instance, be able to recognize the name Hennessy as Ó hAonghusa, or the very Irish Murphy as Ó Murchú, or the very numerous Kelly as Ó Ceallaigh?

When families began to use surnames they very often used, or were inflicted with, nicknames. For instance, Ó Súileabháin means one-eyed, and was subsequently anglicized to O Sullivan. Clarke began as Ó Cléirigh, meaning a clerk, and Ahern began as Ó hEachtiarna, meaning lord of the horse—an animal so important it led to a proliferation of Smiths, anglicized from the Irish name MacGabhann.

I have written a number of books on Irish families, the majority of them published in the USA, where over forty million (or 20% of the population) are said to be of Irish extraction—eight times that of the population of contemporary Ireland, the mother country. I regularly get letters from people asking me to throw some light on their Irish ancestry. This could be a very time-consuming and expensive operation, so I try to set them on course for a "do-it-yourself" effort. I tell them to write to the Chief Herald of Ireland at the Irish Genealogical Office in Kildare Street,

Dublin. This office will then send a form to be completed that asks all the possible sources regarding their Irish origins. It will also advise how much the research will cost them, depending on how deep they want to dig into their roots. If they are prepared to do it in style, the Chief Herald will design them a colourful coat of arms.

In fact, this is—more or less—how this dictionary of Irish names came about. I was asked to provide family histories for a company who were designing coats of arms, requested, mostly, from the USA. I find this type of history fascinating, so I broadened my knowledge of Irish names, and consolidated my knowledge of Irish history as well. I discovered many rare names which normally I would not have been able to include in my books, because there were few representatives of the name still to be found in Ireland, never mind the USA, Canada, Australia, or Europe. These included Ratliss, Lawn, Guidry, Wheat, Peoples, Drohan, Bogg and Battle! Weeks were spent dredging through libraries and archives.

It has to be remembered that Ireland is by no means simply a land of Celts, with a few Vikings and Normans sailing in—not forgetting, and now forgiving, the colonizing British. It is good to have a mixed population and we have also welcomed Quakers, Huguenots from France and Jews from all over Europe, while today we are beginning to accept people from the developing countries and from those countries suffering the effects of tyrannical dictators. There is no standing still.

The demands made on the Genealogical Office have overstretched it to such an extent that it is now in the process of being reorganised. However, there is one contemporary aspect of genealogy that will some day have to be considered—the single parent phenomenon. A child may know his or her mother, but not always the father. And this can engender a further complication—that of brothers and sisters who have different fathers.

The history of a country is reflected in the history of its families. This particularly applied to Ireland, where, from earliest times, each clan or sept had their specific balladeers who recited their genealogies through the generations—very important for a man expecting to be accepted as chieftain. Today, there are still many families with authenticated chieftains, for instance the O Connors, the O Neills and the O Briens, who can trace their male blood line back two thousand years. Some families, like the O Neills or the O Dohertys, settled in Europe following the "Flight of the Wild Geese", when the Irish army was defeated after the battle of the Boyne. Today, many young Irish men and women travel all over the world, and often live and work abroad. The Irish are now a highly educated people, who excel in the worlds of commerce, academia or the arts—literature in particular.

Not everyone will want to read this book from cover to cover. It is for dipping into and finding what interests you. The families are arranged in alphabetical order, ignoring the prefix O. Names beginning with O are listed under the main stem of the name, preceded by the O in brackets—e.g. (O) Reilly is under the "R"s. Also, it should be noted that Mc is simply an abbreviation of Mac, and so they are treated as one. Many families gave up their Irish prefix and anglicized their names, in the bad old days when Irish surnames were outlawed. The prefixes Mac and O denote descent: Mac means son of, while O indicates that the name derives from a grandfather or earlier ancestor.

Another phenomenon to note is that, because of the standardization of spelling, the influx of people of different nationalities and the anglicization of Irish names, there are often many different ways of spelling the same name. This process continued when families emigrated. MacEnenany can now be spelled in at least 25 different ways! With this in mind, I have cross-referenced many alternatives and derivatives in the Dictionary. The main heading for each name is the common anglicized version, and the original Irish is given beneath that. A few of the variants of the name are listed after the Irish version.

Each entry begins with a brief etymology of the given name, related forms, origins, and geographical distribution. I have then given a few examples of famous people who have borne the name, arranged chronologically, relating brief anecdotes about their lives, or explaining their claim to fame, often one of historical significance, in which case I provide some Irish background history.

I would hope that the Dictionary will be of interest to both the serious genealogist and the more casual reader interested in learning more about Ireland's family names, especially those colourful characters who made Irish history. To those living outside the country I would say maybe your interest in your Irish roots will eventually inspire you to make a visit to Ireland, possibly to do your own research.

The study of genealogy is a minefield of minutiae and particulars. Scholars and historians, not to mention devoted family members, lie ready to pounce on the slightest error. Without a doubt, accuracy is absolutely essential in this scientific art and in my painstaking research, I have tried at all times to maintain the highest standards. Nonetheless, I apologise in advance if someone is offended by any detail they find in any way inaccurate. I would warmly welcome their advice or any additional information they can provide for any future edition of what I hope will be a continually evolving work.

Glossary

Barony	An administrative area, smaller than a county, used officially until 1898
Brehon	Brehon Law prevailed in Ireland from about the eighth century until the late middle ages
Chief of the Name	The genealogically prominent member of a Gaelic family
Co-arb	A monastic figure of early Ireland
Crests	Symbols used on the top of armorial bearings
Dáil Éireann	The Irish Parliament
Dalcassians	A powerful sept emanating from east Clare
Erenagh	A lay steward of church land
The Fourteen Tribes of Galway	A group of wealthy merchants who controlled the affairs of the city of Galway. Mostly Norman, their names were: Athy, Blake, Bodkin, Browne, d'Arcy, Deane, Ffont, Ffrench, Joyce, Kirwan, Lynch, Martin, Morris and Skerret. Many of these names still survive
Gallowglass	A mercenary from Scotland who served in Irish armies
Pale	An area from Drogheda to Wicklow in which the writ of the English monarchy ran very strongly
Rapparee	Derived from the Irish *ropaire*. A term applied to the Irish who were dispossessed of their land in the seventeenth century, and who took to the mountains and continued to wage war on the new settlers
Seanad	The Senate (Irish upper house)
Sept	The official term for a group of the same family name. The term clan is used in Scotland.

Acheson

Aitcheson Aitchison Askerson

This is a Scottish name, derived from a diminutive of Adam. From the fourteenth century, the Achesons held high administrative office in Aberdeen.

In 1611, **Archibald Acheson** came to Ireland, where he received large grants of land in counties Armagh and Cavan. In 1628, he was created Baronet of Nova Scotia, where he also acquired land. For many years he was Solicitor-General, Senator of Justice and Secretary of State for Scotland, yet he died in 1634 in Letterkenny in County Donegal.

A descendant of Sir Archibald, born in 1718, was created Baron of Gosford, in Market Hill, County Antrim, and his family went on to become viscounts and earls.

The Acheson who was **2nd Earl of Gosford** in the nineteenth century—he was Governor of Canada—built the first "Norman Revival" castle. It was financed by his wife, a Sparrow heiress, who subsequently returned to Suffolk when they became estranged. When she died, he sent for her body to be buried in Armagh. However, it was lost *en route* through the carelessness of drunken servants. Years later it was found in a church in the English Midlands by a rector who was able to identify her by the coronet she had been wearing.

The **4th Earl of Gosford**, a friend of Edward VII, lived very lavishly and, in 1921, had to sell Castle Gosford and its contents to pay his debts. It has passed through many hands since then, even at one time becoming a base for a circus!

Various branches of the Acheson family filtered through to Wexford, Monaghan and to Donegal, where a **Sir Archibald Acheson** claimed vast territories in the Rosses of Donegal.

The Achesons are most numerous in the Six Counties of Ulster where, until recently, they were linen merchants at Castlecaulfield in County Tyrone.

Agnew

Ó Gnímh

There are a number of different lines to be followed in disentangling the sources of the Agnew name.

In Irish the name is Ó Gnímh (*gnímh* signifies "action"). Scholars have suggested that they left to settle in Scotland but, some generations later, returned as mercenary soldiers to County Antrim. Here they became more literary than military and were appointed hereditary poets to the noble Ó Neills of Clanaboy. In due course, their name was anglicized to Agnew.

From the Bocages of Normandy, the **Baron d'Agneaux** came with the Norman invasion in the twelfth century. He settled in Ulster, where he was given the lordship of Larne and afterwards adopted the name Agnew.

Many Agnews, fighting for the restoration of their Scottish kingdom, left to settle in Scotland. Others remained in Ireland and, until the twentieth century, they held over 10,000 acres of prime land in the Larne district. The Belfast Public Records Office holds many accounts of their pedigrees, lands and mansions in County Antrim, the county in which, by an odd coincidence, Agnews of all the different origins settled.

James Willson Agnew (1815–1901), formerly of Ballyclare, County Antrim, was Premier of Australia.

Spiro Theodore Agnew (1918–96) was the 39th Vice-President of the USA, elected in 1968 and 1972 under the presidency of Richard M. Nixon. However, Agnew was not his given name, but was shortened from his Greek name, Anagnostopoulos!

Over the past two centuries, many of these Ulster Agnews have played a prominent role in the development of Pennsylvania, USA.

Ahern

Ó hEachtiarna

Ahearne Aheron Hearne Heron

There are few Irish names which begin with the letter A and in fact Ahern should not either, as in Irish it is Ó hEachtighearna, which means lord of the horse. It was anglicized to Ahern or Hearne.

Some genealogists believe that the English name Hearne which is peculiar to Waterford could also be a variant of the Irish name, though others suggest it is of Middle-English origin, deriving from heron. It could also derive from the English word hearne or herne, meaning a nook or corner, demonstrated in a quote from the poet Chaucer: "Lurking in hernes and in lanes blind".

In earliest times, the Ó hEachtighearna were connected with the Dalcassians, an important sept whose chieftains were kings in County Clare and County Limerick. One of these, Mathghamhain (d. 976), drove the Norsemen from Limerick. His descendants are the Aherons or Hearnes, who are still to be found most plentifully in their original territories.

In the Genealogical Office in Dublin there is a pedigree of the O Hearns of Hearnsbrook, County Galway, dating from 1650 to around 1700. It is possible that they were banished from their estates during those disturbed times, for there is a long list of Hearns of Connacht whose lands were forfeited. It could be that they also lost their O prefix at about that time, making it almost impossible now to distinguish the original family of Hearnsbrook from the many other recorded Hearns. There are Hearn wills in the Belfast Public Records Office and a confirmation of arms to the descendants of **Lieutenant-Colonel Daniel James Hearn** of Correa, County Westmeath, a grandson of **Daniel Hearn**, Archbishop of Cashel from 1726 to 1766.

Both the Belfast Public Records Office and the Genealogical Office in Dublin have records from the sixteenth century to the present day showing the pedigrees of Hearn and Heron families. Religious persecution drove many of this family abroad, where they found positions as priests, teachers and civil servants in the French courts.

There is a famous old hostelry known as Hearn's Hotel in Clonmel, County Tipperary.

One of the earliest Irish architects was **John Aheron**. Little is known of him, except that he was probably born in Limerick. He published a treatise on architecture in 1754 which he illustrated with his own drawings. It can be seen in the National Library of Ireland, in Dublin.

William Edward Hearn (1826–88) of County Cavan followed a legal career in Melbourne, Australia, where he was Chancellor of the university.

James A. Hearne (1840–1901), son of immigrants who had come to New York as Ahern, was an actor and a very popular playwright.

Patrick Lafcadio Hearn (1850–1904) was born in Greece of an Irish father and a Greek mother. He had an unhappy childhood with relatives in Ireland and made his name as a writer in Japan, where he lived for most of his life.

John D. Hearn served with the Irish-American brigade in 1865. There was also a distinguished lawyer and diplomat, **John J. Hearne** (1893–1969), who helped frame the Irish Constitution and was a high commissioner in Canada and an ambassador to the United States of America from 1950 to 1960.

Bertie Ahern (b. 1951) trained as an accountant and has represented the Fianna Fáil Party in the Dáil since 1977. He took over the party leadership in 1994.

Aiken *see* (O) Hagan

Allen

Ó hAillín

The Allens or Ó hAillíns (*aill* means rock) are widespread in Ireland, particularly in Ulster to which they came from Scotland, brought over as mercenaries by the Ó Donnells. Originally they were MacAllen, a branch of the warlike Campbells. In Counties Donegal and Derry, the original Scottish MacAllen can be traced from MacCallion.

Allen, especially in Counties Offaly and Tipperary, could be an anglicization of Ó hAllín. Sometimes Allen can be a synonym for Hallinan or Ó Hallinan.

The wily Cardinal Wolsey sent **John Allen** (1476–1534) to be Archbishop of Dublin. Later, when he had also become Chancellor, he was assassinated by followers of the Fitzgeralds.

The various Allens must have integrated well, for, as with the native Irish, there are many seventeenth-century records of their houses and estates being confiscated, although they were eventually to get them back. An Allen estate, St. Wolstan's near Celbridge, County Kildare, was confiscated and given to the Earl of Mount Alexander. It was one of the many fine houses designed in the seventeenth century by **John Allen**, a Dutch architect working in Ireland who was much sought after by the nobility.

The Allens acquired many titles, including a viscountcy held by **John Allen**, MP, in about 1685. They were very much of the landed gentry in counties Dublin, Kildare and Cork.

John Allen (d. 1850) was a friend of the patriot Robert Emmet. **William Philip Allen**, possibly of Cork, was one of the "Manchester Martyrs" executed in 1867 for killing a policeman. More recently, **Atwell Hayes Allen** (d. 1939) of Cork was a distinguished mile runner and yachtsman.

Anderson

Mac Aindriú

Anderson (meaning Andrew's son) as a surname is said to have come from Scandinavia to Scotland, and from there to Ireland in the sixteenth century. There is a record from 1588 of expenses paid to **Sir Edward Anderson** for his services to Queen Elizabeth in Ireland.

During the confiscations following William of Orange's victory at the Boyne, the Andersons were granted many forfeited estates. They subsequently spread around Ireland. One of the family whose seat has been at Grace Dieu at Clogheen, County Waterford, for many centuries—the **Reverend Arthur Anderson**—was chaplain in Ireland to William of Orange. Another member of this family, **General Paul Anderson**, was aide-de-camp to Sir John Moore and died with him in battle in Spain.

The papers, pedigrees, letters and wills of the Andersons are well preserved in the Irish and British archives. They had estates in counties Wicklow and Monaghan and in Ulster, where they are very numerous today. Some followed the colonists to India and to the West Indies and the United States of America.

Paris Anderson, born in Kilkenny in about 1790, was a novelist and essayist, and in 1815 served in the Kilkenny Militia.

Over the period of the Land League disturbances, a Crown Solicitor called **Samuel Lee Anderson** was very prominent in the law courts during the prosecutions of the Fenians.

Sir Robert Anderson (1841–1918) had an unusual career as a lawyer and a member of the secret service, advising on political crime. As head of the Criminal Investigation Department at Scotland Yard in London in 1888, he investigated the murders committed by "Jack the Ripper". He wrote many books of reminiscences and was an ardent Presbyterian. Another **Sir Robert Anderson** was Lord Mayor of Belfast from 1907 to 1909.

The Andersons have long been established in Ireland, where they are very numerous. A remarkable number of them have followed the legal profession.

Andrews

Andrew, the first name of one of the Apostles, has always been a popular name in Christian Europe. In the thirteenth century it was monopolized by the Scots, whose patron saint is Saint Andrew. The Andrews (sometimes MacAndrews) came to Ireland from Scotland in the seventeenth century and have been very numerous there ever since, especially in Ulster. Andrews is also to be found plentifully in the United States of America and in Canada.

In the Public Records Office both in Belfast and Dublin, and in the Genealogical Office in Dublin, there is a wealth of wills, pedigrees, letters, etc., relating to various Andrews families. A letter of 1613 from Viscount Mountgarrett accompanies the present of a goshawk to **Sir W. Andrewes** of Ballyne (Ballina?).

Frances Andrews of County Armagh was a provost of Trinity College Dublin in the mid-eighteenth century. For generations, **John Andrews** and Company Limited were flax spinners, millers, soap boilers, chandlers and farmers in and around Belfast in County Antrim.

The Andrews have always been prominent in the public services. **C. S.** (Tod) **Andrews** (1901–85) was a director of Bord na Móna (the Turf Board), of CIE (the Irish Transport Company), and of the Radio and Television Authority. **David Andrews**, his son, a sportsman, barrister and a politician in the Fianna Fáil Party, has held a number of high ministerial posts in Dáil Éireann. His brother, **Niall Andrews**, is also a politician.

The most renowned representative of the name in Ireland was the highly esteemed and greatly missed **Eamonn Andrews** (1922–87). A Dubliner and sports commentator, he became one of the most popular broadcasters and television personalities, with *The Eamonn Andrews Show* and the long-running *This Is Your Life* series.

Archdeacon *see* Coady

Armstrong

The Armstrongs were a warlike border clan of Mangerton in Scotland. They filtered into Ireland in about the seventeenth century and established a number of Armstrong families in Ulster and the Midlands, owning many estates and fine houses. Armstrong is a numerous name in every area of Ireland, most particularly in Ulster. The great poet W. B. Yeats is a descendant of one branch of the family.

Today, their big houses have mostly disappeared or changed hands. Mount Heaton in County Offaly, according to local legend, had to be sold when it was lost in a game of cards to the Prince Regent. It is now the guest-house to a Cistercian Abbey. Gallen Priory, the former home of the Armstrong baronets at Ferbane, County Offaly, is a convent.

In Ireland and abroad, including the USA and Canada, the Armstrongs have been well represented in the Church and in the services. **Sir Alexander Armstrong** (1818–99) of County Fermanagh, a naval surgeon and explorer, accompanied Sir Robert McClure in search of the north-west passage and wrote a personal narration of this important discovery.

James Armstrong (1780–1839) of County Down was a founder member of the Irish Unitarian Society and he wrote an important Presbyterian biography. **George Armstrong** (1846–1906) was professor of history and literature at Queen's College, Cork.

Earlier this century, **Sir William Armstrong** was President of the National Gallery of Ireland. **Lindsay Armstrong** (b. 1942) is a distinguished oboist and was a director of the Royal Academy of Music in Dublin. He was one of the founders of the Irish Chamber Orchestra.

The **Reverend David Armstrong** was driven from his Limavady parish, County Derry, because he went to give Christmas greetings to the local Roman Catholic parish priest during the violence in Northern Ireland.

The Armstrongs are exceedingly well documented in *Burke's Landed Gentry of Ireland* and *Burke's Irish Family Records*, as well as in the many papers in Dublin's Genealogical Office and in the Public Records Offices in Dublin and Belfast.

Arragan *see* Horgan

Arthur *see* MacArthur

Ashe *see* Nash

Athy

It has been suggested that this Norman family adopted its name from the town of Athy in County Kildare, where they may have first settled. In his *History of Galway*, Hardiman writes: "This family is of great antiquity in Galway where there is a tradition one of them erected the first stone house or castle in the town; they were certainly amongst the oldest members of the Fourteen Tribes of Galway and were adherents of Richard de Burgo when he founded the town." The family motto was *Ductus non coactus* (Led not forced).

A **William de Athy** is recorded as being Treasurer of Connacht in 1388, with a fee of £10 yearly. The Athys also filled important roles in other parts of Ireland. **John de Athy** was Sheriff of Kerry and was appointed by Edward II (1284–1327) as Marshal of Ireland.

Later he moved to Ulster, to Carrickfergus in County Antrim, to act as sheriff there. Another **John Athy** was sovereign of Galway in 1426 and again in 1438.

There were serious differences between the Athys and the Blakes, one of the most powerful and enduring of the Galway families. This led to a deadly dispute which, in about 1440, all but exterminated the whole Athy family. The last recorded member of this ancient family was **Philip Lynch Athy**, who was living at Renvyle, County Galway, in *c.*1800.

Other than two entries in the telephone directory for Dublin city and county, the Athy name would appear to be almost extinct.

Aylmer

Aighlmear

The Aylmers (the name derives from a first name) are a distinguished Anglo-Irish family who settled in the thirteenth century in counties Dublin, Kildare and Meath, where they owned considerable estates.

Sir Gerald-George of Donadea Castle, County Kildare, inherited "Lyons", another fine property in Kildare. **Bartholomew Aylmer** rose in the legal profession to become Chief Justice and in 1622 was created a baronet.

The Aylmers followed the fatal Stuart cause in Ireland in the seventeenth century, as a result of which they lost their civil rights and forfeited their property, and many were banished to Connacht. Later, much of their property was restored to them by Charles II.

They were both military and naval men and many achieved high naval rank. **Matthew Aylmer**, a rear-admiral and Governor of Greenwich Hospital, was elevated to the title of Lord Aylmer. A number of his successors were also admirals.

In the army, the Aylmers died in "far foreign fields". **Henry Aylmer**, born in 1776, was drowned at St. Petersburg, while others ended their days in Calcutta or Canada. On the European battlefields, **George Aylmer** of Kildare, a Knight of St. Louis, was wounded in 1775 fighting with St. Clare's Regiment. **Captain Baltazard André Aylmer**, a Chevalier of St. Louis, transferred from St. Clare's to Berwick's Irish Regiment in France.

Sir Fenton Gerald Aylmer, the 15th Baronet of the 1622 creation, lives in Canada. **Michael Aylmer**, the 13th holder of the baronetcy awarded his naval forebear, is a London solicitor.

All branches of this widespread but not numerous family rejoice in the unusual motto "Hallelujah!" Four books, including *The Aylmers of Ireland* by **Sir F. J. Aylmer** published in London in 1931, record the family pedigrees.

B

Bailey

Ó Bealaigh

Baily Baillie

Bailey is an Anglo-Norman name which derives from the word "bailey" (or *le bailiff*), a king's officer or sheriff. It is scarcely to be found in Dublin but is numerous elsewhere, particularly in Northern Ireland, where they came three centuries ago or more with the colonizers. The name is very common in England and Scotland.

Bailey, or Bailie, could also be an anglicization of the old Irish name Bealach (meaning thick-lipped). A son of Bealach is said to have been the second Christian King of Leinster around the sixth century.

The Baileys are very well recorded. Included among the many papers and documents relating to this family is mention of their lands at Grantstown in County Tipperary from 1676 to 1934.

Enquiries were made in 1628 regarding a **W. Baillie** of County Donegal, who was suspected of the treason of letting his land to the "mere Irish"!

In 1649 there were three **John Baileys** serving as clothiers and vintners in the Cromwellian army. **R. Baily** is recorded as being a page to Lord Chesterfield, Duke of Dorset in *c.*1750. In 1902, **George A. Bailie** of Augusta wrote the *History and Genealogy of the Family of Bailie of the North of Ireland.*

Baileys also served in the Irish-American regiments, where there is a record of **Private Daniel Bailey** of the 164th Regiment of New York in *c.*1864. Also in the nineteenth century, the Genealogical Office in Dublin licensed the Reverend Thomas Robert Gage to take the additional name Baillie. **T. R. Baillie Gage** (*c.*1848–1908) was solicitor to the Post Office in Ireland.

The most famous Baily was the British engineer **Sir Donald Coleman Baily** (b. 1901) who designed the prefabricated, mobile bridge which was used extensively during the Second World War and was known as the Baily Bridge.

Baker

Báiceír

Baker, an occupational surname from the Norman *le Bakere*, is very numerous in both England and Ireland. As le Bakere it came first with the Normans in the thirteenth century and, later, with the soldiers of the Commonwealth who acquired confiscated Irish estates.

The Bakers, though never greatly distinguished, have been well recorded. The Public Records Office in Belfast has a great collection of papers connected with a diversity of Baker families. There is a history of the **Cole-Bakers** of Ballydavid, County Tipperary, during the period 1800 to 1950, and also of the **Bakers** between 1620 and 1920.

From 1703 to 1747 there are many papers concerning the Bakers of Ballytobin, County Kilkenny, and a vast selection of papers relate to the Bakers of counties Dublin, Kildare, Kilkenny, Wexford and Wicklow. For 1822, there is preserved an estimate "for building a new chariot for **Abraham White Baker** of County Kilkenny". There are also orders from the Duke of Berwick (1670–1734), the French general and natural son of James II who fought with him at the Boyne, to a **Colonel Peter Baker** to form a regiment at Limerick.

Burke's Irish Family Records (1976) gives the lineage of the Bakers of Lismacue, County Tipperary, whose ancestor, **Thomas Baker**, settled in County Tipperary in around 1640. One of this family was High Sheriff for Tipperary in 1726.

An architect, **Henry Aaron Baker**, succeeded the great James Gandon as Master of the Architects' Society School in Dublin. He designed the charming fountain opposite the National Gallery in Dublin's Merrion Square in 1791.

Bannan

Ó Banáin

Bannon

There were several septs of this name, the more important of which were those of counties Kilkenny and Fermanagh. The derivation of the name is obscure. It is certainly not from the Irish word *bán*, meaning white. There are some who think it may have come from a similar word, without the accent, *ban*, meaning woman.

Leap Castle in County Offaly, once a fortress of the O Carrolls and one of the most haunted castles in Ireland, is said to have got its name, Léim Uí Bhanáin, from a possibly earlier occupation by the Ó Banáin.

Another sept had its territory around Loch Mask in County Mayo, where there is a town named Ballybannon.

In one of the ancient records, the *Analecta Hibernica*, compiled *c.*1712, there are many Fermanagh pedigrees, including almost one hundred pages covering Muintir Bhanán—the Bannan country.

Maelpatrick O Banan was Bishop of Conor from 1152 to 1172. **Gelasius Ó Banán**, an Abbot of Clones in County Monaghan, was Bishop of Clogher from 1316 to 1319.

There is a record of 1585 showing an O Bannaghan as possessing estates in Rathmullan in County Sligo, where the O Bannans were once very important people.

There were Bannons who owned Broughall Castle, near Kilcormac in County Offaly. In the Dublin Genealogical Office there is a record of a grant of arms made in 1911 to the descendants of **Edward Banon** of Rathcastle to his great-grandson, **Christopher James Patrick Banon**, eldest son of **Edward Joseph Banon**, both of Broughall Castle. This family seems to have originated in County Westmeath.

Theresa Bannan (*c.*1776–1847) had a book published by Putnam in New York entitled *Pioneer Irish of Onondaga*. The Onondaga are a native American tribe who have a reservation in New York state.

Barnacle *see* Coyne

Barrett

Baróid

Both in England and Ireland, this is a very numerous surname. The Barretts came to Ireland with the Normans around 1169. Baroid is Norman-French for son of Baraud. There were at one time two distinct families, one of which settled in Connacht, while the other, and by far the most numerous today, became established in Munster, mostly in the County Cork area.

In County Mayo they were lords of Tirawley, where they followed the Irish tradition and founded a sept with a Chief of the Name. The County Cork Barretts who allied themselves with the Irish during the various uprisings held their land until the confiscations of William III in 1691 deprived the head of the family, **Colonel John Barrett**, of twelve thousand acres. He had raised an army for James II and, after the defeat at the battle of the Boyne, he served in France and was killed in action. Some Barretts also served in the Commonwealth armies, while others went to join the armies of North America.

George Barrett (1732–84), born in Dublin, made his name in London as a landscape painter. He was one of the founders of Dublin's Hibernian Academy and was a Master Painter at the Chelsea Hospital.

John Barrett (1753–1821) of County Leix, a clergyman scholar, lived for fifty years in a garret in Trinity College Dublin, where he was a professor of oriental languages. A thorough eccentric, he hoarded his money, never allowing himself any heat in his room, and left all his money "to feed the hungry and clothe the naked", a situation to which he was no stranger.

Richard Barrett (*c.*1740–1810), known as the "Poet of Erris", was an active member of the revolutionary United Irishmen. **Michael Barrett**, a Fenian, was executed for an attempt to blow up a prison. His was the last public execution in England. Another **Richard Barrett** was executed in 1922, at the height of the Civil War in Ireland.

The family is well recorded in the archives. There are a number of Barretts who have assumed a second name, such as Boyd Barrett, Barret Leonard and Barrett Hamilton.

Barron

Ó Bearáin

Barún

Although this surname is derived from the word "baron", it is not, in fact, English. It sprang up spontaneously in two different areas.

In Ulster, the MacBarrons were a branch of the numerous O Neills. In 1598 **Art MacBarron**, an illegitimate brother of an O Neill who was Earl of Tyrone, was one of the chief men of Armagh. Later they dropped the Mac prefix. Barronstown, near Dundalk in County Louth, is a reminder of the name.

In the south they were a junior branch of the Dukes of Leinster, of the FitzGerald family, who were barons of Burnchurch in County Kildare and, up until the seventeenth century, had assumed the name "Barron alias FitzGerald". The Barron name had been in existence long before the arrival of the Norman FitzGeralds.

These Barrons spread throughout Munster where, at one time, they owned approximately ten thousand good acres. They were Catholic and Jacobite, which caused them to lose much of their property. Many went away to join the armies of Europe and America. There are a number of Barron pedigrees in the Dublin Genealogical Office recording their aristocratic connections, especially with France and with the Vatican in Rome. They also owned extensive mines in Mexico.

In County Waterford, Carrick Barron, Georgestown House, Glenanna, Stradbally and Woodstown—where Jacqueline Kennedy stayed—were some of the very fine Barron houses.

Roland Barron, alias FitzGerald, was Archbishop of Cashel from 1553 to 1561. **Milo Barron**, alias FitzGerald, who was Bishop of Ossory, was said to have died in 1553 of grief because of the dissolution of the monasteries.

Henry Barron (b. 1929) was the first of the Jewish faith to be appointed a judge of the Irish high court.

Neither Barrons or MacBarrons are very numerous, though they are still to be found around Ireland.

Barry

de Barra

Barrymore

Two Barry brothers from Wales who took part in the Anglo-Norman invasion of Ireland in 1170 were the progenitors of the innumerable Barry family. They branched out from the vast acreages granted them in County Cork into different septs. There were so many Barrys that they became subdivided and were known as Barry Mór (meaning big, or senior), Barry Óg (young, or junior), Barry Roe (red), Barry Maol (bald) and Barry Láidir (strong). They were ennobled as Earls of Barrymore and Viscounts of Buttevant, a small County Cork town which acquired its French name from the motto on their family crest, *Boutez en avant* (strike forward), the clan rallying call!

Their loyalties were sometimes divided. Some fought with the Irish, while others were on the English side. Like their Irish compatriots, many joined the trail to the battlefields of Europe.

In the eighteenth and nineteenth centuries, they played a prominent part in medicine, law and the arts. The distinguished painter, **James Barry** (1741–1806), was a member of London's Royal Academy.

Drama and acting was a Barry characteristic. The **7th Earl of Barrymore** built a theatre and squandered his Castlelyons estate. He and his two brothers fled to London, where they became Regency rakes. They were such notoriously bad characters that the Prince Regent dubbed them "Hellgate", "Cripplegate" and "Newgate".

Commodore John Barry (1745–1803), formerly of Wexford, is known as the "father of the American navy". Many Barrys emigrated to the USA, where they were active in the army, the public services and on the stage. The trio of Barrymore stage and screen actors, **Ethel, John and Lionel Barrymore**, Philadelphia's "royal family", were but a generation or so away from Cork.

During the War of Independence in Ireland there were two Barry patriot heroes, **Kevin Barry** and **Commander Tom Barry**.

Barrys still abound in Cork and its environs. Their many estates have been mostly dispersed, but Fota Island stands out like a jewel in the crown. It was sold to University College Cork in 1975. The Royal Zoological Society of Ireland looks after the estate, a wildlife park for the preservation of endangered wild animals, including cheetahs. The splendid arboretum pays tribute to former Barry horticulturists.

Battle

Mac Concatha

There are few representatives in Ireland of this rare old Irish name. It derives from *cú catha*, which means hound of battle, or war hound. Reverend Patrick Woulfe, an expert on the history of Irish names and surnames, thinks it was absurdly anglicized to Battle instead of the more euphonious and reasonable MacConcathy.

Until the late sixteenth century the Battles were living in Coolaney in County Sligo.

The Battles, or Battells, who are numerous in England take their name from the old French, de la Bataille. Despite the similarity of the name, there is no connection with the Irish family.

Beaumont *see* Beeman

Beeman

Beauman Beaumont Buamann

This name, which is rarely found as a surname in Ireland, must have suffered a transformation in its crossing of the Atlantic. It is thought to derive from the surname Beaumont. Other variations are Baumann and Buamann, but Beaumont remains the most likely origin. The name is Norman and is frequently found as a place name in France, *beau mont* meaning a fair mount, or hill.

A family of Beauman who were mentioned in *Burke's Landed Gentry of Ireland* owned two manor houses in the nineteenth century, Furness in County Kildare and Tara in County Wexford.

Lady Octavia Beaumont, who married **Sir George Beaumont**, 9th Baronet, was the last member of the Wallis family to live in Drishane Castle in Millstreet, County Cork. This castle, which she had inherited through a previous marriage to a Wallis, is now a convent.

In the Paris archives there are letters from King Henry IV of France to the **Comte de Beaumont**, the French Ambassador, concerning the Catholics of England and the passage of the Spaniards to Ireland in 1605. In 1666, letters from Elizabeth, Queen of Bohemia, to the Archbishop in Ireland, recommend **Dr. G. Beaumont** to be Dean of Derry.

Among the many records of Irishmen who served in the French armed forces at Limoges, it is mentioned that a **P. J. de Beaumont** was there in 1702.

In Britain there are countless Beaumonts—many of them of the nobility—in politics, the arts and sciences.

Begley

Ó Beaglaoich

Morris

Translated from the Irish, this name means little hero. The sept originated in Donegal, where their territory was the barony of Kilmacrenan. Nearby Tulloghobegley perpetuates their name, which is still more numerous in the north than in the south.

A branch of the sept migrated south at the end of the fifteenth century to serve as gallowglasses, or mercenary soldiers, to the MacSweeneys of Cork.

The Begleys followed the usual pattern of confiscation and transplantation. They seem to have transplanted themselves to France, where **Conor Begley**, who lived in Paris, helped Hugh MacCurtin in the compiling of his *English–Irish Dictionary*, which was published in 1732. In this they were also helped by the **Abbé Thadé Begley**, who had a special Irish type cast for its printing.

Henry Begley (d. 1895) of Limerick was a highly respected landscape painter, and in more recent times **John Canon Begley** wrote the valuable, three-volume *History of the Diocese of Limerick.*

For some obscure reason, Morris is used as a synonym for Begley in the Enniskillen area of County Fermanagh.

Donal Begley was for some years the Chief Herald of the Irish Genealogical Office which has recently been moved from its four hundred years' residence in Dublin Castle to new premises in Dublin's Kildare Street, close to the National Library and the Dáil.

Behan

O Beacháin

Beacháin could mean a bee, or it could have been a nickname for a small child. The Ó Beacháins were a Leinster sept whose territory in early times took in parts of the counties of Kildare, Offaly and Leix. They produced two important bishops. **Hugh O Beaghan** was Bishop of Iniscathy, near Limerick, in 1188 and **Donat** (or Daniel) **Beaghan** (d. 1544), a Franciscan, was Bishop of Kildare during the troubled sixteenth century.

A strong literary streak predominates in the Behan family, who have been repeatedly recorded in the great books, including the *Annals of Loch Cé* and the *Annals of the Four Masters.* They were described as "eminent historians", particularly **Donal O Behan** (d. 1411) and **Conor O Behan** (d. 1376).

The father of **Brendan Behan** (1923–64) was a Dublin housepainter who enthralled his family by telling them tales of old Ireland and reading from the English classics. Brendan Behan left school at fourteen to follow his father's trade but was soon active in the IRA. During several periods of imprisonment he learned Irish, read omnivorously and began to write. After his release, he worked for a while for the media. His plays made him one of the most popular and notorious playwrights on both sides of the Atlantic, as well as in England. A brilliant wit was laid low by alcohol and diabetes and he died at the early age of forty-one.

John Behan (b. 1938) is a leading modern sculptor in metal. He has exhibited widely and his many commissions can be seen in offices, hotels and other public places around Ireland.

(O) Beirne

Ó Birn

With or without the O prefix, the Beirnes are an important sept of north Connacht, especially in the County Roscommon area where many have remained until the present day. Although the pronunciation of the name is somewhat similar, they are in no way connected with the O Byrnes of County Wicklow.

The armorial bearings of the Beirnes are particularly colourful. A green lizard sits at the base of an orange tree with a red saltire, or cross, to one side. In the top section of the shield, on a blue background, there is a silver crescent and a smiling golden sun.

In the late eighteenth century, two Beirne brothers were remarkable for their religious divergence. They were sent to France to study for the priesthood and, subsequently, one became a County Meath parish priest, while the other became the Protestant Bishop of Meath!

Many O Beirnes distinguished themselves in the armies of France, Spain and America. A much-wounded, much-decorated brevet **Brigadier-General James O Beirne** from Ireland played a prominent role in the American Civil War.

The Beirnes, or O Beirnes, are still very numerous west of the River Shannon. In Irish the name is Ó Birn or Ó Beirn, which is thought to come from the Norse name Bjorn.

Benison *see* Gildea

Bennett

Bennett is a very numerous name both in Britain and Ireland. It comes from the French name, Benoit, or, in Latin, Benedictus, meaning a blessing.

Benet was the name of an Anglo-Irish family which was prominent in counties Westmeath and Tipperary from at least the thirteenth century. They were landowners, priests, administrators and, in some cases, criminals—such as **Nicholas Bennett**, who was hanged *c.*1295 for stealing. **John Benet** was a Bishop of Cloyne from 1523 to 1536, while **William Bennett** was the Church of Ireland Bishop of Cloyne from 1802 to 1820. **Sir Henry Bennett**, afterwards Lord Arlington, was granted forfeited Irish land by Charles II.

In the counties of Kilkenny and Kildare, there are innumerable bridges, streets and towns bearing the Bennett prefix.

In the nineteenth century there were a number of distinguished Bennets. The son of the Recorder of Cork, **Edward Halloran Bennett**, was a president of the Royal College of Surgeons in Ireland. **Art Bennett** of Armagh was a poet and satirist.

It is thought that the founder of the *New York Herald*, **James Gordon Bennett**, was of Irish, as well as Scottish, ancestry. There were a number of Bennett officers serving with the 69th New York Volunteers.

The journalist **Louie Bennett** (1870–1956) was a pioneering writer for women's rights. In 1932 she became the first woman president of the Irish Trades Union Congress.

It is possible that, in some instances, Bennett is an anglicization of the Irish name Buineáin, which may also have become Bunyan.

Benson

Mac Binéid

Although this surname is fairly common in Ireland, most particularly in Ulster, its origin is English, deriving from the sixth-century Saint Benedict who founded the most famous monastery in Italy, Monte Cassino. Benedict was also the name of fifteen popes!

The Bensons were long established in Westmoreland, England, where one of their properties, The Fault, has been recorded in earliest times. They were ancestors of the Bensons who came to Ireland in the early seventeenth century. They were remarkable for the number of high offices they held in the Church, including a dean of Connor, Monaghan and Belfast, and Archdeacon of Down and Rector of Hillsborough **Trevor Benson** (b. 1790). Many graduated from Trinity College Dublin, including one who was Rector of Blessington in County Wicklow and Adamstown in County Wexford. Descendants of this Westmoreland family have been living for generations near Fermoy, County Cork.

There have been several distinguished Benson architects, prominent among whom was **Sir John Benson** (1812–74), who was born in Sligo. An engineer as well as an architect, he was surveyor in County Cork where he was very active in famine relief works. He designed St. Peter's Bridge in Cork city and the city's waterworks. He was knighted for his design for the prestigious Dublin Industrial Exhibition in 1850.

Dr. Charles Benson, a scholar, was a member of the Royal Irish Academy during the mid-nineteenth century.

One family of Bensons in England produced a remarkable line of authors, archbishops, an actor and a private chamberlain to Pope Pius X.

In more recent times, **Des Benson** (b. 1927), a Gaelic footballer, was the winner of two All-Ireland medals for Cavan.

(O) Bergin

Ó hAimheirgin

Beirgin

The Irish form of Bergin is Ó hAimheirgin and it means descendant of Aimrgin, meaning wondrous birth, which must signify something special about Aimrgin's arrival! In the course of time the name became transformed to Ó Meirgin, Merrigan and Berrigan.

In medieval times, the Bergins were chiefs of the barony of Geashill in County Offaly in the Midlands, where they are still very numerous. However, they have not come to the fore in history. In the records there is an account of "an indenture between Oliver Sentledger and **Rory O Bergin** concerning a grant for four years of Rosconnell and other towns, 1537".

In about 1860, a **G. Bergin** wrote a series of letters concerning the Irish brigade in the papal service. However, the most outstanding bearer of the name was **Osborn Bergin** (1873–1950) of Cork. An eminent Celtic scholar, he was an important contributor to the study of modern Irish. He studied early Irish in Germany, was the first professor of early and medieval Irish in University College Dublin, and the first director of the School of Celtic Studies in the Dublin Institute for Advanced Studies. When he was a student he often cycled as much as eighty miles a day collecting Irish sayings from the old people of the Munster Gaeltacht.

Liam Bergin was editor of the *Nationalist and Leinster Times*, the first Irish newspaper to win a major UK design award.

Patrick Bergin is a well-known actor internationally, while his brother **Emmet** stars in the popular Irish television soap, *Glenroe*.

Bevins

Bevan Bevin Bevand

This surname is not numerous anywhere in Ireland. Although it has been in Ireland for a number of generations, in fact it comes from Wales, where Bevan means son of Evan (i.e. Ab Evan). It has also been credited with being a double patronymic—part Welsh, part English, including the English surname Beddoes in its many variations.

In Irish archives there is a reference to some articles of agreement between the Commissioners "for providing shipping etc. for transplantation of their Majesties' forces to Ireland from Swansea in Wales" in a ship of 203 tons called the *Exchange*, of which **W. Bevan** was the owner in 1690.

In the Dublin Public Records Office, in the encumbered estates files, there is mention of the court rental of lands of Newcastle, Kilconnell, etc., in the barony of County Galway, the property of **William Bevan**, sold in 1854.

The Belfast Public Records Office holds a Deed of Trust of 1892. One of the trustees included Baron Magherамore and there is mention of, among others, **Francis Augustus Bevan**.

Otherwise, one must go to Britain to follow the careers of the tempestuous **Aneurin Bevan** (1897–1960), one of thirteen sons of a Welsh miner who worked his way through trade unionism to become a Labour Party leader, one of Winston Churchill's most irreverent opponents and the man who, as Minister of Health, introduced the revolutionary National Health Service to Great Britain.

Ernest Bevin (1881–1951), born in Somerset in England, was orphaned before he was seven years old. By self-education and his work for the trade unions, from van boy to truck driver to clerk, he rose to become a prominent figure in the British Labour Party. He was a member of Churchill's war cabinet and was a very successful Foreign Secretary.

Birney *see* MacBirney

Bissett *see* MacKeon

Black

Black, a very common name all over Ireland and most especially in Ulster, has a wide choice of origins. It is a common English surname, denoting colour. It is also a collective name of three Scottish clans: Lamont, MacGregor and MacLean of Duart. In Gaelic, whether Scottish or Irish, *dubh* means black.

In 1902, Isaac Ward edited a book on the *Black Family of Ulster*. The majority of the Blacks came to Ireland with the Cromwellians. They are well recorded in Belfast's Public Records Office, where correspondence, travel journals and account books are kept by a Black family who were merchants in Bordeaux, Cadiz, Belfast, London, Edinburgh and Dublin, dating from 1716 to about 1815.

There are also eighty letters from **John Black** to his brother Robert, of Bowman, Black and Company of Cadiz, and to his son, Alexander. These were written from Bordeaux, Belfast and Dublin and relate to family matters, including the wine trade, and date from 1739 to 1766.

There is a record of a Black family in County Sligo between 1764 and 1900 and there are also family papers up to the twentieth century. A pedigree of the Black family of Lurgan, County Armagh, dates from 1783 to 1925.

In 1688, **George Black** worked as a surveyor of an estate in County Fermanagh. Also, a Stuart manuscript contains a letter in French, dated 1699, from Queen Mary to the Bishop of Blois, thanking him for maintaining a Mr. Black and his family.

From 1849 to 1851 **William H. Black** of the Public Records Office in Dublin wrote reports reflecting the sad state of the country brought about by the Great Famine.

Blake

Ó Blácach

Caddell

The original name was Caddell, a Welsh patronymic which, following their arrival with the Normans, was changed to Le Blaca. With the passage of time, this became Blake. Robert Le Blaca, a swarthy man, settled in Galway and there, for six centuries, the family has remained. For several generations they were mayors, sheriffs or burgesses of that five hundred-year-old city. The Blakes were numbered among the élite—the Fourteen Tribes of Galway.

Blakes went on the Crusades and several fought on the Spanish–Irish side at the Battle of Kinsale. Their castles are scattered all over Connacht, where they were powerful landowners with extravagant lifestyles. Menlo, near Galway, which was accidentally burned in 1910, was once the home of a **Sir Valentine Blake** who was pursued by the bailiffs for his gambling and drinking debts. He could only go outside his castle on Sundays—the bailiffs' day off.

When he became a Member of Parliament, he gained immunity from the debt collectors!

One of the Blake family which had settled in County Wicklow in 1832 chartered a ship and sailed with his family and friends for Canada. There he founded a dynasty of Toronto lawyers, one of whom was an authority on the Canadian Constitution.

A Blake from Limerick was governor of five British colonies.

The original Galway Blakes also spread to County Kildare, where there are no less than three Blakestowns. *Letters from the Irish Highlands*, written by **Henry Blake**, paints a vivid picture of nineteenth-century Ireland.

Heralds differ as to whether the Blake family crest is a yellow cat or a leopard. Their motto is *virtus sola nobilitas* (virtue of itself is nobility).

The anglicization of Gaelic names can cause confusion. Blachmhaich was the name of an Irish family in the West of Ireland which became either Blowick or the more numerous Blake.

Bodkin

Boidicín

The Bodkins, who were to be numbered among the Fourteen Tribes of Galway, were descendants of Maurice FitzGerald, who came to Ireland with the first Anglo-Normans. Maurice's son, Thomas, acquired a great acreage of land in Munster, where his descendants became the Earls of Desmond, a branch of the mighty FitzGeralds.

Thomas's son, Richard, in about 1242, went to join Richard de Burgo in Connacht, where he was granted rich properties. It was possibly Richard's grandson, Thomas FitzRichard, who engaged in mortal combat with a valiant Irishman and only succeeded in defeating him by using the short Irish spear called the baudekin. From this incident he earned the name Bodkin, which the family thereupon adopted as their own distinctive name. However, for many generations they continued to use the coat of arms of the FitzGeralds as well as the motto, "Crom aboo", their rousing war cry.

During the time of King Richard II (1367–1400), **Henry Bodkin** was an important administrator in Galway city, owning much property there, where at one time there was a thoroughfare known as Baudekyn's Lane.

During the ravages of the Cromwellian armies, the Bodkins suffered transplantation and confiscation. There were a number of Bodkin officers in the Irish armies of James II. Otherwise, little is recorded of them until the nineteenth century.

A Jesuit priest, **Matthias McDonnell Bodkin**, left his vast collection of novels, poems, plays and essays to the National Library in Dublin. A **Thomas Bodkin** was born in Dublin in 1887 and practised law there for some years before becoming Director of the National Gallery of Ireland from 1927 to 1935. From there he was invited to become the first Director of the Barber Institute of Birmingham. On his retirement, he contributed greatly to the upgrading of the arts in Ireland. With his deep, rich Dublin voice, he became a very popular broadcaster and television personality.

In Ireland today there are very few representatives of the Bodkin name.

Bogg

Ó Buadhaigh

Bogue

This rare surname appears with a variety of spellings, mostly in Munster, in counties Kilkenny, Waterford and Cork. Whether Bogue, Boew, or even Boyce, the name could be an anglicization of Ó Buadhaigh. *Buadhach* is the Irish word for victorious.

The Bogues who came to Fermanagh, probably as planters, are particularly numerous there. They came from Scotland, mainly from Dumfriesshire and Lanarkshire, where for centuries they were important landowners and held many high offices. In Scotland, in Roxburghshire and Perth, there are two towns called Bog.

In Ireland they do not appear to have figured much at all in the archives, although there are mentions of a Bogue whose lands were forfeited in 1657 and of a **Daniel Boig** and a **Dermot O Boig**.

see also Boyce

Boland

Ó Beolláin

Bolan

Ó Beolláin, the Irish form of the name, comes from a Norse personal name. According to genealogists, the *d* at the end of the English version—Boland—is a comparatively recent affectation. The family, which came to Ireland long ago and includes a brother of King Brian Boru in its pedigree, settled first around Lough Derg. Their name is perpetuated in the town of Mountshannon in County Clare which, in Irish, is known as Baile Uí Bheoláin (the town of the Bolands). The other O Bolans are of Connacht, where they had their headquarters at Doonalton in County Sligo.

Although the Ó Beolláins were mentioned in the seventeenth-century *Annals of the Four Masters*, not much has been heard of them since the arrival of the Anglo-Normans.

In 1920, when Eamon de Valera was fund-raising in America and campaigning for international recognition of the Irish Republic, his delegation met Bolsheviks on a similar mission. The Irish had had great success—the Russians had not. So the Russians asked for a loan of $20,000, offering a few of what they said were the Russian crown jewels as collateral. On returning to Ireland, one of the delegation, **Harry Boland**, a deputy for South Roscommon, was given the jewels to mind (Michael Collins, the Free State Army Chief, would not touch them—"There's blood on them; the Czar and his family have been killed," he said). Boland, who was killed in the Civil War, gave them to his mother for safe keeping. Ten years later, when de Valera came to power, the Boland family handed him the jewels, and in 1949 the Irish High Commissioner in London exchanged them with the Russian Embassy for $20,000.

Harry Boland's brother, **Gerald Boland**, who also took part in the War of Independence, was a founder member of the Fianna Fáil Party. He held several ministerial posts, including Minister for Justice during the Second World War when he had to take strong measures to counteract IRA subversion.

Frederick Boland was Irish Ambassador in London in the 1950s. He was President of the United Nations in New York in 1960 when the Russian head of state, Nikita Kruschev, dramatically banged his shoe on the table. He was brought to order by the President banging his gavel so hard that it broke. Afterwards he was inundated with new gavels! His daughter, **Eavan Boland**, is one of Ireland's leading poets.

One of Dublin's oldest bakeries, Boland's Mills, was the scene of much heroic fighting during the Easter rising.

Boyce

Ó Buadhaigh

Boyes

Like many other Irish names, there are several sources to be explored for the surname Boyce or Boyes. It could derive from the old Norman place name, de Bois (of the woods), or it could be an anglicized version of the Gaelic Ó Buadhaigh, meaning victorious.

Bogue or Bowe are other versions of Ó Buadhaigh, a sept located originally in south-west Cork who claim to be kinsmen of the powerful O Sullivans. The numerous Boyces of Donegal and Derry were probably originally Ó Buadhaigh.

Settlers who came from England to counties Meath and Limerick as Boyce or de Boys have long since been assimilated as Irish.

In the archives there are many accounts of grants of arms, including one to the descendants of **Charles Joseph Boyce** of Stranorlar, County Donegal, and Templeville, County Dublin, and to his only son, **Lieutenant-Colonel Charles Boyce, RAMC**.

There is also an interesting journal of 1808, maintained by **Frederick Boyce,** of the proceedings of *HMS Decade* cruising in the East Atlantic and, a few years later, of the *Royal Oak* in the North Sea.

Samuel Boyce (1708–47) was a popular Dublin poet in his day.

The **Reverend John Boyce** (1810–64) of Donegal went to the United States of America, where he became a novelist. His nephew, **Jerome Boyce**, wrote poetry.

Sir Rupert Boyce (1863–1911), who was born in London of Irish parents, was prominent in the development of tropical medicine.

Neither Boyce nor its variant, Boyes, is numerous in Ireland, being mostly located now in north-east Ulster.

see also Bogg

Boyd

Although there is a sprinkling of Boyds throughout the country, the majority are to be found in Ulster, where they came as planters from 1609 onwards. It is thought that the name derives from Bute in Scotland and that it could be synonymous with the Irish word *buídhe* (yellow).

Ballycastle in Antrim was one of the Boyd family's manors. These Boyds distinguished themselves in the services. **Major-General Hugh Boyd** was in the Bengal army at the time of the mutiny and **Sir John Augustus Boyd** saw active service with the navy in the Middle East. Ballycastle Manor has long since become a Barnardo home for children.

The Boyds who were refugees from the persecution of the Huguenots in France came to Kiltra House in County Wexford. According to *Burke's Irish Family Records*, many scattered to Canada, America and Australia. In England, a descendant of this family, **Gladys Boyd**, was at one time editor of *Vogue* magazine, while another daughter, Patricia, an assistant editor of *Vogue* from 1954 to 1958, wrote many novels under her married name, Patricia Moyes.

Middleton Park in Mullingar, County Westmeath, a splendid mansion built in around 1850 by **George Augustus Boyd** (he afterwards assumed the name Boyd Rochfort), made headlines in recent years when it was bought by a keen businessman who put it up to be raffled—an idea not thought to be altogether legal!

Liam Boyd, born in County Down, was one of the founder members of the Irish American Society.

Boyes *see* Boyce

Boylan

Ó Baoighealláin

Boyland

The Boylans, or Boylands, were a widespread sept with territory from Armagh to Louth. When driven out by the MacMahons, they settled in counties Monaghan, Meath and Kildare and are still numerous in this area. The fourteenth-century poet, O Dugan, called them "the bold kings of Dartry", praising them for their horsemanship and blue eyes.

The Church and land have featured significantly in this family. In the eighteenth century, **John Boylan** of the landed gentry, and known as "Seán Lán" (John the rich), stated in his will that, if his "children misbehaved or transgressed by marrying improper persons", they were to be disinherited, nor were they to allow anyone other than a Boylan to have their land. They must have behaved, for they continued to farm their fifteen hundred acres, rearing sheep and cattle. They changed to tillage during the Napoleonic Wars, when there was a big demand for corn.

Patrick Boylan, rich enough to be a yeoman, was threatened with assassination. **Hugh Boylan** joined the rebels in the 1798 Rebellion. His descendant, the poet **Teresa Boylan**, wrote popular songs in the 1890s, including "The Old Bog Road".

One of the family estates was managed by three brothers and their housekeeper whose only outing, once a year, was to the races!

The Boylans are very aware of their ancient pedigrees. Today their descendants own their vast acreages, whereas in the past they were tenants.

In the mid-nineteenth century, **Robert Boylan**, who built a fine house, Clonkeevan, instructed in his will that on his death there were to be celebrations in his house and gardens. There were—and they went on for days!

Mother Columba Boylan, a Dominican nun at Cabra Convent in Dublin, went to Melbourne to found a new convent and stayed in Australia for thirty-five years, until her death in 1910.

Eugene Dom Boylan of Bray first studied atomic physics in Vienna, then joined the Cistercian Order in 1933 and was sent to Australia to found the first Cistercian monastery, near Melbourne. He wrote popular spiritual books and, at Caldy Island in Wales, he got the monks on to a sound economic footing by developing a popular perfume.

Monsignor Patrick Boylan, a distinguished Hebrew scholar and orientalist, was President of the Royal Hibernian Academy in the 1940s.

The biggest footwear industry in Ireland was founded by **James Boylan**, whose family owned a chain of shoe shops around Ireland. **Major Eddie Boylan** of Meath won the prestigious Badminton Horse Trials in 1965 and was European Champion in 1967. **Clare Boylan** of Dublin has made her name as a short story writer and novelist.

(O) Boyle

Ó Baoill

The O Boyles were chieftains in Donegal. Their stronghold was at

Cloghineely, from where they ruled west Ulster with the neighbouring O Donnells and O Doughertys. Translated from the Irish, their name is thought to mean "having profitable pledges". Ballyweel, a town in Donegal, translated means "home of the O Boyles".

Another Boyle family which moved to Armagh about three hundred years ago had a castle at Desert until 1961, when they sold it. They also owned much territory in Derry.

The Boyle family which dominates history sprang from **Richard Boyle**, who came from England in the sixteenth century with little more than a sharp wit. His opportunity came by acquiring property belonging to the outlawed Irish, as well as ecclesiastical lands, and selling it to English adventurers. The historic Lismore Castle in Waterford, once his home, came to the present Dukes of Devonshire through a Boyle marriage. When Richard Boyle died in 1643 he was 1st Earl of Cork and had taken care that most of his fifteen clever children had married into titles. His most distinguished son, **Robert Boyle**, was untitled. He discovered the relationship concerning the compression and expansion of a gas at constant temperature, known as Boyle's Law.

A great grandson, **Richard, 3rd Earl of Burlington**, introduced the fashion for Palladian architecture to England from Italy. Burlington House in London is a prime example.

Another descendant, **Henry, Earl of Shannon**, worked zealously for Ireland. As a member of the Dublin Parliament, he tried to block Ireland's forced financial contributions to the British Crown. He was a great favourite with the people, but this move lost him all his high offices.

Richard Vicars Boyle, an engineer, went to India to build the railroads. He made history during the Indian mutiny, when, with only fifty men, he held out against three thousand rebels. He also helped in the building of the railways in Japan.

John J. Boyle, one of the Ulster Boyles, began life as a stonemason. After studying in Paris, he settled in New York, where he became famous for his gigantic groupings of statuary which include the Indian Family in Chicago and the statue of Commodore John Barry, the Irishman known as the "father of the American navy", which holds a prominent place in Washington DC.

William Boyle, a playwright from Dromiskin, County Louth, wrote *The Eloquent Dempsey*, one of the earliest plays staged at Dublin's Abbey Theatre.

Bradley

Ó Brolcáin

This ancient Irish name means descendant of Brolác, Brolcáin meaning little Brolác. They were long established in County Derry and trace their origins to Suibhne Mean, King of Ireland in the seventh century when their territory was in Clogher, County Tyrone. The family boasted many scribes and learned men.

Scholars describe Bradley as being an anglicization of the old Irish name Ó Brolcáin, or O Brallaghan. Nevertheless, Bradley, whatever its origins, is a numerous name in Ireland, especially in the north, where they probably arrived as soldiers or planters.

In old English, Bradley comes from brad ley (broad meadow).

William Bradley, undoubtedly of English origin, is recorded as serving in Ireland in the Cromwellian army, for which he was granted land in Waterford.

Maelbrighde Ó Brollacháin, a builder who died in 1029, had two sons, **Aedh** (Hugh), a learned professor who died in 1095, and **Maelbrighde**, who was Bishop of Kildare from 1097 to 1100.

Donal Ó Brollacháin, an Abbot of Derry, died in 1203. **Flaibhertach Ó Brollacháin** rebuilt Derry Cathedral and died in 1175.

Denis Bradley (1846–1903) left his native Kerry for the USA, where he became a very popular Bishop of Manchester, New Hampshire.

During the first half of this century there were a number of Bradley writers, including **Bradley the Tailor**, a poet. Looking further afield there were many distinguished bearers of the name, including the philosopher **Frances Herbert Bradley**; a Dean of Westminster Abbey, **George Granville Bradley**; an editor of the *Oxford English Dictionary*; an astronomer; and, of course, the famous **General Omar Bradley** of the US army. **Daniel Bradley** of Ulster was professor of optical electronics at Trinity College Dublin.

Bradshaw

A most numerous and widespread surname in Ireland, originating from a village of that name between Illingworth and Halifax in West Yorkshire, England. Bradshaigh was the original spelling.

Many of the Bradshaw family records have been preserved in various archives. In 1902, Francis J. Bigger published an account of the Bradshaws of Bangor and Mile Cross in County Down. There are many papers dating between 1600 and 1950 relating to Bradshaws who had properties in counties Monaghan, Tipperary and Kilkenny. In 1844 there was a confirmation of arms given to **Robert Bradshaw** of Mile Cross, County Down.

Richard Bradshaw was Lord President of Ireland in 1649 and 1650. In a letter of 1650, he wrote to Cromwell about the plague "which so raged in Ireland, especially in Dublin". This Richard Bradshaw also boasted to a Colonel Husen of Westmeath that he had taken five hundred prisoners and slain more than three hundred! In pursuit of the rebellion, he continued his campaign into Connacht.

Rebecca Bradshaw was a niece of the celebrated Quaker, Sir William Penn (1644–1718), founder of Pennsylvania.

George Bradshaw (1801–53), an English printer, was the originator of the famous *Bradshaw's Railway Manual and Shareholders' Guide and Official Directory* and a host of other travel guides.

Robert Bradshaw of County Kerry, who was a harper, was also secretary of the Harp Festival held in Belfast in 1792. Another Bradshaw who integrated with Gaelic Ireland was Seosamh Bradsthé (**Joseph Bradshaw**), who, in the nineteenth century, wrote romantic Ossianic poetry about the heroes of Ireland.

There were two Bradshaw librarians who collected many invaluable Irish manuscripts. One was **John Bradshaw** of the Bodleian Library in Oxford and the other was **Henry Bradshaw** of the Cambridge University Library, who specialized in Celtic manuscripts: in Irish, Welsh and Cornish.

Harry Bradshaw, formerly one of Ireland's outstanding professional golfers, was from Delgany in County Wicklow.

Brady

Mac Brádaigh

The Brady name derives from a "spirited ancestor", for that is the Irish meaning for this numerous name. Cavan was the homeland of this sept and today they are very widespread. Enforced anglicization caused them to drop the Mac prefix. They are often confused with the O Gradys of Limerick who, in Tudor times, changed their name to Brady.

There have been many religious in the Brady family. From the fourteenth to the sixteenth century there were a number of distinguished MacBrady bishops.

Their most famous scholar, **Nicholas Brady** (1659–1726), left his Cork home for the literary world of London. Most enduring of his compositions is the Christmas carol, "While Shepherds Watched Their Flocks By Night". **Maziere Brady**, great-grandson of Nicholas, also had the Brady gift of verse. He was Lord Chancellor of Ireland and, in 1867, was awarded a baronetcy.

From Cavan came two popular seventeenth-century poets—**Fiachra** and **Philip MacBrady**.

Thomas Brady went to Vienna to study for the priesthood but changed over to the army and was a field marshal during the Napoleonic invasion of Austria. Returning to civilian life, he became governor of Dalmatia.

Shiploads of Bradys sailed to America following the Great Famine. Among other important utilities, **Anthony Brady** opened up the railroads and initiated electrification. He built a vast commercial empire which was inherited by his son, **Nicholas**, who, with his wife, was very active in the Catholic Church. When **Mrs. Brady** became a Dame of the Prestigious Order of Malta, she was ever afterwards known as "The Duchess Brady".

Bradys were also prominent in the legal profession in New York.

It was a Brady who pioneered portrait photography. He was one of the first war photographers and his records of battle and camp scenes during the American Civil War are in the War College.

There were two remarkable Bradys in Australia—on different sides of the coin. **John Brady** was a vicar-general in Western Australia who cared for the aborigines and Irish convicts; **Matthew Brady** was a notorious bushranger.

Liam Brady (b. 1956), a Dubliner, started his professional career as a footballer with Arsenal (1973–9) and was Player of the Year in 1979. He was transferred to the Italian Juventus team for a fee of £600,000. He was capped over seventy times for the Irish international soccer team.

see also (O) Grady

Brandon

Mac Brandáin

The surname Brandon comes from a number of towns and parishes in England, where it was originally de Brandon. They came as settlers to Northern Ireland, where the name is still very numerous today.

Mac Brandáin is a rare County Kerry name, meaning son of Brandáin. Mount Brandon dominates the County Kerry landscape, and there are also Brandon Creeks, Heads, Bay and Points and a Brandon Hotel in the Tralee area. They all celebrate the great local hero, St. Brandan the Navigator, the sixth-century saint and maritime explorer who may even have discovered America.

A manuscript of 1596 mentions "one, Brandon but for whose assistance the wife and children of Florence McCarthy would have starved". Also in the sixteenth century, **James Brandon** received a grant from the Earl of Ormond to build a house for the poor, the old and the sick of Dundalk. He was of an old English family which had settled in County Louth. In Cromwellian times, because they were "papists", many of the Brandons forfeited their lands and were transplanted.

In 1720 Maurice Crosbie of Ardfert Abbey, County Kerry—now a ruin—took the title of **1st Lord Brandon**.

Burke's Irish Family Records gives a pedigree of an important County Fermanagh family of landowners who were also remarkable for having so many ecclesiastics amongst their numbers. In the 1840s, **Lowther Brandon** was Dean of the Falklands. Three of his sisters and a brother were missionaries in India and others of this family held high posts in the army and the navy.

The Brandons also had property in County Kilkenny. Otherwise, except for in Ulster, the name is comparatively rare in Ireland.

Brazil *see* Breslin

(O) Breen

Ó Braoin

MacBreen Brawney

Breen—in Irish Ó Braoin—is derived from *braon*, meaning sadness or sorrow. It is a very numerous surname throughout Ireland, although the O or Mac prefix, once an essential part of the name, has long since been dropped. In the course of time, the name became corrupted to O Brien, and even to Brown or Bruen!

There were a number of Breen septs. At one time they were an influential family in Knocktopher, County Kilkenny, until the Anglo-Norman invasion began in 1169.

The Breens of Westmeath were a more important sept. They owned much land in Offaly, near Athlone. Their chieftains were lords of Brawney and, until the fifteenth century, they were on a par with the great O Conor kings of Connacht and MacMorrogh, King of Leinster.

From the Brawney sept came **Tighearnach O Braoin**, the annalist and, in 1088, Abbot of Clonmacnoise. **Donal O Breen** was Bishop of Clonmacnoise from 1303 to 1324.

Francis Breen of Wexford fought in the 1798 Rebellion.

Elizabeth Breen was with the Irish nuns who were imprisoned during the French Revolution which began in 1793.

By far the most notorious Breen was **Dan Breen** (1894–1969), the son of a Tipperary farmer, who took a leading part in the War of Independence. At one time there was a reward of £10,000 on his head. He was elected a member of Dáil Éireann for Tipperary in 1923. His autobiography recounting his famous guerrilla battles, *My Fight for Irish Freedom* (1924), was a bestseller.

Brennan

Ó Braonáin

The meaning of this name in its original Irish form, as a personal name, remains an enigma: it either means sorrow—or a little drop! There were six distinct septs, all spelling their names in different ways, from Ó Braonáin through to Ó Branáin and Mac Branáin. They were very widespread and are now very numerous, especially in Leinster.

The principal O Brennan sept was in Kilkenny, where they were powerful chiefs until colonization led to confiscation and transplantation. Driven to despair, some formed themselves into bands of robbers who emulated highwaymen, robbing and plundering towns. A full account of the Brenans of Eden Hall in Ballyragget, County Kilkenny, is given in *Burke's Irish Family Records*. They claim descent from the O Brenans, Princes of Idough in Kilkenny.

John Brennan, Bishop of Waterford

and Archbishop of Cashel, like his friend Saint Oliver Plunkett, lived during the religious persecutions. The reports he sent to Rome of these nerve-racking times are a valuable historical record.

The **Abbé Peter Brennan**, an exile in Paris, was executed during the French Revolution.

John Brennan (d. 1830) was probably the last Ossory (Kilkenny) Brennan claiming to be chief of his name. He was known as "the wrestling doctor" because of his satirical attacks on his fellow medical men.

A number of Brennans served with the 69th New York Volunteers in the American War of Independence.

The most notable of the name must be **Louis Brennan**, who left Mayo to work in Melbourne as a watchmaker. He invented the torpedo, sold the rights to Britain and helped manufacture it in England where, during the First World War, he went on to develop monorails and helicopters.

Robert Brennan of Wexford, a journalist and an Irish Volunteer in 1916, was a founder of the Department of External Affairs. He exchanged his directorship of the *Irish Press* for the diplomatic corps where, during the Second World War, he was Minister to the USA. He returned to Ireland to write, and served briefly as Director of Radio Éireann.

The Brennans are prominent in the arts. **Christopher Brennan** (1870–1932) was a classical scholar and acclaimed poet of Australia. **John Brennan** of Wexford writes thrillers with a racing background. **Barbara Brennan**, a stage and screen actress, won a number of theatre awards.

The Gweedore area of County Donegal is home to a remarkable musical family. **Máire Ní Bhraonáin** and her twin brothers form the nucleus of Clannad, a group of traditional musicians who have had worldwide success. Their sister, Enya, who performed for a short time with the group, has also achieved fame in her own right with a number of bestselling albums.

Breslin

Ó Breasláin

Brazil Bresland Breslane Bryce

The Breslins, sometimes spelled Brazil, are one of the principal brehon families—ancient families of judges—and were once centred in counties Fermanagh and Sligo. The name comes from a first name, Breasláin, of which Breasal is the diminutive. Variations include Bresland, Breslane and Breslaun.

The Breslins were a branch of the Cinel Enda clan and were originally chiefs of Fanad in Kilmacrenan, County Donegal. Towards the end of the thirteenth century, they were driven out into Fermanagh, where they settled and were attached to the Maguires, one of the most important septs in Ulster. They acted as lawyers for the Maguires and were administrators of their Derryvullen church.

Another branch were of the Uí Fiachrach of Sligo, where they were chiefs of Kilanly in Tireragh. This branch is now thought to have died out. There are also a number of Breslins in the County Waterford area.

In Donegal, some anglicized their name to Brice or Bryce, a name common in England.

(O) Brien

Ó Briain

O Brian

For centuries the O Briens, the O Neills and the O Conors were the leading Irish aristocratic families. The O Briens took their name from the great High King Brian Boru, who reigned over Munster for thirty-eight years and died fighting the Vikings at Clontarf in 1014. Succeeding O Briens tried to emulate Brian Boru, whose ambition had been to unite Ireland. So far, this has not been achieved.

The O Brien territory of Thomond was around the River Shannon in County Clare. Here they built churches and abbeys and also fought fiercely to defend their kingdom. For their allegiance to the English Crown they were created Earls of Thomond and Earls of Inchiquin. **Murrough O Brien** (1614–74) joined with the Cromwellians in savagely sacking and burning many Munster towns, for which he became known as "Murrough of the Burnings". Later he sided with Charles II, but was spurned as a traitor. Finally he went to Rome to seek pardon from the Pope and spent his remaining years doing penance.

In the late seventeenth century, the O Briens built the handsome Dromoland Castle, which was their chief home, until recently, when it became a hotel. O Briens fought on opposing sides at the battle of the Boyne in 1690. Since the sixteenth century many O Briens have been scattered across Europe. Viscount Clare (an O Brien title) formed Clare's Dragoons, one of the many distinguished regiments serving in France.

The O Briens produced many high-ranking ecclesiastics, scholars, statesmen and parliamentarians. A Dromoland O Brien who had joined the Young Irelanders and taken up arms spent some years in an Australian gaol. His granddaughter wrote a moving account of the conditions on the "coffin ships" which brought emigrants to America.

In the nineteenth and twentieth centuries, Cork O Briens fought for the nationalist cause, agitating through journalism and trade unions. The saga of the countless O Briens is international and full of colourful characters, including two leading women novelists, **Kate O Brien** and **Edna O Brien**. A Thomond O Brien was an author, a round-the-world yachtsman, an architect, a British naval officer and an active nationalist! It was an O Brien sea captain from Cork, **Captain Jeremiah O Brien**, who provoked the first naval engagement of the American War of Independence.

The name is seldom found without its O prefix and fills many pages in the Irish telephone directories. The British royal family can claim an ancestor in King Brian Boru—as can Ronald Reagan and many other notables.

Broderick

Ó Bruadair

Broderick is essentially an English name, which some believe came from a Norse forename. With few exceptions, the Brodericks found in Ireland are of Irish stock. They were Ó Bruadair and anglicized their name to save themselves trouble during penal times.

There were two septs. One was in the barony of Barrymore in County Cork. From here, it is thought, came **Daithí (David) Ó Bruadair** (*c.*1625–98). His family were able to give him a classical education and he was one of the last to be trained in the ancient bardic school. He wrote poetry and prose, as well as a contemporary history of his troubled times, and he was also a genealogist. With the final suppression of the Irish nobility in the 1640s, he was reduced to poverty.

The second sept settled in County Galway, where they are still to be found. From County Galway came **Father Anthony Ó Bruadair**, a Franciscan martyr. There are two townlands in an area between Galway and the Shannon river called Ballybroder.

Sir Alan Broderick from England was appointed Lord High Chancellor of Ireland in the 1660s. He was given considerable lands in County Cork and his descendants took the title of Viscount Midleton from their mansion. A descendant, the **Honourable Charles Broderick**, was Archbishop of Cashel.

David Broderick, the son of Irish immigrants, settled in California. He sat in the Senate and built himself a mansion on San Francisco's Nob Hill.

John Broderick, (1927–89) of Athlone educated himself and ran the family bakery while making a name for himself as a powerful novelist. He emigrated to France and then to England.

Brontë *see* Prunty

Brosnan

Ó Brosnacháin

Bresnahan

The name derives from a descendant of Brosnacáin, who was a native of Brosna in County Kerry. The family has been there for centuries, with 264 Brosnan families located at Brosna in 1961. They are also now fairly numerous in County Limerick.

Brosnans were also recorded in 1133 in Munster, where many O Brosnans were attached to a big estate near Clonmel in Tipperary.

Little more is recorded of them until the early nineteenth century, when **Timothy Brosnan** appears to have been active in the campaign of a fellow Kerryman, Daniel O Connell, the Liberator.

Brosnahan is a variant of the name. In the Genealogical Office in Dublin there is a copy of a grant of arms, dated 1953, to His Lordship, the **Most Reverend Thomas Brosnahan**, Bishop of Freetown and Bo.

One of the largest co-operatives in Ireland, the Kerry Co-operative, was the creation of Kerryman **Denis Brosnan** (b. 1940). The company has several offices in the United States.

Michael B. Brosnan (b. 1933), one of a family of eleven from Gneeveguilla, near Rathmore in County Kerry, went to the USA in 1957 to join five members of his family. Two of his brothers fought with the US army in Korea—one was awarded a Purple Heart. Michael Brosnan became vice-president of the "financial supermarket", Merrill Lynch, New York.

Pierce Brosnan (b. 1953) is an acclaimed actor, who first came to prominence in the television series, *Remington Steele*, and is the new James Bond, in the film *Goldeneye*.

Browne

Brown

Browne is a common name in both England and Ireland. A Le Brun came from Normandy in the twelfth century, landing on the Connacht coast, where his descendants settled, intermarried with the great Irish families, and prospered so well that they were to join the influential Fourteen Tribes of Galway.

Westport House in County Mayo, their Connacht seat, is visited by thousands of people every year since it was opened to the public by **Jeremy Browne**, Lord Altamont, son of the Marquess of Sligo. The family is anxious to preserve this priceless repository of Irish history. One of their ancestors was Grace O Malley—Granuaile, the pirate queen.

The Brownes were pre-eminently clerical and military, making careers in Europe and Russia. **Michael David Browne** was one of the few Irish cardinals to be appointed.

A family of Brownes fled from Limerick, from religious oppression, to join the Czar's army in Russia, where **Count George Browne** rose to be Field Marshal. A kinsman, **Maximilian Ulysses Browne**, who was born in Austria, the son of an exiled hero of the Battle of the Boyne, was a Field Marshal and a Count of the Austrian Empire.

William Browne (1777–1857), son of a humble family who emigrated to Argentina, followed an adventurous naval career and became an admiral in the Argentinian navy.

Arthur Browne, a descendant of a Browne family from Louth, was founder of the Rhode Island college long since known as Brown University.

Alexander Browne, who left Antrim in 1800 to open stores in Philadelphia, New York and Liverpool, has been described as "one of America's first millionaires".

The Brownes who came to Ireland via England settled in Kerry, where they were created Earls of Kenmare. **Valentine Browne**, Viscount Castlerosse and last Earl of Kenmare (1891–1943), the high-living gossip columnist of the 1920s and 1930s, turned the estate into the famous Killarney golf course. His former home is now American owned.

The Brownes have also made their mark in Australia, particularly in the Church.

Perhaps the most dramatic Brown in recent literary history was **Christy Brown** (1932–81). Born into a large, impoverished Dublin family, he was almost completely paralysed from birth. Through his own perseverance, and with the assistance of his mother and Dr. R. Collis, he developed into a fine painter and writer. His autobiography, *My Left Foot*, and his novel, *Down All the Days*, earned him international fame. *My Left Foot* was also made into a highly successful film, starring Daniel Day Lewis.

Bryant

Although this surname was originally Bryan, it has no connection with any Irish name. It was a popular family name in rural Brittany and it came to England when the Bretons joined the Normans in the conquest of England in 1066.

Up until the nineteenth century, the Bryants were to be found mainly in the north of England—in Yorkshire, Westmoreland and Furness. They probably arrived in Ireland with the armies of the Commonwealth, though not in any great numbers. There are only about a couple of dozen to be found in Ireland today. Bryan is a much more common surname.

One of England's most distinguished twentieth-century historians was **Sir Arthur Bryant**. The name is well represented in the professions and in the army and navy lists. A retired **Rear Admiral Bryant** was a manager of Rolls-Royce in Scotland.

The most outstanding Bryants are to be found in the United States of America. **William Cullen Bryant** (1794–1878), a barrister and politician, forged new frontiers in his poetry and also wrote a number of travel books. **A. P. Bryant** is esteemed for his dietary studies with the US Department of Agriculture Office Experimental Stations. In the 1960s, **Beth Bryant**, an American journalist, wrote her travel book, *Ireland on Five Dollars a Day*.

In Ireland in the nineteenth century, **Sophie Bryant** contributed many pamphlets on the history and poetry of Celtic Ireland.

Bryce *see* Breslin

Buckley

Ó Buachalla

Buckley, an essentially English name, has many distinguished entries in *Who's Who*. It can also be an anglicization of Ó Buachalla (*buachaill* means boy).

It has been recorded that "a family of Buckley or Buhilly, resident at Lemanaghan, County Offaly, claimed to be descendants of the cowherd of St. Manahan and were hereditary bearers of his shrine". The shrine is still to be seen in a church in Offaly.

One of the most numerous names in Munster, many of this name were outlawed to Europe following the defeat of James II. "Bulkely" was the name wrongly recorded for **William Buckley**, a royalist who was guillotined during the French Revolution.

There were Buckleys serving America in Meagher's Irish Brigade. The nineteenth-century American botanist, **Samuel Buckley**, probably originated from Ireland.

Liam Ó Buachalla was a cooper in Guinness' brewery, but studied to become a professor of economics and President of the Gaelic League.

Burgess

Brugha

Burgess is an English surname which has been in Ireland, especially Northern Ireland, for many centuries. It originates from the English word for a citizen—a person concerned with the ownership or administration of property in a city or borough—which is what the early bearers of this name who came to Ireland most certainly were.

A Burgess is mentioned as a witness to the Charter of Rosbercon in New Ross, County Wexford, in 1294, while, in 1420, another Burgess is recorded as Assessor for County Kildare. A number of Burgesses came to Ireland in 1649 with Cromwell's armies and were afterwards granted land in lieu of pay.

About 1681, a Dublin priest, **Daniel Burgess**, got into trouble with the law for his libellous attack on the Quakers.

In 1748, the Sheriff of Kilkenny, **Henry Burgess**, was killed in an attempt to capture the notorious highwayman, James Freeney.

Parkanaur in Castlecaulfield, County Tyrone, was a mansion built in the romantic style, between 1802 and 1804, by **J. H. Burgess**. It was sold in 1958 and became a training centre for handicapped children.

Charles William St. John Burgess (1874–1922), a Dubliner, joined the Gaelic League and changed his name to **Cathal Brugha**. He played a leading role in the War of Independence and was Minister of Defence in the first Irish Parliament, Dáil Éireann. He was killed in the Civil War. One of his sons, **Ruairí Brugha** (1917–85), was a Senator and played a prominent part in a number of government institutions, including television, radio and tourism, and was very active in the trade union movement.

In England, the name was made notorious by the infamous traitors, Burgess and Maclean, who eventually defected to the Soviet Union. However, the name has been well redeemed by a prodigal genius, **Anthony Burgess**, a prolific novelist, musician, composer and linguist who also contributed to Irish television with a series on James Joyce.

Burke

de Búrca

Bourke de Burgh

The Burkes are a distinguished and numerous family. They go back thousands of years to King Charlemagne and have blood ties with British and European monarchs. Their entry into Ireland began with **William de Burgh**, who was made Lord Deputy of Ireland by Henry I in 1177. Their name originated from the borough of Caen in Normandy (de burg means "of the borough").

The Normans integrated into Ireland, acquiring Irish land and wives, and contributing their skills in administration and building. The Burkes settled mainly in Connacht, where the two main septs were called Mac William Uachtar of Galway and Mac William Íochtar of Mayo. Minor branches which adopted other family names account for a confusion of spellings.

The Burkes acquired many titles of nobility. By marrying a daughter of the Earl of Ulster, Hugh de Lacy, **Walter Burke** inherited the title. Walter built many fortified castles on the Donegal coast.

To **Richard de Burgo** goes some of the credit for making Galway into a fine city, even though he was not of one of the Fourteen Tribes.

For his allegiance to Henry VIII, **Ulick Burke** was titled Earl and Marquess of Clanricarde.

The pirate queen, Grace O'Malley, took **Richard Burke** as her second husband. Their son, **Tibbot na Long Burke**, went over to the English side at the battle of Kinsale and, in 1627, was created Viscount of Mayo, where he had vast territories.

After the defeat at Kinsale, Burke men and women went into exile and achieved distinction on a global scale, becoming viceroys of India, colonial governors, owners of a Burke Regiment in France and governor of New South Wales. They left their mark on places as far apart as Burgh Quay in Dublin, Burke town and county in the USA, Burke River in Australia and Burk's Falls in Canada.

There were many Burke bishops and pastors, and oratory was one of their talents, exemplified by **Edmund Burke**, the writer and politician who influenced British politics during the French Revolution.

Robert O Hara Burke (1820–61), with his companion W. J. Wills, was one of the first to cross Australia from south to north. However, they died of starvation on the return journey.

There are many books about the Burkes. A family of Burkes brought genealogy to a fine art with the publication of their ongoing *Burke's Peerage*.

Burney *see* MacBirney

Burns

Mac Conboirne

Conborney

Burns is the anglicized form of the old Gaelic name, Mac Conboirne. It is also widely, though not correctly, used for O Beirne, Birrane and Byrne. In the west of Ireland, Mac Conboirne was anglicized to Conborney, a name which now seems to have died out.

By no means a common name, the Burns are still mainly to be found in the place of their origin—the west of Ireland.

Essentially it is a Scottish name, which explains why so many Burns are to be found in Northern Ireland, in east Ulster, where they would have arrived from their Scottish homeland.

Several Burns—but whether Irish or Scottish would be difficult to say—served in the Irish brigade of the New York Volunteers, under General Thomas Francis Meagher, in the American Civil War.

Butler

de Buitléir

Until comparatively recently, the Butlers were one of the most influential families in Ireland, on a par with the FitzGeralds and the Burkes. They came to Ireland with the Anglo-Normans and were given prime land in Limerick, Tipperary and Wicklow. They married Irish heiresses and built many abbeys and fortresses.

Theobald Fitzwalter (d. 1205) was granted the hereditary title of Le Boitilier—the king's chief butler— by Henry II of England. A later Theobald was entitled to one-tenth of the cargo of any wine ship that came to Ireland.

Since medieval times, Kilkenny castle has been a headquarters of the Butlers. Now it holds their archives and hosts their regular clan rallies and the annual Kilkenny festival, while its magnificent stables house the prestigious Kilkenny Design Shop.

The Butlers earned many important titles for their services to the colonial government, including Lords Dunboyne and Marquesses and Earls of Ormond. The 7th Earl of Ormond was the grandfather of Anne Boleyn, Henry VIII's unfortunate second wife who was mother to Queen Elizabeth I. **James Butler** (1610–88), 12th Earl and great Duke of Ormond, founded Dublin's Phoenix Park and many medical and civic institutions still flourishing today.

Butlers served in the armies of Europe and America. A widespread, international and still numerous family, they encompass many well-known personalities, from the temperance pioneer, Father Theobald Mathew, to the great poet, **William Butler Yeats**. There was also the controversial United States politician, **Benjamin Franklin Butler** (1818–93), who championed the rights of the labouring classes and black people.

John Butler (1716–1800), who was a priest, unexpectedly found himself the inheritor to the title of Lord Dunboyne. Believing it to be his duty to provide an heir, he left the Church and, though well advanced in years, married. However, he failed to produce an heir and, on his deathbed, he returned to the Church and left a handsome endowment to Maynooth College.

(O) Byrne

Ó Broin

Byrne (O) Beirne

Branach (*bran* meaning raven) was a son of Maolmórdha, an eleventh-century king of Leinster, and it was from him that the O Byrne name derived. The O Byrne territory was in County Kildare until the arrival of the Anglo-Normans, when they were driven south to the Wicklow mountains. There, for several centuries, they fought valiantly against the might of the Tudor monarchs. Their vast lands, known as Críoch Bhranach (O Byrne's country), included the present-day Newcastle, Arklow and Ballinacor. **Fiach MacHugh O Byrne**, their most heroic chieftain, led raids plundering the castles of the Pale, the area around Dublin controlled by the English. It was in the O Byrne fortress at Ballinacor in 1591 that the sons of the O Donnell and O Neill chieftains found refuge when escaping across the snow-clad Wicklow mountains from Dublin Castle.

Many O Byrnes left Ireland to follow the doomed Stuarts, following the battle of the Boyne. They remained in France, where they became leading citizens in Bordeaux, particularly in the wine business. They also served in the armies of France, both before and after the French Revolution. In the United States of America, the O Byrnes came to the fore in the Church, medicine and literature.

By the eighteenth century, some of the O Byrnes had married into the English aristocracy, assuming the now extinct titles of Leicester, de Tabley and Warren.

One O Byrne family, formerly with an estate at Cabinteely in County Dublin, has a curious crest surmounting its armorial bearings. A mermaid holds a mirror in her right hand and a comb in her left hand. Their motto is *certavi et vici* (I fought and I won).

Today, **Gay Byrne** is a popular and immensely successful presenter of radio and television in Ireland. His namesake, **Gabriel Byrne**, who was born in Dublin in 1950, has starred in many films and has written a delightful memoir called *Pictures in my Head.*

Like many other Irish families, the O Byrnes have a special book in which the poets praise their persons and their deeds. A copy of their *Leabhar Branach* is in Trinity College Dublin. O Byrne is now one of the ten commonest names in Ireland.

C

Caddell *see* Blake

(Mac) Caffrey

Mac Gafraidh

The surname Mac Gafraidh means son of Godfrey. The more usual spelling is Caffrey. They were a branch of the Maguires, once one of the most important septs of Ulster. Their homeland was Ballymacaffrey near Fivemiletown, bordering counties Tyrone and Fermanagh, where today they are no longer very numerous. There is also a townland called Rosmacaffrey.

Apart from the Tyrone historian, the **Reverend James MacCaffrey**, who died in 1875, the Caffreys have not been particularly noteworthy.

Although MacCaffery or Cafferty has sometimes been shortened to Caffery, these are in fact a Donegal and Derry sept and are not related to the Caffreys.

(O) Cahan *see* Keane

Cahill

Cathail

Cathail is the Irish version of the name Charles, meaning valour. From this first name derives Cahill, one of the earliest family names. The O prefix is no longer used by the Cahills. At first they were an important sept in Connacht, where they must have had strong connections with the sea, as their armorial shield features a whale spouting a fountain of water on a blue sea, while their crest is an anchor with an entwined cable.

By the fourteenth century there were several Cahill septs, most of them in Munster, where today they are still most numerous. They have left their name on five different country towns: there are three Ballycahills in County Tipperary, one in County Galway and another in County Clare.

The Cahills were prominent in the Church and, during the eighteenth century, in the armies in Europe, where they served in France with the Irish Regiment of Walsh. In the First World War, three brothers, all from a County Kilkenny family, were killed in action in France.

Caldwell

Ó hUarghuis Ó hUairsce

Horish Houriskey

There are two origins for the Caldwell surname in Ireland. Firstly, it could be an anglicization of the Irish name Ó hUarghuis or Ó hUairsce, which was also phonetically rendered in English as Horish or Houriskey, especially in Tyrone. Secondly, the name Caldwell, which is very numerous in

Scotland and England, is of territorial origin, deriving from lands of that name in Renfrewshire in Scotland. It is worth noting that the Irish word for water is *uisce*, because Coldwell was also a local surname in Yorkshire where, literally, it meant cold well!

Although the name is very numerous in Northern Ireland and less so in the Republic, the Irish Caldwells had to go to the USA to distinguish themselves. Bardsley, in his *Dictionary of English and Welsh Surnames*, writes, "This surname has ramified in the most extraordinary manner in the United States. One of two early settlers must have bred a healthy family of boys, who thrived and married."

James Caldwell (1734–81) came from a Huguenot family which emigrated from Scotland to Ireland and, later, to the USA, where he was born in Charlotte County, MN. He became a clergyman and was chaplain to the army, where he was known as the "soldier parson". His Christianity was described as being of the muscular kind and he was one of the founders of the American Bible Society.

Charles Caldwell (1772–1853) was a son of **Lieutenant Charles Caldwell** of the Presbyterian gentry of County Tyrone. Charles went to the USA, where he qualified in medicine and pioneered medical education in the Mississippi Valley. He was a professor at Louisville Medical Institute.

Alexander Caldwell (1830–1917) left his Donegal parents to volunteer for the Mexican war in which his father had been killed. He later followed a successful career in commerce and politics and was a contractor for army stores west of the Missouri. He promoted the development of the Kansas railroads.

Erskine Caldwell (1903–87), author of many novels and stories, achieved fame with his novel *Tobacco Road*, which was dramatized by Jack Kirkland in 1934. He was very active in social causes, particularly that of impoverished sharecroppers.

(O) Callaghan

Ó Ceallacháin

Callahan

There is a manuscript in Dublin's Genealogical Office showing the O Callaghans' amazingly long pedigree, dating from Milo in about 1400 BC to AD 1614. There is also a manuscript setting out the O Callaghan lands and their chieftains from AD 900 to 1933.

The family took their name from the tenth-century **King Ceallacháin** of Munster—*ceallach* means strife or contention. King Ceallacháin and his fellow chieftains warred continuously, thus enlarging their territories. It was also this king who killed Cinnéide, father of Brian Boru. The Ó Ceallacháins were kinsmen of the leading septs of the powerful Munster Eoghanacht clan.

In the eighteenth century, when large numbers of the Irish were dispossessed, many O Callaghans went to France and to Spain. In Barcelona, a lawyer called **Don Juan O Callaghan** (b. 1934) is the present and authenticated Chief of the Name.

Lismehane, beside the village of O Callaghan's Mills in Clare, was for centuries one of the O Callaghan mansions. A member of the Lismehane family, **Colonel George O Callaghan Westropp** (1864–1944), was aide-de-camp to three of Britain's kings. Returning to Ireland, he headed the Irish Farmers' Union and was a member of the first Irish Senate. Some years ago, Lismehane was razed and a bungalow built in its place.

There have been a number of outstanding members of this far-flung family who, of necessity, made their name abroad. There was an admiral in the British navy; an O Callaghan who wrote the first history of New York; an O Callaghan who compiled the useful reference book, *History of the Irish Brigades in the Service of France*; a Callaghan known as the "Apostle of Vermont"; a Callahan in the American army who fought at Bunker Hill.

At the turn of the twentieth century, **Trixie O Callaghan** (1870–1955) was a popular actress who captivated her audiences with her singing and dancing. **Dr. Pat O Callaghan** was the Olympic hammer-throwing champion at Amsterdam in 1928 and Los Angeles in 1932.

It is thought the O Callaghans in Ulster are not of the same family, their name being a corruption of O Kelaghan or Kealahan.

Campbell

Mac Cathmhaoil

This is a very numerous name in both Great Britain and Ireland, where the Irish name derives from *cathmhaoil*, meaning battle chief. Some Campbells were possibly of Norman origin and their name may have stemmed from the Latin *de campo bello*, while in Scotland it derived from *cam béal*, meaning curved mouth. There is no doubt that in Scotland they were a mighty clan and many of them sought, and found, their fortune in Ireland.

Mac Cathmhaoil (or Campbell) of Tyrone was a descendant of Feradhach, son of Muireadhach, son of Eoghan, son of Niall of the Nine Hostages. This family was a leading sept of the Cenél Feardhaigh at Inishowen, Clogher and Tyrone in Ulster.

In Donegal, where they possibly came as gallowglasses, or mercenary soldiers, the name was Mac Ailín from Mac Cailiún. A descendant of a Donegal family, **Sir Robert Campbell** of Carrick Buoy, Ballyshannon, was ennobled in 1771. In fact, there are ten titled Campbell families in *Burke's Peerage*. They are also well recorded in the annals and archives, and in biographies compiled by various members of their families. Many reached high rank serving in the forces in Europe and America.

In 1599, **Mr. Campbell**, Dean of Limerick, had his living taken from him by the rebels. There are letters written from the administration in London to Dublin saying, "the Duke of Ormond wants to dispose of Campbell and recommends his posting from Dublin to Edinburgh. This is considered advantageous as the Scots in Northern Ireland begin to be troublesome." That was in 1684!

Joseph Campbell (1879–1944) was a Belfast poet and **Patrick Campbell** (1913–80), 3rd Baron Glenavy, was a humorous writer and broadcaster.

Patrick J. Campbell (b. 1918), whose family came from Ballinasloe, County Galway, was General President of the United Brotherhood of Carpenters and Joiners in America.

The catering family of Campbell now owns Dublin's famous Bewley's cafés.

Canny *see* MacCann

Cantwell

de Cantual

The Cantwells came to Ireland in the twelfth century with the Anglo-Normans. They came from Kentwell in Suffolk and were given large grants of land around Kilkenny by the Butlers, who were also Norman knights. They made Cantwell's Court in County Kilkenny their principal seat and became thoroughly hibernicized. During the fourteenth and fifteenth centuries, they had many dealings with their powerful neighbours, the Butlers, Earls of Ormond.

There were various spellings of their name and the Genealogical Office has many of their pedigrees.

They were sheriffs of Kilkenny, soldiers and gentry. Two Cantwells held commissions in the army of James II and they were probably active at the battle of the Boyne in 1690. Cantwells served with the Irish brigades in France and also with the American Irish brigades in 1865.

Above all they were ecclesiastics. During the fifteenth century there were two **John Cantwells** who were archbishops of Cashel. **Richard Cantwell** was Bishop of Waterford and Lismore. **Oliver Cantwell** was Bishop of Ossory for almost forty years (1489–1527). He had the temerity in 1524 to excommunicate the great Earl of Ormond. He it was who built the bridge at Kilkenny. **John Cantwell** was Bishop of Meath at the time of the granting of Catholic emancipation. He helped in the reformation of the diocese. In 1936, Los Angeles' first archbishop was a **Dr. Cantwell.**

Professor Andrew Cantwell (*c.*1705–64) left Tipperary for France, where he became a writer and a physician. His son, **Andrew**, was also a writer, and a librarian in Paris.

The name is still numerous in Leinster and Munster. *A Cantwell Miscellany*, a pamphlet written by **Brian J. Cantwell**, gives an outline of the family and the various spellings of this original Norman name.

Carey

Ó Ciardha

(O) Keary

Ciar is an Irish word meaning dark or black. This sept, whose name was anglicized as O Keary, were kinsmen of the southern O Neills and were lords of Carbery in County Kildare until dispersed by the Normans. Another sept, whose original name was Mac Fiachra, is still to be found in County Galway and the Midlands. Here the name is changed to Carey. Carey is also an adaptation of the old Norman name, Carew. In fact, it is impossible to be sure of an authentic Irish Carey, as so many names have been anglicized to Carey. The name is very common in England and also in Ulster, where many came as settlers.

Dublin was the birthplace of four remarkable nineteenth-century Careys. **John Carey** (1756–1826), a classical scholar, invented the rocket used by shipwrecked mariners. **William Carey** (1759–1839) was a writer, now almost forgotten. **Matthew Carey** (1760–1839), who edited the *Freeman's Journal*, was so outspokenly critical of British rule that he had to leave for America at the time of the American War of Independence. He founded the *Pennsylvania Herald* and published *Carey's American Atlas.* An intellectual, he contributed generously of his talents both to his adopted country and to his homeland.

James Carey (1845–83), a bricklayer and builder who became a city councillor and a Fenian, took part in the Phoenix Park murders. He turned informer and was shot in revenge, subsequently escaping by sea to South Africa.

Governor Hugh Carey of New York was an influential Irish-American.

A seat of the Carey family was named "Careysville", situated on the river

Blackwater in County Waterford. White Castle in Moville, County Donegal, was a later eighteenth-century Carey family home.

Carleton

Ó Cairealláin

Kerrolan (O) Carolan

The O Cairealláins were once chieftains of clan Diarmada in County Derry and they gave their name to Clandermot in that county. This ancient surname is also anglicized as both Carolan and Carleton.

Hugh O Carolan was a distinguished bishop of Clogher from 1535 to 1568, one of the stormiest periods in Irish history.

Turlough O Carolan (1670–1738) is one of the most celebrated of the Irish bards. His family moved from County Meath to County Roscommon, where he was befriended by the wealthy Mac Dermott Roes. At fourteen, Turlough was blinded by chickenpox, whereupon Mrs. Mac Dermott Roe had him taught to play the harp. With the horse and the servant with which she provided him, he travelled the country, earning his living playing in the Big Houses. Many of his songs are still part of the repertoire of Irish folk singers.

William Carleton (1794–1869) was born in County Tyrone, the youngest of fourteen, in an impoverished farming family. He became a scholar and a folklorist, and a wild rover. He wrote many books about contemporary rural life, of which his *Traits and Stories of the Irish Peasantry* is probably the best known.

His son, also **William**, who was born in about 1830, emigrated first to New Zealand and then to Australia, where he published a novel, *The Warden of Galway.* He was considered by the Australians to be one of their best poets.

Denis Carolin was an assistant surgeon in the Irish brigade in New York in 1864.

The name is very numerous in most parts of Ireland. There are papers in the Public Records Office in Dublin relating to a Carolan family of County Louth, and especially to a **Reverend Francis Carolan** in the nineteenth century. There are also letters from a **Miss Anna Carolan** concerning the settlement of her English property between 1832 and 1840.

In the Royal Irish Academy in Dublin, a number of references can be found to the Carolans, sometimes also spelled Kerrolan.

Carmody

Ó Cearmada

This surname evolved from a son of Cearmaidh, a very ancient Irish personal name which still exists in parts of Clare and Munster. Between 1653 and 1654, during the rebellion against the English, seven members of this family were transplanted to Connacht and deprived of their lands. These were **Donnogh** and **Elizabeth Carmadie**, **Honora, Donnogh, Murtagh** and **Philip Carmady** and a **Margaret Carmody**.

In the nineteenth century, six families, mostly from Kilkee in County Clare, made the long sea journey to Argentina. There was **Daniel Patrick Carmody**, an engineer; he married a Brennan and they had nine children. He died in Buenos Aires in 1897. Much the same pattern was followed by all the Carmodys who went to South America, according to Dr. Eduarda Coghlan's comprehensive biography of the Irish in Argentina. Most of them arrived with their wives and they multiplied and prospered. Several owned big estates and horses and cattle.

The Carmodys are also very numerous in Ireland, especially in the south-western counties, the home of their forefathers. They have made their mark in the professions, business, religion and the services, but a Carmody has yet to come to the fore in politics or the arts.

Carnahan

Ó Cearnacháin

Kernahan Kernan

Carnahan originates from the Irish word *cearnach*, meaning victorious. Through the centuries it has had many variations: Kornaghan, Kernohan, Kernahan, Kernaghan and Kernan, for instance.

In medieval times, there was a Kernaghan sept marked on the map of County Donegal. Kernohan appears in Ulster in about the twelfth century and is still very numerous there today. At one time there were Ó Cearnacháin chiefs in Lune in County Meath. A second sept of the name were chiefs of Doe in Kilmacrenan in Tirconnell.

In 1813, in the Belfast Public Records Office, **Samuel Kornaghan** is recorded as assigning a lease of premises in Connor in County Antrim to J. Frew.

Earlier this century, **David Hobart Carnahan** was highly regarded for his research in analytical chemistry. **Ann Carnahan** wrote *The Vatican, the Story of the Holy City* which was published by Odhams in 1950.

Except for in Ulster, the name in all its variants is now very rare and seldom appears in the records.

Carney *see* Fox, Kearney

O Carolan *see* Carleton

Carr

Ó Carra

In England this is a very common surname, especially in Yorkshire, where carr, or kerr, means a low-lying meadow. It is also numerous throughout Ireland, where it can be found as the anglicized form of at least nine different Gaelic names, many of them now extinct. Some Carrs could be descendants of the Cromwellian armies, but in Ulster and Connacht their origins are usually Irish, Ó Carra, *carra* meaning a spear.

From the eighteenth century they are well recorded. Carrs are among a number of families whose papers, relating to their estates at Rathbeale in Swords, County Dublin, are preserved in the Dublin Public Records Office. Also there are copies of a census taken in 1851 which includes Carr families of County Kildare. At about that time, too, several Carrs from Wexford sailed for Argentina.

Charles Carr was a bishop of Killaloe in about 1720. Although **Reverend George Whitmore Carr** (1779–1849) served in the English yeomanry in the 1798 Rebellion, he was later a pioneer of temperance and a supporter of Father Mathew and Daniel O Connell.

Dr. Thomas Joseph Carr, formerly Bishop of Galway, was later Archbishop of Melbourne. **John Carr** was Dean of Armagh.

The Genealogical Office in Dublin has a confirmation of arms to **Colonel Edward Elliott Carr, CB**, and his descendants in Waterford, up until 1908. In 1901 there is a confirmation of arms to **Sir George Carr**, clerk of the Council of Munster. From the eighteenth century, there are many details of exchanges of property belonging to the Carrs in Dublin and its adjacent counties.

A famous twentieth-century Carr is **Joe Carr**, who was born in Dublin in

1922. A golf champion in the 1950s, he won many Irish championships and represented Ireland twenty-three times.

see also Keogh

Carrick *see* MacCarrick

(O) Carroll

Mac Cearbhaill

MacCarroll MacCarvill

The O Carrolls go back to the third-century King Oilioll Olum of Munster. Their name derives from Cearbhaill, who was with Brian Boru in 1014 at the battle of Clontarf.

Their senior septs were the chieftains of O Carroll Ely (Tipperary and Offaly), and O Carroll Oriel (Monaghan and Louth).

Cearbhaill means warlike champion, and this the O Carrolls undoubtedly were. This did not, however, save their Tipperary lands from the Butlers, one of the Norman families who dispersed them in the twelfth century.

Leap Castle, one of their Offaly fortresses, is said to be the most haunted ruin in Ireland. It is good to know that they are also protected by a good spirit, that of Queen Una, their legendary guardian angel.

They were good churchmen and builders of monasteries. When they had to flee Ireland, they fought in the armies of Europe. In America—in Maryland—they founded a distinguished Carroll family.

The owners of Ireland's biggest tobacco company, **P. J. Carroll and Company Limited** of Dundalk in County Louth, are descendants of the Ely O Carroll chieftains. Their coat of arms displays, on a black background, a pair of yellow lions facing each other holding between them a sword.

MacCarvill is an anglicized version of MacCarroll and is mostly to be found in Ulster.

Carson

Corsan

There are two sources for the Carson surname. In England it is thought to have derived originally from the French *garçon*, meaning small boy. In Scotland it was originally spelled Corsan. The Corsans were a prominent Scottish family who provided provosts for Dumfries for several generations.

Today, it is a most numerous name in Ulster, where the Carsons came in the seventeenth century, during the plantations, and acquired much land. They are well documented in the records. *A Short History of the Carson Family of Monanton, County Monaghan*, was published by **James Carson** in Belfast in 1879. In the same year, **T. W. Carson** wrote about the Carsons of Shanroe, also in County Monaghan.

The Public Records Office in Belfast has a pedigree of the Carson family of Belfast for 1844 to 1859. In the eighteenth and nineteenth century, **David Carson** owned lands around Belfast in County Antrim. There is a confirmation of arms to **Lieutenant George Watson Carson** for the descendants of **Thomas Carson** of Sycamore Lodge in Ballylig, County Down. His grandson was **Lieutenant George Carson, MC**, a son of **Thomas Macafee Carson** of Brooklyn, USA.

Joseph Carson was Vice Provost of Trinity College Dublin, where, in the library, there are many of his papers dating between 1867 and 1897. **John Carson, MP, CBE**, was Lord Mayor of Belfast in 1980 and 1981.

The most famous Carson was born in Dublin. He was **Sir Edward Carson**

(1854–1935), a lawyer and politician, Solicitor-General for Ireland and a Member of Parliament for Dublin University. He was also called to the English Bar and made a devastating cross-examination of Oscar Wilde during his notorious trial. Carson led a vigorous struggle against Home Rule for Ireland.

Although there are some Carsons in the Republic of Ireland, the name is still most numerous in Ulster.

Carty *see* MacCarthy

(O) Casey

Ó Cathasaigh

Vigilant or watchful is the translation of Casey, which was a personal name later to be used as a surname by at least six different septs from Belrothery, north of Dublin, further north to Roscommon and Mayo in Connacht, and south to Limerick and Cork in Munster. Today, they are most numerous in the southern counties.

Casey's Lios, near Waterford city, was one of their residences in that county. The Donahies, a fine Georgian County Dublin mansion, was a more recent Casey household, but it has now been demolished.

Whatever their topographical origins, the Caseys have made a significant contribution to the Church, with distinguished bishops at home and abroad, and to literature, particularly poetry. **John Keegan Casey** of Mullingar, a peasant poet and a fervent Fenian, died of tuberculosis in prison aged only thirty-two.

They are recorded in the Genealogical Office in Dublin from as far back as 1662. In the nineteenth century, there were requests from abroad for grants of arms to Caseys from the city of Cork who were in the Indian army and the civil service in Bengal.

Caseys were also active in the armies of Europe. **Joseph Gregory O Casey**, born in 1787 in Limerick, was an admiral in the French navy and Minister of the Marine.

Quite a number of Caseys went abroad to Canada, the Americas and to Australia, where they were especially distinguished. **Cornelius Gavan Casey**, born in Limerick in 1810, practised as a surgeon in Victoria. His grandson was **Richard Gardner, Baron Casey**, Governor-General of Australia in 1965.

Joseph Casey, the son of a Wicklow man, was a medical doctor in Washington. Undaunted by the break-up of his family and considerable hardship, he worked his way through law school and in 1861 was appointed by Lincoln as judge of the United States court of claims. He earned fame as editor of *Casey's Reports*, and went through difficult times in the Civil War.

An army engineer, **Thomas Lincoln Casey**, completed the construction of the Washington monument in 1884.

The most famous of all Caseys, **Sean O Casey** (1880–1964), was nurtured in Ireland. A Dublin labourer, socialist and member of the Citizen Army in the 1916 Easter Rising, he was Dublin's Abbey Theatre's most important playwright.

In Britain there have been many prominent Caseys, especially in the public services. **Walter Frances Casey**, son of a Dublin theatre manager, was editor of the prestigious London newspaper, *The Times*, in 1948.

Cashen

Mac Caisín

Cashin   Casheon   Cassion

The Mac Caisíns were a hereditary medical family of Upper Ossory, now comprising County Laois bordered by Kilkenny and Tipperary. Translated from the Irish, Mac Caisín means son of little Cais (*cas* means pleasant). There are a number of variants of the surname: Casheon, Cashion, Cashin, Cassion and Cassian.

According to records of the time, the Cashens were very numerous in the Midlands, as they still are today. Few settled around Dublin and hardly any in Northern Ireland.

In 1295 **Kenedi Carach Ó Cassion** and his men killed six English soldiers in north Tipperary. The official who should have arrested them kissed the murderers instead and let them go free!

The last recorded Cashin physician was **Conly Cashin**, who wrote a medical book in Latin in 1667.

In Waterford in the last century, the firm of **Cashin, Wyse and Quan** was a big shipowner. This Cashin family was from Kilshane in County Tipperary.

In the National Library of Ireland in Kildare Street, Dublin, there are many deeds relating to the properties of Cashin families in County Limerick in the eighteenth century.

There is a Ballycasheen in the counties of Waterford, Clare and Kerry, the place-name commemorating the family.

Cashman

Ó Ciosáin

Kissane

Cashman is an anglicization of Ó Ciosáin (*cios* means tribute or rent). Essentially now a Munster name, it was transformed to Cashman in County Cork and to Kissane in County Kerry.

Father Woulfe, an early expert on names, suggests that the Ó Ciosáin sept originated in Uí Maine in County Galway and moved south from there. Today the Cashmans are most numerous in Munster, almost all living in the Cork area. The Kissanes have also remained in their original Kerry territory, though they are not as numerous as the Cashmans.

In Dublin's Royal Irish Academy, there are accounts of Ó Ciosáins who were scribes and writers of Irish tales and tracts on Irish grammar.

In the 1930s, **John Kissane**, writing as Seán Ó Ciosáin, translated *The Vicar of Wakefield* and other classics into Irish. Around this same period, the **Reverend Edward Joseph Kissane** was writing bible commentaries.

(O) Cassidy

Ó Caiside

This surname was taken from a first name belonging to a family who, for three hundred years, were hereditary teachers and physicians to the Maguire chieftains of Fermanagh, where there is a town called Ballycassidy. In the early seventeenth century, when the planters from Britain were sent to settle in Ulster, the Cassidys and the Maguires were driven south.

A number of Cassidys followed the much beaten track to Europe, including the poet **An Caisdeach Bán**, who served for a while in the French army where there was also a Cassidy quartermaster with FitzJames' Horse, one of the Irish brigades. Around this time, too, **Thomas Cassidy** was expelled from a monastery and became a soldier of fortune, travelling the roads. He is remembered for his bawdy autobiography.

The family who now spell their name Cassidi in *Irish Family Records* had an ancestor who was a physician in 1650. His grandson also followed the profession in Louth, while another descendant, who served in the British army, became secretary to Viscount Castlereagh, and then chief secretary to the Irish parliament.

In recent years, the Cassidys have had a number of distinguished naval officers, including a captain-surgeon and an admiral who was commander-in-chief of the British Naval Home Command in 1982.

William Cassidy's father emigrated to Albany, New York, where he had a prosperous meat market and was an alderman. William satisfied his political leanings by writing amusing satirical articles. As a newspaper editor, he strongly opposed Lincoln, although he wrote a splendid eulogy when he died. He lacked knowledge of foreign affairs and was very antagonistic towards the English.

Years after their hereditary appointments as physicians had ended, the Cassidy medical tradition lived on in a ludicrous superstition. Until comparatively recently, in Louth or thereabouts, whenever a cow or a horse or any such domestic animal fell ill, the owner went to the nearest Cassidy to beg for a piece of the lining of his coat. This, burned under the animal's nose, was supposed to revive it!

The Cassidys also had a song of their own, called "Cassidy's Corner". The air to which it was sung was adapted by the Orangemen to fit one of their own sectarian songs, gracelessly titled "Kick the Pope".

Caulfield *see* Gaffney

Cawley *see* MacAuley

Church

Eaglais

Aglish

This surname originates from the old English *atte church*, meaning close to the church. It is one of the few English names which have been translated into Irish. *Eaglais* is the Irish word for church.

They came to Ireland in the seventeenth century and settled in Ulster. In County Derry, until the Land Act of 1903, there were fifty-four large landowners named Church. The name is now comparatively rare in Ireland.

Between 1702 and 1703, under the Williamite confiscations, they bought estates forfeited by the local Irish, and many settled in County Cork. They are particularly well recorded in the *Cork Historical and Archaeological Society Journals.* Their history, property and personalities are also thoroughly documented by a member of the family, **Beaufort H. Church**.

John Dearman Church was a high sheriff of Cork. He was the father of **Reverend R. W. Church** of Cork who, in the nineteenth century, was a dean of St. Paul's in London.

Commander William Harvey Church, RN, was born in Cork and died in Bristol. At one time he surveyed the south-west coast of Ireland for the admiralty. His poems are printed in the *Cork Historical and Archaeological Society Journals.*

The most notable member of this family was undoubtedly **Sir Richard Church** (1784–1873), known as the "liberator of Greece". His family were Cork Quakers and he ran away as a youth to join the British army. He served first in the wars around the Mediterranean, where he met the exiled Greek leaders and began to plead their cause in London. After an abortive period of service with the Neapolitan government, he left and joined the Greek revolution, eventually becoming the commander-in-chief. He adopted Greek citizenship and became a member of the Council of State. He lived in Greece for the rest of his life, dying in Athens.

Claffey *see* Hand

Clancy

Mac Fhlannchaidh

Clanchy Glanchy MacClancy

Clanchy, Glanchy, MacClancy—there used to be several versions of this widespread surname, of which Clancy is now the most usual. It derives from an Irish first name, Fhlannchaidh, meaning red-haired warrior.

There were two septs, of which the County Clare family was the most important. The Clancys of Thomond, where they had their headquarters, were hereditary brehons, or judges, to the powerful O Briens and were also kinsmen of the Mac Namaras. Cahermaclancy marks one of their bases in that county. The other sept was of County Leitrim, where they were chiefs of Dartry and Rosclogher until the collapse of the old Gaelic aristocracy in the late seventeenth century.

Boetius was a favourite name and a **Boetius Clancy** represented Clare in parliament in 1585. Another Boetius—**Boetius Glancy**—is recorded as "of the nobility of the diocese of Killaloe".

Many Clancys forfeited their lands following the defeat of the Irish at the siege of Limerick. They joined the flight of the "Wild Geese" to Europe, where they were distinguished in the Irish brigades, especially in the wars in the Spanish Netherlands where there were several Don Clancys holding high army rank.

Their many genealogies, and letters and records relating to the families, are in the archives in England and Scotland, and also in Ottawa, Canada.

Peadar Clancy was executed in 1920 by British auxiliaries during the Irish War of Independence.

Willie Clancy (1921–73), a master carpenter and folklorist from County Clare, was one of the best-loved traditional musicians. His concert appearances in Britain, Europe and the USA, where he would play slow Irish airs on the uileann pipes or the concert flute, attracted large audiences to hear this master of authentic Irish music.

Clarke

Ó Cléirigh

(O) Clery MacAlary MacClery

Cleary is one of the oldest of the Irish surnames, with a lineage going back to Guaire, a King of Connacht famous for his hospitality. Medieval banquets are now held in his enduring fortress overlooking Galway Bay, during the tourist season.

Cleireach, born about AD 820, a descendant of Guaire, initiated the family name. Until they were driven out in the seventeenth century, the O Clerys were poets, churchmen and lawyers in Ulster. The name is quite numerous today, especially since it became fashionable to use the O prefix again. Most of the bearers of this name are now to be found in the south-west.

Cléireach means clerk and this was the dominant occupation of this family, which included the famous O Clerys who helped compile one of Ireland's most valuable books, *The Annals of the Four Masters.*

During the Irish submergence, O Clery was anglicized to Clarke, a common name in England. Nowadays it would be difficult to disentangle a genuine Irish O Clery from a Clarke, many of whom came as English immigrants generations ago.

During the Napoleonic era, two sisters, **Julie** and **Desirée Cleary**, daughters of an Irish silk merchant in Marseilles, made very prestigious marriages, one becoming Queen of Spain, the other Queen of Norway and Sweden.

Thomas Clarke, who was executed in 1916, was the first of the signatories of the Proclamation of the Irish Republic. **Austin Clarke**, who died in 1974, was a popular Dublin poet.

MacClery or MacAlary could also be of this family whose armorial bearings show three green nettle leaves on a yellow background—possibly referring to the physicians in the O Clery clan.

Lieutenant-Colonel Brian Clark (d. 1995) was born in London of a Northern Ireland family. He served with the Royal Irish Fusiliers in the British army during the Second World War, winning a Military Cross at Monte Cassino. He retired to County Wicklow and revitalized the former Royal National Lifeboat Institute, now Irish Lifeboats. He had many friends in the army in Ireland and fought hard against prejudice, for recognition for the many Irish men and women who had fought abroad.

(O) Cleary, Clery *see* Clarke

Coady

Mac ódu

Archdeacon Cody MacGillycuddy

The history of the Coady, or Cody, name is most unusual. Odo le Ercedekne came with the Anglo-Normans and this family was well settled in County Kilkenny from the thirteenth to the seventeenth century. At first they were mentioned in the records as Leveldekne, and then, as Archdeken or Archdeacon. Then some began to be called MacOde, son of Ode. In time, MacOde was gaelicized to MacGillycuddy.

For many generations, Archdeken and Cody were among the leading names in the counties of Kilkenny, Tipperary and Leix.

There was a Jesuit priest, **Richard Archdekin** (1618–93), better known as **Richard MacGillycuddy**, who published a book of miracles.

Most of the Codys who fled to France after the collapse of James II and his Irish army went under the name of Archdeacon. They prospered there in business at Nantes. **Edmond Archdeacon** was a high-ranking naval officer and, although the Archdeacon name is rare in Ireland today, it is still prominent in France. **Nicholas Archdeacon**, Bishop of Kilfenora from 1800 to 1824, although Irish born, was a constant visitor to his French relations.

Although the name MacGillycuddy is also rare, except in County Kerry, it is one of the old families to boast an official Chief of the Name, The MacGillycuddy of the Reeks.

William Frederick Cody (1845–1917), who was born in Ohio, was known internationally as Buffalo Bill and probably came from County Tipperary.

see also MacGillycuddy

Coen *see* Coyne

Coffey

Ó Cobhthaigh

Cowhig

Coffey derives from the Irish name Ó Cobhthaigh (*cobhthach* meaning victorious). There were three main septs—in West Cork, County Galway and South Roscommon.

In Cork because of differences of pronunciation the name became Cowhig or Cowhey. Several place-names record them. In County Cork there is Duncowhey, and there is a Rathcoffey both in County Kildare and in County Leix.

In 1863, **H. Coffey** of Dublin published *Genealogy and Historical Records of the Sept Cobhthaigh.*

An important branch of the Coffeys which settled in Westmeath were famous bards. **Dermot O Coffey** (fl. 1580) was their most distinguished Gaelic poet. At least half a dozen others are well recorded in Irish literature. **Muircheartach** (fl. 1580) was given a mare for every poem of praise he wrote to Manus O Donnell. He wrote twenty poems, so he acquired twenty mares!

Charles Coffey, born in Dublin *c.*1700, was crippled from birth. However, he went to London and had many successes there in the theatre, writing popular plays into which he introduced Irish airs—the first time they were heard on the London stage.

James Charles Coffey (1815–80), a county court judge, was father of **William Henry Coffey** (1854–1943) a county court judge of New South Wales.

James Coffey (1846–1919), born in New York of Irish parents, was a judge in California for thirty-six years.

George Coffey (1857–1916), who came from Rathcoffey in County Kildare and was of the Munster sept, was a highly esteemed archaeologist. **Denis J. Coffey** (1865–1945) graduated as a medical doctor and became the first president of University College Dublin.

The Coffeys are numerous and widespread in Ireland.

Coghlan *see* Coughlan

Cohalan *see* Coughlan

Cohen *see* Coyne

Coleman

Ó Colmáin Ó Clumháin

Clifford Colman

The history of this name is a complex one. Like many other names in Ireland, it is also numerous in England. However, it is thought that the name Coleman was originally Ó Colmáin of the Uí Fiachrach, a leading sept in the counties of Mayo, Sligo and Galway, where many of the name are still to be found.

A branch moved to Cork, where they were known as Ó Clumháin. Some anglicized their name to Clifford. Both the Colemans and Cliffords are very numerous in Munster.

Colm is the Irish word for dove and their name derives from this mystical bird. It would seem they can boast very early ancestry, possibly claiming kinship with the seventh-century **Saint Colman** (*c.*605–76), who was Bishop of Lindisfarne in Scotland in 661. An Irish monk, he was at Iona in 664 when he was called to the Synod of Whitby to settle the dispute between the Romans and the Celts over the dating of Easter. Saint Colman supported the Celts, and lost. With his Columban monks, he retreated to Ireland to settle on Inishbofin in the Aran Islands off Galway, where he built a church and a monastery.

There were two earlier Colman saints. One was a pagan who became a Christian saint and died about AD 600. The other was **Saint Colman Ela** (b. *c.*552), who was a poet before taking holy orders. He was a kinsman of the great St. Columbanus, who was of a royal Donegal family. Saint Colman Ela built a monastery on Iona, from where he spread the Gospel to the Scots.

At some time in the ninth century, there was a poet priest called **Colman** who spent most of his life in a monastery in northern France.

Many Colemans, Colmans and Cliffords are in the records of those who forfeited their lands or who served in the armies, both Irish and English, in the seventeenth century.

(O) Colleran

Ó Callaráin

This is a very rare name in Ireland with only a few families in and around Dublin, rather more in the provinces and hardly any at all in Ulster.

They are known to have originated in Mayo and north County Galway where, in a record dated 1785, eleven families were counted in Ballinrobe.

They have yet to make their name in history or the arts.

Collins

Ó Coileáin Mac Coileáin

Cullane

It would be difficult now to distinguish an Irish Collins from an English immigrant bearing the Collins name, which is equally numerous in Britain. In Ireland it is an anglicization of Ó Coileáin (*coiléan* means a young dog). They were originally based in the Limerick area, where they were lords of Connello. Dispersed by the arrival of the land-hungry Anglo-Normans, they fled further south to West Cork.

In the savage struggle against colonial rule in the seventeenth century, their leading priests took an active part—one suffering martyrdom. An **Ó Coileáin** poet was known as "the silver tongue of Munster".

Many Collins went abroad—to explore the Arctic, to govern Tasmania and to found Sydney. A creative branch of the family prospered in London, one of whom was **Wilkie Collins**, author of *The Moonstone.*

In the USA, Edward Knight Collins (1802–78) was a shipowner who founded the Collins Line, a serious challenge to Cunard.

Michael Collins (1890–1922), one of the most brilliant leaders during the Irish struggle for independence, was tragically killed in an ambush in West Cork during the Civil War.

The Collins armorial shield is red, showing three right hands. In a white chevron there are two green trefoils and a sheaf of corn. The crest is a blue mermaid holding a mirror and combing her long hair.

Colum *see* MacColum

Comerford

Comartún

Quemerford

Comartún is the hibernicized form of the name of an English family who have been prominent in Ireland since 1210. They are said to have come either from Comberton, a parish in

Cambridgeshire, or from Comberford, a village in Staffordshire.

For many generations, they were landed gentry in counties Kilkenny and Waterford. **Joseph Comerford**, Baron of Dunganmore (afterwards Marquis d'Anglune), held the title used by the head of the family. **Margaret Comerford**, of the Kilkenny family, first married Viscount St. Lawrence of Howth and then Jenico, Viscount Preston. She died in Dublin in 1637.

The Comerfords adopted the Irish cause, resisting Elizabethan aggression. In 1585, **Gerald Comerford**, attorney for Connacht, was summoned by the Queen to attend a commission and would fail to attend "at his peril". In Cromwellian times, many Comerfords were transplanted to Connacht. Following the defeat of James II at the battle of the Boyne, fourteen Comerford officers from his Irish army fled to join the armies of Europe.

In Waterford the name was sometimes transformed to Quemerford, and **Dr. Nicholas Quemford** (*c.*1542–99) of that city was the first of sixteen Jesuits to come from there between 1590 and 1640. **Patrick Comerford** (1625–52), Bishop of Waterford, and **Edward Comerford** (*c.*1600) were two of a number of Comerford bishops in Ireland.

John Comerford (1770–1832) painted portraits of leading politicians, including Robert Emmet and Daniel O Connell and many actors of his time.

Maire Comerford (1893–1982), a committed nationalist, was wounded and imprisoned during the Civil War when she opposed the Treaty. In 1961, she published a well received book, *The First Dáil.*

In the USA, **Judge James Comerford**, a former Kilkenny man, was one of the directors of the Saint Patrick's Day parade in New York city.

Commane *see* Hurley

Commons *see* Cummins

Comyns *see* Cummins

Conan *see* Cooney

Concannon

Ó Concheanainn

Conconnon

This very ancient sept of Uí Maine, County Galway, took its surname from **Cuiceannan**, who was killed in AD 991. Translated from the Irish, it means fair-headed hound.

From the eleventh to the fifteenth century, the Ó Concheanainn chieftains were known as the lords of Diarmada, which is near Kilkerrin in County Galway. The Chief of the Name had his headquarters in nearby Kiltullagh. Although today the name is to be found in various parts of the country, Concannon remains a very numerous name in the west of Ireland.

King Cathal O Conor built Knockmoy Abbey for the Cistercian monks in 1189. It is now a ruin, but inside can be seen the fine monumental grave slab erected over the tomb of the fourteenth-century chieftain, **Maurice Ó Concannan**.

During the Cromwellian wars, many of their possessions were taken from them but, until the middle of the last century, the Concannons still owned much property in their original homelands.

Matthew Concannon (1701–48) was one of the first Irish journalists to take London by storm. He attacked its literary establishment, including the great English poet, Alexander Pope. He also wrote comedies and poems and, for his journalistic services to the government, he was appointed attorney-general in Jamaica. He is remembered in Ireland for the anthology of verse he published, much of it translated from the Irish.

Thomas C. Concannon was a very active member of the Gaelic League in its early days. His wife, **Helena Concannon** (1878–1952), born a Walsh in County Derry, was well known for her religious and political writings. She became a member of *Dáil Éireann* and a Senator.

Condon

Condún

Condon, a very common name in Ireland, except in Ulster, derives from the Norman family of de Caunteton who integrated so exceptionally well following their settlement in Ireland in the twelfth century. The chief of the sept, which they formed in the Irish fashion, was known as **An Condúnach**. County Cork was their homeland for a long time where they had a tower house named Cregg Castle.

They fought for the Jacobites, suffered the confiscation of their lands and were forced to emigrate to Europe. In 1690, because they had followed James II, twenty-one Condons were attainted and driven from their lands.

In the seventeenth century, **David Condon** was a popular Gaelic poet.

The Condons of Clonleigh, Barony of Condons and Clangibbon, written by P. Ryan in 1896, gives a full account of the family and there are also many references in local history journals.

The most notorious Condon was **Edward Meagher Condon** (1835–1915) of County Cork, who went to America and fought in the Civil War. Afterwards he returned to Ireland a committed Fenian and took part in the murderous attack on the Manchester prison van, for which he was condemned to death. Because of his United States citizenship he escaped this fate, but was imprisoned for ten years. Returning to the United States, he became a Constitutionalist and wrote *The Irish Race in America*.

Richard Condon (b. 1915), the American playwright and novelist, wrote *The Manchurian Candidate*. He bought Rossenara, a Palladian house in County Kilkenny, and restored it admirably. He lived there for nearly twenty years before going back to Texas.

Colm Condon (b. 1921), senior counsel, was the attorney-general who, in 1970, prosecuted for the state during the famous arms trial when members of the Irish government were alleged to be involved in arms smuggling.

Richard Condon (b. 1937) of Waterford, a leading theatre consultant, administered the Dublin Theatre Festival and has been a successful theatre manager in Dublin and England.

(O) Connell

Ó Conaill

Ó Conaill stems from a personal name meaning high or powerful. One of the most numerous families, they claim a lineage going back to a high king of *c.*280 BC, Eremonium Aengus Tuirneach.

There were three distinct O Connell septs: one was in Ulster, the second in Connacht, while the third and most important was in Munster, particularly Kerry, where they were driven to the Atlantic's edge by the O Donoghues in the eleventh century. Here they were chieftains and hereditary constables of Ballycarbery Castle, near Cahirciveen in County Kerry. In 1650 the castle was demolished by the Cromwellians and some of these O Connells were transplanted to Connacht, where they are still numerous.

From this time began the O Connells' strong and rewarding links with Europe, where they featured prominently in the Irish brigades and at the royal courts. When **Muircheartach O Connell** (1738–1830) entered the Austrian army he changed his name to the more easily pronounced Moritz. During the Seven Years War, his kinsman **Count Daniel O Connell** fought on the opposing side! The Count won the favour of the Empress Maria Theresa and served as imperial chamberlain with three emperors.

Count Daniel Charles O Connell (1745–1833) was the youngest of twenty-two children and served with many armies in various countries. At one time he drew full pay as a general in the French army while acting as a colonel in the British army!

A cousin, **Sir Maurice O Connell** (1766–1848), served with the French army in the early stages of the French Revolution. However, in 1794 he left France to serve in the British army. He was sent to command the forces in Australia, where he settled permanently.

Sir Maurice's nephew was the towering figure of nineteenth-century Ireland, **Daniel O Connell** (1775–1847), "The Liberator". He was reared in Kerry by his uncle, Maurice O Connell, a gentleman smuggler nicknamed Hunting Cap who evaded the penal laws by sending his nephew to France for an education. The young Daniel gave up a successful career at the London Bar to return to Ireland, where his powerful oratory put new spirit into the downtrodden Irish people and, in 1829, he won Catholic emancipation. Always opposed to violence, Daniel O Connell's last years were saddened by the militancy of the Young Irelanders.

The focal point in Dublin's widest street, O Connell Street, is the impressive O Connell monument. His family is very well recorded and the present representative has restored Derrynane House in Killarney, where The Liberator was reared, and its fascinating display of memorabilia can be seen by the public.

Conner *see* (O) Connor

(O) Connolly

Ó Conghaile

Connely

The Connollys were originally a sept in County Galway, where Ballyconeely could well have been one of their homesteads. As the clan grew, they branched south into Cork and Meath, and also north to Monaghan, where **Tirlogha Ó Conghaile** was Chief of the Name in 1591. *Conghaile* means valorous.

A lawyer, **William Conolly** (1662–1729) of Donegal, made a fortune from the lands of the dispossessed Irish after the battle of the Boyne, and was believed to be the richest man in Ireland. He was Speaker in the Irish House of Commons. His was the inspiration for the lovely Castletown Villa in County Kildare, now the headquarters of the Irish Georgian Society.

A Connolly is execrated for betraying the leaders of the 1641 Rising, while another Connolly, **James Connolly** (1868–1916), was one of the martyred heroes of 1916.

Many Connollys went to Europe and also to the USA, where one notorious couple, **Pierce** and **Cornelia Connolly**, earned the headlines because of their acrimonious change of religious faith. When they became Roman Catholics, she went into a convent and founded a religious order, while he joined the priesthood—although not for long.

The great American tennis star of the 1950s, nicknamed Little Mo, was **Maureen Connolly** (1934–69), and one of Ireland's fashion pioneers is **Sybil Connolly** (b. 1921).

The coat of arms of the Connollys of Kildare is a black saltire cross on a white background decorated with five escallops, possibly signifying that they were Crusaders.

(O) Connor

Ó Conchobhair Ó Conchúir

Conner (O) Conor

The name O Connor derives from a personal name which means hero or champion. The O Connors are a very numerous and eminent family, one of the three royal families which include the O Neills and the O Briens. Originally their name was shared by six distinct and unrelated septs in different parts of the country, from Ulster to Munster, several of which are now extinct.

They took their name from Conchobhair (d. 971), King of Connacht. Conchobhair had to submit to the high king, the great Brian Boru, progenitor of the O Briens. A descendant, **Denis O Conor**, is the present chieftain and is styled O Conor Don. This family is uniquely Gaelic. Not a trace remains of their original ancient seat, Belenagare, but their present ancestral home, Clonalis, is still standing in County Roscommon and is in the care of **Pyers O Conor Nash** and his wife, **Marguerite**, who safeguard its invaluable family archives. Clonalis is the only house open to the public that is wholly of the old Irish.

In 1119, **Turlough Mór O Conor** was High King of Ireland. A statesman more than a warrior, he tried to centralize his government, built bridges and castles, maintained a mint and had a fleet of ships on the Shannon and the Atlantic. He married three times and had twenty children, one of whose descendants was Queen Victoria.

Despite the cruel frustrations of the penal laws, the O Connors of Connacht managed to remain in Ireland, producing churchmen, scholars and parliamentarians.

Arthur O Connor (1765–1852) of Cork was a general in Napolean's army. His brother, **Roger O Connor** (1763–1834), was a notorious Irish eccentric who burned down his own house following a suspiciously heavy insurance cover. He subsequently eloped with a married woman and was later tried for robbing the Galway mail train, claiming that he had wanted "to obtain from it some letters incriminating a friend".

The O Connors had artistic genius in abundance. In London, **James Arthur O Connor** (1792–1841) painted landscapes and **John O Connor** (1830–89) revolutionized stage design. **Andrew O Connor**, progenitor of a line of internationally famous artists, was one of America's outstanding sculptors. One of the most popular Irish concert pianists today is **John O Conor** (b. 1947).

The O Connors were also soldiers, physicians and distinguished diplomats all over Europe and the Far East. As early as 1694, an O Connor was physician to the King of Poland. In 1854, at the battle of Alma, an O Connor won a Victoria Cross. It was a Cork O Connor who pioneered Esperanto, an artificial universal language.

Conroy

Ó Maolchonaire

Conary Conree Conry

Conroy is a distinguished Gaelic surname which was anglicized from the Irish, Ó Mulconry, meaning son of Conroy. The Conroys were a remarkably literary family who, for generations, were hereditary poets and chroniclers to the kings of Connacht.

Tanaidhe Ó Maolchonaire (*c.*1100) wrote poems about the legendary Firbolg and Tuatha De Danaan warriors. **Torna Ó Mulconry** (*c.*1250–1310) was chief poet to the O Conor kings of Connacht. His was the inspiration for the somewhat unfortunate seventeenth-century poetry contest between north and south known as the Contention of the Bards. **John Ó Mulconry**, a chronicler and poet of County Clare, presided over a school of poets from 1440 to 1470. **Fearfeasa Ó Mulconry** was one of the scribes who contributed to the famous *Annals of the Four Masters*, a history of Ireland up to 1636.

Florence Conry (1561–1629), a Franciscan monk, spent most of his life in Europe. He was instrumental in founding the Irish College in Louvain in 1607. He came to Ireland, briefly, as a chaplain with the Spanish Armada, from which later he escaped back to Spain with Red Hugh O Donnell. Although he was appointed Archbishop of Tuam, he was never able to return to Ireland. He wrote many spiritual books in Spanish and French.

In the seventeenth century the Ó Mulconrys were gentry, but because they were followers of James II they lost most of their land. **Charles Ó Mulconry** was killed at the battle of the Boyne. Later they converted to the Protestant religion and had much of their land restored. They claim ancestry from Niall of the Nine Hostages (*c.*400). In 1653, **Moylin Ó Mulconry** was accredited 43rd in descent from Niall.

Roderick Conroy (d. 1853) was active in the movement for Catholic emancipation, but he later fell out with the Liberator, Daniel O Connell. In 1864, H. F. Hone published *The O Maolconaire family, unpublished letters from Sir Edward Conry, Bart.*

Conroy is a most numerous name, especially in their original homeland in Roscommon and the west of Ireland.

Considine

Mac Consaidín

Constantine was the anglicized form of the name of an ancestor from whom the family took their name. They are of a Dalcassian sept, the descendants of Domhnall Mór Ó Brien, a king of Munster who died in 1194. Although little is recorded of the Considines, they were a prosperous people in Clare. They suffered transplantation and forfeiture of their lands, which was prevalent throughout Ireland in the seventeenth century. A number of them are mentioned as serving in the armies of Europe.

Séamus Mac Consaidín, who was born in Clare around 1745, was a doctor and scholar. He was also a poet, in the eighteenth-century Irish tradition.

Derk in Pallas Green, County Limerick, is a fine house which was built *c.*1770 and was for many years the seat of the Considine family. **Father Daniel Considine**, a distinguished Jesuit and author of many spiritual books, spent his boyhood there.

Heffernan is a traditional first name of the Considines of Derk, which was sold in 1971. **Sir Heffernan James Fritz Joseph John Considine**, who was educated at Stonyhurst and Oxford, was deputy inspector-general of the Royal Irish Constabulary from 1900 to 1911. His son, **Captain Heffernan James Considine** of the 4th Battalion of the Irish regiment, was killed in action in the First World War.

Many of the family have gone abroad, taking this not very numerous name to South Africa and to Canada. It was to Australia that **Michael Considine** and his mother went from County Mayo in 1890. In Sydney, he became a member of the Socialist Federation of Australia and a union militant. He was president of the Amalgamated Miners' Association and organized many strikes. A strong Marxist, during the First World War he appointed himself acting consul for the new Bolshevik government in Russia.

Dennis Considine, who left Ireland for Australia to study the therapeutic value of the indigenous plants, returned to Cork in 1794 to join the army medical service. He was sent to Edinburgh on a grant to study medicine. He took with him his two natural children, **Constance** and **Constantine**. After graduation, he travelled extensively, studying the curative benefits of plants. For his learned thesis on eucalyptus oil, New South Wales dedicated a tree, *Eucalyptus Consideniano*, to commemorate his pioneer work.

(O) Conway

Mac Connmhaigh

Through the years this name has been spelled in a variety of ways. One of its Irish variants, Connmhaigh, means "head smashing"! There were a number of distinct families of the name, including an Irish sept in County Clare who remained important until the fourteenth century and the Conways who came from Wales.

Gillananal Ó Connmhaigh (d. 1360) was the foremost teacher of music in Thomond, a region which included counties Clare, Limerick and Tipperary.

Early in the fifteenth century, two bishops of Kilmacduagh came from the O Conway family. It was a Jesuit priest, **Richard Conway** (d. 1623), who helped carry out many important reforms in the Church in Ireland at the time of the Reformation.

Jenkin Conway and his three brothers came from Wales in the sixteenth century. They were granted 5,260 acres from the forfeited estate of the Earl of Desmond at Killorglin, County Kerry. In time, they were ennobled with various titles, now mostly extinct. The **Barons Conway** of Kerry were outstanding as progressive landlords, especially during the Great Famine.

The Conways of Cloghane and Glenbeigh in County Kerry provided many distinguished military men, including the first **Count Conway**, who served in France. His son, **Thomas Count Conway** (d. 1800), a major-general in the French army, was a governor of French territory in India. He later became a general in the American War of Independence, where he is remembered for "Conway's Cabal", an attempt by himself and others to oust Washington.

Edward Conway (1894–1968) from Nenagh, County Tipperary, was a leading biochemist who received the Boyle Medal of the Royal Dublin Society, the premier science award in Ireland.

William Conway (1913–77) was born in Belfast. A learned prelate, he was appointed Archbishop of Armagh and Primate of All Ireland in 1963. Two years later he was created cardinal. The formation of *Trócaire*, an agency for aid to the Third World, was partly the inspiration of Cardinal Conway.

Although it would be almost impossible to distinguish between the various Conways—Irish or Welsh—they still seem to be more numerous in Connacht than elsewhere.

Conwell *see* MacConville

Conyngham *see* Cunningham

Cooney

Ó Cuana Ó Cuanacháin

Conan Coonan Counihan

Cooney, a very common surname, comes from the Irish, *cuanna*, meaning handsome or elegant. They were originally settled in Ulster, where they are said to have been an important sept who were chiefs of Clann Fergus. The name is now rare in Ulster, which they left long ago to move to Connacht, where **Diarmud Ó Cuana** (d. 1248) was described in the *Annals of Loch Cé* as being a great priest of Elphin. The Elphin diocese covers Ross, Sligo and Galway. According to Elizabethan records, the Cooneys were still living in the Elphin area in the fifteenth century.

In the 1880s, in both her native Ireland and in the USA, **Mary Cooney** was well known for her poetry.

The *Irish Genealogist* for 1937 contains an account of a **Peter Cooney** who was a printer in Dublin in the eighteenth century.

Little more was heard of the Cooneys until the present day. **Patrick Cooney** (b. 1931) was leader of the Fine Gael Party in the Senate in 1981 and was a Minister of Defence and, in 1986, at the height of the long teachers' strike, he was appointed Minister of Education. **Sean Cooney**, also born in 1931, is a freelance journalist for many publications and specializes in scientific writing.

In County Cork, Cooney can be a variant of Ó Cuanacháin, which has been anglicized to Counihan. Conan is also a variation of the surname, as is Coonan.

In 1864, a **John Coonan** was colonel of the Irish-American brigade in New York.

Cooper

In England there are many distinguished representatives of this common surname, which stems from the trade of coopering, making barrels and casks.

The surname is to be found all over Ireland, where their arrival, to say the least of it, was most ironic. **Austin Cooper**, whose father was at the court of King Charles I, sold all his possessions and, to escape persecution by Cromwell, emigrated to Ireland, where "he layed out gardens", according to *Burke's Irish Family Records.*

An industrious people, the Coopers acquired vast estates, mostly in the west, where they built splendid houses and castles. Markree, a huge castle in Sligo, was the setting for a serialized film on Irish television and is now a hotel run by **Charles** and **Mary Cooper**. Cooper Hill in Limerick and Cooper's Hill in Sligo (now a hotel) are still in Cooper possession.

Edward Joshua Cooper (1798–1863), a distinguished scholar and traveller and MP for Sligo, inherited Markree Castle, where he erected an observatory. He made many valuable discoveries, determining the position of fifty stars, and he wrote valuable books on astronomy. **Major Bryan Cooper** (1884–1930), also of the Markree branch of the family, was a distinguished soldier and MP for Dublin. From 1923 to 1930 he was a member of Dáil Éireann, the Irish parliament.

Austin Cooper, a land agent and an antiquarian, published an important book of his sketches, notes and diaries. **John Cooper** (1836–97) was a telegraph engineer and surveyor to the Sultan of Turkey. He was responsible for the irrigation of much of Asia Minor.

Pedigrees of various Coopers dating from *c.*1650 to *c.*1879 are kept in the National Library of Ireland, together with a collection of their marriage settlements, cash books and rental ledgers.

In 1860, **Charles William Cooper** of Cooper's Hill, County Sligo, assumed, by royal licence, the name and arms of O Hara, in compliance with the will of his uncle, Charles King O Hara of Annaghmore, County Sligo.

Corballis

Cearballis

Not even the present representative of the name in Ireland can throw any light on the origins of this obscure name. He thinks it might once have been spelt Cearballis and that there may even be connections with Saint Colmcille!

The Corballis family were landed gentry in County Meath for several generations in the nineteenth century, and there are townlands in that area bearing their very distinctive name.

Their pedigree, from about 1700, is detailed in *Burke's Irish Family Records*, mentioning their seats at Ratoath Manor in County Meath and Rossanagh in Ashford, County Wicklow. During the nineteenth century, they were champions of Catholic emancipation and papal knights.

Several members of the Corballis family settled in Canada and New Zealand.

Corbett

Ó Corbáin

Corbet

Corbett (sometimes Corbet) is a very common surname throughout Ireland, although it was originally an English name, said to be of Norman extraction. Debrett says: "Corbet, a noble Norman, came into England with the Conqueror, and from his son **Roger Corbet** descends the baronial house as well as the families now existing." Corbett could also be an anglicization of Ó Corbáin, an old Gaelic name which possibly derived from *corb*, meaning a chariot.

The Anglo-Norman Corbetts settled in counties Meath and Offaly, where there are two Corbettstowns and, in the sixteenth century, there was a Ballycorbet.

The Corbetts who came to Ireland were predominantly military, many arriving with the Cromwellian armies, although the first recorded was **John Corbett**, who was constable of Limerick in the time of Edward III (1312–77). **Miles Corbet**, a Cromwellian regicide, was chief baron of the Exchequer in Ireland.

Thomas Corbett served in the army of James II and was a colonel with the Irish brigade in France. His brother, **Thomas**, also an officer with the Irish brigade, was killed in a duel.

Francis Corbet was one of those who, *c.*1750, drew up specifications for the famous St. Patrick's Hospital which is still standing in Dublin. He was also dean of St. Patrick's Cathedral, Dublin.

In Dublin's Genealogical Office there is an account of the granting of a royal licence in 1820 to **Francis Corbet** of Aclare, County Meath, to bear the name Singleton only, resulting from the will of the late Henry Singleton.

In 1805, **William Corbet** published a modern plan of the city of Dublin and its environs, showing paving and lighting.

James John Corbett (1866–1933), known as Gentleman Jim, became world heavyweight boxing champion when he knocked out John L. Sullivan in the twenty-first round at New Orleans in 1892.

(O) Corcoran

Ó Corcráin

Corcoran is a very common name throughout Ireland, except in Ulster. The Mac Corcorans were once an important sept in Ely O Carroll country (the counties of Offaly and Tipperary). They take their name from the Irish word for purple, *corcair*. From the eleventh to the fifteenth century, the O Corcorans whose territory was around Lough Erne in County Fermanagh produced many ecclesiastics.

Brian Ó Corcorain, a sixteenth-century bard, is remembered for his account of the adventures of a boy who was stolen by an eagle.

The most outstanding representative of the name was **Brigadier General Michael Corcoran**, who recruited men for the Irish Legion in the United States of America in 1861. The son of a British army officer from County Donegal, Michael Corcoran had resigned his commission in the Royal Irish Constabulary, refusing to take part in the coercion of his own countrymen. He took part in the famous battle of Bull Run.

O Carolan, the great Gaelic poet, wrote a poem of praise about **Edmund O Corcoran**, a hero of the siege of Limerick in 1601.

In Dublin's Genealogical Office there is a copy of a confirmation of arms, dated 18 August 1928, to the descendants of **James Corcoran** of Oakley Park in King's County (now County Laois), to his sons, **Joseph Corcoran** of Bal Toor, King's County, and **Sir John Arthur Corcoran**. There is also a record of the bankruptcy, in 1878, of **Martin** and **Patrick Corcoran**.

The **Honourable James Desmond Corcoran**, who was Premier, Treasurer and Minister of Ethnic Affairs for Southern Australia in 1979, was undoubtedly of Irish origin.

Corr *see* Corry

Corrigan

Ó Corragáin

Carrigan Courigan

The name indicates a descendant of Corragáin, from a diminutive of the first name, Corra. Other than this, very little is known about the sept, which originated from Fermanagh and who were kinsmen of the Maguire chieftains of that county.

By the sixteenth century, the Corrigans had scattered far and wide, to counties Monaghan, Meath, Offaly and Roscommon. Ballycorrigan near Nenagh, County Tipperary, indicates there must have been an important Corrigan family living there, probably in the seventeenth century. As abbots and ecclesiastics they feature in the *Annals of the Four Masters*, which was compiled in the seventeenth century.

The most distinguished Corrigan was a Dubliner, **Sir Dominic John Corrigan**, a physician whose tradesman father gave him an excellent education at a time when Catholics rarely had this opportunity. He studied medicine in Edinburgh and, on his return to Dublin, became a very able and much loved doctor. He was invited to become a Member of Parliament, although he had little knowledge of the intricacies of politics. He was five times president of the College of Physicians. In 1880, an obituary in *The Lancet* described him condescendingly as the "first prominent physician of the race of the majority in Ireland".

Michael Augustine Corrigan was the grandson of a Meath family. His family, who were grocers, lived frugally to give their children a good education. He was sent to the American College in

Rome for his studies and emigrated to New York in 1828. In time he was appointed Archbishop of New York. He had three brothers—two priests and one doctor—who were always very supportive of him in his administrative duties. He ministered to a diocese of 1,200,000 communicants. Archbishop Corrigan abhorred secret societies and showed no more than a faint interest in Irish politics.

Tom Corrigan left Meath with his family in 1864, bound for Australia. He served his apprenticeship as a jockey and dominated the racetracks of Australia. His honesty made him very popular and when the little man with the huge moustache was killed in a steeplechase he was given a gigantic funeral in Melbourne.

There are still Corrigans in Ulster. **Máiréad Corrigan** of Belfast was co-founder of the Peace People, in response to the deaths of three children in 1976. She was jointly awarded the Nobel Prize for Peace in 1981. She married Jackie Maguire whose wife and children had been killed in the violence.

Corry

Mac Gothraidh

Corr Curry MacCory MacCurry

MacCory, which is quite a rare Irish surname, is an anglicization of Mac Gothraidh (son of Godfrey). There are many variants: MacCorry, MacCurry, Corry, Curry, Corra and Corr. Corry is also a common English surname, meaning a corrie or hollow side of a hill where the game hides.

There are very few MacCorys to be found in Ireland now, but there are innumerable Corrys in Ulster, several of whom have been writers of minor importance. The MacCorys were a branch of the powerful Maguire family of County Fermanagh. During the confiscations ordered by William of Orange after his triumph at the battle of the Boyne, the Maguires, and with them the MacCorys, had most of their estates confiscated and handed over to **James Corry**. Corry was a Scottish ancestor of the Earls of Belmore who, until the Land Acts came into force over one hundred years ago, owned nearly twenty thousand acres in counties Fermanagh and Tyrone.

In Counties Waterford and Tipperary there are Corrys who may originally have been O Currys of Limerick. There was a **Richard Corre** who was Bishop of Lismore from 1279–1308, but he may have been a Norman.

In 1659, Corry was one of the most numerous names in County Meath. It seems impossible now to disentangle the Gaelic from the Scottish–English MacCorrys or Corrys.

Isaac Corry (1755–1813) held many important appointments, including Chancellor of the Irish Exchequer in 1798. With the demise of the Union, this Newry man lost all his political power.

Cosgrave

Mac Cosraigh Ó Cosraigh

Cosgrove MacCusker

This surname is believed to come from the Irish word *cosrach*, which means victorious. There were a number of septs, including the Mac Cosraighs in Leinster who owned lands near Bray, County Wicklow, and were dispersed by the powerful O Byrne and O Toole clans. In the sixteenth century, the Mac Cosraighs of County Wexford were very highly regarded.

In Ulster, the name was spelled Cosgrove and is still common there. In

Connacht, the name was spelled with the O prefix, and **Coningus Ó Coscraigh**, a medieval representative of this sept, was Bishop of Clonmacnoise and died in AD 997. Benedictus O Casey (d. 1325), Bishop of Killaloe, was also of this sept.

In Ulster, another sept of this name were chiefs of Feara Ruis near Carrickmacross. MacCusker is a variant of the name in Ulster.

Cosgrave is one of the families whose documents, of the seventeenth and eighteenth centuries, are in the Paris Bibliothèque Nationale. There is also a Cosgrave pedigree for *c.*1720 to 1938 in Dublin's Genealogical Office, and a confirmation of arms in 1940 to the descendants of **Henry Cosgrave** of Corrstown House, County Dublin, to his great-great-grandson, **Sir William Alexander Cosgrave**, son of **Henry**.

William T. Cosgrave (1880–1965) of Dublin was the first President of the Irish Free State. His son, **Liam Cosgrave**, was Taoiseach of the Republic of Ireland from 1973 to 1976.

Patrick Cosgrave, born in Dublin in 1941 and educated mostly abroad, is a political commentator, novelist and biographer. At one time he was a special adviser to the British Prime Minister, Margaret Thatcher.

Costello

Mac Oisdealbhaigh

Costelloe

Costello (sometimes Costelloe) is a Norman surname which derived from Oistealbh, one of the sons of the famous Gilbert de Nangle. His original surname was de Angulos and this is the first example of a Norman name assuming a Mac prefix (Mac Oisdealbhaigh). On their arrival with the Normans in the twelfth century, they settled in Connacht and gave their name to the barony of Costello in east Mayo.

They were constantly at war with the powerful MacDermots of Roscommon. A tragic love story is told of Una MacDermot, who was locked in an island fortress on Lough Key to separate her from her lover, **Thomas Costello**. Trying to swim to her on the island he was drowned, and she died heartbroken.

In the sixteenth century, their chief seat was at Ballaghadereen in County Mayo. During the seventeenth-century colonization they lost much of their land. In 1666, **Dudley Costello** rebelled and was proclaimed a traitor. He fled to become a colonel in the Spanish service. Although he returned to fight the Cromwellians, he never got back his land. In Dublin's Genealogical Office there are pedigrees relating to the MacCostellos of Mayo and Cadiz in Spain dating from *c.*1550 to 1778.

Nuala Costello wrote a first-hand account of the landing in Mayo of the French General Humbert's expedition to Ireland in 1798.

For their service to France, the Costellos were created Viscounts and Counts of France and Barons of the Holy Roman Empire.

Louisa Stuart Costello (1799–1870) and her brother, **Dudley**, spent their childhood in Paris after their father's death. She helped support her family by painting miniatures and writing. Returning to London, she wrote many popular novels and travel books. Her brother collaborated with her and became a foreign correspondent and an outstanding travel writer of his day.

John A. Costello (1891–1976) was born in Dublin. He was a lawyer and, for a time, attorney-general. He was invited to become Taoiseach and held that post in the first two coalition governments. In 1948, during a visit to Canada, he announced the repeal of the External Relations Act, taking Ireland out of the Commonwealth. A reluctant politician, after his defeat in the Dáil he returned to his practice as a leading counsel. His son, **Declan Costello** (b. 1927), also abandoned politics and became a high court judge.

Paul Costello (b. 1945) is one of Ireland's top dress designers, with an international clientele which includes Princess Diana.

Costigan

Mac Oistigín

Oistigín is an Irish version of the old English name Roger, the pet form for which is Hodgin. The Mac Oistigíns were a branch of a prominent family in the Midlands, the Fitzpatricks of Ossory. This once numerous clan has now considerably dwindled, with hardly a Costigan to be found in Ulster.

In 1510 there was a **MacCostygin** who was rector of Durrow in County Laois. **Patrick MacCostyken** was recorded in 1540 as being a juror in Naas, County Kildare, while the last kern (private Irish soldier) to be mustered by the Earl of Ormond was also a Costigan.

Dermot O Costigan, a gentleman who was dispossessed of his lands during the 1650 rebellions, became a rapparee, or freebooter, living in the woods, carrying out guerrilla attacks on the enemy. However, despite the attempted plantation of the Midlands, he succeeded in getting back his main seat at Grange, and his family held on to it until the Gaelic suppression of the seventeenth century.

Arthur William Costigan, who was living in Europe in the 1780s, wrote letters home which his brother, **C. A. Costigan**, edited under the title, *Sketches of Society and Manners in Portugal.*

In Ottawa, the Public Archives of Canada contain correspondence from the period 1873 to 1916 which includes letters from a Costigan living there, discussing politics and the position of the Roman Catholic Church.

Cotter

Mac Coitir Macoitir

In the form Kotter, this name has long been common in Denmark and Northern Europe. In Ireland it comes from the Norse personal name, Oitir. It is not unusual for Gaelic names to have a Norse origin (such as McAuliffe, meaning son of Olaf). **William Cottyr** (b. *c.*1498) was a son of another **William Cottyr**, who was said to be of Danish origin.

Cotter is still a common name, especially in Munster. The Mac Oitirs or Mac Coitirs were an old Gaelic family of Cork, where their name is perpetuated in Cottlestown and at least eight other place-names.

Sir James Cotter built Anngrove, County Cork, which was still their family home until recently. An admirer of King Charles I, he went to Switzerland with two companions and shot one of the men who had been involved in the King's execution. His grateful widow bestowed Charles's bed on Sir James and this was kept at Anngrove until it was destroyed in a fire. King James II is also believed to have stayed there.

Another **Sir James Cotter** (d. 1705) commanded the king's troops and represented Cork in parliament. His son, **Sir James Cotter** (1689–1720), was hanged for his devotion to the Stuart cause. His son **James** (1714–46) was made an Irish baronet and served in the Irish parliament.

Having changed their religion, in succeeding generations there were a number of Protestant clergymen Cotters in the County Cork diocese.

In the seventeenth century there were two esteemed Cotter Gaelic poets.

The notorious **Patrick Cotter** (1761–1806), born in Kinsale, adopted the more Irish sounding name of O Brien. A pituitary defect caused him to grow to 8' 1" tall (2.46 m). He made a fortune exhibiting himself at fairs all over England and, on his death, left his money to his mother.

Cotty *see* MacCarthy

(O) Coughlan

Ó Cochláin

Cohalan Coghlan MacCoughlan

Coughlan is the anglicized form of the old Irish name, Ó Cochláin, a diminutive of the word for a cape or hood. A most numerous name in the Republic of Ireland, though not in Northern Ireland, it is found in various forms, including MacCoughlan, O Coughlan and Cohalan.

There were two distinct septs or families, one in County Cork and the other, by far the more important, in County Offaly where, until the nineteenth century, they were big landowners. Garrycastle was their headquarters and they had fortified castles in the Banagher and Clonmacnoise areas. They were a Dalcassian sept and their head was styled Chief of Delvin.

Sir John MacCoughlan (d. 1590) was probably one of the ten or so members of this powerful sept mentioned in the history known as *The Annals of the Four Masters*, which was written by monks in the sixteenth century.

Between 1689 and 1790, two Coughlans represented Banagher in the Irish parliament. In the eighteenth century they held 3,400 acres in County Offaly.

Jeremiah Coughlan was a gentleman of slender means with an extravagant wife who augmented her finances by smuggling and thereby building Ardo Castle on the County Waterford coast. She married her daughters to wealthy dukes and earls, one of whose grandsons was the famous Prime Minister of France, Marshal MacMahon. He inherited Ardo, but it has long since been sold and, nowadays, is a prominent ruin on the Waterford skyline.

The Coughlans suffered from the dispossession and transplantation of the seventeenth-century conquests. Many took flight to Europe to serve in Irish regiments in France.

The antecedents of the notorious **Father Charles E. Coughlin** (1891–1979) emigrated to the United States. Known as the "radio priest", he began broadcasting sermons to children in 1930. He expressed increasingly reactionary and anti-Semitic views and, after years of effort, his Church finally silenced him in 1942.

In the 1940s **Sean Coughlan** wrote a number of books on greyhound racing and the now increasingly discredited sport of coursing.

Dr. Eduardo A. Coughlan, a distinguished lawyer of a family long established in Buenos Aires, compiled a huge biographical dictionary of the Irish in the Argentines, which he published in 1987.

Counihan *see* Cooney

Courtney

Ó Curnáin

Courtenay Courtnay

The name Courtney, or Courtenay, is plentiful in every province, particularly Munster. In its original Irish form,

Ó Curnáin derives from an ancient personal name, *cuirnín*, a diminutive of corn or a drinking cup. In early times they were a distinguished literary family in Breffny, which comprised Cavan and west Leitrim. Between 1316 and 1346 they were chroniclers to O Rourke, King of Breffny.

Courtenay, the Norman version of the name, comes from an historic family settled in England for centuries, the Earls of Devon. One of them, **Sir Philip Courtenay**, was knighted by Edward the Black Prince (1330–76). He held the post of Lieutenant of Ireland for ten years. The Courtenay Earls of Devon and peers of Ireland in the eighteenth century owned 33,000 acres in County Limerick confiscated from the FitzGeralds, Earls of Desmond.

There are many Courtenays in northeast Ulster. It is thought some may have changed their name from MacCourt—a name totally unconnected with the Norman name. It is thought that these were settlers who came from England at the time of the plantations. The Belfast Public Records Office holds many papers relating to the Courtenay family of Grange in County Antrim.

The name occurs frequently in the archives, including mention of the account book of a **James Courtenay** who had a scutch mill at Portglenone, County Antrim, and a **Robert Courtenay** who was agent to the wealthy Smith-Barrys of the Barrymore family in County Cork.

see also MacCourt

Cousins

Cúisín

Cuson Cussen

There are a variety of spellings of this surname, which came to Ireland with the Anglo-Normans. At that time it was le Cosyn, meaning the kinsman.

In many instances the old Irish name Cúisín was anglicized to Cousins and it is thought that the Cousins in the southern and western parts of the country stem from that Gaelic name. There are a great number of Cousins in Ulster, but they probably came from England originally. Cussen was a more usual form of the name in the counties of Limerick, Cork and Waterford.

Adam Cuson was one of the fourteenth-century scribes who contributed to the *Book of Hy Many*, a genealogical history of the tribes of County Galway.

Early in the nineteenth century, a period of much religious dispute, the **Reverend John Cousins** gave sermons and published tracts denigrating the Roman Catholic clergy.

Samuel Cousins (1801–87), who was born in Exeter, was a leading mezzotint engraver.

The most famous Irish Cousins were **James H. Cousins** (1873–1956) and his wife, **Margaret**. He was born in Belfast but moved to Dublin where he acted, wrote poetry and plays and taught English. He was an early vegetarian and remained one all his life. He went to India to teach and spent the rest of his life there, producing many books which were published in Madras, including his autobiography, co-authored by his wife, *We Two Together*.

Cowhig *see* Coffey

Coyle

Mac Giolla Chomhgaill

MacIlhoyle

Coyle, also a common name in England, has suffered a confusing number of variations in Ireland. As an ancient Irish name it is MacGiolla Chomhgaill, meaning devotee of Saint Comgal. In Donegal, it has been anglicized in some cases to MacIlhoyle. The MacIlhoyle sept had one of its headquarters at Kilmacrenan.

Anthony Coyle, Bishop of Raphoe from 1782 to 1801, was renowned for his religious writings and his poetry, particularly one poem about the discovery of Moses hidden in the rushes.

The Coyles were driven from their homelands by the many wars and rebellions. They are mentioned frequently in the Archives Nationale in Paris where there is a confirmation from the Dublin Genealogical Office of a granting of arms to the descendants of **Charles Coyle** of Dublin, son of **James Coyle** of Ballintemple, County Cavan, and to his eldest son, **James Vincent Coyle** of Glenburn in Clontarf, County Dublin.

Also, among the Stuart papers written in Latin by James II, there is a mention of "**James Coyle**, now in Paris who is the son of parents of gentle birth, **Eugene Coyle** of Connacht and Catherine Barnewall . . . "

In 1799, part of Sherlockstown, near Naas in County Kildare, was left to **Stephen** and **George Coyle**.

In the nineteenth century, **James Coyle** was a prolific compiler of genealogies and a composer of Ossianic verse.

Willie and **Stephen Coyle** are recorded as living in Kansas in 1875 and, in the early twentieth century, **Kathleen Coyle** of New York was a popular novelist.

Brian Coyle (b. 1934) is one of Dublin's leading auctioneers and valuers. He is also an art historian, writer and lecturer.

Coyne

Ó Cadhain

Barnacle Coen Cohen Kyne

The Coynes were a minor sept of the Uí Fiachrach, a clan rooted in Partry in south County Galway. Essentially a Connacht name, Coynes found in Leinster, especially around Dublin, probably originated from the west of Ireland. The name can be a synonym for Kyne. It has also been anglicized to Coen or Cohen, common Jewish surnames, though in Ireland they are more usually Irish.

Kilcoyne is a form of Mac Giolla Chaoine, meaning son of the follower of St. Caoin. It is not thought to be connected with Ó Cadhain, because *caoin* means gentle, whereas *cadhain* means a wild goose.

Cadhain has also been anglicized to Barnacle—flights of barnacle geese are a familiar sight on the Galway coast. **Nora Barnacle**, whose Irish name was formerly Cadhain, came from that area of County Galway known as Joyce Country. Appropriately, she was the wife of one of Ireland's most famous writers—James Joyce!

Apart from a mention of their service as officers in the army of James II and, in the nineteenth century, the French army, the Coynes feature little in the records, other than as minor writers.

Joseph Sterling Coyne (1803–68), who was born in Birr, County Offaly, went to London where he was very active in the literary world, writing many theatrical farces. His chief claim to fame is as one of the founders of the very successful English humorous journal, *Punch*.

Craford *see* Crawford

Craig

Craig is a very old Scottish name denoting a rock. It has been very common in Ireland since the seventeenth century, especially in Ulster, where they arrived during the plantation which began in 1609.

The Craigs are very well recorded in the Northern Ireland archives, where they have a wealth of pedigrees, papers, wills and leases, etc. In a sixteenth-century manuscript preserved in Manchester, there is a query about land near Mallow in County Cork and its conveyancing to the King by **Sir J. Craig**. Marsh's Library in Dublin holds a petition from **R. Craig**, the owner of a ship built at Ballyshannon who suffered losses in the service of the government in the West Indies between 1702 and 1707.

In 1805 General Maurice Lacy was commanding the Russian troops at Naples. His letters, written in French, to **General Sir J. Craig** are preserved in London's British Museum. In the Belfast Public Records Office there are about twenty letters dated between 1811 and 1815 written from Pennsylvania to the **Craigs** in Lisburn, which contain much information concerning conditions in the USA.

In the eighteenth century, **Rear Admiral William Craig** of Allenstown in County Meath was given a grant of arms on assuming the name Waller only.

James Craig (1871–1940) was born in Belfast, the son of a distillery millionaire. He led the Unionists against Home Rule and organized the Ulster Volunteers. In 1921 he became the first Prime Minister of Northern Ireland and was created 1st Viscount Craigavon.

May Craig (*c.*1889–1972), who was born in Dublin, was one of the leading actresses in Dublin's famous Abbey Theatre. **Maurice Craig**, who was born in Belfast in 1919, is a poet and is Ireland's leading architectural historian. He has written a conversational memoir entitled *The Elephant and the Polish Question.*

Crawford

Craford

The Crawfords came from Scotland and northern England to colonize Ireland. They must have come in great numbers, as the name is very numerous, particularly in Ulster. *The Crawfords of Donegal and How They Came Here*, which was published by **R. Crawford** of Dublin in 1886, may explain their origins.

Personal papers relating to a **George Crawford** who lived during the reign of Queen Elizabeth I include a claim to Rathlin Island off the coast of County Antrim. There are also a number of pedigrees available in Ireland, England, France and America. A pedigree of the Crawford family of Millwood, County Fermanagh, runs to four and a half pages and includes the **1st Earl of Richmond**.

In the Dublin Genealogical Office, dating between *c.*1575 and 1845, there are pedigrees of Crawfords of Cunningham in Scotland, of Ballysavage in County Antrim, of Tullyvanny in County Donegal, of Dublin city and of Wisconsin, USA. There are also pedigrees of Crawfords of Crawfordsburn in County Down and of Lakelands, County Cork, dating from *c.*1650 to 1904.

A pedigree of Crawfords of County Antrim dating from 1680 to 1805 show that family's transition to the name Sharman Crawford. A descendant, **William Sharman Crawford** (1781–1861), was born in County Down. A brave politician, he campaigned for tenants' rights and for Catholic emancipation, though he did not agree with Daniel O Connell.

In France, there are eighteenth-century letters to le curé de Bobigny from his brother, the **Reverend Archambault Crawford**, originally of Limerick and described as **l'Abbé Guillaume Crawford.**

Julia Crawford (*c.*1799–*c.*1860), who was born in Cavan, is immortalized by one song that she wrote, the famous "Kathleen Mavourneen".

Between 1914 and 1925, **Colonel Frederick Crawford** was a prominent figure in the Ulster Volunteer Force and was involved in the Larne gun-running incident.

Cray *see* Crea

Crea

Mac Crea

MacCrea MacRae Ray Wray

There are a variety of permutations and combinations of this ancient Gaelic name, which is also found in Scotland. It can be MacCrea, MacRae, Ray or Wray. It has often been mistaken for the old Irish surname Mac Raith, which was anglicized to MacGrath.

It would seem that the name Crea, or its synonym Rea, was established in Ulster before the plantations, for it is mentioned in the records as early as 1600 and there is also a place-name, Ballymacrea, in County Antrim.

The Crea family were prominent—probably in agriculture—in County Down until comparatively recently. In the Belfast Public Records Office, there is an estate map of 1768 of Ringawiddy, which was owned by Lord Henry FitzGerald, a son of the Duke of Leinster, of which the Creas seem to have been tenants. There are also copies of wills made by several members of the Crea family of Ringawiddy. In 1843, a **W. Crea** applied for a licence to carry arms. There are also farm accounts dating from 1857 to 1893. In 1847, Lord de Ros, a relative of the wealthy FitzGeralds, sent out letters to his tenantry at Ringawiddy thanking them for their support during the Great Famine and this included **Mrs. Ann Crea**.

Today, the Crea name has almost died out in Ireland, though the name is probably perpetuated in McCrea in Northern Ireland, where that variation of the name is very numerous.

Creagh *see* (O) Neill

Crean

Ó Croidheáin

Crehan

The name in Irish derives from *croídhe*, meaning heart. They were a minor branch of the Cenél Eoghan of Ulster who descended from King Niall of the Nine Hostages.

John O Crean of Ballynegare is said to have been head of the family in 1598 while, also in the sixteenth century, the O Creans of Annagh were a prominent Sligo family who were also unusually wealthy merchants. At that time, also, there were two O Crean bishops: one, the Bishop of Elphin, who, perhaps for some misdemeanour, was "removed", and **Daniel O Crean** of Holy Cross in Sligo, Provincial of the Dominican Order, who suffered greatly during the religious persecutions and died in 1616.

Following the confiscations of the seventeenth century, the Creans moved south to Munster, mostly to Cork, where they are still to be found. Others went west to Connacht, many changing their name to Crehan, especially in the area around Ballinasloe.

The Creans were never numerous

and they have yet to feature in the history or literature of Ireland. There was, however, one outstanding character, **Thomas Crean**, who was born in Annascaul, County Kerry, in 1877, near the Dingle peninsula. He joined the British navy at fifteen and sailed with the famous Antarctic explorers, Scott and Shackleton, on three expeditions to find the South Pole. When Scott and his companions were separated from their base ship, Crean was with the search party that found them frozen to death in their camp. In the *Capuchin Annual* for 1952, there is a vivid account of the appalling hardship suffered by the explorers and the outstanding bravery of Crean, who became known as Polar Crean. He lived to retire to Annascaul and open the South Pole Inn, where he died in 1938.

Many of the Creans went to America. **Agnes Crean** married James Bennett from Scotland in New York in 1840. It was this Bennett who founded the *New York Herald*.

Creegan

Ó Croídheagáin

Crean Cregan

Creegan—in Irish Ó Croídheagáin (*croídhe* means heart)—has been confused in parts of Connacht with Crehan. Crean (q.v.) is a historically acceptable variant of Creegan. Throughout Ireland today, Cregan is far more numerous than Creegan.

Martin Cregan (1788–1870) of County Meath worked for the Stewarts in County Tyrone. Recognizing his artistic talents, they paid for his education at art school in London. He exhibited at the Royal Academy there and returned to Dublin, where he became a leading Irish portrait painter.

In the Belfast Public Records Office, there are twenty leases relating to the Cregan family of Ballinatagart, County Armagh, dating from 1793 to 1880. In 1892, the Dublin Genealogical Office issued a confirmation of arms to **Thomas MacMahon Cregan** of County Clare and of Limerick, where he was High Sheriff.

Cregan *see* Creegan

Creighton

Crichton

Creighton or Crichton are the same name, pronounced "Cryton". This family came to Ireland in the sixteenth century at the time of the plantation of Ulster. They came from Crichton Castle near Edinburgh, described by Marmion as "Crichton! though now that miry court, But pens the lazy steer and sheep."

The Dublin Public Records Office holds papers relating to the Creighton family of Dublin, Galway, Fermanagh and Westmeath. There are deeds relating to an **Abraham Creighton** of Clifden in Connemara who was setting up a distillery there in 1824.

The Crichtons built a number of mansions in various areas of the country, the most outstanding of which to this day is Crom Castle in Newtown Butler, County Fermanagh, seat of the Earls of Erne. It was besieged by James II's Irish troops and was vigorously and triumphantly defended by the Creightons in a most bloody battle.

Abraham Creighton, who was created Baron Erne of Crom Castle in 1768, died in 1772. In 1802, **John, 3rd Earl of Erne**, changed the spelling of the name to Crichton. He was Lord Lieutenant of County Fermanagh and a representative peer of Ireland.

John Creighton (1768–1827), born in Athlone, introduced vaccination to Ireland. **Edward Creighton** (1820–74) went to the USA, where he was a pioneer of telegraphy.

A Crichton family of Carrowgarry in Beltra, County Sligo, came from Midlothian in Scotland in the seventeenth century. They were soldiers and medical men for many generations. **Sir Archibald Crichton** (d. 1865) was a physician to Nicholas I of Russia. One of his sons was killed serving with the White Russian army in 1920 and another descendant, married to the heiress of Carrowgarry, was a physician to Alexander I of Russia.

Today the Creightons, or Crichtons, are far more numerous in Ulster than in any of the other three provinces.

Crichton *see* Creighton

Cronin

Ó Cróinín

This Gaelic surname originates from *crón*, meaning saffron-coloured. The Cronins were a sept of Corca Laoidhe in south-west Cork who held an administrative post in the Church and property at Gougane Barra in County Cork. Ballycroneen, also in County Cork, got its name from this family.

The Cronin name appears frequently in the ancient Gaelic manuscripts. O Sullivan Beare (1560–1618), who led the revolt against the English and was defeated at Kinsale, received his schooling from **Father Donogh O Cronin**, who was hanged in 1601.

Lieutenant Philip Cronin died of his wounds while serving with the Irish-American brigade in 1864.

A strong literary talent is found in the many Cronins who, in the nineteenth and twentieth centuries, wrote for magazines and newspapers. The **Reverend Michael Cronin** wrote on many international subjects, including the League of Nations and its problems. In the 1944 *Capuchin Annual*, **William Cronin** wrote "Memories of Fifty Years in the Irish Woollen Trade".

Today's representative of the name is critic and poet **Tony Cronin**, who was born in County Wexford in 1926. He was assistant editor of the now defunct, *The Bell*, a prestigious Irish literary magazine. He has published books of poetry, reminiscences and novels. He also helped instigate *Aosdána*, an organization which helps provide a guaranteed income for a selected number of creative artists.

Cronin—it lost its O prefix during the Gaelic submergence and never regained it—is very numerous in the Irish Republic, rating many columns in the telephone directories, while in Northern Ireland it is scarce. The name is also common in Great Britain, particularly in Scotland.

Crosbie

Mac an Chrosáin

Crosby Cross MacCrossan

This family held the office of chief bard to the O Mores of Leix (Laois), to whom they were also kinsmen. Later they changed their name from O More to Mac an Chrosáin. In the sixteenth century, a member of this family transferred to the English side and anglicized his name to Crosby. He moved south to Ardfert in County Kerry, where he was described as "a very powerful Kerry landlord and also a noted intriguer and one of the Commissioners for the plantation of Ulster".

Sir Thomas Crosbie was a Member

of Parliament, and **Maurice Crosbie** was created the 1st Lord Brandon. Another Crosbie, the 2nd Earl of Glandore's wife, **Lady Diana**, was nicknamed "Owen Glandore" because of her notorious gambling debts.

In 1790, the Crosbies of Ballyheigue Castle near Tralee, County Kerry, were caught up in a scandal of the deliberate sinking of a Danish ship which was loaded with chests full of silver.

The Crosbies, some of whom emigrated to Canada, have had many adventurers. In 1778, one became famous for his exploits as a hot-air balloonist, while another was executed as a rebel in the 1798 Rebellion—they did sometimes stray from their English allegiance!

There was an assistant surgeon called Crosby on the medical staff of the Irish-American brigade in the nineteenth century.

George Crosbie, musician and businessman, is a member of the family who own *The Examiner*, Munster's leading newspaper based in Cork.

see also Crosson

Cross

Mac an Chrosáin

Crosby MacCrossan

Although Cross is an English name, it can, in some instances, be an anglicization of Mac an Chrosáin, or MacCrossan. It can also be related to Crosby or Crosbie.

There were two different MacCrossan septs, one in County Tipperary and the other in counties Leix and Offaly, where they have given their name to the town of Ballymacrossan. They were hereditary bards to the O Mores and the O Conors.

Belfast Public Records Office has a copy of the rentals of the Cross estate in County Armagh dating from 1881 to 1917. There is also a ground plan of their property in Armagh city in 1855 and a map of Newholland Mills, Crossdenned, of 1856.

In the nineteenth century, when **Sarah Jane**, daughter of **Colonel William Cross** of Dartan in County Armagh, married an Innes, he legally assumed the name **Innes-Cross**. When he died, she married a Cooke, who dutifully assumed the name **Cooke-Cross**.

Eric Cross (*c.*1905–80) was born in Newry. In 1942 he wrote a book of short stories, *The Tailor and Ansty.* Considered to be too bawdy, his books were burned, and Eric and his wife were hounded by the clergy and their neighbours.

see also Crosbie, Crosson, MacCrossan

Crosson

Mac an Chrosáin

Crosby Crossan MacCrossan

Crosson is a very rare surname in Ireland. Probably the most prominent representative today is the **Crosson Transport Group** of Drogheda and Dundalk. There are also a few Crossons in nearby County Cavan. The original Irish was Mac an Chrosáin, *cros* being the Irish for cross.

Apart from Crosson, Mac an Chrosáin underwent a number of anglicizations, including Crosby or Crosbie. Later the prefix was dropped and the name became Crossan, a surname which is still numerous in Ireland today.

In the Genealogical Office in Dublin there is a collection of notes and copies of deeds relating to the families of MacCrossan and MacCrosson dating between 1657 and 1810.

see Cross, MacCrossan

Crotty

Ó Crotaigh

When Ó Crotaigh was anglicized to Crotty, it lost its O prefix. This surname came from an Irish word for hunchback, *crotach*. In medieval times the Crottys were a branch of the powerful O Briens of Thomond. Later, they dispersed to Waterford and east Cork, where they are mostly to be found today.

At one time they were prominent in the Church. **Bartholomew Crotty** was a rector of the Jesuit College in Lisbon. In 1790, he returned to Ireland when he was appointed Bishop of Cloyne and Ross. More than a century later, the **Reverend B. Crotty** was the president of the College of Maynooth in County Kildare. The **Reverend Thomas Crotty**, a Dominican priest, was military chaplain to German prisoners during the First World War.

Donnogh Crotty is recorded as being an officer of the Commonwealth army in the 1650s.

The most notorious bearer of the Crotty surname was **William Crotty** of Waterford, a highwayman who was hanged in 1742. In the late eighteenth century, **Julia M. Crotty** published *The Lost Land: A Tale of a Cromwellian–Irish Town.*

Crowe

Mac Conchradha

MacEnchroe MacEnroe

MacConchradha, an ancient surname, derives from an ancestor called Conchradh, an unusual Irish personal name. The motto on the coat of arms of this once leading County Clare family was *Skeagh mac an chroe*, and there is also a place in Clare known as Skaghvicencrowe, meaning the thorn bush of MacEncroe. Their name was anglicized to Crowe, which can easily now be confused with planters from England, where Crowe is a very common name.

There are a number of accounts in the Belfast Public Records Office of these Crowes, including **Charles Crowe** of King's County (County Laois), who was Bishop of Cloyne in 1703. There is a deed partitioning land in Cavan and Monaghan between four Crowes in 1763.

Reverting to the original Irish, it was the **Reverend John McEnroe** (1795–1868) who founded the *Freeman's Journal* of Sydney, Australia.

Dermot McEncroe (fl. 1790) was from the County Clare MacEncroe family which emigrated to France and took the name de la Croix. His Latin poems are highly thought of for their great elegance.

O Beirne Crowe of Cong in County Galway became one of the finest Gaelic scholars of his day and one of the first professors in University College Galway.

Eyre Evans Crowe (1799–1868) was a historian and novelist. His son, **Sir Joseph Archer Crowe** (1825–96), was reared in England and was a diplomat, art critic and war correspondent.

Catherine Crowe, a Victorian novelist, was famous for her powerful ghost stories. Powerful with the tennis racket is **John McEnroe**, famed equally for his outbursts on the courts as for his skills at the sport.

Crowley

Ó Cruadhlaoich

Cruadhlaoch means strong hero, and the family who adopted this name are kinsmen of the MacDermots of Roscommon.

The Crowleys settled in Munster, where their chieftain had his castle at Kilsallow. Between 1641 and 1643, twenty-two Crowleys, all from Cork, are recorded as being indicted for treason. They forfeited twenty-three of their townlands, fourteen of which were appropriated by Richard Boyle, the 1st Earl of Cork—Ireland's first millionaire! This meant the defeat of the Clan Crowley. Some fled as rebels to the mountains, some drifted into day labouring and many went to France, where they distinguished themselves serving in the Irish regiments.

Before the defeat at the battle of the Boyne, **Thady Croly**, chaplain to James II, was one of the many Crowleys championing the doomed Stuart cause. Crowleys also served with the Irish-American brigades in the 1860s.

Benjamin Crawley (or Crowley) built the magnificent Castle Durrow in County Laois for the 1st Lord Castle Durrow. It is now a convent.

In the nineteenth century, the son of a wealthy Dubliner, **Nicholas Crowley**, was a talented painter and exhibited at the Royal Hibernian Academy (RHA) in Dublin at the age of fifteen. For twenty-two years, until his death in 1857, he was also president of the RHA. He painted the portraits of important people of his day, including Daniel O Connell during his imprisonment, Charles Gavan Duffy and the Sisters of Charity.

Peter O Neill Crowley, the son of a Cork farmer, joined the Fenians and was shot in 1867 as he attempted to break into a coastguard station. **Diarmuid O Crowley** of Cork was one of the chief judges in the early days of the Irish Free State.

Today the Crowleys are prominent in the business world. **Niall Crowley**, son of the founder of the accountancy firm of Stokes, Kennedy and Crowley, is chairman of the Allied Irish Bank, director of the Irish Life Assurance Company and has been a president of the Dublin Chamber of Commerce.

Cuddihy

Ó Cuidighthigh Mac Cuidithe

Cuddy MacOda Quiddihy

Cuidightheach is an Irish word meaning helper. Apart from the Irish form of the surname, there are a number of variants, including Cuddy, Quiddihy, Ó Cuidighthigh. There is mention of a Mac Cuidithe in County Cork in 1214. MacOda has also been associated with a Kerry branch of the family.

A manuscript in the National Library in Dublin mentions a **Michael Cuddihy** who, in 1793, was making survey maps of the estates of the Marquis of Clanricarde (a Burke) of Portumna, County Galway, and also of Clanricarde's town and parks at nearby Loughrea.

Neither the Cuddihys nor the Cuddys—now the more usual form of the name—are to be found plentifully in or around Dublin, but are concentrated in the counties of Kilkenny, Waterford and Wexford. In Northern Ireland there is an abundance of Cuddys.

The most remarkable offspring of this Midlands family were the Cudahys who left their native Callan in County Kilkenny with their parents in 1849, at the time of the Great Famine, and settled in the USA. There they progressed from butchering to meat packing in Chicago. **Michael Cudahy** (1841–1910), a partner in the firm of Armour and Company, controlled the plant operations at the Union Stock Yards. Prior to this, it had been strictly a winter business, but Cudahy introduced the refrigeration car which revolutionized the meat industry, enabling meat to be transported all the year round. The

Cudahy family enterprise subsequently spread as far as Omaha, Nebraska, and a number of books have been written on the subject.

Michael Cuddy (b. 1932) was born into a family of livestock exporters and joined the family business in Dublin, rising to the position of managing director. He has been a president of the Leinster branch of the Irish Rugby Football Union and is also a successful racehorse owner.

Cullen

Ó Cuilinn

Culhoun Cullinane MacCullen

Cullion, Culhoun, MacCullen and Cullinane are a few of the variations of this name which, in Irish, is Ó Cuilinn (*cuileann* means a holly tree). They were driven from their roots in Wicklow by the aggressive O Briens and O Tooles. The town of Kilcullen in County Kildare bears their imprint, while Cullenstown was called after a noble Cullen family of Wexford. It is thought possible that the name may have Scottish connections.

The Cullens, who were very active in the Church, can lay claim to producing Ireland's first Cardinal, **Cardinal Paul Cullen** (1803–78) of Ballitore, County Kildare. In Rome in 1848, while rector of the Urban College, he saved some American students by having the college declared an American-sponsored literary institution during the Mazzini revolution.

The Cullens travelled widely and have been numerous in the Argentines for several centuries. There are also many Cullens in Australia.

A mermaid, mirror and comb in hand, sits atop their armorial shield, which is red with three white hands, a white chevron with, inside, a sheaf of corn and two green trefoils.

Cummins

Ó Comáin Ó Cuimín

Commons Comyns Hurley

This surname, which is numerous in every part of Ireland, lends itself to many interpretations. Some say that it comes from the Irish word *cam*, meaning crooked. Others, incorrectly, think it came from the word *camán*, a stick for playing hurling, which caused some people to anglicize their name to Hurley!

In the sixth century, before surnames came into use, **St. Common** came from Ulster and founded Roscommon and a number of other monasteries in the west of Ireland. The Cummins were administrators of the church of **St. Cuimón Fada** of Kilcummin in the bay of Killala in Connacht.

Cormac Ó Cuimón (1703–86) was one of a band of blind bards and storytellers who flourished at that time.

The Comyns who were driven out from County Clare escaped to France, where they were accepted into the French nobility. Here they suffered the fate of their fellow aristocrats and were guillotined during the French Revolution. Other Cummins were more fortunate and fought in the Spanish Netherlands, and were absorbed into the nobility of Spain.

John Cummins, a ship's carpenter, wrote a *Narrative of the loss of HMS Wager During a Voyage to the South Seas, 1740–41.*

Danny Cummins, a Dubliner born in 1914, was for many years one of Ireland's most popular entertainers in pantomime and revue, for which he wrote his own sketches.

Geraldine Cummins (1890–1969)

of Cork was a novelist and biographer of the Somerville and Ross duo who originated the stories of the famous *Irish RM* television series. She also played hockey for Ireland and was famed for her facility for "automatic writing". Her sister, **Ashley**, was also an international hockey player.

A detailed pedigree of the County Cork family of Cummins can be found in the 1976 edition of *Burke's Irish Family Records.*

Cunningham

Ó Cuinneagáin

Conyngham

This could be a Scottish or an Irish name, or a mixture of both. Ó Cuinneagáin means descendant of Conn (using the diminutive of Conn).

One branch descended from Fiachra, brother of Niall of the Nine Hostages and father of the last pagan king of Ireland, and another were kinsmen of the O Kellys. All, from earliest days, were of Connacht. A history of the Clann Uí Cuinneagáin was published in the now defunct periodical, *The Bell*, in January 1943.

The name has been anglicized in a variety of ways, the more usual now being Cunningham or Conyngham. It is very numerous all over Ireland today, particularly in Northern Ireland, where it probably came with the Scottish settlers.

Patrick Cunningham was a fashionable Dublin sculptor who, among other works, made busts of Dean Swift and Frederick, King of Prussia.

John Cunningham (1729–73), son of a Dublin merchant, wrote the farce *Love in a Mist* at the age of seventeen. It was a great success and he continued working for the theatre.

There were Cunninghams in Corcoran's Irish Legion in New York in 1865 and they have been recorded in **Captain J. T. Cunningham**'s *Irish American Brigade—Its Campaigns.*

Lieutenant-General Robert Cunningham (1769–1801) was commander-in-chief of Ireland and was the 1st Lord Rossmore.

The Cunninghams have featured as naturalists, scientists and in the medical profession. **Professor John F. Cunningham** was one of Dublin's leading gynaecologists in the 1930s and 1940s.

Henry, 1st Marquess of Conyngham (1769–1832), an Irish peer, had considerable influence with George IV (his wife was the King's mistress). **Henry, Earl of Mountcharles** (b. 1949), a descendant, holds occasional rock concerts in the grounds of the family mansion, Slane Castle in County Meath. The castle itself was accidentally burned down in 1991.

see also Kinahan

Curley

Mac Turlough

Terry Turley

Curley is an anglicization of this lengthy Gaelic surname, Mac Thoirdealbhaigh, which means son of Turlough or Terence. Terry has also been found as a variant of the original surname.

The name is common throughout Ireland, particularly in counties Galway and Roscommon, from which they came originally. In Roscommon there is a Ballymacurley and Curley's Island, indicating their importance there.

In the 1659 census, Mac Turlough was one of the principal surnames in County Limerick.

The Curleys seldom feature in the

Irish records, but they have been prominent in the United States of America. **James Curley** (1796–1889) was born in Athleague, County Roscommon. He went to the USA in 1817 and became a Jesuit priest there. A most distinguished astronomer, he was a director and historian of Georgetown University.

In 1913, **James Michael Curley** defeated the mayor of Boston, John F. FitzGerald, grandfather of John F. Kennedy. James Curley served four terms as Governor of Massachusetts from 1934 to 1936. A rumbustious Irishman, he wrote an account of his life, *I'd Do it Again: A Record of All My Uproarious Years.* It was published in 1957, about ten years after he had retired from public life.

Curran

Ó Corráin

Although Curran is a very common surname throughout Ireland, it is not well recorded in the archives. In Irish the name is Ó Corráin, meaning descendant of Corrán. In the Middle Ages, they were a distinguished ecclesiastical family.

Simon Ó Curráin, a Dominican friar who died in 1302, was Bishop of Kilfenora. **Andrew Ó Currán**, of the Order of St. Benedict, was the prior of Glascarrig in 1411, while **James O Corren** was Bishop of Killaloe from 1526 to 1546. These were all in the west of Ireland. In the wars and conquests of 1641, **Ulick Curran** of Ballymagrogy had his lands forfeited and given to Lord Mayo.

The most outstanding Curran was **John Philpot Curran** (1750–1817). He came from Newmarket in County Cork, studied at Trinity College Dublin and became a prominent lawyer and patriot. Though a Protestant, he earned fame defending a Catholic clergyman who was unjustly treated. He also defended many of the United Irishmen. When he discovered that his daughter, **Sarah Curran**, had become secretly engaged to the rebel, Robert Emmet, he requested that she leave his house to save him from being accused of treason. Robert Emmet was executed after the rising of 1803. Some time later Sarah married, but died shortly afterwards, in 1808. John Philpot Curran retired to London to join the congenial company of his peers, Thomas Moore, Richard Brinsley Sheridan and Lord Byron. His natural son, **Henry Grattan Curran** (1800–70), was a barrister and a writer.

In the Genealogical Office in Dublin there is a grant of arms to **Thomas Francis Curran**, a solicitor of Annagh, Ballyhaunis in County Mayo, on his assuming by royal licence in 1892 the arms of Tyrell.

C. P. Curran (1880–1975) of Dublin, registrar of the Supreme Court, was deeply involved in the literary and artistic life of the city. He saved much of the magnificent plaster work in Dublin's old houses from those twentieth-century vandals—the developers!

Curreen *see* MacGurrin

(O) Curry *see* Corry

Curtin *see* MacCurtin

Curtis

de Curtéis

Since the thirteenth century, Curtis has been a very popular surname in both England and Ireland. A descriptive nickname, it means a person of courtly manners.

In the archives, there are many references to Curtis families, including their being granted forfeited lands when they came to Ireland. There is a petition of 1642 to the House of Lords from **Lieutenant John Curtis**, who had a lease of land in Queen's County (now County Laois), "now despoiled by the rebels". **Robert Curtis** petitioned for a debt owed to him by the Earl of Clancarty. In 1712, arms were granted to **Robert Curtis**, Member of Parliament for Roscrea, County Tipperary, and auditor of Foreign Accounts.

William Curtis (1746–99) was an illustrious horticulturist and plant historian. He wrote a classic history of the plants of London, *Flora Londoniensis.* He also founded the *Botanical Magazine*, which continues to this day.

In 1822, when **Patrick Curtis** was Roman Catholic Bishop of Armagh, he complained of "a horrible act of placing a calf's head on the altar of the chapel of Ardee".

The outstanding Curtis in Ireland was **Edmund Curtis** (1881–1943), who was born in Lancashire of Irish parents. At the age of fifteen, he went to work in a rubber factory and wrote verses lamenting his unhappy state. Local people rescued him and sent him to Oxford University to get an education. In 1914, he became professor of modern history at University College Dublin. He pioneered in the study of Irish history, using many Irish-language sources. His *History of Ireland*, published in 1936, has long been a repected reference book.

The Curtis name is also very well represented in Australia.

Cusack

Ciomhsóg Mac iosóg

The Cusack name came from the town in Normandy which they left for Ireland in the twelfth century. In counties Meath and Kildare, they acquired lands and prospered, becoming very powerful. Until the eighteenth century, they were prominent churchmen and administrators, but, refusing to conform to the religion of the English establishment, they fell from power.

In their days of glory, they were Lords of Killeen, Gerardstown, Foleystown and Clonard. **Sir John Cusack** of Gerardstown, together with his brothers, led the Irish defeat of Edward Bruce at the battle of Dundalk in 1318. A descendant, **James Cusack** of Clonard, fought for the Stuart King James II at the battle of the Boyne, accompanied by many of his kinsmen.

General and Chevalier **Richard de Cusack**, who fought valiantly against the Cromwellians, later joined the Irish brigade in Europe.

George Cusack's parents intended him to be a monk, but he ran away to sea where he made a living by ruthless piracy. He did not shrink from throwing his crew overboard without mercy if they disagreed with him over the disposal of the plunder!

A distinguished physician, **Dr. James Cusack**, was twice president of the College of Surgeons in Dublin. His niece, **Margaret Anne Cusack**, became famous as the "Nun of Kenmare". With a burning desire to follow a charitable career, she first joined an Anglican sisterhood in London, then switched to the austere Poor Clares in Kerry. She wrote prolifically—books, pamphlets, articles—to support the Order. However, she fell foul of the conservative Irish clergy and reverted to the Anglicans in England. Later, with the Pope's approval, she sailed for the USA, where she founded the Sisters of Peace to look after destitute Irish girls. But her restless spirit drove her back to England and to more religious quests. Today she is regarded as Ireland's pioneer for women's liberation—as well as a campaigner for Ireland's freedom.

Cyril Cusack was the doyen of Irish actors and the father of **Sorcha, Sinéad** and **Niamh,** who have all followed in their father's footsteps.

Cushing

Cuisín

Cushen Cushion Cussen Cussin

Cushing comes from the Norman-French *le cosyn*, meaning the cousin or kinsman. The family has been in Ireland since the thirteenth century and their name, in various forms, has spread throughout the country. Cushen, Cushion, Cushine, Cooshan and Cussin are some of the forms the name took over the centuries. Cushing is also a common name in England, where it is said to have come from a first name, Custance.

Towards the end of the fourteenth century, **Adam Cussin** was one of the scribes who wrote the great *Book of Uí Maine* (the Uí Maine populated large areas of Galway and Roscommon).

A Cussen was Member of Parliament for Athy in 1560. An **Edmund Cushene** and an **Edward Cushine,** both of Cushenstown, featured in the Westmeath records of the sixteenth century. In that century also, the Cussins are listed as having the most numerous name in the Forth area of County Wexford. During the Cromwellian confiscations, many Cussens lost their lands and were scattered, and the name almost disappeared from Ireland.

There have been many very distinguished Cushings in the United States of America, but very few of Irish descent, with the outstanding exception of the late **Richard Cardinal Cushing,** Archbishop of Boston (b. 1895). He was a close friend and adviser to the Kennedys. With J. F. Kennedy, he helped remove the barrier against members of the Roman Catholic Church being elected President of the United States or holding high office. Cardinal Cushing's parents, **Patrick** and **Mary Cushing,** had come to Boston from Glenworth in County Cork at the time of the Great Famine. They had five children, and Patrick Cushing, who was a blacksmith, worked on the railways.

see also Cousins

Cuson *see* Cousins

Cussen *see* Cousins

D

Dalton

de Dalatún

d'Alton

The d'Altons, who originated from Normandy, took their name from Alton in England. The reason they did not arrive in Ireland until the thirteenth century, well after the Anglo-Norman invasion, is a romantic one. Tradition has it that **Walter d'Alton** enraged the King of France by secretly marrying his daughter and had to flee to England and, later, to Ireland to escape his wrath.

The d'Altons acquired rich lands in County Westmeath, where many of their descendants are still to be found. The family also branched out and spread across Ireland, especially to counties Tipperary and Clare. Their chieftain in County Westmeath was known as Lord of Rathconrath. The devastations of the Cromwellian and Williamite wars deprived them of their lands but bound them closer to the long-suffering Irish, so that d'Alton became a thoroughly Irish name.

Many d'Altons went to Europe after the battle of the Boyne and became distinguished military men, particularly in Austria, where, in 1777, the Empress Maria Theresa created **Major-General Richard d'Alton** a Count of the Empire. The d'Altons are well recorded, both in the Irish annals and in the European archives. **John Dalton** (1792–1867) was a notable Irish historian.

John Francis d'Alton (1883–1963) of Claremorris, County Mayo, was Bishop of Meath, Archbishop of Armagh and Primate of All Ireland; he was a cardinal from 1953 until his death.

Louis d'Alton (1900–51), son of **Charles d'Alton**, a comedian and theatre manager, was a playwright and theatrical producer. He contributed a number of popular plays to Dublin's Abbey Theatre.

Dalton is also quite a common name in England.

see also Deaton

(O) Daly

Ó Dálaigh

Dawley

The Daly sept goes back to the third century, to the great High King of Tara in County Meath, Niall of the Nine Hostages, from whom also descend the O Neills and the O Donnells. Ó Dálaigh is the Irish spelling of the name, from *dáil*, meaning a place of assembly, which is what Dáil Éireann is now.

The Dalys are outstanding for the remarkable number of poets and musicians they produced up to the late Middle Ages. They had a bardic school in Westmeath from where they became hereditary minstrels to the noble families of Ireland. Poets can be temperamental people, and one Daly poet killed a critic, while another, a renegade, wrote poems disparaging his country to please the English.

In the eighteenth century, some O Dalys found a new outlet as playwrights and theatre owners and managers, both at home and in America. Some also became colonial administrators in many parts of the globe, including America.

The Barons of Dunsandle and Clan Conal in County Galway, descendants of Donagh, the "Irish Ovid", were mayors of Galway and also, when they emigrated to Britain, became high-ranking officers in the army. A young officer of this family was killed in the IRA massacre of the Household Cavalry in Hyde Park, London, in 1982.

The Daly armorial shield is half white and half yellow, with a half-red and half-black lion and two red right hands.

Cardinal Cathal Daly (b. 1917) became Bishop of Down and Connor in 1982 and retired from this post in 1996.

Danaher

Ó Danachair Ó Duineachair

Danagher

Danaher is a rare name about which little is known except that there was an Ó Danachair chief of his territory near Nenagh, County Tipperary, until they were driven out by the Anglo-Normans early in the thirteenth century.

There appears to have been a succession of poets and storytellers of the name and there is mention of a Gaelic scribe in the eighteenth century who was also a shepherd in County Limerick, where the main branch of the family settled. The manuscripts of some of his poems are in the British Museum.

There are probably approximately one hundred Danahers in Ireland, some with the prefix O, but none in Ulster.

They have never aspired to armorial bearings.

d'Arcy

Ó Dorchaidhe

Darcy Dorcey Dorsey

The name comes from Arci, the original home of this Norman family. The first d'Arcy to reach Ireland was **John d'Arcy**, who came with Edward III in 1341 and was granted his lands in Meath. John d'Arcy married Joan, daughter of Richard de Burgh, Earl of Ulster. At the battle of Crécy he was created Lord d'Arcy de Knayth (his English manor), a title which continues in England to the present day. John's son, **Sir William d'Arcy**, married a FitzGerald and founded Plattyn, their Meath mansion which was demolished in 1950.

A descendant of his, a **Sir William** who was Vice-President of Ireland, had his properties seized by Henry VIII. With his death in 1540, that senior branch of the family became extinct.

Darcy is the anglicized form of Ó Dorchaidhe (*dorcha* means dark). The Darcys were one of the few Gaelic families to be accepted into the Fourteen Tribes of Galway. They were a Gaelic sept, of Partry in County Mayo, of which **James Riveagh** (meaning swarthy) of Kiltulla was Lord President of Connacht and Governor of Galway. His son, **Patrick Darcy**, a lawyer, sat in the Irish parliament of 1640 and resisted the King's attempt to enlist disbanded Irish soldiers to bolster his European wars.

In the seventeenth century, a distinguished bishop, **Oliver Darcy**, held important Sees, including that of Armagh.

Patrick, Count d'Arcy of Galway, was sent to France to be educated. As well as becoming a leading mathematician and a member of the French Academy of Sciences, he also served in the French army during the Seven Years war as maréchal-de-camp. **Pierre Alfred, 2nd Count d'Arcy**, was Receiver General of Finance and an officer of the Légion d'Honneur, but the **5th Count d'Arcy**, chose to become a naturalized British subject in 1919.

A number of Darcys fought and died for the Stuart King James II, many forfeiting their lands and fleeing to France, where **Richard, 1st Baron d'Arcy**, was a colonel in the Irish Brigade.

The d'Arcys of Hyde Park in Westmeath feature prominently in the twentieth century: **Charles Frederick** was Protestant Bishop of Armagh, **Thomas Norman** was a rear-admiral and **Michael**, who served in the Second World War, transferred to the Australian army.

Some Darcys adopted the more fanciful apostrophe of the Norman d'Arcys. To confuse the innumerable d'Arcys or Darcys is excusable.

Daton *see* Deaton

Davin *see* Devine

Dawley *see* (O) Daly

(O) Dea

Ó Deághaidh

The O Deas were once one of the principal Dalcassian septs of counties Clare and Limerick, where the head of their sept owned much land. They are commemorated in County Clare by the townland names of Tully Odea and Desert O Dea—the site of a large battle in 1318.

In Dublin's Genealogical Office there is a record of an O Dea in "*agro Kilkenniense*" who was allied with the famous Geraldines in *c.*1350. There is another record of an O Dea family which shows "a tree of prosperity of Milo *c.*1400 BC to AD 1614".

Like so many other once-powerful families, the O Deas must have been driven into exile for, among the families of Irish origin whose papers are in Paris in the Bibliothèque Nationale, there is a **James O Dea**. There is also mention of an O Dea who was a captain of horse and a **Lieutenant Donough O Dea**, both of General Dillon's Irish regiment and, seemingly, originating from Ballygrefa in County Clare. In the British Museum there are letters written by **Brigadier Denis O Dea** to Cardinal Henry Stuart in 1794.

The O Deas have had many ecclesiastics. **Connor O Dea**, Bishop of Kilmacduagh, is recorded as having a dispute with **Dermott Oge O Dea** and **Daniel O Dea**. And a **Cornelius O Dea** (d. 1434) was Bishop of Limerick. **Reverend Joseph Peter O Dea** (1743–1812), son of Irish exiles, was a distinguished French priest in Nantes.

Jimmy O Dea (1899–1965), though of County Clare origins, was born in Dublin. He qualified in Edinburgh as an optician but, in 1927, he changed career to become an actor and a much-loved comedian on the Irish stage. Pantomime was his speciality and "Mrs. Mulligan, the pride of the Coombe" his most famous song.

Denis O Dea (d. 1978) was for many years an actor with the Abbey Theatre Company. He was married to the celebrated actress, Siobhán McKenna.

Deane

Ó Déaghain

The surname Deane comes from a number of sources, including a Tipperary family who were Ó Deaghain and one from Donegal who were Mac an Deagánaigh. In Irish, the name signifies an ecclesiastical dean. In English, dene means valley. The first of the Deanes to settle in Galway came from Bristol in the fifteenth century. They were variously designated as Allen and as de Den. They were amongst the earliest mayors, chief magistrates and provosts in Ireland and were one of the Fourteen Tribes of Galway.

There is a story of a governor of Galway and a man called Deane who, together, traded profitably in tobacco between Galway and Virginia. When inebriated, the English governor boasted to Deane that his was one of the two pairs of hands which had struck off the head of Charles I—the executioners' names had never been revealed. After the Restoration, Deane let out the secret, whereupon the governor disappeared. Years later, a Galway man called French recognized him begging in London. However, when he tried to befriend him, he vanished again!

Other Deanes who came to Ireland had no connection with the Galway family. Some sided with the Cromwellians, for which, following the Restoration of the monarchy, they had their lands confiscated and were transplanted. There was an **Admiral Richard Deane** who fought in the battle of Kinsale. Under the Williamite confiscations, some Deanes were granted forfeited Irish estates.

The Deanes of Dromore Castle in Cork were descendants of the FitzMaurices, Lords of Kerry. **Matthew Deane** (b. 1626), who was created baron in 1709, moved to Springfield Castle, County Limerick. The **9th Baron Muskerry, Robert FitzMaurice Deane** (b. 1948), lives in South Africa.

From the Deanes of Cork, who designed many of their own homes, came **Sir Thomas Newenham Deane** (1828–99), who was architect of some of the finest houses and public buildings in Ireland, including parts of Trinity College Dublin, the National Museum and the National Library, for which he received a knighthood when it was opened in 1890.

Deaton

d'Alton Daton d'Auton

Deaton is a very rare name in Ireland. There are just a few in the telephone directory, all of them in and around County Dublin.

Edward MacLysaght, who was Ireland's premier genealogist, wrote that the name was prominent in County Kilkenny from the thirteenth century and that it is of Norman origin and has become Dalton by assimilation. It can also be identified with D'Auton.

In the seventeenth century, a **Peter Daton**, "a Papist Proprietor", had his lands confiscated. Between 1653 and 1654, a **Walter Daton** whose family had been banished to Connacht is on the list of those who applied to have their lands returned to them after the Restoration of Charles II.

The Daltons, also of Normandy, have been in Ireland since the thirteenth century, the name coming from Alton, a town in England where they must at one time have settled.

To unravel a Deaton from the comparatively well-documented Daltons would require considerable painstaking research.

see also Dalton

(O) Deegan

Ó Duibhginn

Diggin Dugan Duggan Duigan

Deegan, which in some cases has been anglicized to Duigan, or even Diggin, is a very old Irish surname deriving from the Irish Ó Duibhginn. Translated into English, it means son of the black-headed one (*dubh* means black, *ceann* means head).

In the Middle Ages, the Deegans of Cloncouse in the Midland county of Leix (now Laois) were keepers of the bell of Saint Molus.

At one time there were three distinct families of the name, whose homelands were in the counties of Clare, Galway and Wexford. In Munster, they adopted Dugan or Duggan as the anglicized version of the original Irish Ó Duibhginn.

Although Deegans are numerous throughout Ireland, they have yet to make a name for themselves in the arts or politics.

de Lacy

de léis Ó Laitheasa

de Lasci Lacey Lacy

The de Lacys, who came from Lasci in Normandy, were some of the most famous military men in Ireland in the seventeenth and eighteenth centuries.

Hugh de Lacy (d. 1186) displaced the royal O Melaghlins (now MacLoughlins), becoming lord of 800,000 acres in Meath. He married a daughter of King Roderick O Conor. As a viceroy he showed unusual compassion for the Irish and built the magnificent castle at Trim, today an impressive ruin by the River Boyne. His son, Walter, moved north, where he was created Earl of Ulster, but he joined the O Neills, rebelled against the English and lost his earldom.

There were a number of de Lacy prelates, including **Reverend Hugh Lacy** (d. 1581) who, in the sixteenth century, was Bishop of Limerick. From the family who settled in County Limerick, around Ballingarry, Bruree and Bruff, came the Lacys who, when they were driven abroad, were to become the most famous soldiers in Europe and Russia.

Count Peter Lacy was only twelve when he fought at the siege of Limerick and, after the city's capitulation, left with Sarsfield's troops for Europe. He re-organized the armies of Peter the Great, Czar of Russia, and was the brains behind many Russian victories. His son, **Count Francis Maurice de Lacy**, was a Field Marshal in the Austrian army. Another member of this Limerick family, **Francis Anthony de Lacy**, was a soldier and diplomat in the Spanish services.

Count Maurice de Lacy, a Russian general distinguished by a pronounced brogue, was the last male descendant of the great Hugh and visited Ireland several times. He died unmarried, leaving a fortune to his Limerick relatives. However, they fought through the courts for decades but received nothing. Maurice's sister in Ireland married Terence O Brien, who adopted her name and joined her uncle in Russia. They had a son, **Patrick Count O Brien de Lacy**, whose descendants are numerous and were prominent in Poland. They lost their estates and all their possessions in the Second World War. Many of this family are still in Poland, while a direct descendant of Maurice, **Nellie O Brien de Lacy**, is an outstanding watercolorist in Argentina. She speaks many languages and escaped from Poland during the Second World War.

Brigadier-General Denis Lacy of

Tipperary was killed in action in the Civil War in 1920.

Although they are no longer prominent, the Lacys who stayed in Ireland are numerous in all parts of the country. In the ancient records, the name de Lacy was written de Léis.

de la Haye *see* Hayes

Delane *see* Delany

Delany

Ó Dubhshláine

Delane Delaney

Ó Dubhshláine is a combination of *dubh* (black) and *Sláine* (possibly referring to the river Slaney in County Wexford). The O prefix has long been discarded by this family, who were originally of counties Laois and Kilkenny. In common with most names, there are a variety of spellings, including Delane, which is found in County Mayo.

Felix O Dulany, Bishop of Ossory from 1178 to 1202, built the splendid cathedral which still graces the city of Kilkenny. **Patrick Delany** (1684–1768), a friend of Swift and Sheridan and a preacher and poet, married two rich widows in succession, the last of whom was the popular hostess, craftswoman, letter writer and autobiographer, **Mrs. Mary Delany**, who was influential in seeing that he was appointed Dean of Down. He was also a chancellor of Dublin's Saint Patrick's Cathedral.

In the records and archives there are accounts of diverse Delanys, including a **Captain Delany** who was wounded at Fontenoy in 1745. There are also twenty-five letters to **George Delany**, who was secretary of the Home Rule League from 1876 to 1891.

In 1903, a grant of arms was made to **William Delaney** of Carlow and to **James Delany** of Skrehena, County Laois, descendants of Piers Butler, 1st Viscount Mountgarret, and Sir George Byrne of Tymogue, County Laois.

In 1956, **Ronny Delany**, born in County Wicklow in 1935, won a gold medal in the 1500 metre race at the Melbourne Olympic Games.

Edward Delany of Claremorris in County Mayo is a contemporary sculptor whose metal figures enliven Dublin's parks and streets.

Frank Delany, born in Tipperary in 1942, is a journalist, novelist and TV personality. On BBC's Radio 4, he made his name with the programme *Bookshelf.*

Shelagh Delany, born in Lancashire in 1939, is undoubtedly of Irish origins. She has won many awards for her plays on television. *A Taste of Honey* was one of her most outstanding plays.

Dempsey

Ó Díomasaigh

The name Dempsey evolved from the Irish, *díomasach*, meaning proud. The Dempseys are said to descend from Ros Failghe, eldest son of Cathaoir Mór, a second-century king of Ireland. They were of the same stock as the O Conors of Offaly and were powerful chieftains of Clanmalier in the Midlands.

In 1172, when Strongbow and his Normans arrived, they defeated most of the Irish chieftains, but not the O Dempseys. In 1193, **Dermot O Dempsey**, Chief of the Name, founded the Cistercian abbey at Monasterevan. St. Even was their patron saint. During the penal times, there were many O Dempsey priests.

In the sixteenth century, they changed their allegiance and joined the English planters in the massacre of their countrymen at Mullaghmast in 1577.

The Earl of Essex created **Terence O Dempsey** Viscount Clanmalier and Baron of Philipstown. In later years they returned to the fold and were prominent members of the Catholic Confederation of Kilkenny, which met in 1652. Because of their adherence to the Stuart King James II, they lost their estates.

In both Church and army, they held high rank. **Lieutenant Laurence Dempsey** fought with the English army against Spain in Portugal in 1663. The following year he is recorded as fighting in a duel in Dublin.

Many of them went abroad, especially to France where, *c.*1707, **Reverend C. Dempsey** was president of the Irish seminary at Lille.

Many Dempsey records have been preserved in the Dublin Genealogical Office, including one concerning the Dempseys of Cheshire and Liverpool. There are also grants of arms, and letters from a Dempsey family in Australia.

Denning *see* Dinneen

Dennison

Ó Donnghusa

Dennis

This not very numerous surname boasts a wide variety of origins. In Old French it was *le Danei* (the Dane). It was a popular French first name originating from the early Christian martyr, Dionysius. It could also be an anglicization of Ó Donghusa (the brown choice), an ecclesiastical family in Ulster, where the name is most numerous. It can also be recognized as Dennis, mostly centred in Dublin and its environs.

In the seventeenth century, many Dennisons came to Ireland as troops with the Cromwellian armies. On disbandment, they were paid with forfeited lands. It was a particularly common name in those days in Yorkshire and Northumberland, in England.

There are many references in the archives to Dennis families, but few to Dennison. Dating from 1657, there is a copy of a survey of maps and lands, the property of **Major John Dennison** of the parish of Ferns, County Wexford. Between 1676 and 1843, there are accounts of Dennison ironworks and Dennison ironmongers in Enniscorthy, County Wexford, and in County Derry.

Today, Dennison businesses, mostly in Ulster and Munster, seem to be concerned with the motor trade or other related heavy-metal industries. Strangely, this Dennison characteristic is exemplified in the United States of America, where Dennison, a small town in Tuscarawa, Ohio, is remarkable for its railroad shops, sewer pipe factories and steelcasting foundry!

Devane *see* Devine

Devanny

Ó Duibheannaigh

Devaney Devany Deveney

Translated from the Gaelic, the variations on this name are legion and often cause confusion. Basically the surname derives from the Irish for black, *dubh*, and Eamhain, a place name in County Armagh.

The Ó Duibheannaigh were originally from County Down, while the Ó Duibheamhna, in ancient times, were chiefs of the Uí Breasail of County Armagh.

There is also another sept, Devany of Connacht and of County Donegal who, at one time, were also numerous in counties Mayo and Leitrim. It is thought that the O Devanys were followers of the great chieftain Rory O Donnell. Fortunately for them, they were granted pardons after the rising of 1602. In the census of 1659, the O Devanys of Inishowen, as well as the Devannys of Raphoe, were of the sept who came originally from County Donegal.

So far the only prominent bearer of this surname is Conor, or **Cornelius O Devany**, who was Bishop of Down and Connor from 1582 to 1612. His capture, torture and execution are fully recorded in the famous *Annals of the Four Masters*, a contemporary account of Irish history.

Today Devany and Devaney are the most usual forms of this surname. They are still very plentiful in the west of Ireland and in Ulster, where there is quite a sizeable number both of Devaneys and Deveneys.

They have sometimes been confused with both Devane and Devine, surnames with which they are unconnected.

see also Kidney

Devine

Ó Daimhín

Davin Devane Devin Downes

This is a very widespread Irish name, with a diversity of branches and variations of the spelling, such as Devin, Davin, Devane and Downes.

In 1066 an O Devine was a Church administrator in Derry. Up until 1427, they were chiefs of Tirkennedy, County Fermanagh. They were also distant kinsmen of the powerful northern Maguires.

One branch of the family went to County Meath, where they were lords of Knock before they suffered dispossession and were scattered throughout Leinster. A branch in Corca Laoidhe (south-west Cork), sometimes known as Duane, had their name anglicized to Kidney. The name Devany became very numerous in Connacht, while in Limerick it could be traced back through Downes.

Many Devines of County Clare emigrated to the United States of America in the nineteenth century, where **Professor Edward Thomas Devine** (1867–1948) of Columbia University was renowned for his charitable fundraising.

Dillon

Diolún

Henry de Leon came from Brittany in the twelfth century and his innumerable descendants have long since become thoroughly Irish, bearing the name Dillon. At first they settled on lands granted them around Kilkenny, Longford and Westmeath, which, in time, became known as Dillon's Country. Multiplying rapidly, they branched out to Mayo, Sligo and Galway. Patriots as well as shrewd politicians, they collected titles: Viscounts of Costello-Gallen, Barons of the Holy Roman Empire, Barons of Clonbrock, Earls of Roscommon and Lords of Dromrany.

When they had to flee Ireland, following the battle of the Boyne, they formed the Regiment of Dillon in France which fought valiantly at Fontenoy. In France they were in the upper echelons of the establishment. A Dillon curé who was created archbishop was asked by Louis XVI why he was allowed to hunt, but his clerics were not. His reply to the monarch was, "My vices are the vices of my ancestors, those of my priests are their own!"

A Blake-Dillon family from Connacht bred a succession of patriotic politicians and scholars. Clonbrock

House near Galway and Portlick Castle in Meath, former Dillon strongholds, are no longer in the family.

The coat of arms of the different titled branches of the family invariably display a red lion and three red crescents on the shield, with a red demi-lion on the crest holding a red star.

Dinneen

Ó Duinnín

Denning Dineen Downing Dunning

Ó Duinnín means descendant of Duinnín, which is the Irish diminutive for brown. They were an outstanding literary family in south-west Cork and were, for centuries, historians and genealogists to the powerful MacCarthy Mór. In the Midlands, there was also a landed family of this surname. Ó Duinnín has many synonyms. In Munster it was anglicized to Dineen or Dinneen and also, sometimes, to Downing. In Leinster it could be Dunning or even Denning.

Tadgh O Dinneen was attached to the retinue of the Earl of Clancarty as poet in residence. He was also a leading member of the seventeenth-century school of poetry at Blarney in County Cork.

A number of the Dinneen family emigrated from Cork to Argentina in the nineteenth century. Several became priests, and **Michael Dinneen** was a founder of a college there.

The most outstanding representative of the name was the great **Father Patrick Dinneen** (1860–1934), who compiled the huge *Irish–English Dictionary*. A renowned Irish scholar, he was also actively involved in the founding of the Gaelic League.

Today the Dinneen name remains concentrated in the Munster area. It is comparatively rare in Dublin and rarer still in Northern Ireland.

Dockery

Ó Dochraigh

Dockeray Hardy

In its original form the name was Mac Dháil Ré Dochair and this, in the course of time, the scribes slimmed down to Ó Dochraigh. The name belonged to a sept of Roscommon who, before the destruction of the Gaelic order, guarded the spoils of the kingly O Conors of Connacht. This duty, which they shared with the O Flanagans and the O Beirnes, included the provision of straw for the camp and the horses, as well as beds and furniture for the O Conor household.

Deacair is the Irish word for hard, and in many cases Mac Dháil Ré Dochair was anglicized to Hardy. Hardy is a very common name in England. Today, without documentation, there is probably no longer any hope of distinguishing between the original Irish and the English settlers who bore the Hardy name. There were also some who changed their name from Hardiman to Hardy, but they were mostly of Galway.

The Dockerys, or Dockerays, who are not very numerous, have not made any great impact on history. A few of the name, mostly clerical, have contributed papers to learned religious magazines. In 1909, **Mrs. S. Roope Dockeray** wrote and illustrated a book called *Portugal: Its Land and People.*

The majority of Dockerys are still to be located in their original Roscommon homeland.

Dodd *see* (O) Dowd

(O) Doherty

Ó Dochartaigh

Dougharty MacDevitt O Dogherty

O Doherty has been subjected to many variations, including MacDevitt. The name in Irish signifies obstructive. Their antecedent was the great progenitor, Niall of the Nine Hostages, who ruled from Tara in the fourth century. The O Dohertys left Meath to settle around the Inishowen peninsula in Donegal, where they built their fortress near Buncrana.

It was an O Doherty who, in a fit of madness, foolishly attacked the city of Derry, which was heavily garrisoned by the English. He suffered defeat and death, opening the way for the plantation of the Scottish settlers there early in the seventeenth century.

The O Dohertys who had been Lords of Inishowen fled to Spain, where a descendant in Cadiz is proud to display his pedigree showing he is Lord of Inishowen, eleventh in line from Cahir's brother.

The O Dohertys are well recorded and have a Family Research Association in North America. Their armorial shield bears a springing red stag with a deep green bank on top showing three white stars called mullets. Their motto is *Ár nDúthcas* (our inheritance).

(O) Dolan

Ó Dobhailen

Doolan Dowling (O) Doelan

Ó Dobhailen was the name of a sept whose origins can be traced back to the twelfth century, to counties Galway and Roscommon. They should not be confused with Ó Doibhilin, which was anglicized to Devlin. The variants of the name are O Doelan, Doolan and even Dowling. The Ó Dobhailens branched out to Fermanagh and south to Leitrim and Cavan, where they are now numerous.

Very little has been recorded of this comparatively minor sept. In a manuscript preserved in Dublin's National Library there is mention of **Owen Dolan** who, in 1799, leased lands at Tallymore, County Donegal.

Daniel Dolan served as an adjutant in the 69th New York Volunteers under Major-General Thomas Francis Meagher, during the American Civil War. **Thomas Dolan** (1834–1914) of New York was a very successful Irish-American businessman. The **Dolan Winery** in Redwood Valley is one of a number of wineries owned by Irish émigrés in California.

In modern times, the name came to prominence with **Michael J. Dolan** (d. 1953), a very fine actor at Dublin's Abbey Theatre.

see also Doolan

Donaghy *see* MacDonagh

Donegan *see* Duncan

Donelan *see* Donnellan

Donlevy *see* Dunleavy

Donlon *see* Donnellan

(O) Donnell

Ó Domhnaill

The O Donnells are a most distinguished family. Their ancient lineage includes one of Ireland's patron saints—Colmcille. A powerful clan descending from Niall of the Nine Hostages, they took their name from a tenth-century chieftain called Domhnaill, a personal name meaning world mighty. Indeed, they were mighty fighters through the generations—against their kinsmen the O Neills, and against the English—and when driven abroad they achieved high rank in the armies of Austria, France and Spain.

Of the various O Donnell septs, the main ones settled in counties Clare and Galway, but it is mostly the lords of Tirconnell (Donegal) who fill the pages of history and it is in Donegal that they are most numerous today.

Red Hugh O Donnell (1571–1602), when a boy of seventeen, was enticed aboard a boat in Lough Swilly and abducted. He was imprisoned for three years in the dreaded Dublin Castle. His escape from the castle, across the snow-clad Wicklow mountains, is one of the best-known Irish sagas. His father ceded the chieftainship of the O Donnells to Hugh and he fought successfully against the English at the battle of the Yellow Ford. However, he was later to suffer defeat at Kinsale and he died very young in Spain. A remarkable relative of his, **Mary Stuart O Donnell**, escaped an arranged marriage by running away with her maid, both dressed as soldiers, complete with swords. Whenever it was necessary to allay suspicions of their female identity, Mary would pretend to make love to a serving girl or offer to fight a duel.

A cousin of Red Hugh, Sir Niall Garbh (1569–1626), who had opposed his cousin's election as chief, later turned against the English and was imprisoned in the Tower of London for seventeen years.

The *Cathach*, the battle book of the O Donnells which had been compiled by Saint Colmcille, was found comparatively recently in France and is now lodged in the Royal Irish Academy.

The O Donnells in Austria are descendants of **Major-General Henry Count O Donnell** (of the Tirconnell branch) and of the O Donnells who were formerly of Leitrim. These descendants all filled high posts in the Austrian administration, as well as in the army. Another branch of the family, who went to Spain, produced not only military generals but also a prime minister. Madrid abounds with O Donnells, including the **Duke of Tetuan**, who is heir to the chieftaincy, at present held by a Franciscan missionary. O Donnells are also plentiful in South America.

The O Donnell clan hold regular clan rallies in Donegal.

Donnellan

Ó Domhnalláin

Donelan Donlon

Domhnalláin is a diminutive of the first name Domhnall, or Donal. The Ó Domhnalláins were a distinguished family of poets whose territory was known as Ross O Donelan, near Elphin in County Roscommon, where St. Patrick founded a bishopric over fifteen hundred years ago. In County Galway, Ballydonnellan perpetuates the name of this ancient family which is said to descend from Domhnallán, Lord of Clan Breasail. Their original castle at Ballydonnellan, between Ballinasloe and Loughrea, was built in AD 936 and rebuilt after a fire in AD 1412.

They are lauded frequently in the *Annals of Connacht* and their outstanding poet was **Brian MacOwen O Donnellan** in the seventeenth century, who has been described as the last of the classic bards.

The **Reverend Nehemias Donnelan** (d. 1609) of Galway, a Protestant Archbishop of Tuam, contributed to the translation of the New Testament into Irish.

In the Dublin archives there are many deeds referring to their various land holdings and the different branches of the family, including a **Baron Donelan** of 1702 and a **Reverend Christopher Donnellan** who was rector of Ballymaglasson in County Meath in 1734. A letter from **Thady Donnellan** of Mayo begs Viscount Dillon not to put him off his land because "he had to leave it in charge of his wife's relatives when he went to Kidderminster in England because of the failure of the potato crop in April 1849."

They are also mentioned in the Paris archives. **J. Donnellan** was an officer in the Austrian services in 1669.

In the 1950s and 1960s, **Michael Donnellan** was one of London's leading couturiers.

(O) Donnelly

Ó Donnghaile

In Irish the name falls into two parts: *donn*, meaning brown, and *gal*, meaning valour. They are kinsmen of the royal O Neills of Ulster to whose fighting forces they were hereditary marshals. They are well recorded in their ancient strongholds of Donegal, Tyrone and Antrim by no less than three towns named Ballydonnelly.

Wherever there was a battle there was a Donnelly. **Donnel O Donnelly** was killed while supporting the great Hugh O Neill, Earl of Tyrone, at Kinsale in 1603. In the uprising of 1641, **Patrick Modardha O Donnelly** captured the fine house built on the site of his Ballydonnelly castle by Toby Caulfield, Lord Charlemont, one of the foremost planters in Armagh. **James Donnelly** was among the many prominent people, including bishops, who were killed by the Cromwellian troops at the battle of Ticroghan.

Patrick Donnelly was a Member of Parliament in the government of James II which sat in Dublin in 1689.

The Donnellys followed the trail to Europe with the Wild Geese, where the names of **Don Patricio** and **Don Henriques O Donnely** are recorded among the Irishmen who served in the Spanish Netherlands. They served with the Irish regiments in France, too, and with the Irish-American brigades in the USA, where **Lieutenant-Colonel John Donnelly** was killed at Ream's Station in 1864.

The Donnelly with the greatest claim to fame is **Dan Donnelly**, who was born in Dublin. Originally a carpenter, his enormous strength soon led him into boxing. In 1815, a crowd of forty-two thousand people watched him beat George Cooper, the British champion. This great fight has given its name to Donnelly's Hollow in Kildare, where it took place, and an obelisk marks the spot. A nearby public house is also named after this most renowned of nineteenth-century Irish pugilists, whose life was cut short at the early age of thirty-two.

Charles Donnelly of Tyrone studied at University College Dublin, where he was a member of a brilliant circle of writers before the Second World War. A poet of great promise and a left-wing Republican, he fought in the Spanish Civil War with the Abraham Lincoln Battalion and was killed in 1937 on the Jarama front.

There were several eminent Donnellys in the USA, including **Ignatius Donnelly** (1831–1901), who was Lieutenant-Governor of Minnesota at the age of twenty-eight and an author who merited mention in the *Encyclopaedia Britannica* for his attempts to prove it was Francis Bacon who wrote the plays of William Shakespeare!

(O) Donoghue

Ó Donnchadha Ó Donnchú

Donohoe Donohue

Today the Donoghue, or Donahoe name is widespread. Their family name comes from the personal name, Donnchadh, which is anglicized to Donogh. They descend from a twelfth-century king of Munster who took part in the battle of Clontarf. Their most enduring territory was Cork and Kerry. When the sept divided, several of the O Donoghues spread north into Galway, Kilkenny and Cavan.

The head of the Kerry sept, O Donoghue Mór, had his stronghold at Ross Castle on Lough Lene, Killarney. He is known as O Donoghue of the Glens, as is the present representative, who can style himself The O Donoghue, one of the authenticated old Irish chieftaincies. In his pedigree in *Irish Family Records*, he mentions that his father was deprived of his command in the British army in 1922 for joining a mutiny by the Irish serving in the British army in India and that he subsequently joined the newly-formed Irish army.

When the O Donoghues were forced to flee Ireland, they served with distinction in the armies of Europe. A descendant who settled in Spain, **Juan O Donju**, has been described as "the last Spaniard to rule Mexico".

Their shield is mostly green with two white foxes. The upper section is white with a black eagle. Their crest is an arm in armour holding a sword entwined with a green serpent.

(O) Donovan

Ó Donnabháin

Donnabháin derives from a personal name which is a combination of brown (*donn*) and black (*dubh*). The O Donovans were chiefs of Carbery, near Limerick, where they had their headquarters at Bruree (Brú Rí means King's Fort). However, in the twelfth century the Normans scattered them to south-west Cork, where they found allies in the O Mahonys and became powerful chieftains with extensive lands. Later, the Jacobite wars—between the native Irish and the colonizers—scattered them again, to Kilkenny, Waterford and to Cork, where they are still numerous.

They boast an authenticated Chief of the Name, Morgan Gerald Daniel O Donovan—styled The O Donovan—who lives at Skibbereen in County Cork. The O Donovans are one of the most ancient Irish families, and The O Donovan can trace his forebears back to AD 977 to Ceallachán, King of Munster. They took their name from Ceallachán's son, **Donovan**. Many of their castles are still standing and can be found around their original Cork territory.

In the seventeenth century they were to follow the doomed Stuarts and so were forced to take the well-trodden path to France to join the Continental armies. O Donovan's Infantry was an Irish regiment of considerable distinction.

An **Abbé Donovan** from Cork, chaplain to an aristocratic Parisian family, was caught in the French Revolution, arrested and condemned to death. On his way to the guillotine, an officer heard him praying in Irish and reprieved him, along with seven other Irishmen!

The most distinguished O Donovan was the scholar and historian, **John O Donovan** (1805–61). He translated into English and edited *The Annals of the Four Masters*, a unique record of

Irish history, topography and genealogy up to the seventeenth century. **Edmund O Donovan**, John O Donovan's son, was one of the first war correspondents. He began by joining the French Foreign Legion and travelled widely in the Middle East, sending accounts of his adventures to *The Times* in London and to Irish newspapers. An adept at disguise, he often disappeared for long intervals. He was killed in an ambush in Egypt.

Jeremiah O Donovan (1831–1915) of Cork, famed as O Donovan Rossa, was forced to emigrate to the USA because of his involvement with the Fenians. There he edited the *United Irishman* and wrote about his earlier imprisonment in Britain when he was very badly treated. When he died in New York at the age of 84, his body was brought home for burial at Glasnevin Cemetery. This was some eight months before the 1916 Easter Rising and Patrick Pearse, one of its instigators, made an impassioned speech at his graveside.

Michael O Donovan (1903–66) was one of the foremost Irish writers and translators. He wrote under the pseudonym Frank O Connor.

Colonel "Wild Bill" O Donovan took part in the First World War with the Irish-American "Fighting 69th" and was director of America's first intelligence organization in the Second World War, the forerunner of the CIA.

Doody *see* (O) Dowd

Doolan

Ó Dubhlaing Ó Dubhlainn

Dolan Dooling Doulin Dowling

The Doolans or Doulins take their name from the Irish Ó Dubhlaing, which signifies a challenge, and is mainly a Connacht name, where it is sometimes rendered as Dolan. The name can also originate from the Munster name, Ó Dubhlainn. In Leinster, Doolan seems to have been changed to Dowling.

Very little has been recorded of this sept. Dolin was the name adopted by the world-famous **Sir Anton Dolin,** who was born in Sussex in 1904. A dancer and choreographer with the Diaghilev Russian Ballet, he was born Patrick Healey-Kay (his mother was an Irish Healey).

see also Dolan and Dowling

Doran

Ó Deoráin

Dorran

Translated from the Irish, this very common name means an exiled person. There were two septs, one in County Down and the other originally one of the Seven Septs of Leix, who, in 1609, were transplanted to County Kerry. In Leinster, where they are still numerous, they were a distinguished brehon (legal) family. For generations, they were guardians of the great Irish manuscripts.

In the sixteenth and seventeenth centuries, they were of the landed gentry, centred on their stronghold at Chappell, County Wexford. There, in 1540, they were accused by the English of "succouring rebellious plunderers" by manipulating the Irish brehon laws in their favour.

There were a number of prominent Doran ecclesiastics. In 1523 the Bishop of Leighlin was murdered by Archdeacon Kavanagh. In the nineteenth century, **Edward O Doran** was succeeded as Archbishop of Down and Connor by **Reverend Patrick Dorrian**—an Ulster variant of the name.

Because he was born in London and worked all his life there, **John Doran** (1807–78) is regarded as an English journalist and stage historian. Many of his plays were staged and he edited a number of literary magazines.

Charles Guilfoyle Doran (1835–1909) of Cork was an active participant in the Fenian movement and a writer. There is a record of a grant of arms in 1916 to **Sir Henry Doran**, knight of Clonard in Kimmage, County Dublin.

The Dorans, many of whom must have gone abroad at the time of the persecutions, are well recorded in the European archives.

Dorcey *see* d'Arcy

Dorney

Ó Doirinne

Durney

Dorney is a rare surname and is to be found almost exclusively in County Cork, with a few exceptions in counties Tipperary and Dublin. It derives from a descendant of a woman called Doireann, and in Irish it means sullen. For at least four centuries the sept has been recorded in east Munster, but they have produced none of the usual traditional genealogies. In 1659, O Dorney was one of the principal Irish names in Kerrycurrihy in County Cork.

During the rising of 1641, an O Dorney was outlawed for being on the side of the rebellious Irish. **Owen O Dorney** of County Cork lost his lands and his rights for following the deposed Stuart King James II, who was defeated at the battle of the Boyne in 1691.

Dorney is also thought to be a later form of Torna. The village of Abbeydorney in County Kerry, named after the Dorneys, was made internationally famous in 1985 during the long-running trial of the case of the dead Kerry babies.

Dorsey *see* d'Arcy

Douglas

Dubhglas

Douglas, or Douglass, is an ancient Scottish surname whose origin is lost. This family has a long line of distinguished Scottish soldiers, statesmen, patriots and politicians, many of whom held titles. This surname is numerous in Ireland, especially in Ulster, where they came with the conquerors and were granted forfeited lands. In the records offices in Edinburgh, Belfast and Dublin, there are many papers mentioning their military exploits.

In 1642, **Colonel David Douglasse** conveyed by letter the "exceedingly joyful news of the happy victory of the Scots in Northern Ireland over the arch rebels which included Phelim O Neill and the slaughter of six to seven thousand rebels." In 1689, **Lieutenant-General James Douglas** fought at the battle of the Boyne and afterwards led an attack on Drogheda.

In 1724, **General W. Douglas** wrote concerning a plan of the Irish and the disaffected British on the Continent to establish an impregnable fortress on Lough Bofin in County Galway. He also reveals his discovery of Jacobite plans to mortgage Ireland as security for money lent by the King of Spain's subjects!

An account concerning a Presbyterian family of County Armagh called **Blacker-Douglas** ran through several editions of *Burke's Landed Gentry of Ireland* up to the 1912 edition.

James G. Douglas (1889–1954) of Dublin belonged to a prominent family in the Society of Friends (Quakers). He was so highly thought of by the newly formed Irish Free State that he was made a member of the committee which drafted the Constitution of 1922. He sat in the Irish Senate for many years.

James Douglas, who was born in 1929 in County Wicklow, is a playwright, short-story writer and electrician. **Barry Douglas,** who was born in 1960 in Belfast, is one of Ireland's outstanding pianists.

The most notorious Douglas was **Lord Alfred Douglas**, son of the 9th Marquess of Queensberry and a poet in his own right, whose relationship with Oscar Wilde eventually led to the arrest and prosecution of Wilde for homosexual practices.

(O) Dowd

Ó Dubhda

Dodd Doody Duddy

The O Dowds are a very ancient sept whose name, Ó Dubhda (*dubh* means black), has sometimes been corrupted to Doody, Duddy or Dodd. They claim to be able to trace their ancestry from the Celts who came from Spain with Milesius and his sons. Certainly they are a sept of the Uí Fiachrach, descended from a brother of the famed King Niall of the Nine Hostages, ancestor of the kingly O Neills of Ulster.

Their early territory was extensive, including much of Mayo and Sligo, where they were lords of Tireragh. In *c.*983, **Hugh Ó Dubhda** was King of Lower Connacht. In the thirteenth century, Donnchadh Mór is said to have hired fifty-six ships from various ports in Scotland and its islands to enlarge his fleet so that he could attack Cathal Crobhdhearg O Conor, King of Connacht, who had captured his land. The Ó Dubhdha were always at war with the O Conors of Connacht, raiding and plundering along the coast to sustain themselves.

With the arrival of the Normans in the twelfth century, they were driven out of Connacht. Their ruined fortresses can still be seen along the coast at Easky in Sligo. In 1354, they succeeded for a while in driving the Anglo-Normans out of their territories and so many of their descendants are still living in their old homelands.

Several O Dowds were Bishop of Killala and these were to suffer for their loyalty to the Catholic Jacobite cause in the seventeenth century. In the 1650s the Cromwellians confiscated much of their lands and property and they suffered transplantation. Seeing little hope in their situation in Ireland, many sailed for Europe to serve in the Irish brigades. The head of the sept was killed in 1690 at the battle of the Boyne. He was seven feet tall. Great height is a characteristic of the O Dowds.

Peadar Ó Dubhda (b. 1881), a dedicated Irish scholar, was born in Dundalk. He had a meagre education and taught himself Irish while earning his living delivering groceries. He also studied music and collected folk songs and stories. As an itinerant teacher he earned £50 a year and bicycled an annual eight thousand miles organizing Irish classes. He translated the Douai Bible into Irish and presented it to the National Library of Ireland.

A minor O Dowd sept, long since settled in Derry, spell their name Duddy.

Dowling

Ó Dúnlaing

One of the many versions of this numerous name derives from a word meaning challenge. In earlier times there were two septs. One of these were the Dowlings who were Lords of Leix, members of the powerful Seven Septs of Leix. Their territory around the river Barrow was known as Fearrann na nDúnlaing, meaning O Dowlings' Country. During the confiscations of the sixteenth and seventeenth centuries, many of them lost their lands and were transplanted. The second Ó Dúnlaing sept were of Corca Laoidhe (south-west Cork), where they are still very numerous.

The annals of Duiske monastery, which are kept in Trinity College, Dublin, record the **Reverend Thadeus O Dúnlaing** as being abbot there in the Middle Ages.

In the National Library in Dublin, there are a number of papers relating to the land transactions of the family in Kildare, Wicklow and Roscommon. There was a **James Dowling** who owned land in 1623 in Drogheda and a **Robert Dowling** of Knockcarren, County Tipperary, who leased land from the Earl of Ormond. **Francis Dowling** was active in the Young Ireland movement between 1849 and 1864. **Joseph Dowling** of the Connacht Rangers was court-martialled in London in 1918.

In Dublin's Genealogical Office there is an account written by Margaret E. Dobbs in 1941 called *Women of the Uí Dúnlainge of Leinster*.

Vincent George Dowling (1785–1852), born in London of Irish parents, was the first journalist to publish details of the proposed new police systems, which were later adopted. A parliamentary journalist, he was present when Prime Minister Spencer Percival was assassinated in 1812 in the House of Commons.

Richard Dowling (1846–97) of Clonmel, a versatile writer of novels and short stories, wrote for *The Nation* newspaper. Today, **Donncha Ó Dúlaing** is a popular broadcaster for Irish radio, specializing in live interviews around the country.

The Dowlings are most numerous today in Kerry. In Connacht, the name is often synonymous with Doolan and sometimes Dolan.

see also Dolan, Doolan

Downes *see* Devine

Downing *see* Dinneen

Downey

Ó Dúnadhaigh

Downing Muldowney

The *dún* in this ancient surname refers to a fort. There were two septs of the name, one in County Galway, kinsmen of the O Maddens who were important chieftains until the twelfth century. The name is still numerous in this area, but without its O prefix. A much larger sept were the Ó Dúnadhaigh who were chieftains in Luachair, which covered parts of the counties Limerick, Cork and Kerry. Today this is still an area where the name is quite common, although it is often anglicized to Downing.

Richard Francis Downey (1881–1953) of Kilkenny was famous for two things. At the age of forty-seven, he became the youngest Roman Catholic archbishop in the world when he was appointed to the Liverpool diocese. Although only five feet four inches (1.62 m.) tall, he weighed eighteen stone in 1932. However, by 1939 he had reduced his weight to nine stone, receiving letters of admiration and enquiry from all over the world!

John Downey emigrated from County Roscommon to San Francisco with $10 in his pocket during the time of the gold rush. He opened a drug store, made a fortune and became Governor of California. **L. C. Downey** of

New York wrote *A History of the Protestant Downeys of Counties Sligo, Leitrim, Fermanagh and Donegal* in 1931.

James Downey was a deputy editor of the *Irish Times* in the 1980s. **Liam Downey**, an agricultural scientist, introduced foil packaging for butter, making Ireland one of the first in Europe to adopt this method.

Downey is also recognized as an abbreviation of Muldowney and is often confused with Moloney because of a similarity in the Irish form.

Downing *see* Dinneen, Downey

Downes *see* Kidney

Doyle

Mac Dubhghaill Ó Dúill

Doyelle Doyley MacDowell

The Doyles are very numerous and are found all over Ireland. The greatest concentration of Doyles is in the south-east of the country, particularly on the coast of counties Wexford and Wicklow. Never taking the Irish prefix O, Doyle comes from *dubh ghall*, meaning dark foreigner. This now very Irish surname originated with Norsemen who preceded the Normans in Ireland.

In Ulster, where they arrived from the Scottish Hebrides, they were known as the Mac Dubghaill. So it is that the MacDowells from Ulster and the MacDugalls in Scotland can be said to share the same Norse–Doyle ancestry.

The Doyles are not mentioned in the Irish genealogies, but they feature from the tenth century in the *Annals of the Four Masters*, a seventeenth-century history.

There were Doyles at the battle of the Boyne in 1690 and, later, they followed the Irish brigades to Europe. A dynasty of Doyles from County Kilkenny filled the ranks of the British services overseas from 1760 to 1856. There were six Doyle major-generals, several Doyle naval officers and four Doyle baronets. One was private secretary to the Prince of Wales. When it came to sending out royal invitations, a court official remarked to the King, "I can never distinguish between them." To which the monarch replied, "Perhaps it's just as well that they have taken good care to distinguish themselves."

From Wexford came **James Warren Doyle** (1786–1834), who at one time was an interpreter with Wellington's army in Spain. He returned to Ireland, to the priesthood, and later became a bishop. His many books and treatises were signed with the initials J. K. L. John, Bishop of Kildare and Leighlin.

From one Doyle who settled in England in the nineteenth century descends a galaxy of painters, cartoonists and writers, notably **Sir Arthur Conan Doyle**, the creator of Sherlock Holmes.

A Doyle has also been accredited with building the first bridge over Dublin's river Liffey.

So far, the most notorious Doyle has been the "Gorgeous Gael", **Jack Doyle** (1913–78) from Cork, the heavyweight boxer whose good looks and charm made him the toast of London after he had retired from his boxing career in the USA.

(O) Driscoll

Ó hEidersceoil

The O Driscolls took their name from a Baltimore ancestor whose name means either interpreter or intermediary. Their territory was always in the Cork area, but they had been driven even further west, to Baltimore, by the O Sullivans. They claimed descent from the paternal uncle of Milesius. They were certainly of the Corca Laoidhe (Coralee) who ruled south-west Cork where, in about 1460, the reigning chieftain founded a Franciscan monastery.

It must have been one of their hereditary poets who named their castles so euphoniously—*Dún-na-Seod* (fort of the jewels) in Baltimore, *Dún-na-nÓir* (fort of gold) on Cape Clear, *Dún-na-Long* (fort of the ships) on Sherkin Island, and *Dún-na-nGall* (fort of the foreigners) on Ringaroga Island.

The O Driscolls themselves had sweet-sounding names like Ersevan, Florence and Ffynin. One **Fineen O Driscoll** about whom a ballad was sung, "The scourge of the Sassenach [English] sailor", was the hero of the battle of Moyrath. A **Colonel O Driscoll** died when Mountjoy besieged Kinsale in 1601.

Because of their allegiance to the doomed Stuarts, the O Driscolls lost much but not all of their territory. They were prominent in the Irish brigades in France, and are well recorded in European archives. A **Cornelius O Driscoll** is mentioned as being in the Régiment de la Marine d'Irlande in 1693, while **Jacques O Driscoll** was a chevalier de St. Louis of the Regiment of Walsh in about 1790. **Denis O Driscoll** was Archbishop of Brindisi between 1600 and 1650. They also went even further afield, to America, where they joined the 80th New York Volunteers of the Irish-American brigades.

In the nineteenth century, **John O Driscoll**, a barrister from Cork, wrote about Irish history. He was appointed chief justice to the island of Dominica in the West Indies and was about to return home to collect his wife and family when he died in 1828. His son **William**, also a barrister, went to Dublin to practise. He wrote a life of his friend the Cork-born artist, Daniel Maclise, whose work became very popular in London.

To this day the O Driscolls remain a remarkably numerous family in the County Cork area.

Drohan

Ó Druacháin

Droghan

Drohan is a very rare surname which is still to be found in its place of origin, County Wexford, where there is a high concentration of Drohans. It was adopted as a surname by descendants of Druacháin. Several hundred years ago there was an ecclesiastical Ó Drucháin family at Armagh and some scholars think there may be a link.

In 1569 in County Wexford, **Maurice O Droughane**, a husbandman of Ballincolane, is recorded as having received a pardon. He was probably a rebel.

Daniel Drohan, who was Vicar-Apostolic of Ferns in County Wexford from 1588 to 1624, was generally known as James Walsh—a deception forced on him by the penal laws in force in Ireland and England at that time. Still following the ecclesiastical line, **Dame Elizabeth Druhan** of Lady's Island, County Wexford, was Lady Abbess of the convent school known as Kylemore which was founded in County Mayo by a band of nuns seeking refuge from Belgium during the First World War.

Duane, **Dwane** *see* Kidney

Duddy *see* (O) Dowd

Duffy

Ó Dubhthaigh

Doohey Dowey Duhig O Duffy

Duffy comes from a personal name which, in Irish, means black or swarthy. Monaghan was their original homeland. The Dooheys, Doweys and Duhigs of Ulster were probably at one time Duffys. Lissyduffy in Roscommon commemorates the multitude of Duffys who lived in that area.

In the seventh century, Duffy was the patron saint of Raphoe in County Donegal. The number of O Duffy priests who held high ecclesiastical office is remarkable. They were outstanding as preachers and diplomats in the Church.

In the thirteenth century, there were several excellent Duffy craftsmen, who made many of what, today, have come to be regarded as the treasures of early Irish art.

Following the colonization of Ireland, many Duffys were forced to emigrate and served in the armies of Europe and America.

In the nineteenth century, **James Duffy** founded a Dublin bookselling and publishing company. **Patrick Duffy**, son of a Dublin jeweller, was a landscape painter and a member of the Royal Hibernian Academy.

A talented Monaghan family initiated a dynasty of Duffys at home and abroad. **Sir Charles Gavan Duffy** adopted his widowed mother's name, Gavan, in acknowledgement of her efforts to encourage him in his education. He eventually acquired a legal degree and founded the nationalist newspaper, the *Nation*, and was subsequently imprisoned for a term for his rebellious views. Disillusioned with politics, he went to Australia, where he practised law very successfully and, in 1871, was elected Prime Minister of Victoria. He left many distinguished children in Australia and Ireland. One of his daughters, **Louise Gavan Duffy**, founded a popular Irish language school in Dublin, Scoil Bhríde.

General Eoin O Duffy, at first an army officer and then Commissioner of the Civic Guards, founded, in 1930, the notorious Blueshirts. O Duffy's brigade fought for a short while with Franco during the Spanish Civil War.

For more than three generations, Duffy's Circus has been travelling Ireland, delighting children and their parents.

Duggan

Ó Dubhagáin

Doogan Dougan

The name derives from the Irish words *dubh*, meaning black, and *ceann*, meaning head. There were four important Duggan septs, two in Connacht and two in Munster, where Duggans are still numerous. The principal sept—before the Normans dispersed them—were settled around Fermoy in County Cork, where their chieftain was lord of the extensive territory which was later captured by the Norman Roches and became known as Roche's Country. Near Loughrea, County Galway, they are commemorated by the townland name, Ballyduggan. Duggan is seldom seen now with the O prefix, which was dropped in the seventeenth century when Irish names were anglicized.

There were a number of Duggan poets, the most renowned, **Sean Mór Ó Dubhagáin** who died in 1372, was chief poet to the O Kellys of Galway. He chronicled the distribution of the clan and septs before they were scattered by the Normans.

The Jacobite wars drove the Duggans to join the Wild Geese, which is what the Irish who fled to serve in the armies of Europe were called.

In the nineteenth century, the Duggans are recorded in diverse ways. The great Daniel O Connell had a Duggan as his personal servant at the time of his last illness in Genoa in 1847. *The Brides of Venice*, a three-act opera written by **Francis Duggan**, was staged in 1868.

Pat Duggan, who died of cholera in 1883, came from a long line of Irish priests who had been missionaries in the Middle East for three hundred years. Another **Pat Duggan**, Bishop of Clonfert, was one of the Catholic clergy who were tried for political intimidation during the Galway election of 1872.

Eamon Duggan of County Meath, who graduated in law, fought in the 1916 Easter Rising. He was a member of the first *Dáil*, the Irish parliament, and was one of the delegates who signed the Anglo-Irish Treaty in London. He held a number of ministerial appointments and was also the first chairman of the Dún Laoghaire borough in County Dublin. **George Chester Duggan** of Wicklow was a civil servant in Dublin and was critical of the Anglo-Irish Treaty. He transferred to Northern Ireland, where he held important official appointments. He retired to Cavan, from where he wrote very critically of the politics of the government in Northern Ireland.

In 1926, **Bernardo Duggan** was an early transcontinental pilot. With his companions, he flew 9,376 miles from New York to Buenos Aires.

In Connacht Duggan is sometimes spelled Doogan, while in Ulster it could be Dougan.

Duncan

Ó Duinnchin

Donegan Dunphy MacDonogh

Duncan is undoubtedly a very numerous Scottish surname and the great number of Duncans living in Ulster came originally from Scotland. This surname could also have originated from the Irish Ó Duinnchin, which means son of the brown head. It has been anglicized to Duncan, Donegan, Dunkin, Dunphy, Donogh, MacDonogh and a host of other synonyms.

The Reverend Patrick Woulfe, in his *Dictionary of Irish Surnames*, says the family has three main branches. The first was a branch of the MacCarthys who were chiefs of Duhallow in County Cork, where they owned considerable land. The second was a branch of the MacDermots of Moylurg, who were chiefs in County Sligo, where they had their castle at Ballymote (the famous *Book of Ballymote* was compiled under their patronage). The third is a branch which came to Northern Ireland from Perthshire, where they were kinsmen of the MacDonalds.

In Dublin's Genealogical Office there are extracts from wills and genealogies relating to several landed Duncan families. Also, in the Public Records Office in Belfast, there are many Duncan papers.

William Dunkin (1709–65) was a friend of Jonathan Swift and wrote comic sketches of country life, including a burlesque of the *Aeneid* called *The Murphyeid*.

Ellen Duncan, née Douglas (*c.*1850–1937), who was born in Dublin, brought lustre to the name as an art patron and curator of Dublin's Municipal Gallery. In 1907 she founded the United Arts Club, which still flourishes, and she also campaigned for the return of the Lane pictures from London to Dublin.

Dunleavy

Mac Duinnshléibhe

Donlevy Levy MacAleevy MacNulty

Dunleavy is the more usual spelling of this ancient surname which, in Irish, means fortress of the mountain. They were a royal family of Ulster. When Eochy MacDunlevy, King of Ulidia, was taken prisoner and, despite surrendering, was blinded by the High King Muirchertach in 1166, the other leaders were so shocked at the atrocity that they killed the High King. His place was filled by Rory O Conor who, with Tiernan O Rourke, deposed the King of Leinster, Dermot MacMurrough. This led Dermot MacMurrough to go to France seeking the assistance of Henry II, the Anglo-Norman King of England. And so was precipitated that turning-point in Irish history—the Anglo-Norman invasion.

Although he was styled **Rex Hibernicorum Ultonia** in the thirteenth century, the head of the Dunleavy family was defeated by the Norman, John de Courcy, after which they all fled to Donegal. There they became hereditary physicians to the O Donnell chieftains of Tirconnell.

There are many spelling variants, including Levy, MacAleevy and MacNulty (Mac an Ultaigh), which means son of Ultach (Ulster). In 1395, **Paul Ultach** is recorded as being a Donegal physician, while **Owen Ultach**, alias MacDonlevy, was regarded as "an excellent medical doctor". **Cormac McDonlevy** is remembered for his translations of European medical books into Irish.

Christopher Dunleavy was martyred in 1644. **Reverend Andrew Donlevy** was the superior of the Irish College in Paris from 1728 to 1746. He compiled an Irish–English version of the catechism. **George Dunleavy** (d. 1917), a lighthouse-keeper and a naturalist, was noted for his wide knowledge of rare sea birds.

James Patrick Donleavy (b. 1926) was born in the USA and educated at Trinity College Dublin. He now lives in County Westmeath and has written many novels and plays. His best known work is probably *The Ginger Man*, which was dramatized and made into a film.

Janet and **Gareth Dunleavy** of the University of Wisconsin, USA, spent six summers, from 1977 to 1982, at Clonalis, the headquarters of the O Conor Don family, arranging their vast archives. They published a surname register which has been of great use to people who want to trace their west of Ireland origins.

Dunne

Ó Duinn

Dunn

Donn is the Irish word for brown. Nowadays, the O prefix is seldom used and in Ulster the final *e* is omitted.

The Dunnes originated in County Laois, where they were Lords of Iregan. In the twelfth century, their great poet was **Gillan-na-Naomh Ó Duinn**. They fought valorously in all the attempts to drive out the English and, when they finally had to leave the country, they did well in the armies of Europe and in America, where they also excelled at law. **Finlay Peter Dunn**, the American journalist and humourist, created the well-known Mr. Dooley comic character.

One of Dublin's oldest hospitals, **Sir Patrick Dun**'s, is named after a twelfth-century Scot who was an Irish Member of Parliament and five times president of the Royal College of Physicians in Ireland.

A handsome yellow eagle fills the blue Dunn armorial shield. Their crest, a holly tree, has a lizard at its foot. Their motto, *Mullac abu*, means "Up the summit".

Dunning *see* Dinneen

Dunphy *see* Duncan

Durkan

Ó Duarcáin   Mac Duarcáin

Durcan   Zorkin

This is mainly a Connacht surname and has a variety of spellings, including Zorkin, the only anglicized Irish name beginning with the letter Z. The word *duarcáin* from which the name comes is thought to mean pessimist.

A number of nineteenth-century wills and records of court cases (mainly of family disputes) of the Durkan family are held in the Public Records Office in Dublin.

The **Reverend Patrick Durcan** was Bishop of Achonry from 1852 to 1875.

In the mid 1800s, **Patrick Durkan** of Connacht was writing patriotic poems, including *The Outlaw of the West*, and *Deal*, or *The Peasant's Bride*. A modern poet, **Paul Durcan**, was born in Dublin in 1944 and is a relative of Sean MacBride, the internationally known politician and winner of the Nobel and Stalin Peace prizes. Paul Durcan is a distinguished literary critic who has had several volumes of poetry published and was also included in the *Penguin Book of Irish Verse* in 1979.

Air-Marshall Sir Herbert Durkin, born in Lancashire in 1922, may well have had Irish ancestry.

Sister Regina Durkan, born in County Mayo in 1937 and a member of the Order of the Sisters of Mercy, was a president of the Carysfort College of Education in Blackrock, County Dublin, from 1974. Despite being a very energetic and capable woman, she was unable to save the college from closure in line with economic cuts being imposed by the hard-pressed Department of Education.

The Durkan or Durcan surname, now almost always minus its O or Mac prefix, is still very numerous in the west of Ireland.

Durney *see* Dorney

(O) Dwyer

Ó Duibhir

An early Duibhir (meaning black shirt) gave his name to this important sept, whose origins go back beyond recorded history. From the seventh century until the depredations of the Cromwellians a thousand years later, the O Dwyers were settled in Kilnamanagh (the church of the monks), lords of one hundred square miles of Tipperary's richest land. While resisting the incursions of the English, there were many bloody battles fought between opposing clans in the mountains of that area.

Sheila Burke, an O Dwyer daughter, punished her sister's fall from grace by suspending her by the heels from the castle tower and pouring scalding water down onto her until she died. She rolled unwelcome visitors downhill in a barrel which had been studded on the inside with sharp nails!

One of their many Tipperary strongholds, Killenaule Castle, was well preserved and eventually became a private school.

Following the defeat of the Irish at the battle of Kinsale, the O Dwyers joined the exodus of the exiles to Europe, where they joined the various Irish brigades, rising to very high rank.

One became a governor of Belgrade, while another, one of a family of five brothers, became a major-general in Russia.

In Ireland, **Michael Dwyer** fought in the 1798 Rebellion and, for five years, defied all efforts by the English to capture him at his hideout in the Wicklow mountains. When he was finally forced to surrender, he was transported to Australia. By the time of his death he had risen to the post of high constable in Sydney.

Daisy Bates (1859–1950), who was born an Irish O Dwyer in Tipperary, is a folk hero in Australia because of her single-minded work for the welfare of the aborigines.

Joseph O Dwyer, son of Irish emigrants, was a New York physician, who developed a new treatment for diphtheria.

Bill O Dwyer of Bohola in County Mayo left his clerical studies in Salamanca, Spain, to go to America. He graduated in law and became attorney-general of Brooklyn, a controversial politician and mayor of New York, as well as an army general and a US ambassador to Mexico. **Paul O Dwyer** (b. 1907), his brother and youngest in a family of eleven, joined his brother in America to graduate as a lawyer and become a politician, fighting tirelessly for minority rights. He visited Ireland regularly and built a Cheshire Home on the family land at Lismirrane in County Mayo.

Sir Michael O Dwyer, a lieutenant-general serving with the British army in the Punjab in India in 1924, wrote *The O Dwyers of Kilnamanagh, County Tipperary: The History of an Irish Sept.* Published in London in 1933, and including a map and a pedigree, it is an invaluable account of this old Irish family.

Eason *see* MacHugh

Edmonds

Mac Éamainn

Edmunds Edmundson

In Ireland, Mac Éamainn simply means son of Edmond. Edmonds is a very popular surname in England, but in Ireland it is scarce everywhere except Ulster, where it is very numerous, with a variety of spellings, including Edmundson. The Edmonds came to Ulster with the Cromwellian armies and were also among the planters who settled in Ulster in the reign of Elizabeth I and James I, but there is also mention of a **Marmaduke Edmunds** who was given land in County Cork.

In the Genealogical Office in Dublin there are many letters, written by, and to, an English army administrator, **Sir Francis Edmunds**, concerning plans being made for the arrival of the Spanish Armada and the movements of the Irish in Spain, especially the once powerful O Neills and the O Donnells, who had fled there after the defeat at Kinsale. This correspondence includes a petition from a ship's captain concerning two companies of Irish in the Spanish fleet at Dunkirk who had "too many women belonging to them in the ships".

There are also clear indications that some Edmunds integrated with the Irish. There is an Edmundstown near Ballaghadereen in County Roscommon, and seven Edmonds are on the list of those transplanted from County Limerick between 1653 and 1654 because of their opposition to English rule.

In 1782, **W. Edmonds** is recorded as being ejected from his lands at Coolagh in County Tipperary.

Egan

Mac Aodhagáin

Keegan MacEgan

MacAodhagáin, the Irish version of Egan, comes from the name *Aodh* (Hugh, in English), who was a pagan god of fire. A family of distinguished brehons, or lawyers, for generations they acted as legal advisers to the royal families of Roscommon and Galway, their original territory. Later they had to move to Tipperary, Kilkenny and Offaly. In Dublin and Wicklow, MacEgan was anglicized to Keegan.

When it was no longer possible for them to practise brehon law, the MacEgans turned to the Church. A MacEgan bishop returned from Spain to take part in the battle of Kinsale, where he was killed. Another MacEgan bishop was executed by Cromwellian forces.

They had much success in London in the nineteenth and twentieth centuries as writers and artists, and in the USA they were to the forefront in politics and the diplomatic corps.

The MacEgans hold their clan rallies in their restored Redwood Castle at Lorrha in County Tipperary. Their coat of arms is most colourful, with towers and men in armour and a snake and a swan. Their crest also has an armoured man in a tower holding a battleaxe, while their motto is *Fortitudine et prudentia* (Fortitude and prudence).

Elliott

Eliot

Elliott is a very numerous surname in Ireland, especially in Northern Ireland, where there are at least six columns of Elliotts in the telephone directory. It seems to have no Irish origins, nor does it feature among the famous.

In Scotland, its original home, many Elliotts were titled and held high office. Some believe that the name derives from the Norman, Elias, or Ellis, others that it came from Elwald.

Because of the proliferation of the surname, a rhyme was composed by a medieval Scotsman.

The double L and single T
Descend from Minto and Wolflee,
The double T and single L
Mark the old race in Stobs that dwell.
The single L and single T
The Eliots of St. Germains be.
But double T and double L
Who they are nobody can tell.

From *Annals of a Border Club*

In London in 1906, H. C. Lawlor published his *History of the Family of Cairns or Cairnes and its Connections: Family pedigrees which contain also the Elliot family, the Montgomeries of Lisduff and Ballymagowan; the Moores of Moore Hall.*

In 1641, **Thomas Eliot** was a deputy surveyor-general who was responsible for the transplantation of the Irish to Connacht.

There were many distinguished clergymen of this name, both Protestant and Catholic. **John Elliott** brought a petition from the Roman Catholic inhabitants of Waterford to the corporation of the city, concerning the re-erection of a chapel there in about 1700.

Robert Elliott, who died in 1910, was an art critic, especially of ecclesiastical sculpture. **William A. Elliott** was a leading spinal specialist in the 1980s in Dublin.

Ennis

Ó hAonghuis Ó hAonghusa

Enos Hennessy

The surname Ennis is in no way connected with the town of Ennis in County Clare. It derives from the first name, Aonghuis (Angus), and has a number of variations, including Ó hAonghusa (Hennessy) and Enos. It is sometimes erroneously confused with the Scottish name, Innes. The Ó hAonghuis family were settled mainly in the counties of Kildare, Meath and Offaly.

In 1642, four members of the Ennis family were dispossessed for their part in the rising. **Lieutenant James Ennis,** who chose the opposing side, was a royalist soldier in the Williamite army.

Many of the Ennis family left to serve in the armies of Europe, including **John Ennis**, a major in the French army who returned to serve as lieutenant-colonel in James II's Irish army. After the king's defeat, he was outlawed as a Jacobite.

In the nineteenth century, **Dr. John Ennis**, a Dublin parish priest, was strongly opposed to the setting up of the Queen's colleges in Ireland. **Andrew Ennis** of Dublin, who made a fortune from commercial enterprise and bought property in County Westmeath, was created a baronet in 1866. His son, **Sir John Ennis**, was a governor of the Bank of Ireland and of the Midland and Great Western Railway. He had his town house at 9 Merrion Square.

John Ennis, born in 1944 in Westmeath, is an award-winning poet and has published several collections of his poetry.

Various Ennises have contributed a wealth of pamphlets on history, maps, nature, archaeology, etc., to the archives.

Ervine *see* Irwin

Evans

Ó hÉimhin

Evans could be an anglicization of the Gaelic surname, Ó hÉimhin, meaning son of the swift. They were a sept of Ormond in County Kilkenny. However, the numerous Evans in Ireland today are more likely to be descendants of the Welsh soldiers who came to conquer Ireland in the sixteenth and seventeenth centuries. Perhaps because their name is so numerous, they frequently added a second name, especially when they inherited their wife's property. This has resulted in names such as D'Arcy Evans, de Lacy Evans, Pierson Evans and Carbery Evans. **Sir George Patrick Evans-Freke**, 7th Baron Carbery of County Cork, took his surname from Castle Freke, which he inherited by marriage. It is now a ruin.

In 1650, **Colonel Griffith Evans**, an officer in Cromwell's army, drove the O Mahonys from their Castle Mahon in County Cork. Colonel Evans fell in love with the daughter of their chieftain, The O Mahony. He resigned his commission and retired with her to his Welsh estate, where they married and had three sons.

Many of the Evans came to Ireland with the Commonwealth army and, as was usual, they were awarded the forfeited estates of the Irish. Later, as they prospered, they bought many fine seats throughout the country and played an active role in public life, in the Church and in politics and the services. Their Irish lineage is recorded in *Burke's Landed Gentry of Ireland* (1912) and in the various books on the peerage. In 1864, **W. S. Evans** wrote *The Last Six Generations of the Evans Family.*

In the 1760s, the heyday of high society life in Dublin, when its Georgian buildings endowed it with the grace and charm which endure to the present day, the Evans name was listed among the many engineers and bricklayers.

Sir George de Lacy Evans (1787–1870) of Ireland was a distinguished general in the British army serving in India, the Peninsula wars, America and at the battle of Waterloo. He was a Liberal and represented Rye in the Westminster parliament between 1831 and 1832.

The most illustrious Evans, **Emyr Estyn Evans**, who was born in Wales in 1905, has been acclaimed as an honorary Irishman for his great service to the country, first and for many years with the Department of Geography at Queen's University, Belfast, and then as director of the Institute of Irish Studies. He published many books on Irish folklore, music and history, covering the whole range of the Irish cultural heritage.

Fagan

Ó Faodhagháin

Fegan (O) Hagan (O) Hogan

A very old surname, Fagan is thought to be of Norman, not English, origin, deriving from the Latin *paganus*, meaning pagan. The most notable Fagans descended from William Fagan (*c*.1200), a rich landowner of Feltrim in County Dublin. In a pedigree of this family—also of Faganstown and Deryfagan—they are described as having given the land for Dublin's Phoenix Park. A pedigree dated 1733 shows another Fagan family claiming descent, through the O Hogans, from Niall, the High King of Ireland in *c*.AD 379.

Christopher Fagan fled to Cork in 1497, following the abortive attempt to set up the pretender, Perkin Warbeck, as monarch of England. **John Fagan** was a clerk of Her Majesty's Munitions in Cork, in 1588.

There are extracts of proceedings of a court case for breach of promise held in Drogheda in 1630. The accused, a P. Russell, insisted that she "never had to do with **Sir C. Fagan**, a priest, and had no bastard".

A declaration, in French, by James II states that "**J. Fagan**, formerly of Feltrim, is of good family now residing at Bordeaux." In fact, many Fagans sought refuge in France, where they are well documented. Several Fagans of County Kerry were distinguished in the service of France and were ennobled.

Edmund O Fagan (sometimes corrupted to O Hagan) was an officer in the Ultonia Regiment of the Spanish army in 1778. Fagans also served in America, where **Michael Fagan** was with the 88th New York Volunteers, while **James Fagan** (1828–93), of Irish origin, was a planter, soldier and public official.

Robert Fagan (1745–1816) of Cork was a diplomat and portrait painter. Also in the eighteenth century, **L. Fagan**, a learned Archbishop of Dublin, left money to the Collège des Irlandais in Paris.

The Genealogical Office holds pedigrees of the Fagans of Kerry and Cork, "of the Indian Empire", from *c*.1700 to 1907.

James Bernard Fagan (1873–1933), an outstanding actor-manager and playwright, was born in Belfast. He founded the Oxford Playhouse in 1927 and had many noteworthy London productions.

(O) Fahy

Ó Fathaigh

Faghy Fahey Green

Almost exclusively a County Galway name, translated from the Irish Ó Fathaigh means a lawn or green and, indeed, in a few instances the name Green could originally have been Ó Fathaigh! A sept of the Uí Maine, Loughrea was their headquarters and

Muintir Uí Fhathaigh (Fahysville) described their wide-ranging territory until they were toppled by the Cromwellians.

They have not featured much in history, although there are Fahy papers in the Bibliothèque Nationale in Paris concerning this family in the seventeenth and eighteenth centuries. In 1825, a grant of arms was made to **Rear-Admiral Sir William Charles Fahie**, son of **Judge John Davis Fahie**, President of the Council of Tortola, son of **Anthony Fahie** of the island of Saint Christopher in the West Indies.

In 1864, one of the quartermasters with the Irish-American brigades in New York was **Captain John Fahy**.

Francis Fahy (1854–1935), who was born in Kinvara in County Galway, worked all his life in London in the civil service. Fahy was a songwriter, and his most famous ballad is *The Ould Plaid Shawl*. He founded literary clubs in Southwark, so that children and their parents could keep in touch with their Irish culture, especially the music and literature. He was President of the London Gaelic League.

Francis Fahy (1880–1954), a veteran of the 1916–21 War of Independence in Ireland, was *Ceann Comhairle* (Speaker) of Dáil Éireann, the Irish parliament.

Sean Fahy (b. 1924) was editor of the *Connacht Tribune* newspaper for many years. **Jim Fahy** (b. 1946) is a correspondent for RTÉ, the Irish broadcasting company.

Falconer, Falkiner *see* Faulkner

Fall *see* Lavelle

Fallon

Ó Fallamhain

Falloon

Fallon is a very widespread name in Ireland, particularly in counties Galway and Roscommon. They are most numerous in the area around Athlone in southern Roscommon where, in 1585, the O Fallons held their castle at Milltown in the parish of Dysart, where the ruins can still be found. Until comparatively recently, they owned estates in Ballinasloe in County Galway, claiming descent from the "Chiefs of the O Fallon Country". There were many references to them in the ancient annals, including a record of two medieval Fallon bishops, of Elphin and Derry.

James O Fallon (1749–94), who was born in Ireland, fathered an outstanding family in North America. His son, also **James O Fallon**, was an officer in the American War of Independence, and another son, **Colonel John O Fallon**, was a philanthropist. **Benjamin O Fallon** (1791–1865) was known as Father of the Tribes, because of his friendly relations with the American Indians.

In this century, **Gabriel Fallon**, born in Dublin in 1898, was long associated with the Abbey Theatre, as actor, critic and director. **Padraic Fallon** (1906–74) of County Galway, while both farming and working for customs and excise, wrote a number of important verse plays.

The name is numerous in Ulster, in County Armagh, where it is spelled Falloon.

see also Fullen

Fant

de Fuente   Fante   Ffont

According to Doctor MacLysaght, from the fourteenth century there were Fants in Limerick, where there is also a Fantstown. He suggests the surname could come from the French *l'enfant* or *de la faunte.* Hardiman, in his *History of Galway*, writes that the family of Ffont, or de Fuente, settled in Galway at the beginning of the fifteenth century. They were from Leicestershire and came to Athenry in County Galway at the time of King John, in about 1210.

The Fants were one of the families of the Fourteen Tribes of Galway and intermarried with them for many generations. **Martin Fante** was Mayor of Galway between 1520 and 1521. Some of the family had grants of land in County Galway and others moved to Boyle in County Roscommon.

Scholars think the name Ffonte or de Fuent, meaning barren, could be Norman, or possibly Spanish, in origin. Certainly they seem to have lived up to their name, for the family became almost extinct in the nineteenth century when the last survivor of the Galway family, **Geoffry Ffont**, died there in 1814, aged 105 years.

Today there are only two Fants in the telephone directory system, both in Fermoy in County Cork.

Farley *see* (O) Farrelly

Farquharson *see* Lamont

(O) Farrell

Ó Fearghail

Ferrall

Fearghail is a personal name meaning man of valour. The Ó Fearghail chieftains were lords of Annaly near Longford, once known as Longphort Uí Fearghail (O Farrell's Fortress). A powerful family, they also included parts of Westmeath in their territory. They are kinsmen of the Ó Mordha family, whose most famous heroes were Rory O More and his son Rory Óg (young).

In the helpful Irish genealogy compiled by Michael I. Clery, the O Farrells occupy seven columns in the index. They had many distinguished churchmen, the best recorded being the seventeenth-century Capuchin friar, **Richard O Farrell**.

Ceadagh O Ferrall of Annaly was killed at the battle of the Boyne in 1690. His three sons escaped to distinguish themselves with many other O Farrells in the Irish brigade in France, where an O Farrell Regiment was also formed. Some of the family settled in Picardy.

One of their descendants, Francis Thurot of Burgundy, adopted his maternal grandfather's name and, as **Francis Thurot O Farrell**, he served in the French navy and died in 1760, shortly after the French frigate he was aboard had broken the English blockade of Belfast Lough.

James Farrell, one of Dublin's prosperous eighteenth-century brewers, had a house on fashionable Merrion Square.

Letitia O Ferral was reared at Balyna, the ancestral home of the O More family in Kildare. Daughter of **Ambrose O Ferral**, she joined the Sisters of Charity and gave £3,000 to buy the St. Stephen's Green house which laid the foundation for Dublin's biggest hospital, St. Vincent's. Kildangan in

County Kildare is also a mansion of the More O Ferrall family, famous for its bloodstock and fine gardens.

James Ambrose O Ferrall was a major-general in the Austrian army and a chamberlain at the Austrian court.

Richard More O Ferrall, Member of Parliament for Kildare and Longford, was a staunch supporter of Daniel O Connell, "The Liberator", who won Catholic emancipation for Ireland.

George More O Ferrall was joint producer of the first ever BBC television programme. He produced films for most of the big companies, including Rank and Twentieth-Century Fox. When he was head of drama for Anglia Television, he produced an astonishing number of television plays.

Many O Farrells emigrated in the nineteenth century to the Americas and to Australia.

(O) Farrelly

Ó Faircheallaigh

Farley Fraly Frawley

The name Ó Faircheallaigh, anglicized to Farrelly, originated in County Cavan, where there was a family of abbots and erenaghs (lay lords) at St. Mogue in Drumlane, County Cavan. In the sixteenth century, following the suppression of the monasteries, they lost all their hereditary rights.

In all the provinces except Ulster the Farrelly name is very numerous. It is still among the ten most numerous names in County Cavan and it is also found throughout County Meath. **Feardorcha O Farrelly,** who died in 1740, was an important Cavan poet.

From the fourteenth century, there was mention of an O Farrelly sept in Knockainy, County Limerick, which became extinct by the time of the census of 1695.

Farley, an English name, became synonymous with Farrelly. An example of this transposition is **Cardinal Farley** (1842–1918), born in County Armagh, who became Archbishop of New York.

Earlier this century, **Madeleine King O Farrelly** won fame by composing the music for a popular ballad, "The Old Bog Road". **Patrick Farrelly** was among the Republicans executed in Dublin on 30 November 1922.

Before the standardization of spellings, Frawley, Fraly or Frally could have been a variation of Farrelly in the counties of Limerick and Clare, where these names appear in wills and other records.

Faulkner

Falconer Falkiner

Faulkner, from the name le Fauconer, meaning the falconer, originated in France, from where the name must have come to England with the Normans.

Records from the end of the seventeenth century, during the Williamite confiscations following the battle of the Boyne, show a **Daniel Falkiner** being granted a forfeited Irish estate, while, in 1702, a **John Falkiner** was the purchaser of another forfeited estate.

Caleb Falkiner, a Cork merchant, was the third son of **Daniel Falkiner** of Dublin who was a younger brother of **Daniel Falkiner**, a Lord Mayor of Dublin. In 1812, his great-grandson became **Sir Frederick John Falkiner**.

Among the three hundred Members of Parliament who represented Ireland in the Irish House of Commons in 1797, there was a **Frederick John Falkiner**.

Annemount, overlooking Cork Harbour, was built in the eighteenth century by **Sir Riggs Falkiner**, who named it after his second wife. Mount Falcon, in Borrisokane, County Tipperary, was built in 1720 by **Richard Falkiner**.

The Faulkner name is now fairly common in Ireland, especially in Waterford and Meath. It is very numerous in Northern Ireland.

The only notable representative of the name was **Brian Faulkner** (1921–77), who was born in County Down to a family of shirt manufacturers. The youngest Member of Parliament to be elected to the Northern Ireland parliament in 1949, he was a dedicated Unionist and was instrumental in defeating the moderate Prime Minister, Terence O Neill. In 1971, when Brian Faulkner had himself become Prime Minister, he introduced internment. Following a defeat in 1976, he left politics and, the following year, was killed in a hunting accident.

Fay, **Fee** *see* Foy

(O) Feeley

Ó Fithcheallaigh

Feehily Feely Field Fielding Fihily

The Feeley surname derives from the Irish name, Ó Fithcheallaigh, meaning son of the chess player. Through the centuries it has acquired a great variety of spellings, including O Fihillie, O Fihily, O Fielly, Fihelly, Fihily, Fehily, Fehely, Feehely, Feehily and Feely. During the Gaelic suppression of the fifteenth and sixteenth centuries, like the majority of Irish surnames, it was anglicized and became Field. **John Field** (1786–1837), the Dublin musician who introduced the nocturne and had a most successful career in Russia, may well have had Ó Fithcheallaigh roots. Fielding is a modernization of Field.

It is only in recent times that the spelling of this ancient Irish surname has been standardized. Today Feeley and Feely occur in almost equal numbers and are very numerous, especially in Connacht—in County Roscommon—the homeland of one of the two septs.

The more powerful sept was of Corca Laoidhe in south-west Cork, where their chieftains ruled over Tuath Ó Fithcheallaigh, their vast territory bounded by the sea at Baltimore.

The renowned **Maurice de Portu**, who was Archbishop of Tuam between 1506 and 1513, was a member of this County Cork family. He was very highly regarded by the Church for his great learning, for which he was known as "Flos Mundi".

John Feely was born in Galway in 1810, from where he emigrated to Argentina. In 1857, **Peter Feely**, following the terrible Great Famine, also left Ireland for Argentina. Their descendants there have multiplied.

Canon Fehily, who was born in 1917 in Ballineen, County Cork, was a distinguished army chaplain serving in Germany and Malaysia with the British forces. He was Canon of Motherwell Cathedral in Lanarkshire. **Frank Feely**, who was born in 1931, was Dublin's County and City Manager.

Fegan *see* Fagan

Fey *see* Foy

Ffont *see* Fant

Fennessy

Ó Fionnghusa

Fennessy, an anglicized form of Ó Fionnghusa, probably means the son of the vigorous, fair-haired man (*fionn* means fair and *gus* means vigour).

It is a very rare name, mostly now

found in Munster, especially in the Waterford area. There are a few Fennessys in the Dublin area. Barrack Street was in the heart of Dublin, close to the Royal Barracks which were erected in 1704. In the records of 1820, there is mention of a **John Fennessy** being assigned premises there by John Moran. In 1824, **Catherine Fennessy**, possibly a close relative, is recorded as leasing a house in Barrack Street from John Kane. Barrack Street has since been changed to Queen's Street.

Earlier this century, *A Book of Irish Tales* was written by **Mairead Fennessy** and was published by the Mitre Press.

Fennessys have not featured very much in history, except for one emigrant. **Sir John Fennessy** (b. 1912) is a distinguished representative of the family who must, earlier, have emigrated to Britain. Following service in the Royal Air Force, he became a director of various electronic companies. He was President of the Royal Institute of Navigation and Chairman of British Telecom Research Limited.

Ferrall *see* (O) Farrell

Fidgeon *see* MacGuigan

Field, **Fielding**, **Fihily** *see* (O) Feeley

Finlay *see* MacGinley

Finnegan

Ó Fionnagáin

Finegan

This very old Gaelic name originated from the personal name Fionnagáin, meaning the small fair-haired fellow. In fact there were two Ó Fionnagáin septs (the O prefix is seldom used now). One sept had their territory in the Galway and Roscommon area, where there are two towns called Ballyfinnegan. The other quite separate sept, from which most of today's Finnegans trace their ancestors, is to be found in the area once known as Breffny, covering the counties Cavan, Monaghan and Meath.

James Joyce's novel, *Finnegans Wake*, which has made this, as yet, undistinguished name famous, took its name from an old Dublin ballad.

Seamus Finnegan, who was born in Belfast in 1949, trained as a teacher and is a very prolific playwright who also writes television scripts for British television.

FitzGerald

mac gearailt

Fitzgerald

The name FitzGerald means son of Gerald. The FitzGeralds came from Normandy in 1170. A vigorous family, they integrated rapidly, marrying local Irish women and acquiring vast territories in Kildare, Cork and Kerry, on which they built splendid castles. They acquired exalted titles: Earls of Kildare, Dukes of Leinster and, in Munster, Earls of Desmond. One Earl of Desmond bestowed the titles of Earl of Glin, Earl of Kerry and the White Knight on his three illegitimate sons.

In the sixteenth century, the great **Garret Mór FitzGerald**, was the uncrowned king of Ireland. When he was imprisoned by Henry VIII for burning the cathedral of Cashel, he told the King, "If I had not been told that my Lord Archbishop was inside, I would not have done it," to which King Henry replied, "All Ireland cannot govern this Earl, then let this Earl govern all Ireland."

Because of their militant preference for Irish rule to English, four FitzGeralds were imprisoned and died in the Tower of London. Henry VIII also executed eight of them at Tyburn.

At Kilkea Castle in County Kildare, once a FitzGerald stronghold and now a hotel, the so-called **Wizard Earl of Kildare** is said to emerge from the lake, riding a white horse shod with silver shoes. When another FitzGerald castle, Woodstock in County Kildare, caught fire, the heir, a baby, was rescued by a pet monkey, which is why there is a chained monkey on their armorial bearings.

Finding their castle at Maynooth too shabby, **Robert**, 19th Earl of Kildare, commissioned Richard Castle to build nearby Carton, a palatial house. **James**, 20th Earl of Kildare and 1st Duke of Leinster, built Leinster House in Kildare Street, Dublin, as his town house. Leinster House is now where Dáil Éireann, the Irish parliament, sits. One of James's twenty-two children was the patriot leader **Lord Edward FitzGerald**. Following a military career in America and France, he joined the United Irishmen, was betrayed and died of his wounds.

One of the Earls of Desmond, **George Robert FitzGerald** (1748–86), a rake and an eccentric, tortured his family, tying his father to a pet bear and locking him up for days. His private army was the terror of Mayo.

The FitzGeralds were prominent in Europe, where they had their own regiment. They distinguished themselves in America in many spheres. *The Great Gatsby* was written by **F. Scott FitzGerald**.

Desmond FitzGerald, 29th Knight of Glin, an antiquarian and historian, has beautifully restored his ancestral castle at Glin, beside the Shannon estuary.

The FitzGeralds continue to dominate Irish politics. **Garret FitzGerald** (b. 1926) was three times Taoiseach with a coalition government.

FitzGibbon

Mac Giobúin

Fitzgibbon

The FitzGibbon surname came from Normandy. Fitz, meaning son, Gibbon, a diminutive of Gilbert. There were two branches, one of which descended from Gilbert de Clare and the second which is connected with the Burkes of Mayo, who were also of Norman origin.

From the fifteenth century, they held one of the three hereditary knighthoods in County Limerick. These were the Knight of Kerry (FitzGerald), the Knight of Glin (FitzGerald) and the White Knight (FitzGibbon). These three titles were bestowed by an autocratic FitzGerald on his own three illegitimate sons. The titles of Knights of Kerry and of Glin still exist, but the White Knight title has long been dormant. **Maurice Desmond FitzGibbon**, who emigrated to Australia in 1927, considered claiming this title at one time.

Undoubtedly, **John FitzGibbon** (1749–1802), 1st Earl of Clare and Lord Chancellor of Ireland, was the most outstanding of the FitzGibbons. He was the most powerful man of his day and also the most reviled. He helped to bring about the union with England, thus losing Ireland her independent parliament, and he opposed the emancipation of Catholics. He built a magnificent mansion in County Limerick, Mountshannon, which is now a ruin.

Gerald FitzGibbon was a distinguished member of the Irish Bar and his son, **Edward** (1803–57), was one of the most remarkable fishermen of his day. He was born in Limerick and died in London. He published books on the art of angling which are considered to be classics.

The FitzGibbons travelled far afield, to India, the Americas, Toronto, Lisbon,

Bordeaux. Many served in the British army or navy, or the consular services.

Constantine FitzGibbon (1919–83) was born in Massachusetts, USA, and died in Dublin. He served with both the British and American armies in the Second World War. He spoke fluent French, German and Italian and wrote many plays, documentaries and history books. He married four times.

The name of FitzGibbon is very numerous in every part of Ireland except the North.

FitzHenry *see* Henry, MacHenry, MacEnery

Fitzpatrick

Mac Giolla Phádraig

Kilpatrick MacGillapatrick

This is the only Fitz surname which is Irish rather than Norman. Anglicized from Mac Giolla Phádraig to Fitzpatrick (and Kilpatrick and other variations), it means son of a follower of St. Patrick. Their pedigree is a long and distinguished one, stretching back to Heremon, son of Milesius, the King of Spain who conquered Ireland in the sixth century BC.

In the tenth century, when their chieftain was Giolla Phádraig, they were Lords of Upper Ossory (Kilkenny). They lost most of their position of power because of their loyalty to the ill-fated Stuart King, James II, and also because of their Butler neighbours, the Earls of Ormond.

Sir Barnaby Fitzpatrick, an intimate of the kings of England and France, was knighted in 1558.

Brian Fitzpatrick, the Vicar Apostolic of Ossory, saved the *Book of the O Byrnes* from destruction by transcribing it, and was subsequently murdered by Cromwellian soldiers in 1652. Also in the seventeenth century, **Colonel Fitzpatrick** raised an Irish regiment for service in France.

Sir Jeremiah Fitzpatrick, who was born about 1740 in County Westmeath, was a medical doctor and Inspector of Health for the British army. He was an early pioneer in the improvement of living standards for the troops.

The Fitzpatricks managed to hold on to their twenty-two thousand good acres in Kilkenny and Leix until the nineteenth century. In that century, too, a Fitzpatrick was the abbot of the renowned abbey at Clonmacnoise.

William John Fitzpatrick (1830–95), a wealthy Dubliner, published biographies of several famous romantic Irish characters of the eighteenth and nineteenth centuries.

In both Ireland and England there have been a number of distinguished Fitzpatricks in politics, the army and, latterly, the Royal Air Force. They have also featured prominently in the USA, Australia and Barbados.

(O) Flaherty

Ó Flaithbheartaigh

(O) Flaverty Laverty

The O Flahertys were always an important sept in west Connacht, and "bright ruler" is the translation of their ancient name. At the height of their power they ruled over more than a quarter of a million acres. Their history is exemplified in their armorial bearings, which show a ship with oars, the red hand of the O Neills—their partners in many battles, and the mythical lizard which would warn a sleeping O Flaherty of an approaching enemy.

The O Flahertys were much inclined to warfare. They had to fight to preserve their possessions against the encroachments of the Normans, especially those who were numbered among the élite Fourteen Tribes of Galway, who described them as "the ferocious O Flahertys from whom God defend us".

The remains of their palatial castle of Aughnanure near Oughterard in County Galway is an example of the great splendour in which they lived. According to the records, they were attended by a large and varied staff, including a physician, lawyers, poets, learned men, a master of the revels and several beekeepers.

The first husband of Granuaile (Grace O Malley), the great Irish pirate, was an O Flaherty. He was killed in battle.

In Elizabethan times, the O Flahertys' power began to wane. They were on the losing side in all the battles. Following the disaster at the Boyne in 1690, they lost practically all their possessions. Although they joined the exodus to the Irish brigades in Europe, they do not seem to have produced any outstanding commanders.

Their last chieftain, **Roderick O Flaherty**, died in poverty in Moycullen in 1718, but he left behind an invaluable Latin history of Ireland.

Colman O Flaherty was chaplain to the American expeditionary force in the First World War and was killed in Europe. In the Second World War, a **Monsignor Hugh O Flaherty** in Rome was one of the famous "Scarlet Pimpernel" priests who helped allied soldiers to escape from German-occupied Italy.

Robert J. Flaherty, the son of Irish emigrants, pioneered the filming of the lives of primitive people, for which he earned the title "father of the documentary". In Ireland, he filmed the classic *Man of Aran*.

Liam O Flaherty (1896–1984), born on the Aran Islands to Irish-speaking parents, left to become an internationally acclaimed novel and short story writer.

There is also an O Flaherty sept based in Kerry. In Ulster the name has been transposed to Laverty.

Flahiff, Flahive *see* Laffey

(O) Flanagan

Ó Flannagáin

Flannagáin was the name of the hereditary poet and steward at the court of the O Conor kings of Connacht, where they were also regarded as "royal lords". Translated from the Irish, *flann* probably means red-haired. Apart from the Galway sept, there were others of the name in counties Fermanagh and Offaly.

In the fourteenth century, the saintly **Conough O Flanagan** was famed for his bountiful hospitality. A **Captain Flanaghan** of the Regiment of Dillon was wounded at the battle of Fontenoy and **Sergeant Luc O Flannagan** was, at that time, serving with the Regiment of Bulkely. A Flanagan who went further afield, **Roderick Flanagan**, founded the *Sydney Chronicle.*

There were many ecclesiastical writers, including **Michael O Flanagan** (1876–1942), the republican priest who caused trouble wherever he went. An active member of *Sinn Féin*, he was silenced by his bishop. He left a trail of incidents in the USA and he was deported from Australia. Eventually, when he finally settled back in Ireland, he spent his last years editing John O Donovan's fifty-volume *Archaeological Survey.*

In Dublin's National Library, there are many unsorted papers belonging to a **Captain Woulfe Flanagan**, including some from Calais in 1716 concerning Jacobite affairs. Elsewhere there is a certificate confirming **Marguerite O Flanagan**'s right to a pension in Paris *c.*1750.

Flanagan is a widespread name all over Ireland, including Ulster, whereas O Flanagan is not so numerous now.

Flaverty *see* (O) Flaherty

Fleming

Pléamonn

Late in the eleventh century, Belgium's flat eastern coast was flooded. Many people fleeing from the floods found shelter in Scotland and Wales, where they became known as Fleming, the name of the area from which they had come. Some came with the Anglo-Normans to Ireland, where they were given land and built Slane Castle in County Meath. In the seventeenth century, they were driven from there because of their adherence to the Catholic religion.

Later, more Flemings came with the various invasions to County Cork and to Ulster, where they are still most numerous. Today, many distinguished Flemings crowd the pages of biographies internationally. The Dublin Genealogical Office holds records of many Flemings, including the Barons of Slane and of Magno Porto in Spain, from *c.*1300 to 1721 and from 1571 to 1902. There are still claimants to this now defunct title.

An Irish pirate called Fleming is recorded as having been captured in 1617. Many Flemings also filled high ecclesiastical office. In the seventeenth century, **Archbishop Fleming** of Dublin wrote to Rome describing the massacre of three hundred helpless women in Wexford by Cromwellian troops. A number of Cromwell's soldiers subsequently settled in Ireland.

The Flemings, many of whom became rich and important, built fine houses all over the country, most of which have since been demolished.

In the eighteenth century, a **Field-Marshall Count Fleming** served in Saxony. Many more Flemings served in the armies of Europe and in the Irish-American brigades. The Irish Flemings settled mostly around Philadelphia.

There were literary men, including **John Fleming** (1814–96) of Waterford, a teacher and scholar. **John Fleming** (1830–1908) of Carlow was a royal chaplain whose sermon for the funeral of the Duke of Clarence became such a profitable bestseller that it stimulated the clergy to print many more sermons.

Lionel Fleming, a son of a County Cork canon, was a journalist and an overseas broadcaster for the BBC.

Flemings married into many old Irish families. One branch claim to be kinsmen of the distinguished Somerville-Large family of County Cork. A number of historical memoirs have been written by various Flemings about their ancestors.

Flinn *see* (O) Flynn

Flood

Mac Maoltuile Ó Maoltuile

Tully

The surname Flood is to be found mostly around counties Galway and Cavan. Formerly it was Ó Maoltuile, which was anglicized to MacAtilla or MacTully, meaning son of the Flood. Tully and Flood at one time were interchangeable.

The Ó Maoltuile, spelled in a variety of ways, are recorded as being hereditary physicians to the O Conor kings of Connacht and to the O Reillys of Breffny. In County Longford, near Granard, Tullystown commemorates the Ó Maoltuile who were physicians for the O Reillys.

There are letters in the national archives concerning **Matthew Flood**, alias Tully, who had a pension in 1606 from the King of Spain and was a retainer of O Donnell, Earl of Tirconnell.

Henry Flood (1732–91), an illegitimate son of **Warden Flood**, attorney-general and chief justice of the King's Bench, was an Irish statesman and a patriot. He was one of the finest orators of his day. A hot-tempered man, he killed an opponent in a duel and had to be restrained from challenging the great Henry Grattan.

In 1806, Frederick Solly, a grandson of **Sir Frederick Flood**, Member of Parliament for Wexford, was given a grant of arms to assume the name **Solly Flood**. Flood Hall in Thomastown, County Kilkenny, home of the great **Henry Flood** and later of the **Solly Floods**, was demolished in 1950.

Reverend Dr. Peter Flood (d. 1803) was a president of St. Patrick's College, Maynooth. **William Henry Grattan Flood** (1807–1928), author of *The History of Irish Music*, was an organist and a composer of liturgical music.

In 1921, **Frank Flood** was sentenced to hang in Dublin's Kilmainham Gaol.

Joseph Mary Flood (1882–1954) was professor of English and Roman law at University College Galway. He wrote many enduring books on Irish history and legend.

Flood is also an English name, and many Floods came to Ireland with the colonists. It would be difficult now to separate the Gaelic Tullys or Floods from the Anglo-Irish Floods.

see also Tully

(O) Flynn

Ó Floinn

Flinn (O) Loinn (O) Lynn

Flynn comes from the personal name, Flann, meaning ruddy complexion. Several families of this name sprang up independently in various counties. In Munster, the O Flynn stronghold was Ardagh Castle, not far from Skibbereen in County Cork. Another O Flynn family, also of Cork, were lords of Muskerrylin (Muscraidhe O Floinn).

In Connacht, the O Flynns were centred in Roscommon, where they were important administrators in the church of St. Dachonna in Boyle. The head of this family was so highly respected that he had the privilege of sharing a horse belonging to the O Conor king.

In modern Irish, because of the aspiration of the letter *f*, the name has become O Loinn, or O Lynn in Ulster. This family claims descent from Colla Uais, King of Ireland in the fourth century.

The Flynns were prominent in the Church in France, and they also served in the Irish brigades.

Jeremiah O Flynn, a Franciscan friar, was a pioneer and a fiery missionary in both Australia and the USA. **John Flynn** (1880–1951), a Presbyterian minister, founded Australia's Flying Doctor Service and was known as "Flynn of the Inland".

Edmund Flynn (b. 1847) was Premier of Quebec in Canada. **William James Flynn** (1867–1928) was head of the US Secret Service and, later, the FBI. **Elizabeth Gurley Flynn** (1890–1964) was leader of the Communist Party in the USA and died in Moscow.

James O Flynn (1881–1962) was "Father O Flynn of the Loft", from the name of the theatre he created over a sweet factory in Cork. Here, he promoted Shakespearean plays and the Irish language.

Errol Flynn (1909–64), who came from Tasmania, was a swashbuckling star of many romantic Hollywood films in the thirties and forties, until he destroyed his health through over-indulgence.

Fogarty

Ó Fógartaigh

Gogarty

It is thought that the Irish word *Fogartach* derives from an older word which means either exiled or expelled. The Ó Fógartaigh were of the Dalcassian sept of County Tipperary, and their long-since lost headquarters were at Castle Fogarty. They have left their name to the barony of Eliogarty near Thurles in County Tipperary.

The seventeenth-century **Malachy O Fogarty**, who was born at Castle Fogarty, was a distinguished scholar at the University of Paris. In more recent times, there was an important ecclesiastic, Archbishop **Michael Fogarty** (1858–1955), who was Bishop of Killaloe for fifty-one years.

For many years the Fogartys dominated the architectural scene, from their headquarters in Limerick. **J. Fogarty and Sons** built St. Mary's Catholic church in Limerick and the Wesley College in Belfast, as well as a great number of offices and public buildings.

Earlier this century, **Lily Fogarty** wrote a number of publications on Irish patriots, including the Young Irelander, Fintan Lalor. **George J. Fogarty** (d. 1914) wrote profusely on archaeology and wildlife.

Professor Michael Fogarty was born in Burma in 1916 of Galway parents. He was a director in London of the Economic and Social Research Institute, and Vice-President of the Liberal Party. He has published a number of books on economics. **Robin Fogarty** (b. 1928) was one of the delegates who, in 1972, effected Ireland's entry into the European Economic Community. He has been Irish Ambassador to Japan and to the Federal Republic of West Germany.

Gogarty—Mac Fhógartaigh in Irish—can sometimes be synonymous with Fogarty.

Foley

Ó Foghladha

Translated from the Irish, this name means a plunderer! Originating in Waterford, where the name is still numerous, the family has spread through Munster and south Leinster. There is a distinguished English family of the name who are thought to have had Irish origins, possibly as far back as the seventeenth century.

Maolisa O Foley (d. 1131) was archbishop of that most important and royal seat of the hierarchy, Cashel, in County Tipperary.

Like many of their countrymen during the Commonwealth period, there were Foleys serving in the English army. There were also Foleys in the Irish-American brigades during the American Civil War.

May Foley, a daughter of **Dr. William Foley**, was the mother of Sir Arthur Conan Doyle, who was born in Edinburgh and died in 1930. He was the creator of the eccentric detective, Sherlock Holmes.

John Henry Foley and his brother **Edward** were born early in the nineteenth century and were Dublin's foremost sculptors in their time. John's many commissions included the statues of Burke and Goldsmith outside Trinity College Dublin, and Albert, Queen Victoria's Consort, on London's gigantic Albert Memorial. John died before he had time to complete the landmark of Dublin's O Connell Street—the memorial to Daniel O Connell.

In the nineteenth century, the **Reverend Daniel Foley** produced his Irish–English dictionary, while, in the musical world, **Alan James Foley** delighted his audiences under the stage name of Signor Foli!

In Ulster, Foley could be a synonym of MacSharry—*searrach* being the Irish word for foal.

(O) Foran

Ó Fuaráin

Ford Forde Forhan Fourhane

Ó Fuaráin was an old Gaelic sept which got its name from a Fuaráin antecedent. Fuaráin is a diminutive of *fuar*, meaning cold. This surname belongs to the province of Munster, where it is very numerous. It is also now quite numerous in Leinster, especially in Dublin city and county.

Perhaps through a slip of the pen, some of the Forans of Cork had their name changed to Ford, or Forde, which has led to considerable confusion, because the name Ford belongs to a different sept. Before the standardization of surnames, the Foran name could also be recognized as Forhan or Fourhane.

One of the Foran name who came to prominence in early times was **Lawrence Foran**, a Waterford scribe who, in the 1780s, compiled *The Book of Portlaw*, celebrating his native county.

There were also two outstanding ecclesiastics: **Nicholas Foran**, a mid-nineteenth-century Bishop of Waterford and Lismore, and an Augustinian monk called **Thomas Foran** who wrote extensively on Church history and sacred art.

In 1918, **Thomas Foran** was President of the Irish Transport and General Workers' Union. He was one of the leaders of the general strike in Dublin during April 1920.

Forbes

Mac Firbisigh

The ancient Gaelic surname Mac Firbisigh (meaning son of a man of property) was anglicized to Forbes.

In medieval times, they were a distinguished literary family of Connacht. **Giolla Iosa Mac Firbisigh** (*c.*1360–1430) belonged to a family of scribes who provided chronicles and pedigrees for the O Dowds.

A descendant of his was the famous teacher, **Dubhaltach Mac Firbisigh** (1585–1670). He continued the family tradition and compiled many important manuscripts, including the invaluable *Book of Lecan*. When he was driven from his Galway estate by the Cromwellians, he fled to Dublin, where he continued working on his manuscripts. When his patron, Sir James Ware, died, he became destitute and set out on foot for Sligo. Sadly, he was murdered by a crazy youth along the way.

Forbes is also a Scottish name, now mostly to be found in Northern Ireland. They were, and still are, an important family in Aberdeenshire.

Sir Arthur Forbes, 1st Baronet of Castle Forbes in Granard, County Longford, came to Ireland in 1620. For generations, his descendants have held high office in the judiciary and the services at home and abroad.

It was Sir Arthur Forbes, colonel of his own Irish regiment of foot, who suggested to Charles II the foundation of the Royal Military Hospital at Kilmainham, which has recently been beautifully restored and is a popular centre for the arts and for conferences. **Bernard Arthur Forbes**, 8th Earl of Granard, was a lord-in-waiting to King Edward VII and Master of the Horse for many years. He was a member of the Senate in the Irish Free State from 1922 to 1934 and a member of the Council of State of Ireland in 1946. He generously donated many fine pieces of furniture to Dublin Castle. Castle Forbes is still occupied by his family, many of whom now live mostly abroad.

Forde

Ford MacEnawe MacKinnawe

Forde is a common name in England. Many Fordes came from Devonshire to County Meath in the fourteenth century.

Ford can also be a mistranslation of a number of Irish names. For instance, in Connacht, it comes from Maigiollarnath, a name meaning son of the devotees of the saints. A more fanciful translation comes from another Connacht sept, the Mac Consnámha, meaning son of the swimming hound, which became Ford! Phonetically, this has been anglicized as MacKinnawe or MacEnawe. This family, which had much land, were chieftains of Muintir Kenny. One of their sons was the **Cornelius Mac Consnámha** (d. 1355) who became Bishop of Kilmore.

In County Cork, Ó Fuaráin, or Foran, once signified Forde. Today the name Forde predominates.

The Fordes who came to Ireland at the time of Charles I, in the early eighteenth century, were high sheriffs of Seaforde in County Down. Their descendant today is known as Lord of the Manor of Teconnaught and was born as recently as 1940. An ancestor was a colonel with the first regiment of the King's troops to go into India.

There is much information in the Irish archives about the pedigrees, properties and wills of the Fordes of County Down, from *c.*1670 to 1948.

Patrick Forde (1837–1913) was born in Galway. He was a journalist and politician who emigrated with his parents to Boston, where he edited the *Boston Sunday Times* and founded and edited for forty-three years the *Irish World*, the voice of the Irish who had settled in America.

Henry Ford of motor car fame also had Irish origins.

see also (O) Foran

Forkin

Ó Gabhláin

Forkan Forken Goulding

A very rare name, Forkin is said to have come from the Irish name Ó Gabhláin; the Irish name for a fork is *gabhal*. Originally from Galway and Mayo, in some instances Forkin has been used as a substitute for Goulding, a much more common name in Ireland.

Today, Forkin is mostly to be found in County Mayo, though there are a few representatives of the name in County Dublin and in some other areas of the country, with the exception of Ulster.

As is usual with names that were formerly Irish, it has a variety of spellings, including Forken or Forkan.

Fourhane *see* (O) Foran

Fox

Ó Catharnaigh

Carney Kearney

The chief of Teffia in County Meath who died in 1084 was Tadgh Ó Catharnaigh. He was known as The Fox, a name adopted by this branch of the family, who claim to be descendants of Niall of the Nine Hostages and, consequently, kinsmen of the great O Neills.

Until the depredations of the Elizabethan armies, they owned much land in Offaly. Although it was restored to them, they lost it again in the 1641 uprising. Land in County Meath remained with the family, where their seat was the handsome Galtrim House until they left for Australia, where the head of the family still styles himself The Fox.

Other branches of the original family who kept the Ó Catharnaigh name spread into almost every county and can be detected under a variety of anglicizations, including Carney and Kearney. Fox is also a common name in England, from where many settlers came, especially to the Limerick area, where their territory was known as Mountfox.

The Foxes figure prominently among the officers who were with King James's armies and, afterwards, with the Irish regiments in France and the USA.

In an old manuscript in London, there is an account of a Fox from Ireland "who was tried at Chester for treasonable words, for which he stood four hours in the pillory and lost his ears".

Around 1568, **Sir Patrick Fox** of Westmeath was a state interpreter of the Irish language. In 1797, **Luke Fox** was a Member of Parliament in the Irish parliament.

James Fox and Company (cigar merchants), one of the oldest specialist tobacconists in Ireland, are still in their original Dublin shop in Grafton Street.

Foy

Ó Fiaich

Fay Fee Fey Fye

Fee, Fey, Foy and Fye are all anglicized versions of the Irish surname Ó Fiaich, meaning the raven. The most numerous versions of the name today are Fee, which is to be found mainly in counties Fermanagh and Cavan, and Foy, found in north Connacht and also in Cavan. Today, Foy—sometimes spelled Foye—is numerous all over Ireland.

Fay is sometimes a synoym of Foy and Fee. In the Middle Ages, the O Fays were administrators of a church near Enniskillen in County Fermanagh.

On 23 November 1689, **Nathaniel Foy**, Protestant Bishop of Waterford and Lismore, was praised for the sermon he preached in Christ Church in Dublin, on the anniversary of the Irish rebellion which had broken out on that same day in 1641.

In 1787, **James Foy** at Ballinrobe, County Mayo, was accused of treason for "procuring, stirring and provoking Andrew Craig and others to murder Pat Randall McDonnell and Charles Hyson".

In 1829, **General Foy** who lived in France with the **comtesse Foy**, wrote a history in French of the Peninsula wars under Napoleon. During the 1840s, **Martin Wilson Foye** published a number of books on the early Irish Church. In the 1950s, the **Reverend Thomas Foy** wrote regularly on Roman Catholic Church affairs.

The outstanding representative of the name was **Tomás Ó Fiaich**. He was born in County Antrim in 1923 and was ordained in 1948. A dedicated Irish language revivalist, he has written many books and has also translated the Bible into Irish. He was Archbishop of Armagh and Primate of all Ireland in

1977, and was created Cardinal two years later. He died in 1990.

Fraly, **Frawley** *see* (O) Farrelly

French

de Freyne Ffrench

The French family came from Normandy to England with William the Conqueror, and from there to Ireland, where they were known first as de Freyne (of the ash trees), referring to their origins in Normandy. Another branch were known as French, or ffrench (the two small *ff*s represented capital *F* in the sixteenth and seventeenth centuries).

Patrick, the first arrival, settled at Wexford, while a kinsman went to Galway, where the family became very important, enough to be included among the Fourteen Tribes of Galway. There, between the fifteenth and sixteenth centuries, they had sixteen French Mayors of Galway. In good Norman tradition, they built many fine houses in Connacht, as did their kinsmen in Wexford.

Nicholas French was Bishop of Ferns, County Wexford, when priests were being driven to hide in the mountains. He went to Rome, and to various other European capitals, to seek help for his oppressed flock, but always his efforts were blocked by powerful influences in Ireland. He was forced to remain in Europe, where he held many high ecclesiastical offices.

The French family earned various titles, many still extant, including the Barons de Freyne of Sligo and the Lords French, formerly of Frenchpark in Roscommon. In 1734, when a de Freyne died at the age of 86, he left a huge sum of money, insisting that his body be laid in state in the park for three days and nights and that the country people should feast around it—which they cheerfully did!

Lord French of Castle French, who refused to take rents from his Galway tenants during the Great Famine, became bankrupt and was forced to sell his castle. In 1919, it was bought back by his descendants.

Many Frenches travelled worldwide. In the seventeenth century, **Peter French**, a missionary, spent thirty years with the Indians in Mexico. Pedigrees of the many who fled during the Irish suppression can be found in the archives of Europe's capitals. **Viscount French**, a British General and Lord Lieutenant of Ireland between 1918 and 1921, was the brother of Mrs. Charlotte Despard. She worked in London for the poor and campaigned for votes for women. At the age of 70, she joined Maud Gonne MacBride in Ireland in her campaign for republican prisoners, causing great embarrassment to her brother!

Percy French, who died in 1920, still has the power to delight us with his comic songs. He abandoned his civil engineering degree to become a highly successful entertainer. "The Mountains of Mourne" was one of his earliest and most popular songs. He was also an excellent watercolourist.

Friar, **Friary** *see* Prior

Fullen

Fallon Fullan Fuller Fulloon

Edward MacLysaght, who wrote a series of dictionaries on the origins of over four thousand Irish surnames, took the view that this name, now very rare, came to Ireland via County Tyrone in Northern Ireland—the only area where it is still to be found in any numbers. He suggests that Fullen could be a variant of the English Fulloon, which come from the English fullen, or fuller (pronounced fooler), meaning one who cleanses and thickens cloth. Fuller's earth is a type of clay used as an absorbent in fulling cloth. Perhaps these Fullens came to Ulster to work in the days when linen growing and weaving was a thriving industry there? A few Fullens are still to be found in the Dublin telephone directory, but not in those for the rest of the Republic.

Before the standardization of Irish names, there were many confusing variants of a family's name. This led some to believe that Fullen, in some cases, could possibly be a variant of Fallon (q.v.).

Fulloon *see* Fullen

Fye *see* Foy

G

Gaffney

Ó Gamhna

Caulfield

Edward MacLysaght, who was the leading expert on Irish family names, admits that "Gaffney is one of the most confusing of all as anglicized." He concludes that "it could be Ó Gamhna, Ó Caibheanaigh, Mac Conghamhna, Mac Carrghamhna or Mag Fhachtna." These Irish names are anglicized to, among others, Gaffney, Caulfield, Keaveney, MacCarron or Gaughney!

The principal Ó Gamhna sept (*gamhain* means calf) was of Ossory, in the Kilkenny area. But there, today, as in many other parts of the country, the ancient Gaelic name has been transformed to Caulfield!

Gaffney is numerous west of the Shannon, as is Caulfield. Both versions are also numerous in Dublin, but in Northern Ireland Caulfield predominates.

Austin Gaffney, who was born in Dublin, is one of Ireland's most popular singers and has made a name for himself internationally, especially singing in musicals.

The Gaffneys travelled to America and have given their name to a town in Cherokee country in South Carolina, where Gaffney was incorporated in 1874.

(O) Gallagher

Ó Gallchobhair

The Gallaghers of Donegal were a very ancient senior clan, descendants of the fourth-century Niall of the Nine Hostages. *Gallchobhar* means foreign help. Their territory included a wide area of Donegal and their chieftains had their seats at Ballybeit and Ballynaglack. For three centuries they held high rank in the armies of the neighbouring O Donnells. Although they later served in the Irish-American brigades, they are chiefly renowned for their remarkable number of bishops.

The monastery at Raphoe, which is said to have been founded by St. Colmcille, had six Gallagher bishops between the fifteenth and eighteenth century. These were undisciplined times in the Church and one of their earliest bishops was far from being a worthy prelate. Another Gallagher was a renowned preacher. One Gallagher bishop suffered martyrdom for rescuing some of the men from the Spanish Armada, wrecked off the Donegal coast. **Hugh Gallagher** was a nineteenth-century pioneering bishop in America.

Frank Gallagher (1898–1962), a Cork-born journalist, fought in the Irish War of Independence. He worked in Radio Éireann, the Irish broadcasting company, and was the first editor of the *Irish Press*, the party-political newspaper of Eamon de Valera. He was on the staff of the National Library of Ireland and wrote several autobiographical novels.

Patrick Gallagher (1873–1964) was the eldest of eight children raised in poverty on a Donegal bog. He suffered great hardship as a hired labourer, working in Scotland and England. From the poet, painter and agricultural writer George Russell, he got the idea of co-operative agriculture and set up the first co-operative in Donegal in 1906. This met with great opposition, as it cut the high profits of the middle men, known as gombeen men. Despite every attempt to blacken his character he persisted, travelling abroad to learn more about the method and making so great a success of his co-operative that he became known as "Paddy the Cope".

Gallahers Limited in Dublin were one of the earliest tobacco manufacturers in Ireland.

Gardner

Gardiner Garner

Gardner—sometimes Gardiner, or even Garner—is essentially an English name, which came to Ulster in the sixteenth century. Originally from Normandy, they were named from their trade, le Gardener.

Sir Robert Gardiner was chief justice of Ireland in 1585, and there was a **Sir Robert Gardner**, who was a justice of the peace and high sheriff of Dublin as recently as 1914.

Some sons of this family may not have been Loyalists, for there are accounts of Gardners who were transplanted to Connacht during the uprising of 1653 to 1654. However, there were also Gardner officers in the armies of the Commonwealth, in Cromwell's time.

Matthew Gardiner (*c*.1710–*c*.1745) was a popular author of verse plays and ballad operas.

A banker called **Luke Gardiner** (d. 1755) bought and developed much of the north side of Dublin. Gardiner Street and Mountjoy Square are a few of the magnificent squares and streets of houses built by him and named after his family, who became Earls of Blessington and Viscounts Mountjoy.

Charles Gardiner, Earl of Blessington, brought literary notoriety to the name when he married Marguerite Power, the novelist and journalist known as "the gorgeous Lady Blessington". She was helped by her friend, Count D'Orsay, to squander the family wealth. The title became extinct when her husband died in 1829. There are pedigrees of these Gardiners in Dublin's Genealogical Office, dating from 1623 to *c*.1816. There are also accounts of them in the Bibliothèque Nationale in Paris. They owned much land in County Tyrone in Northern Ireland, where the name is very numerous.

The Public Records Office in Belfast has a letter from **Daniel R. Gardner** to his wife in Belfast, describing his voyage to Australia.

In 1598, **Sir Richard Gardner**, Mayor of Chester, wrote requesting that urgent despatches for Ireland would no longer be delayed for fair winds but be sent via Holyhead.

There are a number of distinguished Gardners and Gardiners recorded in *Who's Who*, including **Baroness Gardner of Parkes**, whose listed hobbies include gardening!

Garrett

Garret

This is both a first name and a surname. It is most numerous in England, from where it came originally, via the Normans. It can be traced to Gerrard or Gerald, which in turn links it to FitzGerald. A recent Taoiseach (Prime

Minister) in Ireland was **Garret FitzGerald**.

There are a number of genealogical references, including a pedigree of the Garretts of County Carlow which dates from *c.*1600 to *c.*1845.

In *The Genealogists' Magazine* of 1956, there is an account of a **Captain Garrett** who was killed at Cahir Castle *c.*1583, fighting the rebel Irish. In 1592, **Jeane Garret** took, at Waterford, "one hundred vialls of plate off the *Adelantado* to serve in the gallies".

There are letters from the great nineteenth-century British statesman and philosopher, Edmund Burke (b. 1729 in Dublin), to a **Mr. Garrett**, advising him about the education of his children. Between 1789 and 1823, the famous Quaker family of Leadbetter kept up a correspondence with **Edward** and **Elizabeth Garrett**.

In the nineteenth century, many Garretts travelled abroad. **Tydell Edmund Garrett** wrote about his South African travels and he also translated Ibsen.

In 1871, **John Garrett**, who was a director of public administration in Mysore, wrote a classical dictionary of Hindu mythology. In 1876, **Rhoda** and **Agnes Garrett** were pioneering the field of interior decoration in their *Art at Home* series, published by Macmillan.

There were a number of Garretts with the invading English armies in Ireland and also with the New York Volunteers and in the Irish brigades in the USA.

Garrett is widespread in all the counties, but it is particularly numerous in Ulster.

Garrihy *see* MacGarry

Garrity *see* Geraghty

Garry *see* MacGarry

Garvan *see* Garvey

Garvey

Mac Gairbhith

Garvan

The Garvey nomenclature stems from the unpromising *garbh*, the Irish for rough. Their pedigrees in the Dublin Genealogical Office run from AD 300–AD 1842 and encircle the globe. They were lords of Morrish and of Tully in County Mayo, they had castles in County Down and Kilkenny, and they were people of standing in Jamaica, Rouen, Bordeaux, Cadiz, New Zealand and Texas!

The principal Ó Gairbhith sept had its seat at Oneilland in County Armagh. Garvin (Ó Gairbhin) was the original name, which became corrupted to Garvey when they were driven from Meath to Connacht by the Anglo-Normans.

John Garvey (1527–1605) of Mayo had a very successful ecclesiastical career once he adopted the establishment religion of Queen Elizabeth I, which put him "in great favour with the higher powers". He was eventually to rise to the position of Archbishop of Armagh.

Callagh Garvan (1644–1735) was a physician to the unfortunate royal Stuarts.

Edmund Garvey (1740–1813) emigrated to London, where he became a successful landscape painter and was elected to the Royal Academy.

Sir Terence Garvey, born in Dublin in 1915, entered the British diplomatic service and was High Commissioner of India from 1971 to 1973 and of the USSR from 1973 to 1975.

Sir Ronald Garvey (b. 1903), a colonial governor, was also a member of the famous Hispano-Irish sherry family which was founded in 1780 when **William Garvey** from Kilkenny, on a journey to Spain to buy sheep, was wrecked off the coast near Cadiz. He met one of the Gomez family who had a sherry bodega at Jerez and was persuaded to remain. He married a Gomez daughter, and so was founded the great sherry firm of Garvey, which still flourishes.

Gavan *see* Gavin

Gavigan *see* MacGuigan

Gavin

Ó Gábháin Ó Gábhín

Gavan

An ancient surname which has long since lost its O prefix, it is thought that Gavin stemmed from the Gaelic word for want. Originally there were two septs—Ó Gábháin of west Cork and Ó Gáibhín of Connacht. This explains the two different spellings, Gavin and Gavan.

The records contain occasional brief references to the name. In 1428, a **Walter O Gawane** of Clonmel was mentioned, and, in 1584, a **Gavin** of Ballynerene in County Limerick was recorded as being "in rebellion".

In the Hearth Money Rolls of 1665 to 1667, eleven families of Gavan were recorded in County Tipperary, while six families were recorded in Mullingar, County Westmeath.

Today this surname is very numerous, especially in the west, while in Ulster it occupies over twenty columns in the Northern Ireland telephone directory.

Father Cormac O Gavane, a medieval Franciscan friar, has the distinction of receiving a number of references in the *Analecta Hibernia* (volume VI), a contemporary history of Ireland.

Towards the end of the seventeenth century, an eccentric named **Antonio Gavin**, calling himself Gabriel d'Emiliane and seemingly living in Italy, wrote many tirades against the wickedness of popery.

The death of **Luke Gaven** in 1790 led to his will being disputed in the family. This continued into the nineteenth century, when it went to an appeal in the House of Lords.

Earlier this century, **William Gavin** was a minor poet. In the 1960s, **Tadgh Gavin** produced a stream of religious prose and hagiographies.

The name Gavan has been perpetuated by the Gavan Duffy family of Ireland and Australia. **Sir Charles Gavan Duffy**, patriot, writer and Prime Minister of Australia in 1871, honoured his County Monaghan mother by adopting her Gavan maiden name, and this continues to be passed down through his descendants.

Geoghegan *see* MacGuigan

Geraghty

Mag Oireachtaigh

Garrity Gerity

There are no less than seventeen variants of this ancient Irish surname. Originally it was Ó Roduibh, and these were chiefs of Muintir Roduibh, a territory in the county of Roscommon, until their dispossession in the sixteenth century. The Ó Roduibhs took the name of a son of a family named Oireachtaigh, for whom they changed their name to Mag (Mac) Oireachtaigh (*oireachtach* means a member of a court or an assembly).

The Mag Oireachtaigh were a sept of the Uí Maine, located in the counties of Roscommon and Galway, and kinsmen of the royal O Conors. Up to the thirteenth century, they were head of one of the four royal chiefdoms. Athlone was the seat of The Mag Giriaght, who was Chief of the Name.

They are still most frequently found in the Galway area, where many followed the priestly vocation, especially in medieval times, when they had a number of bishops. In 1744, **Father Geraghty** was Dean of Elphin. **Monsignor Richard Joseph Gearty** (*c*.1864–1938) was a very active member of the Church in the Argentines.

Gibbon *see* Gilbert

Gidery *see* Guidera

Gilbert

Gibbon

Gilbert is a very old personal name of Norman origin. In England, where it is recorded in the *Doomsday Book*, it has long been widespread and there are at least twenty surnames based on Gilbert. Gib was a nickname for Gilbert from which came the diminutive form Gibbon. The Irish, Giobán, was adopted for this surname by the Anglo-Normans.

In the twelfth century in England, there was a religious order of Gilbertines and numerous allied convents, which were broken up during the suppression of the monasteries.

There are many Gilbert pedigrees and accounts of various Gilbert families in Ireland's National Library, most of which were army officers or administrators from England. There are also letters from **Sir Humphrey Gilbert** (1537–83), the famous English navigator whose "good service against the Irish rebels" earned him a knighthood and the government of Munster in 1570. He writes about the gallowglasses (mercenary soldiers) and where he would garrison them in Munster, and how to get one hundred soldiers from Chester to Derry.

In 1601, **Sir John Gilbert** complains in his letters of delay in providing shipping from Plymouth, where he has raised men for service in Ireland and, "by way of Charity", gives them five shillings at the time of embarking.

Sir John Thomas Gilbert (1829–98) was born in Dublin and educated in Bath in England. He was an eminent historian and antiquary who made valuable contributions to Irish archaeology. He inspired the founding of the Public Records Office and his great collection of Irish historical and archaeological material was acquired by the corporation for Dublin's City Library. **Lady Gilbert** (1841–1921), his wife, a novelist under her maiden name, Rosa Mulholland, published his biography in 1904.

One of Ireland's foremost couturiers in the 1960s was **Irene Gilbert**, who died in 1985.

Gilbert is not a common name in Ireland, where, apart from a scattering in Munster, it is mostly concentrated in north-east Ulster.

Gildea

Mac Giolla Dhé

Benison Guilday Kildea MacGillegea

Gildea, or Kildea, is the anglicization of an ancient Irish name, Mac Giolla Dhé, which means a devotee of Christ. They were once very numerous in Tirconnell and in the province of Connacht. Today they seem to be more numerous in Ulster, on both sides of the border. At one time, in County Leitrim, they went under the name Benison, a Latin rendering of their name!

In the Middle Ages, they were followers of the powerful O Donnells of Donegal where, in 1601, those following the flag of Rory O Donnell were listed as Conor, Owen, Brien and **Edmund MacGillegea**, a Donegal anglicization of Gildea.

In 1624, a Daniel Guilday was Vicar-General of the diocese of Killaloe. There is a Ballydildea in County Clare and a Ballydilladea in County Galway.

In the Dublin Genealogical Office there is a confirmation of arms to the **Reverend George Robert Gildea**, a descendant of **James Gildea** of Fort Royal in County Mayo, son and heir of **James Gildea** of Gologh and grandson of the former James, the **Reverend George Robert Gildea**, Provost of Tuam in 1884, eldest surviving son of **Thomas Gildea**.

Sir James Gildea (1823–1920) of County Mayo, who served with an ambulance in the Franco-Prussian war, was a philanthropist who raised vast sums of money for soldiers' widows and orphans. He was one of the founders of the St. John Ambulance Brigade. He died in London.

Gillen

Ó Giolláin

Gillan

The name stems from the Irish word *giolla*, meaning a lad. They were a family of the Cenél Eoghain, descendants of Eoghan, son of Niall of the Nine Hostages, and were mainly located in Sligo, Donegal and Tyrone, where today far more Gillans and Gillens are to be found than in the rest of Ireland.

In 1488, **Enog Ó Gillain** is recorded as translating into Irish a Latin life of Saint Patrick.

In the nineteenth century, there was a remarkable family of Gillens in Australia. **James Gillen** (1856–1912), one of the children of a farm labourer and his wife who emigrated from Cavan in the year of his birth, became the stationmaster in Alice Springs for Post and Telegraphs. A boisterous character with a great social awareness, both of the deprivations in his father's country and for the aborigines in Australia, he teamed up with the famous anthropologist, Sir Baldwin Spencer, and together they traversed Australia, writing books on their travels and studying what they called the Stone Age People.

James's brother, **Peter Paul Gillen** (1855–96), a shopkeeper and politician, was Secretary of the Irish Land League Committee and was also a member of a number of Catholic societies. He was, for a while, Minister for Crown Lands and Immigration, but an ailing heart, the legacy of childhood polio, cut short his life. He is commemorated by Gillentown, near his home in Clare, and Gillen on the Murray River.

Professor Gerard Gillen, born in Dublin in 1942, is an organist of international renown. He has performed widely, including broadcasts for RTE (the Irish broadcasting company) and BBC, and has won many awards. He runs the Dublin Organ Festival, which is held every July.

Gilmartin *see* Martin

Gilsenan *see* Leonard, Nugent

Ginley, **Ginnell** *see* MacGinley

Ginty *see* MacGinty

Gleeson

Ó Glasáin Ó Gliasáin

Glisane Glasone Glissane

Glas is the Irish word for green or grey. The Ó Gliasáin family came from the same stock as the O Donegans of Ara, County Tipperary, who had arrived there from Muskerry in County Cork.

Until the mid-seventeenth century, when the Cromwellian armies devastated the country, the Gleesons had been prosperous landowners. They were among the thousands of landed gentry who had their lands confiscated and were transplanted to Connacht.

Although the Gleesons have not been prominent in history, there is mention of a **Dermot F. Gleeson** who edited the *Annals of Nenagh, 1336–1528.*

In Dublin's Public Records Office, there is mention of Gleesons, between 1840 and 1844, in papers referring to property of the Grace family at Balla Bryan in County Waterford and at Clonmel.

In the 1860s, Brigadier-General Gleeson wrote articles on Fenianism, including portraits of prominent Fenians, and on Orangeism, as well as writing ballads. The once-thriving Athlone Woollen Mills was founded in the 1880s by a **Dr. Gleeson**.

The Gleeson surname is very numerous in every part of Ireland, yet it is in the United States of America that they have had their most outstanding achievements. There, **Father William Gleeson** is regarded as being the founder of the Roman Catholic Church in California; **Edward Blakeney Gleeson** was one of Rochester's millionaires; **Frederick Grant Gleeson** (1848–1903) composed music; **Monsignor Joseph M. Gleeson** (1869–1942) was a distinguished educator and historian.

There are many variations of the name, including Glisane, Glissane and Glasone—but never Leeson, as some would have it!

Glisane, Glissane *see* Gleeson

Glynn *see* MacGlynn

Godwin *see* Goodwin

Gogarty *see* Fogarty

Golden, Golding *see* Goulding

Goodwin

Ó Goidín

Godwin

This is a fairly numerous name in Ireland, particularly in Ulster. One version of the surname comes from the Old English words *god*, meaning good, and *wine*, meaning friend. It can also be a synonym of many Irish names, including O Dea. The eminent Father Woulfe believes it to derive from the surname Ó Goidín, diminutive of *god*, Irish for stammerer.

Many Goodwins came with the Cromwellians. Prominent among these were **Sir Robert Goodwin**, who was appointed commissioner for the government of civil affairs in Ireland in the 1650s. He wrote profusely to his superiors in England concerning "the bad state of the Protestants in Ireland" and he gave an account of the siege of Ballinakill in County Dublin in 1643.

Bryan Goodwin, who was obviously a rebel, was dispossessed of his estates and banished to Connacht.

In the Public Records Office in Dublin, there are papers relating to property in Dublin belonging to the Goodwin family between 1703 and 1898. The Genealogical Office holds draft pedigrees for MacGodwin of Philadelphia between 1763 and 1940.

In the mid-eighteenth century, **Timothy Goodwin** was Bishop of Kilmore and Ardagh.

In 1865, **Charles Goodwin** was a captain with the Irish-American brigade in New York.

In the nineteenth century, a number of fine old Irish houses were built to the designs of the distinguished English architect, **Edward Goodwin**.

(O) Gorman

Mac Gormáin Ó Gormáin

Grimes MacGorman

Gorman comes from the Irish word *gorm*, meaning blue. Originally the name was MacGorman, but when the Gaels were compelled to drop the prefix from their name they became simply Gorman. Later, with the revival of all things Irish in the nineteenth century, many of the family adopted the O prefix. Today, Gorman and O Gorman are very numerous, while there are comparatively few MacGormans.

The earliest MacGormans came from Slievemary in County Laois, not far from Carlow town. Their chieftains were lords of Slievemary. When driven out by the Normans, they fled to west Clare and Monaghan. In County Clare, the head of the MacGorman sept was hereditary marshal to the forces of the great O Brien of Thomond.

Finin MacGorman, a twelfth-century Bishop of Glendalough, was the compiler of the celebrated collection of stories and poetry known as the *Book of Lecan*.

In the fifteenth century, the MacGormans of Ibrican in County Clare were remarkably wealthy and extended warm hospitality to all the Gaelic poets.

By the seventeenth century, many MacGormans had joined the exodus to Europe. The colourful **Chevalier Thomas O Gorman** (1732–1809) from Clare set the fashion for this version of the name. He graduated as a physician in Paris and married the heiress to the d'Eon vineyard in Burgundy, which he later inherited. Serving in an Irish brigade, along with many others of the same name, he was conferred with the title "Chevalier" by Louis XV. A keen Irish scholar, he paid regular visits home to compile pedigrees for his fellow émigrés in France and Spain. However, the French Revolution was to ruin him, and he returned home to be supported by his relatives.

Nicholas O Gorman (1820–95) joined the Young Irelanders.

In 1867, the Nationals of Washington, led by **Arthur Pue Gorman**, made the first baseball trans-Allegheny tour as far as St. Louis. Later, this Gorman became a Senator in Maryland.

In Ulster, the name Gormley has sometimes been transformed to Gorman.

see also Grimes

Gormley

Ó Gormghaile

Gormely MacGormley

Gormley is a very numerous name in Ireland, particularly in Ulster where their tribe name was Cenél Moen. In the fourteenth century they were driven from their territory in Raphoe, County Donegal, by the O Donnells. Having fled to the Tyrone side of the river Foyle, they continued an unequal struggle with the powerful O Donnells, Earls of Tirconnell.

In 1609, with the beginning of the ruthless plantation of Ulster, they began to have their lands confiscated. Some went abroad, and there is a record of a **P. Gormely** who served as adjutant with the 63rd New York Volunteers in the Irish-American brigades between 1861 and 1865.

In the Public Records Office in Belfast, there is an unproved will of **J.**

Gormely of Inishmagh, County Tyrone, dated 1802.

In the middle of the last century, **Richard B. Gormley** was one of Dublin's leading organists.

Earlier in the twentieth century, **Frank M. Gormley** wrote such popular folk songs as "Song of the Motherland" and "Achushla Machree".

There was a family of O Gormley of Lough Key in County Roscommon who, it is thought, had no connection with the O Gormelys of County Tyrone. There are also a few MacGormleys, and others who have changed their name to Gorman, or even to Grimes.

Gormleys are very numerous throughout Ireland, but most particularly so in Northern Ireland.

Goulding

Ó Góilín

Golden Golding

Goldwane, an Anglo-Saxon personal name, arrived in Ireland with the Normans. In time the spelling changed to Golding or Goulding, and it was also gaelicized as Góilín. The Gouldings or Goldings settled in Dublin, Kildare and south Munster.

The Irish name Mag Ualghraig, anglicized to MacGoldrick, has sometimes been transformed to Golden or Goulding.

In the records there is mention of a **Nicholas Golding** of Castleknock in County Dublin who, in 1314, was king's victualler. Another **Nicholas Goulding** was a quartermaster sergeant in Cromwell's army in Ireland. There were also papist Gouldings who, in the seventeenth century, forfeited their lands in County Kerry and were transplanted to Connacht.

The Genealogical Office holds a pedigree of the Gouldings of Churchtown and of Piercetown Laundy in County Meath of 1400 to 1550, and a pedigree of the Gouldings who were baronets in Birr, County Offaly, and Summerhill, County Cork, of 1650 to 1904.

The Genealogical Office also has a confirmation of arms to the descendants of **Joshua Goulding** of Birr, eldest son of **Lieutenant William Goulding** of the Roscrea Cavalry, made for Joshua's grandson, **William Joshua** of Roebuck Hill, County Dublin, and of Summerhill, Cork City. He was the eldest son of **William Goulding**, who was a Member of Parliament for his county in 1902.

Sir Basil Goulding (1909–82), was chairman of his family's Cork fertilizer firm, **W. and H. M. Goulding**. He was a director of a number of banks and other institutions. A man of many talents, literary and artistic, he had a sculpture garden at his County Wicklow home and a collection of modern Irish paintings. He has been succeeded by his son, **Lingard** (b. 1940), who is headmaster of Headfort School in County Meath. Another son, **Timothy** (b. 1945), who lives in County Kerry, is one of Ireland's leading painters.

see also Forkin

(O) Grady

Ó Grádaigh

Brady

The Ó Grádaigh name means illustrious, and it was from this noble forebear that they trace their origins back to the Dalcassian sept which included the royal O Briens of Clare. In the thirteenth century, clan warfare drove them south to Limerick, where their chieftain had his headquarters beside Lough Gur at Kilballyowen and where his descendants still live.

As the O Gradys increased, they divided into at least six new Munster septs, centred at Cappercullen, Elton, Grange, Lodge, Cahir and Mount Prospect.

In Tudor times, to preserve their land, some O Gradys changed their surname to the less obviously Gaelic, Brady. However, the O Gradys of Kilballyowen soon reverted to their original name, if not to their original faith. There have been an impressive succession of O Grady bishops, including bishops of Cashel, Tuam and Killaloe.

To save his lands, **Donough O Grady** pretended to be a Protestant. He fell in love with Faith, the only daughter of his good neighbour Sir Thomas Standish. On their marriage, Sir Thomas arranged to have O Grady's land returned to him and, for this brave and generous gesture, the O Gradys have kept both Faith and Standish as family names.

Standish O Grady, who was Viscount Guillamore and Baron O Grady, was an attorney-general and acted for the prosecution at Robert Emmet's trial. His titles are now extinct. Another **Standish O Grady**, the son of an admiral, was for thirty years an engineer in the United States of America. He retired to Ireland to work on ancient manuscripts, contributing invaluably to Irish historical archives. Confusingly, a cousin who was yet another **Standish O Grady** (1846–1928), wrote a number of popular novels based on the ancient folk heroes of Celtic mythology.

Today the O Gradys are numerous in Canada and the USA. They fought in the American Civil War and a New York O Grady, **Henry Woodfin O Grady**, reported on the war for the *New York Herald*.

Perhaps the most remarkable O Grady descendant is **Cassius O Grady Clay** (Mohammed Ali). His Clare ancestor a century ago married a black American lady who was so proud of her O Grady name she passed it on to her children.

Lieutenant-Colonel Gerald O Grady, an authentic Chief of the Name, conscientiously preserved the family archives in the modern home he and his American wife built close to the old O Grady castle shortly before he died.

Graham *see* Grimes

Grant

The Grants came to Ireland from Speyside in Scotland, where they were a numerous clan. The greatest concentration of Grants is now in the north of Ireland; few ventured west to Connacht. In Munster, they are frequently mentioned in the records, sometimes as le Graunte, which gives a hint of possible Norman origins in the distant past, or perhaps a different branch of the family altogether.

They suffered all the disasters of the native Irish in the sixteenth century, including confiscation of their lands and transplantation from their own territory. They also joined the Wild Geese to serve in the armies of France, where they distinguished themselves in the regiments of Clare and Dillon, and died on the battlefield of Fontenoy.

However, the Grants cannot be blamed for **Albert Grant** (1830–99). Born in Dublin with the name Gottheimer, he went to London, took the name Grant, and became a heartless swindler of shares, preying on innocent widows and clergymen. Despite this, he got himself elected to parliament, presented Leicester Fields to the London authority and gave Landseer's portrait of Sir Walter Scott to the National Portrait Gallery.

John Grant of Buncrana in Donegal is now the only independent manufacturer of snuff and pipe tobacco left in Ireland.

Grayhan *see* Grimes

Grealish *see* MacGrealish

Green

Ó hUaithnín

Greene

The Green(e)s are numerous in England and in Ireland where many could be of English descent. However, those with roots in Connacht, or in the south around County Cork, could be natives whose name was anglicized from Ó hUaithnín (*uaine* means green). They were of the ancient Dalcassian sept. The Irish Greens of Ulster can be traced to MacGlashan (*glas* means pale green). Even Fahy, anglicized from Ó Fathaigh, has a green touch: *faiche* means a lawn—hence the mistranslation to Green!

Sometimes Ó hUaithnín was changed to Honeen or Houneen, which explains why, early in the eighteenth century, an admiral in the Spanish Navy called **Daniel O Huonyn** can be traced back to a County Clare family.

Although there are few really outstanding Greenes, they are very well recorded in the archives, and histories have been written by several members of the Green families.

Will Green was one of those who victualled the army under an agreement with the English establishment in the Pale, the English area around Dublin. Greens were high officers in the army of King James II, and there were also Greens in Cromwell's Commonwealth armies—although these were undoubtedly mostly from England.

The family of **Colonel Charles Greene** occupies five pages in *Irish Family Records* (1976), and spans the world.

Harry Plunket Greene (1865–1936) was a singer of international fame. **Alexander Green** of Dublin married the famous London fashion designer, Mary Quant.

Greene's Bookshop in Dublin's Clare Street has been a mecca for generations of book lovers, including the young W. B. Yeats and James Joyce.

see also Fahy

Greer

Mac Grioghar

Greeve Grierson Grieves MacGregor

Greer is the usual form of this name in Ireland, although its many variations include Grier, Grierson, Greeve and Grieves. All are anglicizations of the Scottish name MacGregor, of the "wicked clan Gregor", epitomized by the famous Rob Roy (Red Robert), the Highland chief who died in 1734. Endlessly harassed by other Scottish clans, the MacGregors were probably glad to take part in the plantation of Ulster in the seventeenth century. They anglicized their name and acquired much land and it is there that they are still mainly to be found.

In the Belfast Public Records Office there are many deeds, leases, rentals and general notes dating from 1630 to 1900 relating to the Greers of County Tyrone. They were members of the Society of Friends (Quakers) and, for generations, were linen traders in County Tyrone. This family and its many branches scattered throughout the globe and occupy twelve columns in *Burke's Irish Family Records.*

There were Greers who were grain merchants and distillers in Lurgan, County Armagh. Many of these emigrated to the USA and Australia, and one could wonder whether the well-known feminist writer and broadcaster, **Germaine Greer**, once of Melbourne, is a descendant of this family of the clan MacGregor.

Greers are also to be found recorded in several editions of the now defunct *Burke's Landed Gentry of Ireland*.

Greeve *see* Greer

Grehan *see* Grimes

Grierson *see* Greer

Grieves *see* Greer

Griffey *see* Griffin

Griffin

Ó Gríobhtha

Griffey Griffith

This family derives its name from the Irish word *gríobhtha*, which means griffin-like (i.e. fierce warrior). They were a Dalcassian sept who were chiefs in Thomond (parts of Clare and Limerick), where their castle was at Ballygriffey, near Ennis. A minor sept who had their territory in Kenmare, at Ballygriffen, were overcome by the powerful O Sullivans.

Although some Griffins came from Wales following the Anglo-Norman conquest, their Welsh origins were soon absorbed. Griffin, and its variants, is now a very numerous name in Munster.

Griffins were active in the many uprisings and there were at least nine of them in the army of the Stuart King James II at the time of the battle of the Boyne in 1690. They were also soldiers in the Commonwealth armies and, later, officers in the Irish-American brigades.

Richard Griffith (*c.*1704–88) of Dublin collaborated with his English wife in writing a series of popular novels in the form of letters.

Sir John Griffith (1784–1878) of Dublin, a geologist and civil engineer, is esteemed for his survey of the Irish boglands and his advice on the design of some of Dublin's most important buildings.

Gerald Griffith (1803–40) of Limerick wrote *The Collegians*, one of the most powerful novels of its time.

Arthur Griffith (1872–1922) was a strong believer in passive resistance to British Rule. He invented the name Sinn Féin (meaning We Ourselves) and edited newspapers advocating the nationalist cause. In 1921, he led the Irish delegation which went to London to sign the Anglo-Irish Treaty. When Eamon de Valera opposed the Treaty and resigned as President, Arthur Griffith became the first President of the Irish Free State. The Civil War followed and he died soon after, it was said of grief.

Griffith *see* Griffin

Grimes

Gorman Graham Grayhan Grehan

A very common English name, it is also found in Ireland in great numbers, particularly in the north, where it occupies nearly seven columns in the Northern Ireland telephone directory. Its origins are difficult to trace and there are no genealogies. In many cases it is known to be an anglicization of Ó Gréacháin, a Connacht name which has also been anglicized to Grehan, Graham or Grayhan. In County Tyrone it is an anglicization of the Irish name Ó Gormghaile, or Gormley.

The Grimes in Ireland have thrown up no heroes, statesmen or villains, but they do have a wide-ranging collection of scholars. **Seamus Grimes** wrote about the rural landscape of his native North Leitrim. **Michael Grimes**, a professor of microbiology at University College Cork, retired in the 1960s.

During the 1930s, **W. F. Grimes**, an archaeologist, wrote extensively on his subject in the *Ulster Journal of Archaeology*. He also published essays on the archaeology of Britain and Wales, with a special study of a phenomenon known as Grime's Graves.

Many Grimes in the USA served in the army and a few were writers. A number of them are recorded in the American dictionaries of biography.

see also (O) Gorman

Guerin *see* Sharpe

Guidera

Mac Giodaire   Mag Fhuadaire

Gidery   Guider   Guidry

This is an extremely rare Irish surname. It can be traced from a variety of anglicizations, possibly from Mag Fhuadaire (*fuadaire* means rambler), or from Mac Giodaire. Variations of this name include Gidery, Guidry and Guider. Today, there would appear to be less then twenty remaining of the Guidera name and none with the Guidry spelling. The Gaelic form of the name, Mac Giodaire, is used in County Derry.

In a seventeenth-century census, a **Gidery and Gidery** are recorded in County Tipperary, where at one time the name was fairly numerous.

Between 1653 and 1654, during the Cromwellian usurpation, **Edmund and Margaret Guider** were transplanted from County Limerick, probably to Connacht. The name Guidera is still occasionally found in County Galway today.

In its various forms, it has been recorded in Clogheen and Clonmel, County Tipperary, in a number of seventeenth-century birth registrations.

Guidry *see* Guidera

Guilday *see* Gildea

Guinness *see* Magennis

H

Hackett

Haicéid

Hacket

The Hackett name came to Ireland with William de Haket, who accompanied King John of England following the Norman invasion in the late twelfth century. Since then, the Hackets have been distinguished in the army and the Church and have served abroad, in Canada, the USA and Australia. Today's representative, **General Sir John Winthrop Hackett**, was educated in Australia, where his father was Lord Mayor of Adelaide and Attorney-General of South Australia.

There is a Hacketstown in County Cork, a Ballyhackett in County Dublin, a Castle Hackett near Tuam in County Galway and the Hackett Memorial Hall near Bray in County Wicklow which commemorates one of the many Hackett churchmen. Other distinguished men of the Church include **Peter Hackett**, who was Archbishop of Cashel between 1385 and 1407, **David Hackett**, who was Bishop of Ossory from 1460 to 1479, and **Reverend John Baptist Hackett** (d. 1676), a Dominican priest who was a close friend of Pope Clement. In this century, **Bernard Hackett** was a Bishop of Lismore, County Waterford.

County Kilkenny produced a family of Hacketts which included **Florence Hacket** and **Felix E. Hackett**, both writers. **Francis Hackett** (1883–1962) was a journalist and novelist who worked in Dublin and New York before going to live in Denmark when one of his novels was banned in Ireland.

The Hacketts owned many fine properties in Ireland, one of which, Lakefield in County Tipperary, built in the 1830s, is said to have been lost to the family after a game of cards.

Hackett's Dublin Illustrated Family Almanac was a popular read in the 1860s.

This once Norman family, which derives its name from the humble hake, is a numerous and interesting one, which has left its mark on Ireland in many positive ways. It is also a numerous name in England.

(O) Hagan

Ó hÁgáin

Aiken Hogg

It is believed that this surname may originally have been O Hogan (Ó hÓgáin). The O Hagans were an important sept of Ulster. There are a few variants of the name, such as Aiken and Hogg. The O prefix has seldom been dropped from this ancient Gaelic name.

The O Hagans had the hereditary right to perform the elaborate inauguration ceremony for the O Neills, who were kings, or overlords, of Ulster. This ceremony took place at Tullaghogue, their clan headquarters. Though despoiled by the invading English, the ceremonial stone has been restored and is now on view at the Ulster Museum in Belfast.

Ivor O Hagan of Armagh taught St. Malachy in *c.*1100. The O Hagans owned much land in Antrim, Armagh and Monaghan, but had it taken from them during the Elizabethan and subsequent wars.

Three O Hagan rebels were hanged at Carrickfergus in 1722.

Turlough O Hagan, Chief of the Name, travelled the long journey south to County Wicklow to rescue Red Hugh O Donnell, the young son of the Ulster Earl of Tirconnell. In December 1590, Red Hugh was recaptured after escaping from Dublin Castle, but the following December he escaped once again and trekked through the snow across the Dublin mountains to safety.

At least five O Hagans fought beside the great Earl of Tyrone, Hugh O Neill, at the fatal battle of Kinsale. Afterwards, in 1612, they lost most of their rights and property. A number of the O Hagans who fled abroad after Kinsale served in Irish regiments in France.

Thomas O Hagan (1812–85) was the first Catholic lord chancellor of Ireland since the time of James II.

John O Hagan (1822–90) was a patriot poet and a judge.

Mary O Hagan (1823–76) was the abbess who founded the order of the Poor Clares.

see also Fagan

Haggerty *see* Hegarty

Halfpenny *see* Halpin

(O) Halloran

Ó hAllmhuráin

The Ó hAllmhuráin name derives from a word meaning pirate, or stranger from overseas, referring to a very early forebear of this ancient family. They may have been seafaring people, as they were certainly very prominent on the Atlantic coast in Galway until the arrival of Henry II, who began the English conquest of Ireland in the twelfth century. At one time the O Hallorans held dominion over twenty-four villages on the east side of Lough Corrib, not far from Galway. Near Barna, just outside the city, there are the remains of an old O Halloran castle which the Lynch family acquired through marriage.

There was another O Halloran sept in Clare, who were in no way related to the Galway family. In fact they were kinsmen of the MacNamaras and had their headquarters on the shores of Lough Derg, from where they spread south to Limerick.

It was this Limerick family which, in the eighteenth century, produced the more outstanding O Hallorans.

Sylvester O Halloran studied medicine in Paris and Leiden and practised in Limerick, where he had plenty of opportunity to develop his surgical skills attending to the injuries suffered by faction fighters! A distinguished eye specialist, he published many text books on the subject and was one of the founders of Dublin's Royal College of Surgeons in 1784. His other great interest was the promotion and preservation of Irish manuscripts. His brother, **Joseph O Halloran**, a priest of the Jesuit order, was a professor of philosophy at Bordeaux in France.

Sylvester's son, **Joseph O Halloran**, sailed to the Far East as a midshipman and joined the British army in India. He ended his fifty years abroad as a major-general, with a knighthood from

William IV. On his return to Limerick, he was given the freedom of the city. His eight sons also went into the service of the army. His sixth son, **William Littlejohn O Halloran**, served in both India and Belfast and, in 1840, went to serve the colonial government in Australia.

An adventurous member of the clan, **Laurence Hynes O Halloran**, was a poet, teacher and sailor who was transported to Australia, where he put his talents to good use as headmaster of a school in Sydney.

Halpenny *see* Halpin

Halpin

Ó hAilpin Ó hAilpine

Halfpenny Halpeny Halpine

Alp, from the Irish word for lump, was the origin of this fairly unusual surname, which surfaced as Ó hAilpin in County Monaghan, where the sept was prominent at one time. It is a three-syllable name where it appears further south, anglicized to Halpeny or even Halfpenny.

In 1539, **Robert Halpenny** was a hereditary standard bearer to the Flemings, Lords of Slane in County Meath. In 1541, **John Halpeny** was a juror in north Meath. In 1544, there were twenty-seven Halpennys, including a captain, recruited for service under the King of England.

Thomas Halpin was among the insurgents in the 1798 Rebellion. However, he saved his life by turning informer.

William Halpin (b. 1825), a Fenian, distinguished himself in the American Civil War.

Nicholas John Halpine (1790–1850), a Shakespearean critic, was a bitter opponent of Daniel O Connell. His son, **Charles Graham Halpine** (1829–68), a brigadier-general, later edited the *New York Times*, sometimes writing satirically about the war.

Patrick Halpin (fl. 1755–87) and his son **John** (b. 1764) were painters and engravers. **George Halpin** (1779–1854) was an architect and an inspector of lighthouses. He was the architect of the Corn Exchange at Burgh Quay, Dublin.

Anthony R. A. Halpin, one of Cork's leading business- and sportsmen, is a director of several liquor companies and a member of the Cork Harbour Commissioners.

There is a selection of papers in Dublin's Genealogical Office relating to various Halpins.

Hamilton

The very numerous Hamiltons in Ireland come from many different sources. Some are from Hambledon in England, but very many came from Scotland at the time of the plantation of Ulster. One of the leading Hamilton families in Scotland today are the Dukes and Earls of Abercorn.

In the course of history, the Hamiltons acquired many titles of nobility, including Earls of Arran, Barons of Lunge in Sweden, Barons of Glenalley and Earls of Clanbrassil. In earlier days the Earls of Abercorn were Jacobites, but later they changed their allegiance to the Protestant William III (William of Orange). A Viscount Boyne was one of William of Orange's generals.

Burke's Guide to Country Houses lists a great variety of residences owned at various times by Hamiltons, including the magnificent Baron's Court in County Tyrone, ancestral home of the Abercorn Hamiltons. In *Burke's Irish Family Records* (1976) there are copious accounts of the Hamiltons of counties

Laois, Louth and Meath, and also the **Rowan-Hamiltons** of the legendary Killyleagh Castle in County Down.

A member of the Catholic branch of the family, **Count Anthony Hamilton** (1645–1719), left Roscrea Castle with his parents at the time of the Cromwellian invasion to settle in France. He distinguished himself in the army and at the court of Louis XIV and returned to Ireland to raise a Régiment d'Hamilton for the French king. This Hamilton was also a writer and his most famous work is the French classic, *Mémoires de Grammont.*

James Archibald Hamilton (1747–1815) of Ulster was an important astronomer. The **Reverend William Hamilton** (1755–97) was an outstanding naturalist.

Hugh Douglas Hamilton (1739–1808) of Dublin trained in Dublin and went to London, where he was much in demand as a portrait painter at the time of George III.

Sir William Rowan Hamilton (1805–65) of Dublin showed, from infancy, a prodigious intellect. He mastered mathematics, languages and astronomy, and was Astronomer Royal for Ireland. He published many papers, including the outstanding "Elements of Quaternions". He also wrote poetry.

Hand

Claffey Lafan Lavin MacGlavin

Hand was originally an English name and is very numerous throughout Ireland. Whether Hand, Hands or Hance, the name originally came from the Dutch Han, or Hans, meaning son of John.

It is possible that some bearers of the name were true Gaels whose name suffered a crude mistranslation from Mac Láimh, *lámh* being the Irish word for hand. In fact, because of varying pronunciations in different parts of the country, it became Lavin or Lavan in County Roscommon, a sept who were of some importance in the sixteenth century as followers of the chieftain MacDermot Roe. MacGlavin is to be found in parts of Connacht. Other variations are Claffy, Claffey, or Lafan.

Many Hands have been prominent in the military field. A **William Hand** is recorded as serving in the army of James II. **Edward Hand** (1744–1802) of Offaly went to the USA, where he played an important role in the revolutionary army and afterwards became a member of Congress. **James Hand** was with the Irish-American brigade in 1865.

At home, the most important representative of the name was **John Hand**, who, in 1842, founded All Hallows College in Dublin for the training of priests for missionary work.

(O) Hanley

Ó hÁinle

Hanly

Hanley, or Hanly, a very numerous surname, derives from the Irish word *áinle*, meaning beauty. The original Ó hÁinle sept were centred on the river Shannon in County Roscommon, where they gave their name to the town of Doohyhanly. They were military chiefs in the army of the royal O Conors of Connacht.

Donal O Hanly was Bishop of Dublin from 1085 to 1096. In 1347 there was a **Sir J. Hanley** who came to an agreement with Henry VI for the government of Ireland for six years.

Between 1661 and 1665, three Hanleys are recorded in the armies of the Spanish Netherlands: **Don Dionisio,**

Don Alferez and Don Maurisco Haneli.

In the Stuart archives, a certificate dated 1700, written in French, from James II, records that "**Peter Hanley**, now in the Duke of Lorraine's Body Guard, is the son of gentle parents"—meaning he was entitled to armorial bearings.

An opera and a novel have been written about the unfortunate **Ellen Hanley**, the "Colleen Bawn" who was murdered in the 1840s in County Limerick.

Gerald Hanly (b. 1916), a writer and traveller, has published a number of successful novels, including *The Consul at Sunset*. His brother **James** (1901–85), following an adventurous career at sea, also published several very successful novels.

David Hanly, who was born in Limerick in 1944, is a respected radio journalist with RTE, the Irish broadcasting organization.

(O) Hanlon

Ó hAnluain

The Ó hAnluain (*luain* means champion) were an important sept in east Ulster. They were located in County Armagh, in Oneilland and Orior, where they were lords of Orior.

In 1537, their chieftain, **Oghie O Hanlon**, agreed to the English system of surrender and regrant and so were able to keep their lands. He gave up his chieftancy in exchange for a knighthood.

Despite the Ulster plantations, for some time they remained conciliatory towards the English and so continued to hold their estates. They were appointed royal standard-bearers north of the river Boyne. However, following the ruthless Cromwellian invasion, they were reduced to outlawry. Their last chief, **Redmond "Count" O Hanlon**, lost everything and retreated to the hills, from where he would swoop to exact retribution from the usurpers. A big price was offered for his capture, which attracted a kinsman to inform on him, and so Rory's head was spiked on the gate of Downpatrick Gaol in 1681.

Tanderagee, a mansion built on the site of the ancient O Hanlon castle, changed hands many times and is now a potato crisp factory.

O Hanlons who fled from Ireland served in the Spanish Netherlands and also with the Irish brigades in France and at Fontenoy.

John O Hanlon (1821–1905) of Stradbally, County Laois, went to the United States of America at the time of the Great Famine where he was ordained a priest. He was a writer of Irish-American history, and his major work was *Lives of the Irish Saints* in ten volumes.

O Hanlon, more so than Hanlon, is widespread throughout Ireland. They are well represented in medicine, the law and the newspaper and publishing industry.

Hanly *see* Hanley

Hannan, **Hanneen**, **Hannen** *see* Hannon

(O) Hannigan

Ó hAnnagáin

Hannagan

This surname is numerous throughout Ireland. Its Irish form, Ó hAnnagáin, refers to a descendant of Annagán, which is a diminutive of the Irish word for delay. According to the experts, this ancient surname is of uncertain origin. It could have originated in two widely separated areas:

County Waterford in Munster and County Tyrone in Ulster.

In the Belfast Public Records Office, there is a fee-farm grant of property in Cultra, County Down, to a **William Hannigan** in 1852. His will is also held there, dated 1888.

Edward Allen Hannigan (1807–59), who was probably a descendant of an Ulster family, as he was a Presbyterian, was born in Hamilton, Ohio. He trained as a lawyer and, having survived many vicissitudes, he was elected to the Senate of the USA in 1841. He was a brilliant and aggressive orator, so when he lost his seat he was sent as Minister to Berlin. However, alcoholism, against which he had fought long and hard, caused him to be sent home in 1850.

Margaret Hannagan, wife of Seamus Glandillon, one of the early directors of Radio Éireann, edited and translated several books of songs of the Irish Gaels.

The **Right Reverend James Hannigan**, Roman Catholic Bishop of Menevia, has been a bishop in Wales since 1983. He was born in Donegal in 1928.

James Edgar Hannigan (b. 1928), who probably had Irish antecedents, lives in Eastbourne in England. He was Deputy Secretary in the Department of Transport in the United Kingdom from 1980.

Hannon

Ó hAnnáin

Hannan Hanneen Hannen

This ancient surname originates from a first name and signifies descendant of Annán, which is a diminutive of *annadh*, meaning delay.

The Hannans or Hannons, who dropped their O prefix, never to retrieve it, were established in County Limerick for many generations. It was also a very common name around County Galway in the sixteenth century.

There are a variety of spellings of this comparatively simple name. It can be Hanneen in the west of Ireland, where they are believed by some scholars to be descendants of Ainchín, which could be a variation of Ainghein, which means unborn.

They are not much in evidence in the chronicles, with the exception of **Maelissa O Hannen**, a prior of Roscommon who died in 1266.

In the seventeenth century, they were also numerous in Athlone, as well as Roscommon. During the Cromwellian devastations, many lost their lands and suffered transplantation.

There is a famous **Patrick Hannan** of County Clare who emigrated to Australia. It was he who, in 1888, discovered the fabulous Kalgoorlie gold field in Western Australia which was calculated to be “the richest square mile in the world”.

A few extracts from records in the Genealogical Office in Dublin might be of help to family researchers. In 1848, shortly after the Great Famine, **Brian Hannon** and his wife, Ellen Price, emigrated to the USA, but their son, **John**, and daughter, **Mary**, remained in Ireland. The Genealogical Office also has a draft confirmation of arms to **Berchmans Hannin** of Mullingar, County Westmeath, made in 1933.

Hannan or Hannon is a very numerous name, especially in Munster and Connacht, its original homelands. Hannen is usually found to be of English origin.

(O) Hanrahan

Ó hAnracháin

The Ó hAnracháins are of the ancient Gaelic Dalcassian sept, whose territory was Thomond in County Clare. The Dalcassians embraced many kindred septs, including the mighty O Briens. Ó hAnradháin is recognized as a variant of the name and has been anglicized to O Hourihan. These are also of the Dalcassian sept, but their roots are in north Tipperary.

E. H. Hanrahan has published many treatises on scientific agriculture, specializing in soil mechanics.

Norah Hanrahan wrote a number of very popular books with a strong Catholic ethos.

Many Hanrahans have resumed the O prefix. They are numerous throughout Ireland, with the exception of Ulster, but they have yet to come to prominence.

O Hara

Ó hEaghra

The name Ó hEaghra signifies a descendant of Ara, who was a chieftain of the family of the kings of Munster. The name, which is seldom seen without its O prefix, was anglicized to O Hara.

In the fourteenth century, they divided into two septs: O Hara Boy (*buídhe* means yellow) of Collooney, and O Hara Reagh (*riabhach* means brindled) of Ballyhara, both in County Sligo. Later, another branch settled in County Antrim.

They were all dispossessed by the Cromwellians, except for some of the Sligo O Haras who went over to the English side. At one time they had more than twenty-one thousand acres and some very fine mansions, including Annaghmore, which is still in the family (in Sligo). They produced many bishops, Members of Parliament and high sheriffs and were created barons of Tirawly.

One of these Tirawly O Haras, **Kean O Hara** (1714–82), who was known as "Cruel Tall O Hara" because of his great height, was a playwright and is credited with the invention of the burlesque genre.

Following the subjugation of the Irish nation in the seventeenth century, many O Haras served in the armies of Europe and Russia.

John O Hara, son of an Irish doctor who had settled in Pennsylvania, leaped to fame in 1934 with his novel, *Appointment to Samarra*. He preferred to overlook his Irish origins.

The O Haras are well recorded in the Irish genealogies, one—**Milo of Art**—from *c.*BC 1400 to AD 600! One of the front covers of the Irish Georgian Society's magazine (Jan–Jun 1986) was adorned with a colourful Chinese export plate, made for the O Haras and displaying their arms and their motto, "Try". The plate can be seen in Dublin's Heraldic Museum.

Hare *see* (O) Hehir, MacGarry

Harnedy *see* Hartnett

Harney

Ó hAthairne

Hartney

Patrick Woulfe, a priest of the diocese of Limerick and a member of the Council of the National Academy of Ireland, whose dictionary *Irish Names and Surnames* was published in 1923, says the Hartneys "were descendants of

Atairne (fatherly or paternal), a rare and scattered surname".

They appear to have originated in County Roscommon and they can still be found there in Connacht, as well as in County Tipperary, though they are still not numerous.

The name was anglicized to Hartney or Harney, and the outstanding representative so far is the Irish politician, **Mary Harney**. She was born in Dublin in 1953 and was the first woman auditor of the centuries-old, all-male College Historical Society of Trinity College Dublin. While still in her early twenties, she became the youngest ever member of the Senate when she was nominated to the upper house by the Fianna Fáil party, whose leader was Jack Lynch. She later moved to the Progressive Democrats and is now leader of that party.

Harrington

Ó hLongardail

In the seventeenth century, many Harringtons came from England, first as soldiers, then as settlers, having been given forfeited Irish land in lieu of pay.

The Harringtons who are very numerous in counties Cork and Kerry were originally of the Irish Ó hIongardail sept, which was first anglicized to O Hunderell and, later, to Harrington. In Connacht, Ó hOireachtaigh was incorrectly anglicized to Harrington, instead of the correct Heraghty. In County Kerry, Ó hArrachtáin has sometimes become Harrington. The name derives from an Irish word meaning a number of things, including tall, mighty, brave or heroic.

The history of the Irish Harringtons remains obscure. It is the Harringtons from England, mostly from Cumberland, who feature most in Irish history. In Irish archives there are letters written by **Sir Henry Harrington**, who ruled "the counties of the Birnes and Tooles", people he found to be in "a pitiable condition". Nonetheless, it was the O Byrnes who defeated Sir Henry in County Wicklow in *c.*1596.

R. Harrington showed great compassion when, in *c.*1643, he petitioned the House of Lords for a collection to be made for the distressed city of Londonderry.

There is a letter in the manuscript collection of Dublin's National Library regarding **William Stanhope, 1st Earl of Harrington**, a distinguished military man. It says that "Lord Harrington is most talked of as Lord Lieutenant of Ireland but I doubt how it will be as he is too stout or too lazy to go directly to the Closet for it." However, Lord Harrington must have made an effort, for he was Lord Lieutenant and Governor-General of Ireland from 1746 to 1751. Harrington Street in Dublin commemorates him. His family must have taken to Ireland, because, for generations, there are records of their marriages to leading Irish men and women, including the Barrys who were Earls of Barrymore, County Cork, and the FitzGeralds who were Dukes of Leinster. In 1806, the **3rd Earl, Lord Charles Stanhope Harrington**, commanded the forces in Ireland.

The only Irish Harrington to make the pages of history was **Timothy Charles Harrington** (1851–1910) of County Cork who, in 1877, founded the newspaper, the *Kerry Sentinel.* An active member of the Land League, he was also a Member of Parliament and supporter of Parnell. He was a barrister and defended many political prisoners. He was Lord Mayor of Dublin from 1901 to 1904.

Harris

The English surname Harris was adapted from the first name Harry, which is an English corruption of the French first name, Henri. It is a very common name both in England and in Ireland, where it is mostly to be found in Ulster.

In various issues of the *Cork Historical and Architectural Society Journal* there are accounts of the 1722 will of **Joseph Harris** of Cork, and also of the Harris Affair, being "an account of the death of **William Harris** as a result of being tossed in a blanket".

Some of the Harris family must have gone over to the native Irish, for there are seventeenth-century records of their lands being forfeited for "treachery". On the other hand, **Lieutenant Edward Harris** and **Lieutenant William Harris** were officers in the Cromwellian armies in Ireland.

General Sir George Harris, born in 1740 in Kent and a hero of the capture of Seringapatam, was awarded a peerage in 1815. He married a daughter of Robert Handcock-Temple of Waterston, County Westmeath. He prefixed the name Temple to Harris when he inherited Waterston.

The most outstanding representative of the name was the notorious **Frank Harris** (1856–1931). He was born in Galway, the son of a naval commander in the revenue service. A journalist and wild genius, he tried many careers and, for a period, owned and ran a highly successful political weekly, *The Saturday Review*. *My Life and Loves*, his scandalous sexually explicit three-volume autobiography, shocked many of its readers.

Sir Ian Cecil Harris, born in 1910, managed his Ballykisteen stud in County Tipperary. Born in Limerick, **Richard (St. John) Harris**, poet and actor, has made a big name in films and television, including roles in *The Guns of Navarone*, *Mutiny on the Bounty*, *The Field* and many, many more successful productions.

Harrison

Mac Annraoi

Harrison is an old English surname which means son of Henry. The Harrisons came to Ireland early in the seventeenth century with the soldiers of the Commonwealth. Following the Cromwellian conquests, they were given numerous grants of land which had been confiscated from the Irish.

In the late seventeenth century, the **Reverend Theophilus Harrison** was Dean of the monastery of Clonmacnoise in County Offaly.

For three centuries the Harrisons of Castle Harrison, County Cork, were prominent in Irish public life. The **Honourable William Harrison** was a revenue commissioner for Dublin in 1728.

They were also prominent in the learned professions. Earlier this century, **Henry Harrison** was a distinguished historian, **J. Heslop Harrison** was a naturalist and **Sam Harrison** wrote poetry. There were also several Harrison medical men.

In the Irish archives there are a variety of papers relating to the many branches of this now very numerous family, including a request to the Genealogical Office in Dublin for confirmation of arms to the descendants of **Captain James Harrison**, "whose father, **James Harrison**, removed from County Antrim to South Carolina in 1767, and his great-grandson . . . **Lieutenant-Colonel Walter Archibald Harrison**".

During the nineteenth century, **C. W. Harrison and Sons** were prosperous ecclesiastical sculptors. It was a Harrison son who, apart from many other artistic commissions, carved the famous riverine figures on Carlisle (now O Connell) Bridge in Dublin.

Today, in Ireland, the Harrison name is most numerous in Ulster. They are also to be found all over the United States, to which they emigrated in the nineteenth century.

(O) Harte

Ó hAirt

Hart

Harte is common to England, Scotland and America, as well as to Ireland, where it derives from a personal name, *Art*, meaning martial man. Art was a son of King Conn of the Hundred Battles and was a kinsman of the O Neills. The O Harts were one of the Four Tribes of Tara. One family were chiefs in County Meath, while another were chiefs in Sligo in the sixteenth century.

With the arrival of the Normans, the O Harts were scattered but, until the seventeenth century, when they suffered religious persecution, they owned vast estates and were among the leading families of Connacht.

During the plantation of Ulster, many Harts came from England to settle. A Harte took over Doe Castle at Cresslough, County Donegal, a former stronghold of the MacSweeneys. They also came with the armies of William of Orange in 1690. They are well recorded in the military archives, and among manuscripts in the National Library of Ireland there is a letter of 1590 from Queen Elizabeth I which directs that "**P. Harte** be released from Exeter gaol on condition that he serves in Ireland"!

Sir Robert Harte (1835–1911) of Portadown, County Armagh, an inspector-general of Maritime Customs in Peking, brought many people from Ireland to serve in China.

The Harts are extremely lucky, not only in that several books have been written about their lineage by various members of the family, but also because of the illustrious **John O Hart** (1824–1902) of County Mayo, who produced several volumes of Irish pedigrees, including his own very detailed one. The armorial shield of the Irish Harts shows only one heart, while that of the English Harts shows three; John O Hart suggests that the Irish family is the senior, and is progenitor of all the Harts, including those long since settled in America.

Hartigan

Ó hArtagáin

The Irish name Ó hArtagáin means son of Artagáin, which is a diminutive of the first name, Art. They were a Dalcassian sept whose territory was in east County Clare.

Cinéad Ó hArtagáin (*c*.910–975) was one of a band of poets and bards who wrote about their native county. **Dúnlaing Ó hArtigáin** fought beside the great King Brian Boru at the battle of Clontarf in 1014—one of the turning points in Irish history. He was regarded as one of its heroes.

From County Limerick came **Father Matthew O Hartigan**, who recruited men for the order of priests known as the Society of Jesus. He was an emissary for the Catholic Confederation to France in 1643. Later he went further afield, to the West Indies, where he looked after the Irish who had been exiled there.

The Hartigans were deprived of many of their possessions in the seventeenth century. Among one sorry list of the names of those who suffered transplantation are **Edmond, Daniel, Ellen, Donnogh, Anstace** and **Alson Hartigan**, all of whom lost their lands between 1653 and 1654.

Many Hartigans went to Europe to serve in the armies of France and Spain. **Don Dermicio O Hartagain** is mentioned as serving in the Spanish Netherlands under the Conde de Inchiquin, who was a fellow countryman, an O Brien from County Clare who commanded his own regiment, the Clare Dragoons.

A few emigrated to Australia, where the name was brought to fame by **Father Hartigan**, who is regarded as a leading Irish-Australian poet, writing early this century.

Usually without the O prefix, the Hartigan name today is numerous, especially in their ancestral homelands in Munster and Connacht.

(O) Hartnedy *see* Hartnett

Hartnett

Ó hAirtnéada

Harnedy (O) Hartnedy

Ó hAirtnéada derives from a first name which is thought to mean either battle-bear or battle-stone. It is a very old west Munster name and it is in this area that the majority of those bearing this name, anglicized to Harnedy or Hartnett, are still to be found. O Hartnedy occurs frequently in sixteenth-century records.

In the Genealogical Office in Dublin, there is a will made by **James Fuller Hartnett** of Aghamore, County Kerry, and there are also pedigrees of this family dating up to 1874.

In the 1901 census, there were fifty Hartnetts in County Kerry. Until the transfer of land from landlords to tenants, there were four Hartnett families who owned considerable land in Munster.

Apart from in Munster, the name is comparatively rare today, nor has it made any headlines, either famous or infamous.

Michael Hartnett, who was born in Newcastle West in County Limerick, is a considerable poet, writing in both Irish and English. From 1976 to 1978 he was a lecturer in creative writing in Thomond College, Limerick.

Hartney *see* Harney

Harvey

Ó hAirmheadhaigh

Harvey is a very old English first name which has long since been used as a surname. It first came to Ireland during the plantations of Ulster. It is thought that some Gaelic families of Harvey may have taken it as an anglicization of the Irish name Ó hAirmheadhaigh, which meant owners of a herd of cattle.

Burke's Irish Family Records gives a comprehensive pedigree of the Harveys of Bargy Castle in County Wexford, dating from *c.*1600 to the present day. From this family came many distinguished administrators, both at home and abroad, including Buenos Aires, Argentina and Australia.

The most illustrious of the Harveys was **Beauchamp Bagenal Harvey** (1762–98), a wealthy young barrister who supported Catholic emancipation. Chosen to lead the rebellious United Irishmen, it was with great reluctance that he took part in the tragic 1798 Rebellion, having issued orders that there was to be no plunder or other excesses. Following the defeat at New Ross in County Wexford, Bagenal Harvey was hanged on the bridge at Wexford.

From this family comes **Chris de Burgh**, the popular singer and composer, who is a graduate of Trinity College Dublin and who was born in Argentina.

There was a **Harvey de Montmorency** (1864–1908) who went to Ontario, and there is still a Harvey family at Bromley House in County Wexford.

The Harveys have been prominent in medicine, science and natural history. Today, Harvey is a most numerous name in every area of Ireland.

Haughey *see* Keogh

Hayes

Ó hAodha

de la Haye (O) Hea

Aodha is a personal name meaning fire. The equivalent English name is Hugh, which is why some descendants of the Ó hAodhas can be traced to Hughes, mainly in Ulster. There was a multitude of O hAodha septs, some of which anglicized their names to Hayes while others became O Hea. They are most numerous now in Munster. In Wexford there was an Anglo-Norman family of de la Haye who built many fine castles on their large estates.

From the twelfth to the sixteenth century, a plenitude of Hayes were bishops of Lismore, and of Cork and Ross.

In the seventeenth century, many Hayes featured in the commercial life of Dublin. One owned a ship, the *St. Stephen*, which was bound for Dublin with Spanish wines when it was impounded off the Isle of Man. Another was mining for gold in Wicklow and had thoughts of a project for a mint. **Sir James Hayes**, in 1671, held an important post with the revenue commissioners.

Since the eighteenth century a succession of **Sir Samuel Hayes** have occupied Drumboe Castle in Donegal. Crosshaven House, County Cork, was the home of the descendants of a Hayes family who bought the lands from a Cromwellian officer in 1656 for £247 10s 0d. It is now a community centre.

Sir Henry Hayes of Vernon Mount in Cork was sentenced, in 1801, to transportation, for attempting to abduct a rich heiress. Far from being poor, he made the journey to Botany Bay with his manservant and a comforting amount of luggage. Nine years later, his daughter gained him a pardon from the Prince Regent.

Sir John MacNamara Hayes, an eminent physician and surgeon from Cork, was with the British forces during the first American war.

Catherine Hayes, a poor Limerick girl, became a leading soprano, with the assistance of the Protestant Bishop of Limerick. She gained international recognition, singing in all the world's opera houses. People paid $1,000 to hear her sing in New York.

Michael Angelo Hayes of Waterford and his contemporary, **Edward Hayes**, were celebrated and versatile painters. **Canon John Hayes** founded the very successful Muintir na Tíre co-operative to encourage the improvement of rural life.

Michael Hayes, a professor of languages who fought in the 1916 Easter Rising, later held a ministerial office in the government and was elected Senator.

Richard Hayes, a remarkable scholar, made important contributions to the bibliography and archives of the National Library of Ireland when he was its director.

In the USA, **Archbishop P. J. Hayes** was made a cardinal in 1924.

see also Hughes

(O) Hea *see* Hayes, Hughes

(O) Healihy *see* (O) Healy

(O) Healy

Ó hÉalaighthe Ó hÉilidhe

Hely (O) Healihy

In Munster the Irish form of this name is Ó hÉalaighthe, while in north Connacht it is Ó hÉilidhe. Nowadays it can be either Healy or Hely. It consists of two words which mean ingenious claimant. Ballyhely on Lough Arrow in Sligo was the seat of the Connacht sept. The Ó hÉalaighthe sept had their Munster territory at Donoughmore in County Cork.

There were two separate chieftaincies, both presiding over large territories. In the seventeenth century, the Cromwellians dispossessed them of all their lands.

The Healeys boasted many priests and a number of archbishops. When **John Hely-Hutchinson** of Cork married an heiress, he assumed her name. He was one of the most progressive, as well as sometimes the most outrageous, provosts of Trinity College Dublin. One of his sons, who sat in the House of Lords in London, took his title, **Earl of Donoughmore**, from the family homeland. A descendant, **Mark Hely-Hutchinson**, was Managing Director of Guinness and a director of the Bank of Ireland.

The paintings of **John Healy**, the artist who tragically died young in 1771, are very highly valued today. Windows by **Michael Healy**, an artist in stained glass, can be seen in a number of Irish churches.

Tim Healy of Kerry was a towering figure in nineteenth-century politics. As correspondent for an Irish newspaper, he knew all the Irish Members of Parliament at Westminster. He became involved with Parnell in the movement for Home Rule. He was called to the Bar and developed into a powerful orator. Following the split over Parnell's affair with Kitty O Shea, Tim Healy was expelled from the Irish Party. He left a successful legal career in England to return to Ireland after the 1916 Easter Rising. From 1922 to 1927 he was first Governor-General of the Irish Free State. His brother **Maurice** and his son **Joseph** were both barristers, and great Irish "characters".

John Healy, a Drogheda barrister and journalist, was, for twenty-seven years, editor of the *Irish Times*. **Cahir Healy** of Donegal, a littérateur, was an unusually level-headed leader of nationalism in Ulster.

Hearne *see* Ahern

Heather

de Fraoc

Heather is a common surname in England, where Heather is the name of a parish in the county of Leicestershire, near Ashby-de-la-Zouche. Although the name has been in Ireland for a long time, it is not to be found in the usual surname records. A member of the family—one of a couple of dozen concentrated in the County Dublin area—thinks it was an anglicization of de Fraoc (*fraoch* is the Irish word for heather).

It is possible that the Heathers came with one of the various armies from England, or they may have come during the plantation of Ulster, for there was a family known as **Campbell Heather** which settled in one of the northern counties. One of this family was a vicar in the Church of Ireland.

For many years there were also Heathers in County Galway, mostly living in the far west of Connemara, where, recently, a member of the family who was searching for the graves of their ancestors at Errislannan found a Campbell Heather gravestone, clearly establishing Ulster origins for this name.

The Heathers of Dublin were, and some still are, members of the Society of Friends (Quakers). They had a prosperous shoe factory in the city. Three Dublin brothers enlisted in the British army during the Second World War, greatly displeasing their father, as Quakers are strictly non-militaristic.

The name is a rare one in Ireland today. Heather pedigrees can be traced in the headquarters of the Society of Friends in Dublin.

Heelan *see* Hyland

Heffernan

Ó hIfearnáin

Ó hIfearnáin means descendant of Ifearnáin and is anglicized to Heffernan. Originally from Corofin in County Clare, where nearby Muintirefernáin commemorates their name, they were chiefs of Owneybeg until the fourteenth century. When they were displaced by the Ryans, they moved on from Clare to Limerick and the borders of Tipperary. They must have rallied, because in the sixteenth century they were described as being the most important sept in the barony of Clanwilliam.

From 1543 to 1553 **Aeneas O Heffernan** was Bishop of Emly.

From the troubled times of the seventeenth-century invasion by Cromwell's armies, there are records of **Catherine, Connor and Edmond O Heffernan** being transplanted to Connacht, together with at least fifteen others of their kin.

Their more illustrious representative was **Liam Dall Ó hIfearnáin** (1720–60) of Tipperary. Although born blind and always suffering great poverty, he studied at the famous bardic school at Limerick and became an esteemed scholar and poet. **Dr. Paul Heffernan**, an eighteenth-century dramatist, was regarded as one of the great characters of his time.

There was a Heffernan officer in Dillon's Regiment, serving with the Irish brigades in France between 1783 and 1784.

In 1970, **Father Brendan Heffernan** of Dublin became the first Roman Catholic chaplain to be appointed to Trinity College Dublin.

Following the penal times, the O prefix was dropped and has seldom been reinstated.

(O) Hegarty

Ó hÉigceartaigh

Haggerty

The O prefix is seldom used now with this ancient Gaelic name, which comes from the Irish word, *éigceartach*, meaning unjust. The Hegartys originated in Ulster, where they were a branch of the Cenél Eoghain, who were descendants of Niall of the Nine Hostages from whom came the great O Neill chieftains.

Maolmuire O Hegarty died at the battle of Kinsale in 1602, fighting with Hugh O Neill's army.

The Hegarty name was frequently to be found among the lists of priests who were persecuted during the severe period of the penal laws. Hegarty's Rock at Killygarvan near Lough Swilly commemorates the murder there, in 1715, of **Father James Hegarty**.

Many Hegartys fled to France, where they distinguished themselves in the Irish brigades. **Lieutenant-Colonel Hegarty** of Lally's Regiment had his services rewarded with a governorship of the Isle of Bourbon.

Daniel O Hegarty, a shipbuilder in Dunkirk in 1721, founded the first Freemason Lodge in France. Its members were mostly Jacobites, intent on restoring the Stuart monarchy to England!

Patrick Sarsfield O Hegarty (1879–1955), who was born in Cork, took part in the Irish War of Independence. He was secretary to the Department of Posts and Telegraphs and was a pioneering editor of nationalist books, also writing many volumes of Irish history. His son, **Seán Sáirseál Ó hÉigeartaigh**, was a Gaelic scholar and a civil servant in the Department of Finance. With his wife he founded a publishing firm, Sáirseál agus Dill, which revolutionized the publishing of books in the Irish language, encouraging a whole new generation of writers. His early death was a great loss.

A variation of the name, Haggerty, is popular with Irish-Americans, but it is seldom found in Ireland.

(O) Hehir

Ó Haichir

Hare

O Hehir—quite a rare name today—derives from the Irish word *aichear*, meaning bitter or sharp. They were an ancient Dalcassian sept who lived around the counties of Clare and Limerick.

A Thomond (County Clare) family at the end of the eleventh century were lords of Magh Adhair, which is between Ennis and Tulla. They afterwards settled on land around Ennis and the Slieve Callan mountain.

In the sixteenth century, an O Brien pedigree mentions the marriage of Donogh O Brien with **Honora O Hehir**, daughter of the Lord of Ire Cormaic.

Many O Hehirs were transplanted to Connacht during the bad Cromwellian times, between 1653 and 1654. With the restoration of the monarchy in England, records show that some had their land restored to them.

In the nineteenth century, several scholarly gentlemen were writing verse in Irish and English, including **John Hehir** of the Royal Irish Academy and **Padraigh O Hehir** of Trinity College Dublin.

Dublin's **Micheál O Hehir** (1920–96) was one of the most outstanding bearers of the name. Early in his career in journalism he veered towards sports reporting—horse racing in particular—and was racing correspondent for a number of newspapers, including the *Irish Independent*. He progressed to broadcasting on radio and television and quickly became RTE's best-known commentator, with his distinctive voice communicating the excitement of the moment. For a while he also managed Leopardstown Racecourse. He broadcast on many networks besides RTE, including the BBC and NBC. One of his most memorable commentaries was his coverage of the funeral of President John F. Kennedy.

Hely *see* (O) Healy

Henchy *see* Hennessy

Hennessy

Ó hAonghusa

Henchy Hensey

Aonghus, a personal name, is the root of the Hennessy name, which, in Irish, is Ó hAonghusa. It has taken several other forms, including Hensey and Henchy. The O prefix has not been restored.

There are two leading septs, and at least half a dozen Ballyhennessy place-names testify to their Connacht and Munster origins. One branch of the family was in Offaly, while the other settled for a while between Meath and Dublin. Later they were driven south by the Normans, who began to arrive in 1170.

In the seventeenth century, they joined the exodus to France, where, as outstanding military men and administrators, they were admitted to the French nobility—a rare honour for a non-French national. A battle-worn army officer, **Richard Hennessy** (1720–1800), retired to Cognac and discovered the restorative powers of brandy. He sent a sample to Ireland, where it was greatly admired, and set up a distillery in Cognac, which earned the Hennessy name worldwide fame. This French family of Hennessy also sponsored the Hennessy Gold Cup and have been successful horse breeders.

A member of the **Pope-Hennessy** family from Cork was the first Catholic Conservative to hold an Irish seat as a Member of Parliament. While serving as governor in the British colonial services, he is said to have planted the seeds of colonial independence. **Sir John Pope-Hennessy** (1913–94) of this Youghal family held many posts in the art world, including consultant chairman of European Paintings in the Metropolitan Museum, New York. Specializing in Italian art, he won many awards for his books and articles.

The Hennessys in England have also distinguished the name in the arts, publishing, politics and television. The 3rd Baron Windlesham, **David J. C. Hennessy** (b. 1932), was Minister for State in the Home Office and held a number of appointments with English television companies.

see also Ennis

(O) Henry

Ó hInnéirghe

FitzHenry

Henry is a numerous name in Ireland, the majority of which are to be found in Ulster. Variations of the name included MacEnery (q.v.) and O Henry. In Ulster, the original head of the Ó hInnéirghe sept was a chief of Cullentra in County Tyrone. The FitzHenrys came from Normandy to Wexford and in time their name was also shortened to Henry.

The pedigrees of the Henrys in the Irish archives include some who emigrated to Paris in the eighteenth century, including **A. S. Henry**, whose Belfast company were linen manufacturers from 1847 to 1955, **P. S. Henry**, who was the first president of Queen's College Belfast, and **Mitchell Henry**, formerly of Loughbrickland in County Down, who built the magnificent Kylemore Castle, now a school and abbey, at Letterfrack, County Galway.

Mrs. FitzHenry was a popular eighteenth-century actress.

Plants named Henryana commemorate the famous County Antrim botanist, **Augustine Henry** (1857–1930).

Paul Henry (1877–1958) was an outstanding artist, whose painting of the Connemara landscape was made into a railway poster, making both the artist and its subject extremely popular!

Hensey *see* Hennessy

Herbert

Hoireabard

Saint Herbert was Archbishop of Cologne in about AD 1000. His name became a popular one for sons of the French nobility. **Herbertus Camerarius** came to England with William the Conqueror, and his descendants became Earls of Powis, Lords Herbert of Cherbury and Herbert of Muckross. They also had several untitled branches of the family in England, Wales and also in Ireland, where they arrived about 1659 with the Elizabethan colonists and settled in County Kerry. They were also Earls of Pembroke, a name familiar to those who know their Dublin street-names.

Muckross House in Killarney, County Kerry, was magnificently rebuilt between 1839 and 1843 by **Colonel, the Right Honourable H. A. Herbert**. It changed owners several times, until 1932, when it was presented to the Irish nation and became known as the Bourn-Vincent National Park.

For generations, the Herberts have lived in Kerry. One member of this once large family who was born in 1770 and died in 1829 was a popular diarist and wrote *Retrospections of Dorothea Herbert.*

J. D. Herbert, an architectural student who turned to the stage, wrote an amusing account of Dublin life in the mid-nineteenth-century *Irish Varieties.* In the same period, **Lady Lucy Herbert** was prioress of the Augustinian Cannonesses of Bruges.

Victor Herbert (1859–1924), who was born in Dublin, played his cello in the orchestra of Johann Strauss before becoming lead cellist with the Metropolitan Opera Company's orchestra in New York. He also composed comic operas and that very popular song, "Ah, sweet mystery of life".

Patricia Herbert of Dublin, a concert pianist and teacher, married the conductor of the Radio Telefís Éireann orchestra, Eimear O Broin, in 1959.

The Herbert name is not very numerous today in any part of Ireland. In the Ballsbridge suburb of Dublin, there is a beautiful little park called Herbert Park.

Heron *see* Ahern

Heslenan *see* Heslin

Heslin

Ó hEislin

Heslenan

Formerly Ó hEisleanáin, and anglicized to Heslenan, this is a rare old sept of Breffny whose territory was in the neighbourhood of Mohill in County Leitrim. In the course of time, the name was abbreviated to Ó hEislin and Heslin. The name comes from an ancestor whose first name was Eisleanáin.

In the sixteenth century, they were fairly numerous in counties Leitrim and Longford.

In the seventeenth century, a **Father Haslenane** is recorded as being a Franciscan in Louvain.

When Phelim O Byrne was a rebel hero operating in the glens of County Wicklow, a **Cormack O Heslenan** was arrested for trying to prevent a witness giving evidence against him.

There are very few representatives of the Heslin name now in the Republic of Ireland, and practically none at all in Northern Ireland.

Hewson *see* MacHugh

Hickey

Ó hÍcidhe

This ancient and very numerous surname means healer and, for generations, the bearers of this distinguished name were physicians to the kingly O Briens of Thomond in the counties Limerick and Clare.

They are very well recorded. Two of the still enduring branches of the original families are in *Burke's Irish Family Records* (1976). These were the Hickeys who were once physicians and were driven out by the Tudors, and the Hickies of Slevyre (now a convent) in County Tipperary, who have had outstanding careers in the armed forces of the former British Empire.

At home and abroad, there are innumerable distinguished Hickeys, many of whom settled in India, where they remained for generations. **Professor Anthony Hickey** (d. 1641), a Franciscan priest, presided over Irish colleges in Rome and Louvain.

In the eighteenth century, there were two Hickey brothers, **John**, a sculptor, and **Thomas**, a painter.

William Hickey (1749–1830) was an attorney who travelled widely and who wrote, both scandalously and amusingly.

Early in the eighteenth century, following the capitulation of Limerick, many Hickeys fled to France to serve in the Irish brigades. Also in the eighteenth century, **William Hickey**, a clergyman and philanthropist of Wexford, was a pioneer of agricultural education.

Dr. Michael O Hickey (1860–1916), a priest and professor of Irish at University College Dublin, was a fanatic believer in the revival of the Irish language by making it a compulsory subject, antagonizing even his bishop by his single-minded zeal.

Ballyhickey in County Clare was one of the principal seats of this family, who have many pedigrees in Dublin's Genealogical Office, including "A fabulous account of the origins of the name made in 1690."

(O) Higgins

Ó hUigín

Ó hUigín (*uigín* means knowledge) is an Irish name which was transformed into Higgins. It is not, however, connected with that name, which is also common in Britain. Originally they were of the same family as the Westmeath O Neills, but they later dispersed, mainly to County Sligo.

An outstanding literary family, for three centuries they were illustrious poets. Eight of them were among the best of their time. Following the suppression of the ancient culture, they changed to become prominent in the sciences.

In Chile, there is an O Higgins province named after **Bernardo O Higgins**, whose father was Viceroy of Peru, while Bernardo himself was known as the liberator of Chile.

The Higgins contributed two members to the list of Irish eccentrics. One was a cleric, **Reverend Francis Higgins** (1669–1728), who went to London, where he advocated sedition from the pulpit and kept a brothel. The other, also a **Francis Higgins** (1726–1802), and known as the "Sham Squire", made his money by manipulating the law and journalism, and by marriage to a wealthy lady whom he deceived into believing that he was of the landed gentry! He also made money by gambling, and probably by collecting the £1,000 reward offered for informing on Lord Edward FitzGerald.

Kevin O Higgins, patriot and founder of the Civic Guards, was shot dead in 1927.

Alex "Hurricane" Higgins (b. 1950) from Belfast is renowned for his top-class snooker playing.

The O Higgins heraldry is unusual, having three black towers on a black strip across the shield, which is speckled black. A demi-griffin, sword in claw, emerges from the black tower on the crest.

Hill

Cnoch

Hill is a very numerous name, whose topographical origin is obvious. In Ireland it is to be found mainly in Ulster, where Hills came as soldiers or planters. Cnoch (*cnoc* is the Irish word for hill) was the surname of an old Irish family whose name had been anglicized to Hill. A somewhat similar surname, MacCnogher, has been anglicized to Hillyer, Heller and Hillers.

Hill is the family name of the Marquis of Downshire, or, to accord him his full appellation, **Arthur Wells John Wellington Blundell Trumbell Sandys Rodes Hill**, Earl and Viscount of Hillsborough, Viscount Kilwarlin and Baron Hill of Kilwarlin. Through the generations, the family made many advantageous marriages, which explains the plurality of surnames.

The progenitor of this powerful Ulster family was **Sir Moyses Hill**, who came to Ireland with the English army in 1573 to suppress Hugh O Neill's rebellion against Queen Elizabeth's rule. He distinguished himself as a soldier and magistrate, and married Alice, a sister of the great Scottish chieftain, Sorley Boy MacDonnell. A descendant of his distinguished himself by wounding Oliver Cromwell. Another was created Marquess of Downshire in 1789 for his contribution towards trade and the plantations. Their family home, Hillsborough Castle in County Down, became the seat of the government of the Six Counties until it was abolished in 1973. Hillsborough is one of the prettiest villages in Ulster.

Hill Mount in County Antrim was built by the Hills who had a linen bleaching mill there. In the nineteenth century, a Hill family of architects based in County Cork designed many fine houses in that locality.

Derek Hill (b. 1916), portrait painter, stage designer, gardener and organizer of exhibitions worldwide, has donated his beautiful home, St. Columb's in County Donegal, to the nation. It is a focus for his wide-ranging collection of paintings and *objets d'art*. It was he who "discovered" the naïve painters of Donegal and introduced their work to the contemporary world of art.

Hodges, Hodgeson *see* Hodgins

Hodgins

Hodges Hodgeson Hodgkins

This English name derives from an English pet name for Roger, "Hodge". Very numerous in Ireland since the seventeenth century, the Hodgins (sometimes Hodgeson) probably came to Ireland with the Cromwellian armies, rather than the plantations, for they are not numerous in Northern Ireland.

In the National Library of Ireland in Dublin, there are records of a number of wills relating to the Hodges family, who seem to have been wealthy Dublin merchants in County Dublin. A **Henry Hodges** owned the well-known hostelry, The Yellow House, at Rathfarnham, in the nineteenth century. A **William Hodges** owned Millton House.

There are abstracts of wills of Hodges of London and Shanagolden in County Limerick dated 1655 to 1788. A letter of 1675 was from **John Hodges** of Dublin, who wanted to create free ports in Ireland for supplying English ships. In 1703, a **Richard Hodges** was admitted to the freedom of Kilkenny.

The British Museum in London has a diary which was kept by **T. L. Hodges**, a captain in the West Kent Militia serving in the south of Ireland during the 1798 Rebellion. It is an account of his social life, for he took no part in the fighting.

The Genealogical Office holds a pedigree of Hodgins of Ballymackey, County Tipperary, dating from 1770 to 1907.

There are many variations of the name, including Hodge, Hodges, Hodgeson, Hodgin, Hodgins, Hodgings and Hodgkins!

Hodgkins *see* Hodgins

Hoey *see* Keogh

(O) Hogan

Ó hÓgáin

Hogan comes from the Irish word *óg*, meaning young. There were three Ó hÓgáin septs, the more important one descending from Casrach, an uncle of Brian Boru, the last high king of all Ireland.

The Hogans—the O prefix has been mostly lost—have made history in a variety of ways.

Maurice O Hogan was Bishop of Kildare from 1281 to 1298.

"Galloping Hogan" has joined the ranks of the folk heroes for his co-operation with Patrick Sarsfield in blowing up the English ammunition train at Ballyneety in 1690.

Michael Hogan (1823–99), known as the "Bard of Thomond", began life in his native Limerick as a wheelwright but soon found his métier to be writing popular verse based on ancient legends.

In America, in 1858, **Father John Hogan** began building a settlement to house the poor Irish labourers in the railway camps of St. Louis. Cut short by the Civil War, it was never completed, leaving only the name—the Irish Wilderness.

A most illustrious Hogan was **John Hogan** (1800–58) of Waterford. His artistic talent was recognized by philanthropists, who sent him to Rome to study sculpture. There he settled and received many commissions, until revolution broke out in 1848 and he had to leave Rome. Back in Ireland, after a difficult start he received many commissions to sculpt famous people of the day, including Father Mathew and Daniel O Connell.

Edmund Hogan (1831–1917) of Cork, a professor of Irish and history, made an invaluable contribution to Irish history with his *Onamastican Goeddelicum*, an index of Gaelic names and tribes.

Patrick Hogan (1886–1969) of County Clare fought in the Irish War of Independence and afterwards became the first Minister of Agriculture in the new Irish Free State. He was also called to the Bar.

Sir Michael Hogan (d. 1986) of Dublin, a man of outstanding intellect and an all-round sportsman, was a lawyer with an international reputation who filled many exalted posts, including, for a while, Officer Administering the Government of Malaya and Chief Justice of Hong Kong. In recognition of his services, he was awarded many high honours.

Desmond Hogan (b. 1951) is an actor, teacher and writer.

see also Fagan

Hogg *see* (O) Hagan

Holden

The name Holden means residence in a narrow valley. In Bardsley's dictionary of surnames, Holden is described as "an estate in the parish of Haslingdon in the County of Lancashire from which a family name spread worldwide". At times, Holden has been confused with the Welsh name Howlin. The Holdens must have come to Ireland in the sixteenth century, for there is a record in the British Museum of an election of a **Thomas Holden** as Canon of St. Thomas the Martyr in Dublin.

In 1681, the marriage of **Walter Holden** of Killyon, County Meath, is recorded. In the seventeenth century there were also Holdens in County Kilkenny, where there was a Holdenstown, as there was also in County Wicklow.

In 1805, one of *Holden's Triennial Directories* was published.

Smollet Holden of Waterford, who died in 1813, composed military music and moved to Dublin, where he made instruments and edited several music publications. His son, **Francis Holden**, a Doctor of Music, assisted the distinguished George Petrie in the collection of Irish airs.

The name Holden is quite numerous in Ireland today.

Holland *see* Houlihan

Horgan

Ó hArgáin

Arragan Hourigan

Horgan, in Irish Ó hArgáin, is almost exclusively connected with Munster, particularly counties Cork and Kerry. When some of this sept moved to Limerick, the name became Hourigan, while in the counties of Waterford and Tipperary it has sometimes evolved to Arragan. They were also an important family in County Kerry—important enough to have four townlands named after them—all Ballyhorgan!

There is a record of a pardon granted in 1551 to **David O Horegane** of Leix (Laois). He was a kern—a lightly armed Irish soldier.

The **Reverend Matthew Horgan** (1777–1849), parish priest and a native of Whitechurch in County Cork, was not only a poet and a Gaelic scholar of distinction, but also a learned antiquary.

A map of a survey of Finure in the barony of Imokilly in County Cork was drawn up to show that this land was transferred by lease to **Daniel Horgan** *c.*1794. The Horgan family of County Cork, where the name is very numerous, were very active in politics at the time of Charles Stewart Parnell, and also in the nineteenth and twentieth century. The family holds many letters from leading statesmen.

John Horgan (1881–1967), a County Cork solicitor, was chairman of Cork Harbour Commissioners and played an important role in public affairs. He supported the Gaelic League and was an active patron of the arts. He wrote a number of books including, in 1918, the notorious *The Complete Grammar of Anarchy*, the first edition of which was confiscated by the British government.

(O) Houlihan

Ó hUallacháin

Holland Nolan Whoolahan

Ó hUallacháin, an old Gaelic name, derives from the Irish word *uallach*, meaning proud. There were two septs, one in County Offaly and the other which spread throughout Connacht, where they were chiefs of the Síol Anmchadha. According to a census of 1659, the Ó hUallacháins seem to have moved in great numbers to County Kilkenny. In County Offaly, the O Holohans shared the lordship of clan Colgan with the O Hennessys.

Through the centuries, the name Ó hUallacháin, apart from being anglicized to Houlihan, suffered no less than seventeen variations, including Oulcháin and Whoolahan, while in Connacht, for some unknown reason, the name was transformed to Nolan, and even to Holland—an English name.

Their greatest celebrity was **Dermot O Holohan** who, when Donal O Sullivan Beare (1560–1618) was making his epic march to his friends in Ulster following the battle of Kinsale, helped him build the bridge at Portumna which allowed O Sullivan Beare and his followers to escape from their pursuers.

Many Houlihans moved south to County Cork, where they anglicized their name to Holland. **John Holland** (1841–1914), the American inventor, was from County Clare.

John Houlihan came from the Ó hUallacháin family of County Kildare. He was one of the leaders of the United Irishmen in Kildare during the 1798 Rebellion, in which his son, **Simon Houlihan**, was killed. This John's grandson, **Richard Houlihan** (b. 1822) left Dublin for the USA in 1849, eventually becoming a major with the Irish Legion and fighting in the Civil War. Afterwards he served in the Treasury Department in Washington DC. Many of his descendants are still in the USA.

Hourigan *see* Horgan

Houston *see* Hutchinson

Howley

Ó hUallaigh

Whooley

The old Irish surname, Ó hUallaigh (*uallach* means proud), has been anglicized to Howley and, in some cases, Whooley. It can also be an English name, though this is rare. There was an Archbishop of Canterbury in 1842 called **William Howley**.

Robert Howley, who was an abbot of Mothel in County Waterford, is recorded as granting land to E. B. Power in 1440.

John Howley is listed as an officer in Butler's infantry regiment, in the service of the army of King James II. There were also at least two other Howley officers serving in this regiment, which was based in the counties of Kilkenny and Tipperary.

William Howley was the parish priest of Fethard in County Tipperary and was the vicar-general of the archdiocese of Cashel in about 1744.

Henry Howley of Roscrea, County Tipperary, was executed for his part in the rising led by Robert Emmet in 1803.

Early in the nineteenth century, **John Howley** of Rich Hill, Limerick, married a daughter of William O Shea, also of Limerick, who had close family connections with several grandee families in Spain. John Howley and his wife had three sons.

Howley is a common name throughout Ireland, with the exception of the province of Ulster, where it is rarely found.

Hoy *see* Keogh

Hughes

Ó hAodha

Hayes (O) Hea

Hughes is a most numerous name in England and in Ireland, particularly in Ulster. It probably derives from one of the many saints of the name. A noble family of Wales, originally from Normandy, the Hughes came to Ireland with the Cromwellians and acquired considerable confiscated land, both in Ulster and in counties Tipperary and Wexford.

It would be impossible now to distinguish the former Welsh Hughes in Ireland from the Irish Ó hAodhas who anglicized their name to Hughes. In fact, there are said to be at least twelve distinct septs of Ó hAodha. O Hea and Hayes are a few of the more usual variants.

In the archives there are a number of manuscripts setting out the pedigrees of the Hughes of County Wexford, dating from 1580 to 1950, and the Hughes of County Tipperary, dating from 1640 to 1820. In 1694 a number of priests, including **Father James Hughes**, were accused of smuggling spies and deserters through Rotterdam on merchant ships.

A Hughes family has been settled for centuries in County Wexford. One of this family, **Sir Frederick Hughes** of Ely House, was a Knight of the Persian Order of the Lion and Sun. His father, **Robert Hughes**, had been Baron of the Exchequer, and several of the family were mayors of Wexford. Many were military men who served abroad in India and the Far East.

The Hughes name also features among those who served in the Irish-American brigades in the American Civil War.

Reverend John Hughes (1797–1864), the son of a family who had emigrated from County Tyrone to New York, was a dynamic administrator who cared for the famine-stricken Irish exiles in his city. He was founder of Fordham University and he laid the foundation stone of St. Patrick's Cathedral in New York.

John Hughes (1865–1941) of Dublin was one of Ireland's leading sculptors.

In the nineteenth and twentieth centuries, the Ó hAodha name has been distinguished by many Gaelic scribes and poets, including **Micheál Ó hAodha** (b. 1918), the poet and playwright and Abbey Theatre director who came from County Clare.

Hunt

Ó Fiachna

This common English surname probably came to Ireland with the Cromwellians and is now found all over Ireland. In Ulster, it is usually of English origin, but in the rest of the country, particularly in Connacht, it can be an anglicization of the Irish word *fiach*, meaning hunt. As a reward for their services to the Crown, the military Hunts were granted much land during the Williamite confiscations.

From early in the seventeenth century, the Hunt pedigrees are well recorded in Dublin's Genealogical Office, showing the extent of their land holdings, most of which were in Munster.

In 1749, **Lieutenant-General John Hunt** of St. George's Regiment of Dragoons is recorded as having taken the oaths and subscribed to the declaration against popery. In 1787, a **Sir John Hunt** became a freemason.

In the Genealogical Office in Dublin, there is a record of 1911 of a confirmation of arms to the descendants of **Captain John Hunt**, including **Surgeon Colonel Samuel Hunt** of Limerick, grandson of **Vere Hunt** of Friarstown in County Limerick. These descendants moved to Winnipeg, Canada, in 1932.

In 1756, the **Right Honourable Percival Hunt** was Lord Mayor of Dublin.

Sir Vere Hunt of Limerick, who succeeded to the baronetcy in 1818, adopted the name **de Vere**. A popular landlord and a poet, he was father of the famous **Aubrey de Vere** (1814–1901) of Curragh Chase, County Limerick, a prolific poet and a brother of **Stephen de Vere**, who wrote *The Snowy Breasted Pearl.*

John Hunt (1900–76), who was born in County Clare, was an outstanding scholar of medieval sculpture and an antiquarian who inspired the restoration of many ancient sites and castles, including Bunratty Castle. He bequeathed his collection of antiquities to the National Institute of Higher Education in Limerick, now the University of Limerick.

Hunter

Hunter, or Hunt, is a common name both in England and in Ireland, where it is particularly numerous in north Ulster, which suggests that the Hunters may have come during the plantations. Le Hunt, or Hunter, is thought to be of Norman derivation, though there are no genealogies to confirm this.

Other Hunters settled in Ireland when the Cromwellian armies were disbanded.

There were Hunters serving in the Irish-American brigades in the United States.

Alexander Hunter (fl. 1777), a medical doctor, wrote on geology and published recipes for “modern cookery with medical commentary”.

John Hunter served in the British navy, where he rose to the rank of admiral.

In the nineteenth century, **Sir William Wells Hunter** served in the government of India. About the same time, there were a number of scholarly Hunters in Ireland. **Arthur J. Hunter**, a linguist, translated from many languages, including Latin and Greek.

H. Hunter, probably a plant biologist, wrote extensively in Ulster journals on how to improve the flax and cereal crops in Ulster.

In the 1940s, **Barbara Hunter** was a popular Ulster poet.

A number of Hunters emigrated from Ulster to the USA, including **Thomas Hunter** (1831–1915), who left Ardglass for New York, where he became an outstanding teacher and founded the first high school. Hunter College is called after him.

Whiteside Godfrey Hunter (1841–1919) of Belfast, a physician, emigrated to the USA, where he served as a Union soldier and became a Kentucky legislator. For several years he was Minister to Guatemala and Honduras.

Hurley

Ó hUrthuile Ó Muirthile

Commane

There are two Hurley septs, the Ó hUrthuile of Clare and the Ó Muirthile of Cork. The name comes from Urley, an extinct first name. A very ancient Gaelic family, the Hurleys of Clare claim descent from the Dalcassians, one of the earliest, most powerful septs of Thomond in south-west Ireland. They were chiefs of Knocklong in Limerick, where the remains of their castle and church can still be seen. In Limerick and Tipperary, where they moved in the fourteenth century, their other headquarters were at Rath Hurley and Killcullane Castle.

When Sir John Perrot, who was executed for treason in 1592, was Lord Deputy in Ireland during Elizabethan times, **Thomas Hurley** of Knocklong served in his parliament.

In the churchyard at Emly, County Tipperary, a gravestone inscribed in Latin commemorates **Maurice Hurley**, who died in 1632. It also shows an oak tree, the ancient seal of the Clare O Hurleys. A namesake, **Sir Maurice Hurley** of Knocklong, was a member of the Supreme Council of Kilkenny in 1647 when the Irish tried vainly to oust the usurpers.

With the arrival of the ruthless Cromwellians in 1649, O Hurley lands were forfeited and many were transplanted to Connacht, while others followed the military profession in the army of the Stuart King, James II.

Hurleys also went to America, where a **Major Hurley** and a **Lieutenant Hurley** were on the medical staff of the Irish brigades between 1861 and 1865.

In the late 1600s, there was an unsavoury Hurley, **Patrick Hurley** of Clare, who ennobled himself as "Count of Mountcallan" in order to conceal his infamous career as informer and racketeer.

During the height of the religious persecutions in the sixteenth century, three Hurleys suffered martyrdom: **Dermot, Archbishop of Cashel; Thomas, Bishop of Ross** and the Franciscan brother, **Donagh O Muirthile**. Even in the twentieth century, **Dr. Denis Hurley**, Catholic Archbishop of Durban, barely escaped prosecution by the South African government in 1985.

During the anglicization of Irish names, one Hurley family emerged as Commane—the Irish for the hurley stick is *camán*! The Hurleys are very numerous in County Cork and are well recorded by their kinsmen.

see also Cummins

(O) Hussey

Ó hEodhusa

de Hosey

The Husseys, originally from Normandy, came to Ireland with Strongbow in around 1169. They were given generous grants of lands in counties Dublin and Meath, where they assumed the title of Barons of Galtrim.

Sir Hugh Hussey received a knighthood of Palatine origin which was not recognized in England. Succeeding generations continued to use this title.

The Ó hEodhusa of Connacht were hereditary bards to the MacGuires of Fermanagh. **Eochaidh O Hussey** (1569–1612) was the last of these bards.

Bonaventura O Hussey left Ireland to become one of the first Franciscans in the Irish College at Louvain in Belgium.

The Husseys supported the deposed James II, with the result that they suffered much persecution, losing their estates and being forced to flee abroad. Their names appear on the rolls of the many Irish regiments in France in the seventeenth century.

They are also well recorded in the Genealogical Office in Dublin, including a grant of a quartering of arms in the name of **Valentine John Hussey** of Mal Hussey in County Roscommon and Canby in France, for his wife Ellen O Brien.

In 1695, a **Colonel Maurice Hussey** reported discontent among the Irish officers in France. He also did some intelligence gathering, for which he regularly asked payment.

Walter Hussey was sheriff of Kerry in 1602, an area to which some of the Husseys had migrated.

Philip Hussey (1713–83) of Cork was a popular painter in Dublin.

Thomas Hussey (1741–1803) was Bishop of Waterford and Lismore.

Dermot Hussey is the financial controller of a large group of companies, while his wife, Gemma, was very active in politics and was a former Minister of Education.

Hutchinson

Mac Úistin

Houston Kitchen MacCutcheon

The Hutchinsons originated in Scotland, where they were known as Mac Úisdin, while in Irish they were Mac Úistin, meaning little Hugh. Many of this name settled in Ulster. Apart from Hutchinson, the name has had at least nine different anglicizations, including MacWhiston, Houston, Kitchen and, probably the most numerous, MacCutcheon.

In Great Britain, there have been many distinguished bearers of the Hutchinson name. Their lineage in Ireland can be traced to a family in Derby, England, two of whose sons settled in Ulster, where **Dr. Francis Hutchinson** (d. 1720) was Bishop of Down and Connor. **Samuel Hutchinson** (d. 1748) of Portglenone was with Lord Forbe's Regiment at the battle of the Boyne. His four sons and their descendants were distinguished churchmen and wealthy landowners.

Francis Hutchinson of Castle Sallagh in County Wicklow was made a baronet of Ireland in 1782. This family became associated with the distinguished Synge family by marriage and assumed their name. Christina, a wealthy daughter of the family, married the provost of Trinity College Dublin, who added her name to his. He was the famous **John Hely-Hutchinson** (1724–98), whose descendants are the Earls of Donoughmore, County Tipperary.

Francis Hutchinson (1694–1746) was born in County Down and educated in Edinburgh, where he became one of the most esteemed philosophers of his day. It was he who coined the phrase "the greatest happiness to the greatest number".

Today, the Hutchinsons and the MacCutcheons are still numerous in Northern Ireland.

Hyland

Ó Faoláin Ó hAoileáin

Heelan Phelan Whelan

Ó hAoileáin and Ó Faoláin (Phelan or Whelan) seem to come from the same root, *faol*, meaning a wolf. Although not numerous, Hyland is distributed all over Ireland, including Ulster. There are records which suggest that it could have originated in Laois and Offaly in the sixteenth century.

There is an account of leases in County Waterford being granted between 1483 and 1485 by a **David Hyland**.

In Dublin's National Library, a manuscript records abstracts of wills of a family of Hylan and Hyland of Dublin city and of County Kildare, dating between 1731 and 1795.

During the American Civil War, **Captain Joseph Hyland** served in the 88th New York Volunteers.

Hyland's Mammoth Hibernian Songster: Over Five Hundred Songs Dear to the Irish Heart was published in Chicago, USA, in 1901.

Because of the differing pronunciations in Munster, Hyland can also be found as Heelan, while in Ulster Ó hAoileáin has sometimes been anglicized to Holland.

Hynds *see* Hynes

Hynes

Ó hEidhin

Hynds (O) Heyne

Eidhean is the Irish word for ivy, from which the leading sept of Hynes took their surname.

Ó hEidhin was a descendant of Guaire the Hospitable King of Connacht. The chief of the O Heynes shared with his kinsmen, the O Shaughnessys, the lordship of Aidhne, a territory which stretched from Gort to Oranmore. **Mulroy O Heyne**, Lord of Aidhne, was the father-in-law of King Brian Boru. With the O Kellys he commanded the Connacht forces at the battle of Clontarf in 1014.

From the seventh to the early eighteenth century, the head of the O Heynes was chief of a territory in south Galway in the barony of Kiltartan—an area made famous by the writings of Lady Gregory, friend of W. B. Yeats.

In 1608, the O Heynes owned 8,640 acres near Kinvara in County Galway. As recently as 1878, the head of the O Heynes family is recorded as owning 4,169 acres near Ballinasloe, also in County Galway. Apart from being outstanding landowners, the Hynes do not often appear in the records. They were, however, remarkable for an abundance of missionary priests.

In the twentieth century, **Garry Hynes** is an outstanding representative of the Hynes family. With dynamic enthusiasm, she has raised theatre in Galway to an international level with the groundbreaking Druid theatre company.

Hynes is now a very numerous name throughout Ireland.

I

Igoe

Jacob Jago MacIago MacKigo

This surname, which originated in Cornwall in south-west England, has a variety of synonyms, including Jago and Jacob. It has been known in Ireland since the sixteenth century as either MacEgo or MacKigo and, sometimes, MacIago.

Branches of this family are to be found in Counties Cork and Roscommon. In County Longford, the O Hanlys were kindred of the Igoes. Today Igoe is a rare surname, and no more than a couple of dozen are to be found in Ireland and, probably, none at all in Ulster.

In the Act of Settlement and the Act of Explanation, both passed in the reign of Charles II (1660–85), there is mention of **Charles Igoe** having been granted land in Ireland.

In 1920, *Notes of Jago Families of Cornwall, Cork and Dublin* was compiled by H. Guinness, who had a theory that they were allied to the Guinness family.

Jago is as rare in Ireland as Igoe. There is a pub in Ballybrack, County Dublin, called the Igo Inn, but that is probably no more than a play on words!

Irvine, Irving *see* Irwin

Irwin

Ó hEireamhóin

Ervine Irvine Irving

Irwin and its variants, Irvine, Irving and Ervine, although numerous throughout Ireland, is concentrated in counties Armagh and Antrim. Edward MacLysaght, the authority on genealogy, says that "Although a sept of O Hirwen, i.e. Ó hEireamhóin, did exist in County Offaly, nearly all Irwins in Ulster and County Roscommon are of planter stock, their name being derived from the Old-English *oforwine*, boar friend." He suggests that, although the Irvine and Ervine variants have been confused with Irwin, they are in fact of Scottish origin and were established in Ulster in the seventeenth century.

The Irwins were undoubtedly an influential family who, as recently as the nineteenth century, held thousands of acres in Ulster and County Roscommon. Their pedigrees are very well recorded in the Genealogical Office, particularly the Irwins who came to Roscommon *c.*1580, some of whom emigrated to America *c.*1650.

In the eleventh century, **Aedh (Hugh) Ó hEireamhóin** was Bishop of Kildare, while **Dr. Alexander Irwin** (d. 1779) was Bishop of Killala in County Mayo.

On the whole, the Irwins were military men. In the archives there are letters written in French regarding a plan by an Irwin for raising a battalion of

Irish Catholics in 1760. **Lieutenant-General Sir John Irwin**, commander-in-chief of the land forces in Ireland, expressed his concern, in a report of *c.*1766, about recruiting Roman Catholics to fight in America.

William Irvine (b. 1740) came from Fermanagh and was prominent in the American War of Independence. A **Colonel Irwin** was acting Governor of West Australia *c.*1848.

Mount Irwin was one of a string of Irwin mansions scattered across the north of Ireland. In *Burke's Irish Family Records* (1976) there is a full pedigree of the family, beginning with **Robert Irwin,** one of whose seats in 1580 was Rathmoyle in County Roscommon.

Ivers *see* MacKeever

J

Jacob, **Jago** *see* Igoe

Jennings

Mac Sheóinín

In Ireland, the name comes from the Norman Burkes of Connacht. The Irish version is Mac Sheóinín, meaning son of Seónín (Little John) Burke, which was anglicized to Jennings. The name Jennings is numerous in Britain too, also meaning Little John.

From 1441 to 1450, **John Jennings** was Archbishop of Tuam in Connacht.

They are a well-documented family, with pedigrees showing their descent from Charlemagne to Burke to Jennings, from 814 to 1911. The Irish Genealogical Office holds many of their pedigrees, and abstracts of wills from 1579 to 1793 of Jennings in England, Ireland and the USA. Among their many letters is one from **Gabriel Jennings**, complaining of his imprisonment in Dublin.

Up to the late sixteenth century, they owned extensive property, including Dunmore in County Galway and Kilmaine in County Mayo.

Charles Edward Jennings (*c.*1752–99), Lord Kilmaine, a distinguished soldier in the French service during the Revolution, chose his title from his homeland. His brother, **Father James Jennings**, was imprisoned during the French Revolution.

Sir William Jennings is recorded as "coming with King James II out of France" to Ireland, where he fought at the battle of the Boyne. After that defeat, many Irishmen joined the Irish brigades in France. **Lieutenant-Colonel Ulick Jennings** and **Lieutenant Ulick Albert Jennings**, both of Ironpool in County Galway, were descendants of Sir William Jennings.

Sir Patrick A. Jennings (1830–77), who was born in Newry, County Down, was Governor of New South Wales.

Johnston

Johnson

This is a numerous surname, especially in Ulster, where there are twenty columns in the Northern Ireland telephone directory. In every part of Ireland, the spelling Johnston outnumbers Johnson. The name is of Scottish origin, but it can sometimes be a translation of MacShane, a branch of the powerful O Neills of Ulster.

From this family probably came the famous **William Johnson** of County Meath (1715–74) who was taken by his uncle to North America, where he became a colonel in the army fighting the French colonists. He was an able mediator with the Indian tribes and was created a baronet.

The Johnstons are well recorded in *Burke's Irish Family Records*, where **Richard Graves Johnston** (b. 1914) of County Armagh claims to be a descendant of the senior branch of the Scottish house of Annandale who first came to Ireland in *c.*1626 as ministers of the Scottish kirk.

A **Colonel Johnston**, with other officers under Lord Inchiquin, was shot in Cork in 1680 for deserting from the Cromwellian forces.

General Christopher Johnson of County Meath was in the service of the emperor of Germany in 1802.

In Ulster, there were Johnsons who were linen merchants, Orangemen, government officials and mayors of Belfast in the nineteenth century.

Francis Johnston (1760–1829) moved from his native Armagh to Dublin, where, as architect to the Board of Works, he designed many of the finest buildings still to be seen in the capital city, including the GPO building which was the focus of the Easter Rising in 1916.

Joseph Johnston (1890–1972) of County Tyrone was an economist with an international reputation who pioneered agricultural economics.

Denis Johnston (1901–84), son of a supreme court judge, was a barrister, director of the Gate Theatre, the BBC's war correspondent and its director of programmes. He was also a major Irish playwright. His daughter, **Jennifer Johnston** (b. 1930), is also a playwright and a prolific and popular novelist.

Jones

Mac Seóin

Johnson Jonson

Jones is one of the most numerous names in England and Wales. Originating in Wales, it has been translated into Irish as Mac Seóin, meaning son of John. It can also be represented by Johnson or Jonson.

The Jones came to Ireland with Cromwell's army and were given forfeited land to make up for arrears of pay. For compiling a record of Cromwell's campaign in Ireland, **Dr. Henry Jones** was awarded a yearly £200 from 1650.

Sir Theophilus Jones, a soldier of the Commonwealth, settled in Limerick. He was one of the three hundred Members of Parliament who, in 1797, represented Ireland in the Irish House of Commons.

The Jones are to be found in every part of the country. In the eighteenth and nineteenth century, there were a number of talented men of this name. **Henry Jones** (1721–70) of Drogheda, who began his working life as a bricklayer, was encouraged to develop his literary talents. He became a successful poet and playwright in London, until his dissipated life caused his downfall. A wagon ran over him and killed him outside the theatre.

Frederick Edward Jones, a wealthy high society man, had little success as a theatre manager. However, his extravagant personality captivated the Dubliners and they named Jones' Road, on the city's northside, after him.

John Edward Jones (1806–62) of Dublin was an engineer and sculptor. He became fashionable for his sculpted busts and was even commissioned to do one of Queen Victoria. **Sir Thomas Alfred Jones** (1823–93), a foundling, became one of the most popular and esteemed portrait painters.

Henry MacNaughten Jones (1845–1918) of Cork, a surgeon, was involved in the founding of several new hospitals there and wrote a best-selling textbook, *Diseases of Women*. The family of **Mark Bence-Jones**, a prolific writer and architectural historian, has been settled in Cork for generations. The Bence-Jones family occupies a record thirteen pages in *Irish Family Records*.

Kenneth Jones (b. 1936) is an engineer, turned organ builder, in County

Wicklow. His company exports worldwide and is on the road to becoming the world's top organ builder. The cathedral of the Madelaine in Salt Lake City, Utah, and the university church in Cambridge, England, contain examples of his work.

Jordan

Mac Siúrtáin

MacJordan

This ancient surname has a long and well-recorded history in Ireland, where it is very numerous. It is said to have originated at the time of the Crusades. The family who came to Ireland adopted the name to commemorate an ancestor who fought in a battle between the Christians and the Saracens on the banks of the River Jordan. The Jordans came from England to Ireland, and were known as d'Exeter, from the town from which they came. To integrate with the Irish, many changed their name to Mac Siúrtáin. They built castles and churches, and for many years they possessed much land in Connacht.

In Mayo, they anglicized their name to MacJordan. Their Mac Siúrtáin chieftain had his residence at Athleathan, near Gallen, an area known as MacJordan's Country. There was also a Jordan's Castle at Ardglass, County Down, which **Simon Jordan** defended for three years when it was besieged by rebels in 1611.

Jordan pedigrees include **Father Fulgentius Jordan**, a priest of the Augustinian Order who was martyred in 1652.

During the seventeenth-century rebellions, much of their lands were forfeited. Some went abroad, and there is mention of a **Jordan of Mervani** in France and a **Don Edmundo**, a colonel in the service of the Duke of Lorraine in Spain.

Dorothea Jordan of Waterford (1762–1816), a popular actress in London who adopted the name Jordan, became notorious as the mistress of William IV (formerly the Duke of Clarence). She bore him five sons and five daughters, all of whom took the name FitzClarence. The eldest was created the Earl of Munster.

Kate Jordan (1862–1926), the American novelist and playwright, was born in Ireland. **John Jordan** (b. 1930) is one of Dublin's poets, critics and novelists.

Neil Jordan, born in 1951 in Sligo, has won a number of prestigious literary awards and has directed several films, including *Company of Wolves*, *The Crying Game* and *Michael Collins*.

Joyce

Seoigh

Jorse Joyes

The Joyce name came to Ireland with the Normans in the twelfth century. Scholars believe their name derives from the French personal name, Joie, which, of course, means joy. On arrival, they lost no time in marrying high-born ladies of Connacht, where they settled and multiplied. A part of Connemara even became known as Joyce Country. As prosperous merchants who were numbered among the Fourteen Tribes of Galway, they were many times mayor of that city. They have always been renowned for their tall stature.

There were many distinguished Joyce churchmen, one even contributing to the founding of the Dominican College at Louvain.

A **William Joyce**, while travelling in Europe, was captured by Saracens and, when he escaped, was led by an eagle to buried treasure which, when he got home, he used to build the walls of Galway city. His granddaughter, known as **Margaret Joyce** and nicknamed Margaret na Drehide (of the bridges), built bridges all over Connacht while her husband was away trading in Spain. She also encountered an eagle, which dropped a rare jewel into her lap. This is why the Joyces have two eagles on their coat of arms.

Another Joyce spent many years in captivity in Algeria, where he became a gold- and silversmith. On his return to Galway, his skill made him a wealthy man. It is thought that it was he who made the first of the famous Claddagh rings.

As the Joyces spread through Ireland, they produced a stream of scholars, historians, linguists and folklorists. One of the towering figures of English literature, **James Joyce** (1882–1941) of Dublin, was a poet, novelist, playwright and author of several famous books. *Ulysses* is possibly the most famous, and *Finnegans Wake* the most enigmatic, of his novels.

During the war, a sinister voice used to be heard on the radio, saying "Germany calling, Germany calling". This was the mysterious **William Joyce**, known as Lord Haw Haw, who was born in America of an Irish father and English mother. He embraced fascism and, when captured by the Allies, was convicted for treason and hanged for this crime.

The Joyce pedigrees are both international and fascinating. There are Joyces also in Britain, but they are not related to the Irish family.

K

Kane *see* Keane

Kavanagh

Caomhánach

Cavanagh MacMurrough

A famous branch of the MacMurroughs, Kavanagh is an important name in Irish history. It was the much-maligned **Dermot MacMurrough**, King of Leinster, who encouraged the Anglo-Norman invasion. His seat was at Ferns in County Wexford and he sent his son **Donal** to the nearby monks at Cill Caomháin (St. Kevin's Church) for his education. Donal changed his name to Caomhánach, which was anglicized to Kavanagh, a derivation of the saint's name, Kevin. Although he did not succeed to his father's title, he inherited much of Wexford and Carlow, where the Kavanaghs are still rooted. A later king of Leinster, **Art MacMurrough Kavanagh**, reigned for forty-two years and was succeeded in the title, until it was abolished by Henry VIII.

Following the Stuart cause to its bitter end, a number of Kavanaghs had followed the beaten path to Europe to join the armies of France and Austria, where they were remarkable for their stature no less than for their ability.

Borris Castle in Carlow is still the seat of the Kavanaghs, whose chief is styled **The MacMurrough Kavanagh**. Here, in the nineteenth century, was born the most outstanding of the many Art MacMurrough Kavanaghs. A thirteenth child, born with only rudimentary arms and legs, he was greatly encouraged by his mother and developed into a sportsman, a world traveller, a Member of Parliament and head of his illustrious family. He fathered seven children.

There have been a number of Kavanagh writers, but, in modern times, a man from a humble Monaghan farm, **Patrick Kavanagh** (1905–67), has been recognized as a leading twentieth-century Irish poet.

The fine Kavanagh Castle at Enniscorthy in County Wexford is now a museum.

A red lion with two red crescents below its feet forms the Kavanagh heraldic crest.

Kealy *see* (O) Kiely

Keane

Mac Catháin Ó Catháin

Kane (O) Cahan MacCloskey

This family name is an amalgam of several septs which originated from the personal name Cian. One sept, the Kanes, had their territory mainly in Ulster, while the Keanes are of Connacht and, more numerously, of Munster.

Several variations of the name were adopted. For instance, the descendants of **Bloskey O Kane**, who killed the heir of a king of Ulster, was an ancestor of the MacCloskeys, while Aibhne Ó Catháin's descendants are today's MacEvinneys—both families were from Derry. Ó Catháin was also anglicized to O Cahan. Their last chieftain, **Donnell Ballagh O Cahan**, died in the Tower of London in 1617.

A most distinguished harpist in the mid-eighteenth century was **Echlin O Kane**, who was invited to play at the courts of European royalty.

Many Kanes and Keanes commanded the armed forces in Europe and, later, the Middle East and India.

The celebrated actors, **Edmund Kean** and his son **Charles**, are members of a Waterford family. Despite deafness and other physical infirmities, Edmund Kean became the greatest Shakespearean actor of the nineteenth century, sometimes acting with his equally talented son.

Sir John Keane, who came from the titled Keane family of Cappoquin in Waterford, was, for twelve years, a member of the Irish Senate from its inception.

The popular publican and playwright, **John B. Keane** (b. 1928), is from Listowel in County Kerry. His play, *The Field*, was adapted as a successful film, starring Richard Harris as Bull McCabe. He has also written numerous novels and short stories, including *Durango* and *The Bodhrán Makers.*

The Kean, or Kane, family has produced a number of distinguished scientists and artists, as well as two of the many Irish bishops of Dubuque in Iowa.

Their armorial bearings are also many and varied, usually including stars, salmon, a cross, several heraldic beasts and, on the crest, a cat. Their motto is *Felis demulcta mitis* (The stroked cat is meek).

Kearney

Ó Cearnaigh   Ó Catharnaigh

Carney   Fox

To achieve brevity, coupled with clarity, in an account of this numerous family poses problems. Deriving from a number of septs, Kearney is now widespread.

The Ó Cearnaigh (*cearnach* means victorious) were of the Uí Fiachrach sept of Mayo, Sligo and south Galway. Another sept, that of the Dál gCais, inhabited Clare, Limerick and Tipperary. The name of these septs was anglicized to Carney or Kearney.

The Ó Catharnaigh (meaning warlike), whose name was anglicized to Kearney, were chiefs of Teffia and of Kilcoursey, in Meath. **Tadgh Ó Catharnaigh**, their chief, who died in 1084, was dubbed Sionnach, meaning The Fox. Since then, the head of that family (the current chief lives in Australia) has styled himself The Fox. Fox is sometimes an anglicization of Ó Catharnaigh.

They do not feature much in the records until the sixteenth century, when there were many important Kearney ecclesiastics, including an Archbishop of Cashel and an **Abbé Kearney** who was a royalist during the French Revolution.

Men bearing the names Carney, Kearney and Fox accompanied the retinue of James II. Several of the Fox and Kearney families fought with the Irish brigades in France, and one was killed at Fontenoy. They also held appointments in the French courts.

From the Kearneys who migrated to County Tipperary came a succession of politicians and lawyers, and several Members of Parliament.

Peadar Kearney, who was a house-painter and uncle of the playwright Brendan Behan, wrote the words of *A Soldier's Song*, the Irish national anthem.

The Kearneys owned a number of fine houses, mostly in Munster, including Arbutus Lodge in Cork city, which is now an award-winning restaurant and hotel. Garretstown House, which was built in Ballinspittle in County Cork in the eighteenth century, was never completed and is now a ruin.

The Kearneys, like the O Connells and the Nolans and other families living along the Irish coast, were said to have acquired their wealth by smuggling.

Kearns

Ó Céirín Ó Ciaráin

Kern (O) Kieran (O) Kerin

There is no letter *k* in the Irish alphabet—the letter *c* is its equivalent. Father Woulfe, who was an expert on Irish names, says that the name Kearns derives from Ó Céirín (*ciar* means black or swarthy). He describes the Ó Céiríns as ancient lords of Ciarraighe na-nAirne in the barony of Costelloe, County Mayo, and says that they were very widespread in the sixteenth century.

Dr. MacLysaght, the respected genealogist, also describes the Ó Céirín sept as owners of great areas of land in County Mayo. In time they moved further north, to Sligo and Donegal, during which time their name acquired a number of variations, including O Kieran, O Kerin, Kern, Kerrane.

Another thing to note is that "kern" is the word used to describe the lightly armed soldiers who accompanied their chieftains into action. However, as the Irish word for a kern is *ceithearnach*, one can only suppose that the name has been shortened to Céirín. Incidentally, Cairns, which was originally a Scottish place-name and has sometimes been substituted for Kieran, is a very numerous name in Ulster.

There are a number of legal papers and wills concerning the Kearns family in the Public Records Office in Dublin. In the National Library of Ireland, there is a letter dated 1695, stating that "**Mr. D. Kearnes**, barrister, is lately come out of Ireland to negotiate some grand affair for the republican party of that kingdom."

In Ennis Abbey, there is a tomb belonging to **Teige O Kerins**, who died in 1685.

A priest called **Moses Kearns** was hanged in Paris during the French Revolution. The rope broke and he was saved, only to be executed when he returned to Ireland as one of the leaders of the 1798 Rebellion.

William Henry Kearns (1764–1846) of Dublin was a violinist and composer.

Richard Kearns (1842–1916) emigrated with his family from County Meath to the USA, where he was involved with building railroads.

Keating

Céitinn

MacKetian

Some believe that the Keatings who came with the Anglo-Normans were originally from Brittany, where their name would have been Étienne. Other scholars suggest that they came from Wales and that their name might have been Cethyn. As many Normans passed through Wales before crossing to Ireland, there is something to be said for this theory. They settled where they landed, in County Wexford, before moving on to County Laois.

In the Bibliothèque Nationale in Paris, there is a pedigree of *c.*1575 to *c.*1750 relating to the Keatings, described as Barons of Nicholston, County Tipperary, and Baldwinston,

County Wexford, and also of Brittany in France.

From 1302 onwards, the Keatings had become a great sept in the Midlands, where they filled many administrative posts. In 1539, an indenture between Piers, Earl of Ormond, and **John Keating** agrees "that John Keating shall have a man's part of the leading of any kerns (soldiers) of the Earl in County Tipperary and in return the Earl will receive any goshawks breeding in the wood called Glenegarry". In 1542 a nest of goshawks was discovered!

Doctor Geoffrey Keating (1570–1644), alias **Seathrún Céitinn**, one of four priestly brothers of Tubbrid in County Tipperary, was educated abroad because of the penal laws. A great Irish scholar, he wrote a history of Ireland to refute scurrilous histories written by English historians.

John Keating (*c.*1635–95) was Lord Chief Justice and a Member of Parliament. Another branch of the family included **Maurice** and his son **Richard Keating**, both judges of the probate court in Ireland.

Anne, created **Baroness Keatinge** of the Papal States by Pope Pius in 1875, died unmarried. **Seán Keating** (1889–1977) was a remarkably fine painter of Connacht and its people.

Keaveney *see* Gaffney

(O) Keeffe

Ó Caoimh

The O Keeffes originated in Cork and there they remain. They descend from Caom (*caomh* means noble or gentle), the son of King Fionghuine of Munster who was slain in 902. At first they settled around Glanmore and Fermoy, until the Normans drove them further south, into the Duhallow barony, which subsequently became known as Pobal O Keeffe (of the O Keeffe People).

They had few outstanding characters until the seventeenth century, when **Owen O Keeffe**, a poet who was held in high regard, was elected president of the bards of north Munster. He abandoned the literary life to become parish priest of Doneraile, after the death of his wife.

In the wake of the defeat of King James II, they left for France, where many O Keeffe officers are recorded in the army lists. One, **Constantine O Keeffe**, had to send home for his pedigree, proving his aristocratic Irish lineage, in order to be accepted in an élite regiment. After several generations in France, their name was transformed from O Keeffe to Cuif.

With the abolition of the penal laws, some O Keeffes who had remained in Ireland, dropping the Irish O prefix from their name, came to the fore in the arts. **Daniel Keeffe** studied art with the Dublin Society and exhibited later in London's Royal Academy. Overwhelmed with his success in Dublin and London, he declared his Irishness by restoring the O to his name. However, this did not prohibit him from being granted a state pension when he grew old. His brother, **John Keeffe**, became an actor but was forced to give up when he lost his sight. Assisted by his novelist daughter, **Adelaide**, he wrote many popular plays, one of which, *Wild Oats*, was staged at London's National Theatre.

A number of O Keeffes, including the Lanigan O Keeffes, settled in Australia. **Eugene O Keeffe** of Bandon in Cork founded the successful Victoria Brewery there in 1861. He was also appointed president of a bank and was honoured for his charitable works by being appointed private chamberlain to the Pope.

Belle Isle in Tipperary and Glenville Park in Cork, two former O Keeffe mansions, are still standing but are no longer in the hands of the family.

Georgia O Keefe (1887–1986) was an acclaimed artist of New Mexico, USA.

Keegan *see* Egan

Keeley *see* (O) Kiely

Keenan

Ó Cianáin

Keenan, in Irish Ó Cianáin, is a numerous surname throughout Ireland, especially in Ulster, where it originated.

From the middle of the fourteenth century to the beginning of the sixteenth century, the Keenans distinguished themselves as ecclesiastics and historians to the Maguires in their territories encompassing the counties Fermanagh and Monaghan. Because of the traffic between Ulster and Scotland, the name is also to be found there.

In the eighteenth century, **John Keenan** was a popular harpist in Dungannon in County Tyrone. **Frank Keenan** (1858–1929) was the son of an Irish immigrant to the USA. From humble beginnings, he became a successful actor, playing in comedy and character parts both on stage and film. He married three times.

James Keenan (1838–1913), who described his father as an "Irish gentleman", was born in England but went to the USA at the age of fourteen. The Comstock silver find provided the basis for his career as a stock exchange speculator. He won and lost a series of fortunes, both in the money market and on the turf. He loved horses and bred many winners.

Thomas Keenan (1860–1927), an actor and entertainer, using the nom de plume Tom Conway, wrote a stream of popular ballads: "Mother Machree", "If You're Irish, Come Into the Parlour", "Hello Patsy Fagan", etc.

Sir Patrick Keenan (1829–94) was Chief Commissioner of National Education in Ireland. **Sir Norbert Keenan**, who was born in Dublin in 1866, emigrated to Australia to become one of that country's leading statesmen. **Joseph Keenan** (b. 1900) was an authority on thermodynamics.

Around 1986, **Brian Keenan**, a Belfast teacher, was kidnapped in Beirut, Lebanon, for over four years. Much of his imprisonment was spent in solitary confinement. After his eventual release, he wrote an extraordinary book, *An Evil Cradling*, describing his harrowing ordeal.

Kehoe *see* Keogh

Keily *see* (O) Kiely

Kelleher

Ó Céileachair

Keller

The surname Ó Céileachair derives from *céileach*, an Irish word meaning companion. The first to use the surname was Céileachair, son of Dunchuan, brother of Brian Boru, the 175th monarch of Ireland who died at Clontarf in 1014. The Ó Céileachairs were of the great Dalcassian sept of County Clare and, in the fourteenth century, they migrated to counties Kerry and Cork where they owned much land up to the sixteenth century and are still very numerous.

The original Kelleher pedigree has been lost, but it is known that a Kelleher parish priest of Glanworth in County Cork represented the senior branch of the sept. A younger branch was headed by another Corkman, Alderman Keller. Although Keller is a common Austrian or German name, it has sometimes been used as a misspelling of Kelleher.

Donogh O Kelleher, who succeeded St. Kiernan of Saiger as Bishop of Ossory, died in 1048. Several Kellehers served in the Irish-American brigade, under General Thomas Francis Meagher, in the American Civil War.

Early in the twentieth century, following the Irish literary revival, there were many Kelleher poets, mostly writing in Irish.

Daniel Lawrence Kelleher, who was born in Cork in 1883 and educated at University College Cork, was a schoolteacher who wrote many books on travel and poetry, some of which have been reprinted in the USA. His play, *Stephen Gray*, had a successful run at Dublin's Abbey Theatre. Where and when he died remains a mystery.

Donncha Ó Céileachair (1918–60) of Cork retired from schoolteaching to help prepare an important English–Irish dictionary. He also wrote biographies with his sister, Iognáid. Yet another schoolteacher of Cork, **Seamas Ó Céileachair** (b. 1916), migrated to Clare, where he wrote poetry and rhymes for children and edited various poetry anthologies and textbooks.

Edward Kelliher (b. 1920) of Tralee, a former Managing Director of Easons, the booksellers, was a yachtsman who took part in the 1964 Tokyo Olympics. **Richard Kelliher** emigrated from Tralee to Australia in 1933. He joined the Australian army and fought against the Japanese in New Guinea and, for his bravery under heavy fire, he was awarded the Victoria Cross. He died at the age of fifty-two from malaria.

Keller *see* Kelleher

(O) Kelly

Ó Ceallaigh

Kelly comes second to Murphy as the most numerous surname in Ireland. It goes back over a thousand years, as does the Kelly coat of arms, which has as its crest a mythical green beast, the enfield. When the Kelly chieftain, **Tadgh Mór Ó Ceallaigh**, was killed at the battle of Clontarf in 1014, the enfield is said to have come out of the sea to guard Tadgh Mór's body until his kinsmen could give him an honourable burial.

The O Kellys were a powerful family in Connacht, where they ruled over a vast territory. When they were not fighting, they built churches and castles and they held high rank in the Church. They have been a shaping force in the long saga of Irish history and when they could no longer fight for their own country they went abroad to Europe and America. Today, there are far more Kellys in the USA than there ever were in Ireland.

In 1863, **Colonel Patrick Kelly** commanded the Irish brigade at Gettysburg. In 1893, **Michael Kelly** was the US baseball champion. **"Honest" John Kelly** was the first Irish Catholic head of Tammany Hall. There were also the Kellys of Philadelphia. **Jack Kelly** was the first American oarsman to win an Olympic Gold Medal in 1920. His daughter was the much-loved **Grace Kelly**, film star and Princess of Monaco. **Captain Colm Kelly** was the US pilot of the bomber which destroyed a Japanese battleship at Pearl Harbour. **James Edward Kelly** is known as "the sculptor of American history".

In Austria the Kellys served the Empress Maria Theresa so well she awarded them the title of counts of the Holy Roman Empire, which they still hold. In Australia they have achieved dubious fame with **Ned Kelly** and his brothers, the outlawed bushrangers. They also had a bishop of Sydney.

The Kellys have also been outstanding in the field of literature. Since the last century there has been a throng of Kelly dramatists, journalists, actors and novelists.

Kenneally

Ó Coingheallaigh

Kenealy Kennelly

Kenneally or Kennelly are some of the variations of the old Irish surname Ó Coingheallaigh or Mac Coingheallaigh (*coinníoll* means pledge). This family were employees of the O Davorens of West Cork, from whom they held lands at Drinagh, near Drimoleague. They also spread north into Ormond in County Kilkenny. Another branch, who settled in the barony of Connello in County Limerick, were driven out by the FitzGeralds following the twelfth-century invasions by the Anglo-Normans.

There was a Kenneally lieutenant in King James II's regiment of infantry at the battle of the Boyne in 1690. Following that disaster, many Irish men and women left for France. A Kenneally brigadier is recorded in the Irish brigade in France and **Joseph Kenneally** was a Sous-Lieutenant in 1763 in Dillon's Regiment.

In the nineteenth century, the **Reverend Dr. Kenealy** was the first Archbishop of Simla in India.

William Kenealy (1828–76) was Mayor of Kilkenny.

Edward Vaughan Kenealy (1819–80) was born in Cork and graduated in law from Trinity College Dublin. He practised at the English Bar and was notorious for his violent conduct in defence of his clients, which led to his disbarment. He published a newspaper, described as "scurrilous", and also much prose and verse which he claimed he had translated from eleven languages.

Brendan Kennelly (b. 1936), who was born in Kerry, has been professor of modern literature at Trinity College Dublin since 1973. He has written a number of novels and is one of Ireland's foremost poets.

Cork city and county is still where most of the Kenneallys are to be found today.

(O) Kennedy

Ó Cinnéide

There are possibly twenty thousand Kennedys and O Kennedys in Ireland. Kennedy is also a Scottish name, although it is thought that these may have had Gaelic roots. In Ireland, the Kennedys have an impeccable genealogy, descending from Dunchaun, a brother of King Brian Boru who died in 1014.

The Irish name, Ó Cinnéide derives from *ceann éidig*, meaning helmet head, which they inherited from Brian Boru's father. Three helmets are displayed on their coat of arms.

The Kennedys were of the aristocratic Dalcassian sept, related to the powerful O Briens of County Clare. Killaloe, the royal seat of the Dalcassian kings, was their home until quarrels with their neighbours drove them across the Shannon to counties Tipperary and Kilkenny, the area then known as Ormond. For four hundred years, they were Lords of Ormond, resisting the usurping Norman Butlers. By the middle of the eighteenth century, they ruled over twenty thousand acres, but they were finally driven abroad, and fought in the Irish brigades in France.

Ulster was fertile soil for a number of the Kennedy sept, who included in their ranks a colonial governor, an admiral and a master of Dublin's famous Rotunda hospital.

Many Kennedys have achieved fame in the USA. In the 1960s, **Jimmy Kennedy** from Ireland was a popular songwriter who made a fortune from royalties on songs such as "Red Sails in the Sunset" and "South of the Border".

John FitzGerald Kennedy was a member of the wealthy Kennedys of Boston and became President of the USA. During his visit to Ireland, shortly before his death, he was presented with some authentic Ormond deeds. Both he and his brother, **Robert Kennedy**, died at the hands of assassins.

Kennelly *see* Kenneally

Kenney *see* Kenny

Kenny

Ó Cionaoith

Kenney

The Reverend Patrick Woulfe suggests that this surname derives from *cionadh*, meaning firesprung! Undoubtedly there are a number of distinct septs of this name, including a distinguished family from Somerset in England who came to Ireland over four centuries ago. One of the Irish Kenny septs of County Galway married into the Kenny family from England, enriching them with vast tracts of land.

Ballinrobe in County Mayo was built *c.*1740 by the Kennys and is the family seat of the well-known concert pianist, **Courtney Kenny** (b. 1933). He was a founder of the renowned Wexford Opera Festival.

The majority of the Kennys—or Kenneys—came from counties Galway or Roscommon, but they are very numerous today in Munster and Leinster.

Two clergymen, contemporaries of each other, followed very different paths. **Reverend Arthur Kenny** (1776–1855) was outspokenly anti-Catholic, while **Peter Kenny** (1779–1841) founded Clongowes College, one of Ireland's premier boys' schools.

James Kenney left Dublin for London with his family. There he became the manager of the famous Boodle's Club. His son, **James Kenney** (1780–1849), wrote dozens of operas and plays, including the hugely successful *Raising the Wind.* A friend of Charles Lamb, he named his son **Charles Lamb Kenney** (1821–81). This son was born in Paris, where his father subsequently died, and became a translator and a librettist for the opera.

Sean Kenny (1933–73) was an outstanding architect and stage designer. Despite a relatively short life, he had many adventures, including sailing across the Atlantic from Dublin in a small shrimping boat with three friends.

John F. Kenny (b. 1884) wrote the important *Sources for the Early History of Ireland.*

Today, there are Kennys in journalism, radio and television, while **Ivor Kenny** of Galway was the recipient of an Economist of the Year Award. Kenny's Bookshop and Art Gallery in Galway is a mecca for book lovers and art lovers.

Kenny is also a common name in England.

Keogh

Mac Eochaidh

Haughey Hoy (Mac)Kehoe Hoey

In Irish, Keogh is a real tongue-twister—Mac Eochaidh—which derives from a personal name. It has been anglicized with a variety of spellings.

One of the Keogh septs had their territory around Limerick and Tipperary, where there was a townland called Ballymackeogh. Another sept were lords of Moyfinn, which comprised sections of Westmeath and Roscommon and was known as Keogh's Country. The third sept were the Keoghs of Leinster, who were hereditary bards to the O Byrnes. In succeeding generations, they boasted many fine poets, of which the sixteenth-century **Maolmuire MacKeogh** was the most highly regarded. Following the Norman invasion, they moved further south and, in Wexford, they are now more commonly known as Kehoe.

A Dubliner called **John Keogh** paved the way for Daniel O Connell's Catholic emancipation campaign.

A Roscommon man from Keoghville, **William Keogh**, became a hated and reviled judge, when he sentenced the Fenians Luby, O Leary and O Donovan Rossa to death.

Myles W. Keogh (1848–76) from Carlow was an experienced soldier who went to serve in America, where he met his death at the hands of the American-Indians in the battle of Little Big Horn.

Until the Great Famine of the mid-nineteenth century, there was a family of landed gentry near Limerick who spelled their name **K'Eogh**. O Hoey and Hoy are also variations on Keogh and claim descent from the kings of Ulster.

The MacKeoghs of Connacht's heraldic shield displays a red lion with a red hand and red crescent. Their crest shows a large, very blue, boar.

(O) Kerin, Kern *see* Kearns, Kieran

Kernan *see* Carnahan, Kiernan

Kerr

Ó Carra

Carr Ker

The majority of the Kerrs in Ireland are descendants of immigrants to Ulster, where, seven centuries after their arrival, they are very numerous. The surname is thought to have come from the English word for a low-lying meadow. In some cases, Kerr could be an anglicization of the Irish name, Ó Carra (a spear).

This Gaelic family is mentioned in the *Annals of Ulster* and by the Four Masters and it is also found in County Galway, where Carr is one of its variants.

In 1370, a **Richard Kerr** is described as a collector of taxes in County Tipperary.

The Kers of Portavo were descendants of **David Ker** (b. 1500). They came from Middleton in Scotland and are now a prominent family in County Down.

Many prosperous Kerr families and their pedigrees and possessions are listed in the Public Records Offices of Belfast and Dublin. There are also papers relating to a **Lady Anabel Kerr**, who wrote the *Life of Cesare, Cardinal Baronias of the Roman Oratory, 1538–1607.*

David Kerr was one of the three hundred Members of Parliament in the Irish House of Commons in 1797, only a few years before its abolition.

Virginia Kerr (b. 1954) of Dublin is one of Ireland's classical singers. She has appeared at home and abroad on many concert platforms, as well as on television and radio.

Many Kerrs emigrated to America, where they became missionaries, physicians and engineers.

Kerran, Kerrane *see* Kearns, Kieran

Kervick, Kerwick *see* Kirby

Kidney

Ó Dubháin

Devany Downes Duane Dwane

Kidney is a straight translation from the Irish surname Ó Dubháin. *Duán* is the Irish word for both a fish hook and a kidney! Duane is accepted now as the anglicized form of Ó Dubháin and it is not at all a numerous name.

In earlier times, there were Kidneys in at least four different locations, especially County Meath, where they were Lords of Knowth, near the world-famous neolithic burial chamber at Newgrange. There was also a family in south-west Cork. It was this family that changed their name to Kidney. Although there are only a couple of dozen Kidneys in Dublin and other parts of the country, including Northern Ireland, they are most numerous still in County Cork. In Connemara, another Ó Dubháin clan may have changed their name to Devany. In Limerick, Ó Dubháin has changed to the surname Downes.

A family of Kidneys were owners of Jury's Hotels in Dublin for many years. There have also been a number of architects and doctors in that family.

(O) Kiely

Ó Cadhla

Kealy Keeley Keily Kiley Queally

Kiely derives from the Irish name Ó Cadhla (*cadhla* means graceful). Through the twists and turns of history, it has acquired a variety of spellings, including Kealy, Keeley, Kiely, Keily and even Queally. A **Dr. Malachy Queally** was Archbishop of Tuam in County Galway.

In the Public Records Office in Dublin, there is a pedigree of the Kiely family dating from 1743 to 1882. The Genealogical Office in Dublin holds a pedigree of Kelly, more probably Kealy, of Tomgarty in County Galway dating from *c.*1720 to *c.*1790. Incidentally, this very numerous surname has sometimes been confused with O Kelly, with which it has no relationship.

In the Middle Ages, the head of the Ó Cadhla family was a chieftain in Connemara, while another bearer of this name was a chieftain in Thomond (Limerick).

Walter Kiely, "a doctor of Physic", represented Gowran in County Kilkenny in 1689, in the short-lived parliament of the ill-fated Jacobean King, James II.

Tom Kiely of Carrick-on-Suir was the great Irish sportsman who, at the St. Louis Olympics in 1904, was the first Olympic champion in the all-round event which was later to become the Decathlon.

Jerome Kiely, who was born in Kinsale and ordained in Maynooth in 1950, is a widely travelled priest, as well as being a poet, novelist and literary prize winner. He is published in both England and the United States of America. **Benedict Kiely** (b. 1919) is also a distinguished literary man, celebrated for his short stories, plays and novels, and for his appearances on radio and television. He was also a university professor and has lectured in universities in the United States of America.

Kieran

Ó Ciaráin Ó Céirín

Kearns Kierans (O) Kerin

This ancient Irish name is Ó Ciaráin or, sometimes, Ó Céirín. In Irish, *ciar* signifies black or very dark brown.

The Ó Ciaráin family once owned much land in the barony of Costelloe in County Mayo, from which they were forced to move to the counties of Sligo and Donegal. One important branch of the family settled in County Clare in 1420, a county in which they are still to be found to this day.

A private collection of papers in the custody of P. J. O Flaherty, solicitors of Enniscorthy in County Wexford, relates to a number of families since 1676, including Kierans who had lands in counties Wexford, Laois and Tipperary.

The Genealogical Office in Dublin has a draft pedigree of Kieran of Drumshanbo in County Leitrim of *c.*1830 to 1943. In the National Library of Ireland there are papers regarding the trial of Cox v **Kiernan** in 1853.

There are a number of variants of the name, including Kearns, Kierans, O Kerin, Kerrann.

see also Kearns

Kiernan

Mac Thighearnáin

Kernan MacTiernan Tiernan

The Irish word for lord is *tighearna*, and the Mac Thighearnáins were chiefs of Tullach Donnchadha, now Tullyhunco, in County Cavan. Thirty-three of their chieftains were sufficiently important to have their obituaries recorded in the famous *Annals of the Four Masters.* They were kinsmen of the high-ranking O Rourkes of Breffny.

Another sept of this name in County Roscommon were descended from Tiernan, the grandson of Turlough Mór O Conor (1088–1156), High King of Ireland. The name has gone through a series of modifications, including MacTiernan, Tiernan, Kiernan and Kernan. It has no connection with Tierney.

For twenty years, the **Reverend Edward Kernan** (d. 1844) was Bishop of Clogher. **Frances Kiernan** (1816–92) was a senator in the USA.

Thomas J. Kiernan (1897–1967) of Dublin was a director of Radio Éireann before becoming Minister to the Holy See. He opened Ireland's first diplomatic mission to Australia and was Irish Ambassador in West Germany, Canada and Washington. His wife was the famous ballad singer, Delia Murphy. On retiring, he administered the Ireland–America Foundation in the USA and wrote about finance and history.

Dr. Eoin McKiernan was born in 1915 in Manhattan of first-generation Irish parents. As president, and prime mover, of the Irish-American Cultural Institute—the largest Irish organization in the USA—he said that, of the forty-four million who claimed Irish origin in the last US census, he would like to see one million caring Americans—"That way we could accomplish something." Already the organization has accomplished much in raising the image and status of the Irish in America and affording financial help to the arts in Ireland. **Ethna Maeve McKiernan**, one of Dr. McKiernan's nine children, is a poet. She also runs Irish Books and Media, one of the largest suppliers of books of Irish interest in the USA.

Kilbane

Mac Giolla Bháin

White

Kilbane is a rare Irish surname, which was originally Mac Giolla Bháin. This family was a sept of the important north Connacht Uí Fiachrach clan.

Giolla means servant or son, while *bhán* means white, which explains why, in some instances, the name was anglicized to the ubiquitous White.

Kilbane is seldom found outside Connacht, where there is a remarkable concentration of them around Achill Sound, off the Mayo coast.

Kildea *see* Gildea

Kiley *see* (O) Kiely

Killeen

Ó Cillín

Killen Killian MacKillen

Killeen, which is now a very popular name in all the provinces except Ulster, originated in Connacht, where there is a town in County Mayo called Ballykilleen. Killeen could be a diminutive of *ceallagh*, the Irish word for strife. This is a word which hardly applies to the many ecclesiastical dignitaries of this name, which, as far back as 1106, was represented by **Cormac O Killeen**, bishop of the important monastery of Clonmacnoise, while a namesake was archdeacon of that diocese in 1026.

Some of the recognizable variants of the name are Killian, MacKillen and Killen. In the nineteenth century, there were several leading Presbyterian ministers of the name in Belfast, including **Thomas Young Killen** (1826–86) and **Reverend William Dane Killen** (1806–1902), a historian who published books on the history of his church.

From County Antrim came **James Bryce Killen** (1845–1916), an active Fenian and land reformer. A New York lawyer, **Doran Killeen**, was also a member of the revolutionary movement in America.

Earlier in the nineteenth century, during an attempted rebellion in Ireland led by Robert Emmet, **John Killen** was hanged, falsely accused.

Michael Killeen (b. 1928) was born in Galway. He was a director and chairman of many important business enterprises: the Irish Export Board, the Central Bank, the Irish Management Institute, and Irish Distillers. His early death at the height of his career was universally mourned.

Killian *see* Killeen

Kilmartin *see* Martin

Kilpatrick *see* Fitzpatrick

Kilroy *see* MacIlroy

Kinahan

Ó Coinneacháin

Cunningham Kinagan Kiningham

This is a difficult name to disentangle from its many variants. In Irish it was Ó Coinneacháin, a family very numerous at one time in the Midlands as, indeed, they are still today, taking the form Kinahan.

During the seventeenth and eighteenth centuries, many Irish families adopted names which sounded English or Scottish, which made life easier for them under English rule. Thus, Ó Coinneacháin became Cunningham (Scottish) or Kinahan or Kiningham, and a host of other somewhat similar variants.

The pedigrees of the old County Offaly families can be found in the Dublin Genealogical Office. Kinahan is not a common name in Ireland, especially in Ulster, yet there are records of several distinguished Kinahans.

George Henry Kinahan (1820–1908) of County Down was an outstanding geologist and engineer, whose writings fill many specialist columns.

Charles Henry Grierson Kinahan

is now retired from the directorship of a number of international companies, including Dunlop Malayan Estates and **Lyle Kinahan** of Belfast. He was also Harbour Commissioner and a senator of Queen's University, Belfast.

Major General Oliver Kinahan served with the Royal Irish Fusiliers during the Second World War, and also with other regiments in the Far East, retiring when he was the army's Paymaster General.

Sir Robert Kinahan was Lord Mayor of Belfast from 1956 to 1961 and has been Lord Lieutenant of Belfast since 1985. With **Lady Kinahan** he restored the historic sixteenth-century Castle Upton in Templepatrick in County Antrim.

Kindellan *see* Quinlan

King

Conry

This is a very numerous surname throughout Ireland. It is thought that in some cases it may have been an anglicization of the Gaelic name Conry (*rí* means king). But who, today, can separate the original Gaelic Conry, or King, from those Kings who came to Ireland with the Commonwealth armies, many of whom distinguished themselves, especially in the Church?

Three outstanding King families were ennobled at various times, including the Kings of Charleston, County Mayo. From this family came **Edward King** (d. 1638), Bishop of Elphin for many years, who raised it from penury to prosperity and left fifteen children. His descendants were Earls of Kingston and Viscounts Kingsborough. A present-day descendant was **Commander William Leslie-King** (b. 1910) of Oranmore Castle, County Galway. In 1973 he sailed solo round the world and has written many books.

In *c.*1628, the **Reverend R. G. S. King** was Dean of Derry, while the **Reverend Paul King** (d. 1665) was a Franciscan monk.

The Kings of Corrard, County Fermanagh produced the famous Archbishop of Dublin, **William King** (1650–1729). An illustrious scholar, he encouraged the promotion of the Irish language in Trinity College Dublin and supported Dean Swift in his campaign against the spurious coinage known as "Wood's Halfpence".

Many Kings appear in the archives in France. Many were East India merchants. **Henry King** of County Wicklow was a deputy surgeon-general in Madras in India *c.*1788.

William King (b. 1809) was a doctor of science and geology at Queen's College, Galway, and was the first to identify Neanderthal man as a distinct species.

Rockingham in Boyle, County Roscommon, once the home of the **Stafford King Harmons**, Earls of Kingston, is now the Lough Key Wildlife and Forest Centre and is open to the public, a popular recreation area during the summer. Rockingham was beautifully restored in 1995 by the Office of Public Works.

Kiningham *see* Kinahan

Kinsella

Cinnsealach

This is one of the few Irish names which has never been prefixed by O or Mac. It originated from **Enna Cinsealach**, one of the many illegitimate sons of Dermot MacMurrough, the king of Leinster who, in the twelfth century, brought the Anglo-Normans to Ireland.

A **Cinsealach** was also a grandson of Cathair Mór, a king of Ireland and forty-eighth in descent from Hermon, son of Milesius, the sixth-century king of Spain.

In their pedigree it is recorded that, "In 1552 **Edmund Duff Kinsella** . . . found his followers much oppressed and impoverished by the Kavanaghs, their County Wexford neighbours." They entered into an agreement with the Lord Deputy to keep their lands and pay the king a yearly tribute. The Kinsellas forfeited their possessions after the rising of 1641, despite their apparent submission. However, what land they had—and most of it was in north Wexford—they were allowed to hold by descent, unlike the Irish custom where a chief had to be chosen.

Aeneas Kinsella was a member of the Supreme Council which sat at Kilkenny in 1646.

Bonaventure Kinselagh was an officer in Kavanagh's Infantry Regiment, which fought with King James II's army in Ireland at the battle of the Boyne in 1690.

Among the Kinsellas who left Ireland at the time of the Great Famine was **Thomas Kinsella** (1822–84), who rose from the humblest of beginnings to be editor of the prestigious Brooklyn *Daily Eagle.*

One of the foremost poets in Ireland, **Thomas Kinsella** was born in Dublin in 1928. He has won many prizes for literature and has been a professor of English at Temple University, Philadelphia, since 1990. He also edits literary magazines and lectures on poetry.

Kirby

Ó Ciarmhaic

Kervick Kerwick

The name Ó Ciarmhaic is descriptive of the son of a dark brown father (*ciar* means dark or swarthy). Their original homeland was County Limerick. A branch of the family who settled in County Kilkenny anglicized their name to Kerwick, or Kervick. An ancient family, they were chiefs of the Eoghanacht clan of Munster, descendants of Eoghan, son of King Oilioll Olum. They presided over the district of Knockany in County Limerick, an area where they are still numerous.

There are many records relating to the family in the National Library in Dublin. In 1690, **Richard Kirby** wrote about the revolution in Ireland. **Major-General S. Woodburn Kirby** compiled a military history of the Far East battlefields of the Second World War.

Writing about medicine, architecture and history, the Kirby name appears frequently, especially in England, where they must have gone early in the seventeenth century.

In 1701, there is mention of a **"Temperance" Kirby** and a House of Lords appeal. In 1781, Dame Jane Ormsby was concerned with an appeal against lands in County Limerick which were tenanted by Thady Quin.

Joshua Kirby, who was President of the Society of Artists in London, was a friend of the great painter, Thomas Gainsborough (1727–88).

William Kirby (1759–1850), born in Suffolk and in holy orders all his life, was the leading entomologist of his day. A naturalist writer, he had a special interest in butterflies.

Robert Kirby was a publisher in London in the nineteenth century.

William Kirby (1817–1906) wrote *The Golden Dog*, a fascinating romance about the early days in Quebec, Canada. A pirated edition was published in 1877 and was so popular it has often been reprinted.

Rollin Kirby, earlier this century, was a very popular cartoonist with the New York *World Telegram.*

Perhaps it was an Irish exile who patented those useful hair restrainers known as Kirbigrips?

Kirwan

Ó Ciardubháin

Kirovani Kyrvan Kyrwan Quirovan

The Kirwan lineage stretches back before Christ, to the Milesians who came to Ireland from Spain. In Irish their name is Ó Ciardubháin (*ciardhubh* means dark black). At first they settled in Louth, but it was when they came to Galway that they became rich and important. With the Darcys, they were the only native Irish to be counted among the Fourteen Tribes of Galway.

Their connection with the Church also goes back a long way. Their bishops, both Catholic and Protestant, were numerous. A Kirwan Bishop of Killala in the seventeenth century rebuked a man who had left his wife, insisting that he was risking damnation. "I could bear the flames of hell better than my wife's company," complained the husband. But when the Bishop urged him to sample it by putting his hand over a candle flame, he returned to his less painful wife.

The Kirwans were prominent in France, both in the Church, the army and the royal court, where one of their physicians looked after Louis XV. Some were absorbed into the nobility, while another family produced the very well-known Château Kirwan wine.

The most eminent Kirwan, **Richard Kirwan**, came from Cregg Castle in Galway. Ordained a Jesuit priest, he left the Church and became a scientist, a philosopher and a wonderful eccentric who was the first president of the Royal Irish Academy.

The Kirwans have been explorers, from the North Pole to the Antipodes, and their abilities have been appreciated not only in the armies of Europe, but also in many other spheres. Their pedigrees are well recorded in the international archives and in Ireland, especially by their own descendants.

Their patriotism was epitomized by a Dublin Kirwan who was executed with Robert Emmet in 1803. There are many reminders of the family to be found on the buildings and tombstones of Galway, where their unusual armorial bearings are easily recognizable. Three red-legged crows surround a black chevron on their shield, while another black crow forms their crest. Their motto, probably acquired in France, is *Mon Dieu, Mon Roi et Ma Patrie* (My God, my King and my Country).

Kitchen *see* Hutchinson

Kiverkin *see* MacGurrin

Knight

Mac an Ridire

MacKnight Ruderry

Knight, a rare name in Ireland, is to be found mainly in Ulster. They mostly arrived in the seventeenth century with the Cromwellian armies, or, later, during the plantations, when they were granted considerable amounts of land.

Knight is also to be found in England and Scotland. Father Woulfe wrote "Mac an Ridire, the son of the knight (*ridire* = knight), is the Irish surname assumed by the Fitzsimons of County Westmeath and perhaps also by offshoots of knightly houses in other parts of Ireland."

Although the Knights have not contributed significantly to the arts, sciences, politics or industry, they are quite well represented in the archives, dating from about 1614, when a soldier, **William Knight**, who "had served in the wars in Ireland was granted a pension of £4". The Genealogical Office in Dublin holds pedigrees relating to Knights of Dublin, Brickfield, Limerick, Ballynoe and Charleville in County Cork.

In the seventeenth century, **Sir Richard Knight** was Principal Secretary of State in Ireland and Chancellor of the Exchequer.

About 1776, **Lady Philippina Knight** left an interesting collection of her letters to the archives. There was also a **Robert Knight** who was Baron of Luxborough.

In *c.*1871, **Richard Goold Knight** was a member of the Council of Santa Cruz in the West Indies.

In 1932, there is a record of arms being granted to **Lieutenant Frederick Boniface Knight**, only son of the **Reverend Frederick William Knight** of Drumcree Rectory in County Westmeath.

Knowles *see* Newell

Kyne *see* Coyne

L

Lacy, Lacey *see* de Lacy

Laffey

Ó (F)Laithimh

Flahive Lahiff Lahive (O) Flahiff

This is a very rare name. Originating as Ó Flaithimh, it signified son of the lord, or ruler (*flaitheamh* means ruler). In the sixteenth century, it was more numerous than it is today and could be found thinly scattered in the counties of Galway, Clare, Tipperary, Kilkenny and Wexford.

During the course of history, it was anglicized, assuming a variety of spellings. With the dropping of the O prefix, it became Laffey and Lahiff. It can also be recognized as O Flahiff or Flahive.

Perhaps because of its comparative rarity, bearers of this name have not yet come to any prominence in the Irish manuscripts or history books.

Lally *see* Mullally

(O) Lalor *see* Lawlor

Lambe

Ó Luain

Lamb (O) Loan(e) (O) Lowan

Ó Luain was anglicized to Lamb, a direct translation from the Irish word for lamb (*uan*), though there are some scholars who believe that the original name meant a hound, hence a warrior (*luan* means hound).

There were several septs, one of whose chiefs were Lords of Deisbeg in County Limerick. In the thirteenth century, they were dispersed by the Anglo-Normans and spread throughout Munster. Another sept, that of Oriel (County Monaghan), were also similarly scattered.

Lamb is also a numerous English name and many Lambs, or Lambes, in Ireland are descendants of Cromwellian and other English settlers.

In the National Library of Ireland, there are eighteenth-century papers relating to a **Reverend F. J. A. Lamb** of Julianstown Rectory in Drogheda, County Louth. There are also many Lamb papers in the Royal Irish Academy, including some pedigrees dating up to the twentieth century.

In 1801, the Genealogical Office issued a royal licence to George Audouin of County Wicklow, allowing him to add Lamb to his surname. **Lieutenant George H. Lamb** has left a diary of his exploits serving with the army in Ireland from 1852 to 1853.

The firm of **Lamb Brothers** were in

the jam business for many years and had their fruit farm at Moone in County Kildare.

The most outstanding bearer of the name is **Charles Lamb** (1893–1964), who was born in Portadown, County Armagh. The son of a house decorator, he studied art and, in 1938, received the accolade of membership of the Royal Hibernian Academy. He settled in Connemara, which he popularized in his paintings, which have been exhibited internationally.

In Ulster, where both Lamb and Lambe are very numerous, they can also be of the same nomenclature as O Luan, O Lowan, O Loan and Loane.

Lamont

Mac Laghmainn

Farquharson Lammon Lamond

This is the clan name of a leading Scottish family, a branch of which settled in Ulster, where they are still numerous. It is thought to be of Norse origin, *logmaor* means lawman, or a person with judicial powers.

There are many variations of the name. As Lamond, it is found in the thirteenth century in Lancashire. It can also be traced to Farquharson in England, from the Scottish MacFarquhar. To add to the variety—and confusion—in County Derry, Mac Laghmainn was anglicized to MacLamond or MacClement, and even to Clements. The name is also found in the eleventh-century Doomsday Book as Laghemann.

The Lamonts were a Scottish-Irish family of Argyllshire, of the same stock as the MacSweeneys and MacLaughlins, all descendants of the great O Neills of Ulster. In Scotland, the clan Lamont have their own green and black tartan. They once held appointments in the court of the Stuart kings. The Lamont harp is preserved in Edinburgh. A Clan Lamont Society was founded in 1895. In 1938, with contributions from American admirers, they produced a fine book titled *The Lamont Clan: Seven Centuries of Clan History from Record Evidence.*

Frederic Lamont (1868–1948) of Glasgow was a pianist and composer. **Johann von Lamont** (1805–79) left his native Braemar in Scotland to work in Germany, where he became professor of astronomy at Munich University.

Lane *see* Lehane

Langan

Ó Longáin

Long

This surname comes from the Irish *long*, meaning long or tall. In some cases the name was anglicized to Long, a name which derived from le Long, which came into Ireland with the Anglo-Normans in 1172. Today, Long is a very common name in England.

In ancient times there were several different Ó Longáin septs. In Ulster, they were chiefs in County Armagh, from which they were later driven west to County Mayo. There was also an ecclesiastical Ó Longáin family in County Limerick. These were administrators of the monastery of Ardpatrick and one was a bishop of Cloyne. After the destruction of the monasteries, they were scattered and many forfeited their lands.

In the eighteenth century, there were three generations of Langan poets. **Michael Langan** (d. 1770) was the father of another **Michael** (1765–1837), a United Irishman. His three sons, **Peter**, **Paul** and **Joseph**, followed in the family tradition and were all writers.

Joseph M. Langan (1815–92), who was a poet, antiquarian and politician, translated many early Irish poems into English.

In the Belfast Public Records Office there is mention of "a messuage [mansion house] in Kilmainham, County Dublin" being leased to **William Langan** in 1538.

There are several small townlands called Ballylanigan in various parts of the south, which may have been connected with the Langans, who are very numerous, except in Ulster.

Lanigan

Ó Lonagáin

The origins of this name are uncertain. Lonagáin, the Irish form of the name, means a little blackbird. The greatest concentration of the name is to be found in their original territories of counties Kilkenny Tipperary and Limerick, where there are two Ballylanigan townlands.

There was a Lanigan rebel who was outlawed in 1297. The Genealogical Office in Dublin has a pedigree of Lanigan's of Ballykeife and of Grange, both in County Kilkenny, between *c.*1720 and 1826.

The outstanding Lanigan was **Reverend Dr. John Lanigan** (1758–1828), an ecclesiastical historian who was born at Cashel in County Tipperary. He studied for the priesthood at the Irish College in Rome. He was teaching in Italy, at Pavia, near Milan, when he was driven out by Napoleon's troops. On his return to Ireland, he was not well received by the clergy, who suspected him of heresy. He was given work by the Royal Dublin Society as a translator, eventually reaching the office of librarian at £3 a week. He is remembered for his four-volume book, *An Ecclesiastical History of Ireland.*

Another translator, also a doctor, **John Lanigan**, a veterinary surgeon, is thought to have translated, among other books, *Instructions for Shepherds and Proprietors of Flocks.*

In 1895, the Genealogical Office granted arms to **Stephen Martin Lanigan** of Glengyle in County Tipperary and Delville in County Dublin, the eldest son of **John Lanigan** of Glengyle by Frances, daughter of Charles O Keeffe and niece of Dixon Cornelius O Keeffe of Richmond House in Templemore, County Tipperary, on his assuming under royal licence the name and arms of O Keeffe. There are several families of Lanigan O Keeffe living in counties Kilkenny and Dublin.

Larkin

Ó Lorcáin

This very numerous surname derives from *lorc*, meaning rough or fierce. There were four distinct septs. Ó Lorcáin of Leinster, who was considered to be of royal blood, was put out of his Wexford territory with the arrival of the Anglo-Normans in 1169.

The Oriel Uí Lorcáin, who were chiefs of Farney and of west Uí Breasail, had their territory in County Armagh. The Galway Ó Lorcáins were of the same stock as the O Maddens. Lorrha in County Tipperary was the headquarters of the Ó Lorcáins who were administrators of the local churches and abbeys.

The O prefix has long since been dropped from the name.

Cornet James Larkin of Kilkenny and **Lawrence Larkin** are both recorded as serving in the Commonwealth armies in Ireland in 1649.

In 1867, **Michael Larkin**, while attempting, with others, to rescue Fenian prisoners from a police van, killed a police constable. For this they were all summarily executed and are commemorated as the "Manchester Martyrs".

The most famous Larkin is **"Big" Jim Larkin** (1876–1947), whose statue stands in Dublin's O Connell Street. He was born in Liverpool of Irish parents and began life as a seaman. He introduced trade unionism and the "blacking" of goods—he even got the police out on strike! He was imprisoned in the USA for his too vigorous trade unionism. Coming to Dublin in 1908, he founded the Irish Transport and General Workers' Union (ITGWU) and confronted the newspaper and businessman tycoon, William Martin Murphy, bringing 100,000 workers out on strike for eight months. Following Home Rule, he was appointed a Dáil deputy.

Big Jim's eldest son, also **James** (1904–69), succeeded him as a trade unionist and a politician. He studied at the Lenin School in Moscow and was Chairman of the Communist Party of Ireland. His brother, **Denis** (b. 1908), was a member of the Dublin Corporation for thirty years. In the 1950s he was twice Lord Mayor of Dublin and a member of the European Trade Union Conference Executive.

Lavan *see* Hand

Lavelle

Ó Maolfhábhail

(Mac)Fall (Mac)Paul Melville

Although Lavelle may normally have French connotations, it also has very authentic Irish origins. Originally Ó Maolfhábhail (*fáball* means movement), it suffered various anglicizations, to Lavelle, Lawell, Melville, MacFall, Fall, MacPaul and even to Paul.

The Ó Maolfhábhail family were of the noble Cenél Eoghain, the clan name of the great O Neills of Ulster. They descended from Fergus, grandson of Niall of the Nine Hostages, and were chiefs of Carrickabraghy in north-west Ulster, near the Inishowen peninsula in County Donegal.

The branch of the family which became Lavelle moved to Connacht, where they are now most numerous. They are also to be found in County Dublin and in and around Belfast. Because they separated into such a variety of septs and names, there is scarcely a mention of the Lavelle branch in the records, though plenty of Melville—also the name of an historic Scottish family.

An outstanding kinsman was **Father Michael J. Lavelle** (1856–1939). He was born in New York, where he had a distinguished clerical career, first as Rector of St. Patrick's Cathedral, and then as Vicar-General of New York.

A remarkable number of Lavelles of the present day would appear to follow the medical profession.

Lavery *see* Lowry

Laverty *see* (O) Flaherty

Lavin *see* Hand

Lawlor

Ó Leathlobhair

Lawler (O) Lalor

There are at least three different ways of spelling this fairly common name. Translated from the Irish, *leath* means half and *lobhar* means sick, suggesting that it was probably a nickname for a half-sick person—possibly an early description of a hypochondriac! The name was borne by two early kings of Ulidia in County Down, families that are long since extinct.

Like their kinsmen the O Mores, the O Lalors were one of the Seven Septs of Leix (Laois). Their early settlement was near the famous Rock of Dunamase, the ruined but still impressive castle of the O Mores. In 1577 the O Dempseys, aided by English planters, massacred the O Lalors and their neighbours. **Harry Lalor** is remembered as the hero of Mallaghmast, the place in County Laois where this savagery took place. In Elizabethan times, most of the Seven Septs of Leix forfeited their territory. The Lalors who were peasants remained and Lalor's Mills, a property of theirs in 1609, commemorates their territory.

Following the suppression of the native Irish, the Lalors dropped their O prefix and many of their nobility chose exile. There are records of two **Don Ricardo Lalors** who served in the Spanish Netherlands in 1661.

Numbered among the prominent members of this family in the nineteenth century were **James Fintan Lalor** from Laois, a Young Irelander and influential journalist whose famous slogan was "the land of Ireland for the people of Ireland". A near cripple, he died prematurely. His younger brother, **Peter Lalor**, graduated from Trinity College Dublin in civil engineering. He emigrated to Australia, where he was involved in the gold miners' uprising at the Eureka Stockade in Victoria. He was badly wounded, losing an arm. In due course he became Speaker of the Legislative Assembly at Victoria.

John Lawlor of Dublin trained at the Royal Dublin Society before going to London, where he became an eminent sculptor. He was commissioned by the architects working on the Houses of Parliament and the Albert Memorial, and also by Queen Victoria herself.

Alice Lalor was the Mother Teresa of early nineteenth-century America.

The golden Lalor shield is filled with a red lion standing upright.

Lawn *see* Lehane

Leahy

Ó Laochdha

Leahy, a numerous surname, is an anglicization of the old Gaelic *laochda*, meaning heroic. It is still most widespread in its original homeland, the province of Munster.

Using a variety of earlier spellings, it is well recorded in the archives. **John O Lahy** was hanged in 1581 for helping a Jesuit priest to escape to France and for refusing to renounce his faith. **Edward David Leahy** (1797–1875) was a fashionable portrait painter in both Ireland and England.

The **Reverend Patrick Leahy** (1806–75) was Archbishop of Cashel and helped build Thurles Cathedral. A distinguished scholar, he also strove to prevent intemperance and to put a stop to local faction fighting, which had got out of control.

In the mid-nineteenth century, a number of Leahys left Munster for Argentina, where they were successful in medicine, agriculture and the Church. In fact, a remarkable number of Leahy women became nuns.

The Genealogical Office in Dublin has a pedigree of Leahys of South Hill in Killarney, County Kerry, from 1737 to 1917. There is also a confirmation of arms to the descendants of this family, which includes **Professor A. H. Leahy** of Sheffield University, **Major H. G. Leahy** of Carriglea, County Kerry, and **Captain T. B. A. Leahy**, all of whom were sons of **Colonel Arthur Leahy** of Flesk in County Kerry.

The Leahy family of Mallow in County Cork who prefixed Carroll to their surname are recorded in *Burke's Landed Gentry of Ireland* of 1958. This family's former mansion, Woodfort, is now a hospital.

Walter D. Leahy, an admiral with the US navy, has written an account of his time as chief of staff to both President Roosevelt and President Truman.

(O) Leary

Ó Laoghaire

The O Leary name comes from the first name, Laoghaire, which was once very popular. It is one of the most numerous names in Ireland. The family originated in County Cork, where they ruled as chiefs at Inchigeela under the mighty MacCarthys of Muskerry. With the arrival of the Anglo-Normans, they were driven from their territories. In County Cork there are two towns called Ballyleary.

They played a prominent part in the wars against British rule, for which they were outlawed. In the eighteenth century, their name featured widely in the Irish regiments in France and Austria.

The tragic love story of **Art O Leary** and Eileen Dubh, his wife, inspired her to write one of the most poignant love poems. He was formerly a colonel in the Austrian army, but after his return to Ireland he was killed, in 1773, because he would not sell his famous horse to an English soldier.

One of the most distinguished of the O Learys was **Father Peadar Ó Laoghaire** (1839–1920) of Cork. A superb scholar, he was one of the first Irish writers of the Gaelic League. There were also many songwriters in the O Leary family.

John O Leary (1830–1907) went to America to seek support for the Fenians. On his return he was arrested and spent nine years in prison. After his release he exiled himself to Paris but, later, he returned and inspired the great poet, W. B. Yeats. He wrote many books on Ireland.

Daniel O Leary (1846–1933) was one of America's leading long-distance runners. And it was **Mrs. O Leary**'s cow which knocked over the bucket which started the fire which destroyed the city of Chicago in 1871!

Liam O Leary, who was born in Cork in 1910, was Ireland's leading film archivist. He also wrote a number of books on the cinema.

The most illustrious of the family was **Laoghaire**, King of Ireland at the time of Saint Patrick. Dún Laoghaire in County Dublin commemorates his name.

Lee

Mac an Leagha Mac Laoidhigh

Mac an Leagha means son of the physician, and the bearers of this descriptive name were once very distinguished medical men who were hereditary physicians to the O Flahertys of Connacht. In the fifteenth century, they wrote on medicine in both Irish and Latin.

Lee is a very widespread name in both Ireland and in England, where it means a grassy plain. Without a reliable pedigree, it would be impossible now to distinguish the Irish from the Anglo-Irish Lees.

There were several Irish septs, the most numerous of them being in County Cork. Until the Cromwellian suppressions, they were big landowners in many areas of the country.

In the thirteenth century, **John O Lee**, a Dominican, was Bishop of Killala. In about 1560, **Father John Lee** from Waterford had established himself as a leading teacher in Paris, while a kinsman was sheriff of his native Waterford.

Many Lees distinguished themselves in the armies of Europe, including **Colonel Andrew Lee** (1650–1734), who was a soldier in the Irish brigade in France. The Lees also served in the American War of Independence.

As prosperous landowners until comparatively recently, their pedigrees appeared regularly in the now defunct *Burke's Landed Gentry of Ireland.*

Leech

Ó Laoghóg

Logue

In England, leech used to be the word used for a medical doctor (the Middle-English word *leche* meant physician), probably because of their excessive use of this bloodsucking worm as a cure-all. The name came to Ireland via Scotland and the north of England, particularly Cheshire.

The Mac an Leagha family's name was also sometimes anglicized to Leech. They were highly esteemed physicians who ministered to the important chiefs and their retinues. In Derry and Donegal the name Leech was sometimes used by the Ó Laoghóg family, which was often transformed to Logue, which is still numerous.

The Leeches who were English settlers and the Leeches of Irish descent have merged thoroughly, so that it would now be difficult to deduce their national origins.

In Dublin's Genealogical Office there are deeds relating to Leech properties in Dublin, Meath and Cork. There is mention of the conferring of arms on the descendants of **John Leech** of Mayo in 1860.

A **W. Leech** whose family for generations operated a ferry across the River Liffey claimed compensation from a **John Henry Leech** of Wicklow, who was part proprietor of the new Butt Bridge across the river.

In 1875, **Arthur Blennerhassett Leech** is recorded as being an Irish rifleman in the USA, one of a number of military Leeches who served abroad.

The most famous Leech was **John Leech** (1817–64), who was born in London. His Irish father was a scholarly man and at one time the wealthy owner of a coffee house on Ludgate Hill. John Leech was an artist and humorist whose cartoons delighted the readers of Britain's *Punch* magazine from its very first issue.

(O) Lehane

Ó Liatháin

Lane Lawn Leyne Lyons

The origin of this surname is most confusing. It can be traced to a variety of anglicizations, including O Lehane, Lehane, Leyne, Lane and Lyons. *Liath* is the Irish word for grey. Liatháin is a diminutive and it probably meant the small, grey man.

At one time there were two distinct families using the same name. One had its territory in County Cork, while the other was in the north-west, in County Sligo. Ó Liatháin is still common in Cork, although it has assumed a variety of spellings and has even been anglicized to Lyons. The Sligo family belonged to the prominent Uí Fiachrach race who had their territory in the parish of Dromard. The name has long since faded from Sligo and its bearers have moved further north to County Donegal, where they also anglicized their name to Lyons.

It would seem possible that another anglicization of Ó Liatháin, i.e. Lehane, was corrupted in the course of time by misspelling to Lawn, a very rare name in any part of Ireland except Ulster. As Lawn, this surname has not come to prominence yet, unlike Lyons, of which there have been a number of prominent people at home and abroad.

Another anglicization of the surname is Lane. The most distinguished representative of this name was **Sir Hugh Lane** (1875–1915), the famous art collector from County Cork who was drowned when the *Lusitania* was torpedoed. His legacy of paintings has been divided amicably between Dublin and London, after many legal disputes.

Lenihan

Ó Leannacháin

Lenaghan Linehan

The surname Ó Leannacháin is a diminutive of the Irish word *leann*, meaning cloaked or mantled.

Although Lenihan in its various forms is numerous throughout Ireland, it originated in County Roscommon, where **Maelciaran Ó Lenechan** (d. 1249) of Tuamna in Boyle was an outstanding priest, highly praised by the Four Masters in their history of Ireland known as *The Annals of Loch Cé*.

In Ulster, where the name is usually spelled Lenaghan, there are also MacClenaghans and MacLenaghans, whose names are thought to be anglicized forms of Mac Leannacháin.

Maurice Lenihan (1811–95), who was born in Waterford, was a journalist and editor who campaigned for Irish nationalism in his newspapers. When he moved to Limerick, he wrote a *History of Limerick*, which, although it was subscribed for, completely drained his financial resources.

The Genealogical Office in Dublin holds a copy of a grant of arms to descendants of **James Lenihan** of Waterford which was compiled by **Maurice Lenihan** (1845–1974). They also have a confirmation of arms to **William Burke Lenihan**, a family of Eyre Square in Galway, made in 1938.

Brian Lenihan (1930–94) of Dundalk, County Louth, son of a politician, was a barrister and Member of the European Parliament. He was deputy leader of the Fianna Fáil Party, in which, when it was in government, he held more ministries than any other politician. His son, also Brian, has followed the political path too.

Lennane *see* Lennon

Lennon

Ó Leannáin

Lennane Linane

For Lennon, a numerous surname throughout Ireland, a variety of origins are suggested. Some say it derives from the Irish word for cloak, while others say it means paramour!

In Scotland, it is a shortened version of MacLennan. In Ireland, there are several distinct Lennon septs, the most numerous of which is of Glandore in County Cork, who use the spellings Lennane or Linane.

In counties Galway and Mayo it is anglicized to Lennon. The O Lennons of County Fermanagh were Church administrators at Lisgoole, near Enniskillen, where, between 1380 and 1466, they produced six priors or canons.

Like many another family, the Lennons travelled abroad, including a **John Lennon** who was notorious as a daring sailor. **John Brown Lennon** (1850–1923) was prominent in the labour movement in America.

The most famous of all the Lennons was **John Lennon** (1940–80) of the Beatles, who was born in Liverpool, probably of Irish blood. Lennon and Paul McCartney (also with Irish origins) wrote the music and lyrics which fuelled the worldwide "Beatlemania". John Lennon was murdered outside his New York home by a deranged young man called Mark Chapman.

Leonard

Ó Leannáin

Gilsenan Linnane Lunny MacAlinion

St. Leonard was a very popular saint in France and England, from where came the surname Leonard. It has suffered such a variety of gaelicizations (*leann* is a cloak or mantle) and anglicizations it would be impossible to distinguish it from the Ó Leannáins who were an ecclesiastical family in County Fermanagh, and two other Gaelic septs of the same name, one of Killala in County Mayo and the other who supported the powerful O Kellys of Galway. The name has many variants, from Lennor, Linnane, Lineen, Lunny, Gilsenan, MacAlinion to Nannany—depending on local pronunciation.

There are few accounts of the Leonards in Ireland until the seventeenth century, when there is mention of a **Lieutenant-Colonel Francis Leonard** who was with the army of King James II in 1690, for which "treason" he forfeited his land.

The Dublin Genealogical Office has pedigrees of many propertied Leonard families, including four in County Meath and two in County Dublin, dating from about 1750 to 1950. They were also estate owners in counties Kerry and Limerick. There is a map of the estate of **John Leonard** of Moneen, Ballyduff and Gowran of County Kilkenny, made in 1823. There is also an interesting certificate written in Latin by James II stating that **Paul Leonard** and his brother, **Stephen**, both from Waterford and now in Spain, were of gentle birth. They probably needed an aristocratic pedigree to be accepted as officers in the Spanish army, like many others of the "Wild Geese".

Between 1828 and 1869, **J. P. Leonard** gathered a wealth of papers on the Irish brigades in France.

The internationally celebrated playwright, **Hugh Leonard** of Dublin, changed his name from Byrne.

Leslie

The original Leslies were Scottish and were noted for "a chronic adventurous poverty". They "adventured" to Ireland in the seventeenth century as supporters of the royal Stuarts. On the other side there were the Leslies of Kerry, who were awarded much property in Ireland for their support of William of Orange. P. L. Pielou published *The Leslies of Tarbert, County Kerry* in 1935.

Charles Leslie (1650–1722), born in Dublin, was a chancellor of the Cathedral of Connor until deprived of his office for not signing the oath of allegiance. This drove him to join Prince Charles in France.

In 1913, **Seymour Leslie** published *Of Glaslough in the Kingdom of Oriel and the Noted Men who Have Dwelt There*. Glaslough, or Castle Leslie, in County Monaghan, is a palatial mansion which was the home of a string of distinguished Leslies, including many ecclesiastics.

John Leslie, while a subaltern in the Life Guards, won the grand military steeplechase and also painted a picture which was hung in the Royal Academy.

His son married one of the Jerome sisters of New York, and the other Jerome sister married Randolph Churchill. Thus it was that the Leslies became cousins of the Churchills.

Sir Shane Leslie (1885–1971) was a historian, a poet and, above all, a teller of ghost stories. His son, **Desmond Leslie** (b. 1921), wrote *Flying Saucers Have Landed* which, since it was published in 1953, has been translated into sixteen languages. His sister, **Anita Leslie King** (1914–86), was a historian and a writer of a number of books on the Churchills. At her request, she was buried in the Castle Leslie demesne.

Thomas Edward Cliffe Leslie (1827–82), who was born in Wexford, was a professor of economics and jurisprudence, and one of the founders of the theory of political economy.

Burke's Irish Family Records (1976) contains pedigrees of the Leslies of County Kerry and County Antrim. The name is not numerous in Ireland, other than in Ulster.

Levens *see* Livingstone

Levy *see* Dunleavy

Leyden *see* Lydon

Leyne *see* (O) Lehane

Liddane, Liddon *see* Lydon

Linane *see* Lennon

Linehan *see* Lenihan

Livingstone

Levens Livingston

The name Livingstone comes from a parish in the burgh of Linlithgow in Scotland.

There is an American family which descends from the 5th Lord Livingstone, who was guardian to Mary Queen of Scots. This family emigrated to North America in 1673 and settled in Albany.

The most famous Livingstone, **David Livingstone** (1813–73), the missionary and explorer who discovered the Victoria Falls of the Zambezi River in Africa, came from Scotland.

About 1609, **Sir George Livingstone** was one of the officials appointed to administer the plantation of Ulster, for which he was awarded two thousand acres. He was threatened with a fine of £400 if he failed to populate the country with immigrants from Scotland, but he was far from unsuccessful, judging by his many namesakes living today in Northern Ireland. The name is rare in the Republic of Ireland.

Both in the Public Records Office in Belfast and in the National Library in Dublin, there are records going back to the seventeenth century concerning this family.

William Livingston (1723–90) was Governor of New Jersey, and his brother **Philip** signed the Declaration of Independence.

Peadar Livingstone of County Fermanagh published, in 1969, a well-documented history of his native county, from its earliest times to the present day.

The Livingstones were great travellers and wrote copiously about the various parts of the world they explored. In the United States of America they were revolutionary patriots and soldiers. They are very numerous today in the USA, where they hold many high offices.

(O) Loane *see* Lambe

Loftus

Loughnane

This ancient English surname is very well recorded. A pedigree dating from 996 to 1840 gives their descent from the Earl of Anjou to Hugh Capet, King of France.

A Loftus is recorded as being first Bailiff and then Mayor of Limerick from 1422 to 1444. But mostly they came from Swineshead in Yorkshire as Elizabethan planters or soldiers of the Commonwealth. They spread throughout Ireland, becoming very influential and owning many fine properties.

Adam Loftus (*c.*1533–1605) arrived in Ireland as chaplain to the Earl of Sussex in 1560. He was appointed Archbishop of Armagh and Dublin and it was mainly through his influence with Queen Elizabeth I that land was granted for the founding of Trinity College Dublin, of which he was the first provost in 1591. He took good care of his nephews, one of whom, another **Adam**, became the 1st Viscount of Ely and Lord Chancellor of Ireland.

An orientalist called **Dudley Loftus** had a strange arrangement with an Italian lady, Maria Plunketta. They were to live near each other and to visit each other regularly, even after death!

The Loftus family were viscounts and marquesses of Ely. One of their properties, Ely Lodge near Enniskillen, was blown up in 1870 by the 4th Marquess during his 21st birthday celebrations. He built a huge windswept mansion called Loftus Hall by the sea, near Wexford. Like many of their mansions, it is now a convent. Mount Loftus in County Kilkenny, which was built in 1750 by the **1st Viscount Loftus**, has been rebuilt three times.

In Connacht, where this surname is very numerous, it could be a synonym for Loughnane, assumed during the suppression of Gaelic names.

Logan

Ó Leogháin

Loghan Lohan Loughan

It is a difficult to discover the exact origin of the Logan name. There was an ancient family who were Ó Leogháin chieftains and Lords of Morgallion in County Meath until they were driven west by the Anglo-Normans. There were also de Logans who came to Ireland with the Normans about 1190.

Logan is a common name in Scotland, and many came from there in the seventeenth century at the time of the plantations, which is why today there are many more of that name in Ulster than in any other part of the country.

In County Galway, Ó Leogháin was anglicized to Lohan. It was also foolishly anglicized to Duck. The Irish word for duck is *lacha*, which bears little resemblance to the original!

There are four Loughanstowns in Westmeath, a Loganstown in Meath, and a Loughan's Park in County Galway.

From 1254 until 1283, **Maurice O Loughan** was Bishop of Kilmacduagh.

A most distinguished Logan was **James Logan** (1674–1751) of Antrim, and possibly of Scottish origin. The son of a Quaker schoolmaster, he was an astute businessman who caught the attention of William Penn, the Quaker founder of Pennsylvania, who made him his secretary. He lived in Pennsylvania for fifty years, making a vast fortune in trade, as well as becoming a justice of the supreme court. He had an enormous estate, a huge library and wide and esteemed botanical knowledge.

Cornelius Logan (1806–53), whose parents had emigrated to the USA from Ireland, was an actor and dramatist. His daughter, **Olivia**, followed a successful acting career, while his son, **Ambrose**, was a physician who played an active role in American politics.

Loghan *see* Logan

(O) Loghlen *see* (O) Loughlin

Logue *see* Leech

Lohan *see* Logan

Londrigan *see* Lonergan

Lonergan

Ó Longargáin

Londrigan

Longargáin, in ancient times an Irish first name, translated into English means strangely fierce. It was from this somewhat frightening ancestor that the Lonergans derived their unusual name.

In pre-Norman times they had their headquarters in County Tipperary. Inter-tribal warfare between themselves and their more powerful neighbours, the O Briens of Thomond (mostly Limerick and Clare) and the MacNamaras, combined with the encroaching Butlers of Ormond, drove them south to the rich lands of Cashel and Cahir in County Tipperary.

The Lonergans were both a musical and an ecclesiastical family. For centuries they were harpers to the O Kellys of Galway. Between the twelfth and the fifteenth century, they could boast three Archbishops of Cashel, two Bishops of Killaloe and one Bishop of Clare. From then on, they seem to have been submerged by the cruel wars of the sixteenth and seventeenth centuries.

An Irish nun called **Anne Lonergan** suffered imprisonment during the French Revolution. **Thomas Lonergan** (b. 1861) was an Irish-American poet and politician.

Long

Ó Longáin

Long, a most numerous name all over Ireland, has a number of origins. In Norman-French it was de Long and in Irish it was Ó Longáin, the word *long* meaning tall.

Many of the Longs in Ireland today are descended from English soldiers who came in the seventeenth century with the Cromwellian armies. They were given land and, through the centuries, they have distinguished themselves in the military, the Church and the professions.

In Ulster, there was a family of Ó Longáin who were chieftains in Armagh. Another Ó Longáin family were important Church administrators in Munster. Following the destruction of the monasteries, they lost their lands and were dispersed, some of them joining in the flight to serve in the armies of Europe.

Many fine houses were built by the various Longs, both English and Irish. Mount Long at Oysterhaven in County Cork was built by **Doctor John Long**, who was hanged for his part in the rising of 1641. It is now a ruin.

John St. John Long (1798–1834) of Limerick studied art in Dublin before emigrating to London, where, for a while, he was a very successful painter. He turned to medicine, claiming to be able to cure all the common diseases, until the death of several of his patients put an end to this spurious career.

In the eighteenth century, **Micheál** and his son **Micheál Óg Ó Langáin** were outstanding Gaelic scholars. A collection of their poetry is in Harvard University library.

In 1989, **Denis O Long** of Garranelongy, who lived at Farnanes in County Cork, had his claim to chieftainship of the O Long authenticated. He was officially installed as The O Long of Garranelongy in 1990.

see also Langan

(O) Loughlin

Ó Lochlainn

(O) Loghlen

This was an important Dalcassian sept of Thomond (counties Clare and Limerick). Their chieftains were lords of Corcomroe and at one time they were close kinsmen of the royal O Conors of Connacht. Their name derives from their ancestor Lochlainn, Lord of Corcomroe.

Conghalach Ó Lochlainn was Bishop of Corcomroe (now known as Kilfenora) from 1281 to 1300.

With the arrival of the land-hungry Elizabethan adventurers, they lost much of their land and retreated into a much smaller territory at the Burren in County Clare. Until comparatively recently the head of the O Loughlins was known locally as the "King of Burren".

Before the arrival of the Cromwellians, twenty-two castles were listed as belonging to the O Loughlins. Even after the restoration of King Charles I their property was not restored.

Sir Michael O Loghlen (1789–1842) of Drumconora in Ennis, County Clare, a distinguished lawyer at the Irish Bar, was created a baronet. He was a solicitor-general and a master of the rolls. He was the first Roman Catholic since 1688 to be raised to a judicial office in either England or Ireland. His eldest son, **Sir Colman O Loghlen** (1819–77), was a Member of Parliament for County Clare and a campaigner for Catholic emancipation. His second son, **Sir Bryan O Loghlen** (1828–1905), emigrated to Australia, where he became Prime Minister of Victoria.

The O prefix has been dropped from the surname in some cases, mostly in Northern Ireland. The name has no connection with MacLoughlin or MacLaughlin (q.v.).

Loughnane *see* Loftus, Loughney

Loughney

Ó Lachtna

Loughnane Maloughney Molony

The Irish name Ó Lachtna (*lachtna* means dark grey) was anglicized to Loughney. They were of the ancient Uí Fiachrach sept of Connacht, where they were chieftains of Two Bacs and of Glen Nephin in Tirawly in County Mayo. Loughney, now a very rare name, has long since been replaced by Loughnane.

It could also be related to Maloughney and Molony and the Irish name Ó Maoldhamhnaigh, meaning descendant of the servant of the church. It has always been a thoroughly Gaelic name, but one which has received little mention in the archives.

The Genealogical Office in Dublin has a pedigree of Loughnan, and of Maher Loughnan from 1610 to 1919. There is also a confirmation of arms to **Lieutenant Francis Loughnan**, son of **Andrew Loughnan** of London, grandson of **J. Loughnan** of Ferrol in Spain. This is dated 1846.

(O) Lowan *see* Lambe

Lowry

Ó Labhradha

Lavery

Ó Labhradha was an old Ulster family which divided into three septs. Their name was anglicized to Lavery and, later, to Lowry, and they were known as the Baun-Lavery, the Roe-Lavery and the Trin-Lavery (*bán* means white, *rua* means red and *tréan* means strong). Through mistranslation, the Trin-Lavery name was transformed into Armstrong. The word *labhraidh* means a spokesperson.

The most famous Lavery was **Sir John Lavery** (1856–1941), a landscape and portrait painter who was born in Belfast. He designed the first Irish bank notes, using a portrait of his wife, **Hazel**, a great beauty, to adorn them.

The Lowrys of Ulster are a junior branch of the Earl of Belmore's family. During the seventeenth century, **James Lowry** came from Scotland and settled in County Tyrone. His son **John** was present, with his wife, at the siege of Derry. In succeeding generations, these Lowrys were Members of Parliament, clergymen and lawyers, and they built themselves several fine homes.

Arthur Lowry Corry, Member of Parliament for County Tyrone (b. 1740), assumed his wife's family name. He was created 1st Earl Belmore of Castle Coole, County Fermanagh. His descendants were Lords of the Admiralty, Governors of Jamaica and holders of many high civic posts.

A very military family, the Lowrys of Glasdrummond House in County Down have served all over the former British Empire in the army and the navy.

Lieutenant-General Robert Lowry (b. 1844) held over eighteen thousand Irish acres. He was High Commissioner of Corfu and of the Ionian Islands. He also commanded a force against the Fenian raids at Fort Erie in 1866. A son of his became a fruit grower in California.

The most remarkable twentieth-century Lowry was **L. S. Lowry** (1887–1976). A Manchester painter with a distinctive style, his Lancashire industrial scenes are easily recognizable.

Today, the Laverys and the Lowrys are most numerous in Northern Ireland.

Lucas

Lucas is the older form of Luke, the name of the Apostle. This ancient surname is scattered throughout Ireland. One family of Lucas in *Burke's Irish Family Records* (1976) supposes their lineage to go back to an ancestor who came to Cork with Sir Walter Raleigh in 1580. For generations, their home was in Ardbrack in Kinsale, County Cork. However, in the archives there is a grant by **Issyn Lucas** to Meryk and David Walsch of land in Inishtioge in County Kilkenny, made in 1409.

Lucas is well recorded in the Genealogical Office and in the Public Records Offices in Dublin and Belfast, where there are pedigrees of various, not necessarily related, Lucas families, including one family of Castle Shane in County Monaghan, one of Coote Hill in County Cavan, and also several in the counties Clare, Carlow and Laois. The **Reverend Edward Lucas** of Castle Shane married a wealthy Clements heiress and, in 1823, changed his name to Lucas Clements.

Many Lucas men were soldiers in the Cromwellian armies, for which they were rewarded with grants of land. **Sir Thomas Lucas** told of a letter which related how five thousand Irish rebels were slain in Cork and one hundred prisoners executed! However, many of the named were themselves rebels and forfeited their land and were transported to Connacht.

The most celebrated Lucas was **Charles Lucas** (1713–71) of County Clare, an apothecary. He accused the government of abuses in the sale of drugs and campaigned against corruption. He also advocated parliamentary independence for Ireland, for which he had to emigrate to Leiden, where he graduated in medicine. Years later he returned and became a Member of Parliament for the city of Dublin, but he continued to write about injustice. His statue can be seen in Dublin's City Hall.

Lucey

Ó Luasaigh

Lucy

This fairly uncommon name belongs to a family who came from Oxfordshire and settled in Fermanagh. In some instances, the name possibly derives from the fourth-century **St. Lucy**, a virgin martyred at Syracuse at the time of the Emperor Diocletian. Her feast is December 13 and she is the patron saint of the blind. In the Middle Ages, there were also Norman de Lucys who were prominent in England.

In Ireland, the Lucey name is now very much centred in County Cork and Laois and is an anglicization of Ó Luasaigh.

Ronayne's Court in Douglas, County Cork, a seventeenth-century mansion built by John Ronayne, has been for some time the home of **Lieutenant-Colonel John Lucy**.

The **Most Reverend Dr. Lucey**, Bishop of Cork, was famous for his conservative Catholic convictions.

Lunny *see* Leonard

Lupton

Lupton is an English name which came unobtrusively to Ireland, where it is neither numerous nor prominent.

This family originated from the town of Lupton in Westmoreland, from where they crossed over into Yorkshire. There have been a number of distinguished English Luptons who were writers and clergymen, including a **Donald Lupton** (d. 1676) who was chaplain to the English forces in the Low Countries, probably including Prussia. In 1632, he returned home to settle in London as a fairly undistinguished writer.

Roger Lupton (d. 1540), a provost of Eton, was the founder of the renowned Cumbrian public school, Sedbergh. It was he who had to surrender the leper hospital at St. James in Westminster, including its many acres, to Henry VIII, in return for a meagre amount of land elsewhere.

A few representatives of this rare name can be found in Ulster, but the majority are mostly distributed around Munster.

Lydon

Ó Loideáin

Leyden Liddane Liddon Lyden

Very little has been recorded about this name other than that its roots are definitely in the counties of Galway and Mayo and that it derives from a first name, Lodán. For a comparatively simple name, it has gone through a great variety of anglicizations, from Ó Loideáin to Liddane, Liddon, Lydden, Lyden, Leyden and Ludden. The Leydens are more likely to be found in Sligo and Clare, while the Liddanes are peculiar only to Clare.

It is believed that the **Abbot Ó Lotáin** mentioned in the *Annals of Loch Cé* in 1216 was of this sept. He is described as "a paragon of piety and learning".

There is a record of two Liddons in Castlebar, County Mayo, who forfeited their estates because of their allegiance to King James II.

It is probable that the nineteenth-century book illustrator, **A. F. Lyden**, who made colour plates and wood engravings, was originally of this sept before emigrating to Britain.

The Lydon name is most prominent in Galway city, where **H. J. Lydon and Company**, the bakery and confectionery of Lydon House in Shop Street, also have a restaurant and bars. They have extended their business to Limerick and Tipperary. Their Shop Street restaurant is notable for the collection it has on display of the stone carved armorial bearings of the old Galway families which used to be set into the doorways or chimney pieces of their houses. The Lydons must be given credit for saving this Galway heritage.

Lynch

Ó Loingsigh

The anglicized Lynch surname comes from two quite distinct sources. One was Labradh Longseach (*longseach* means mariner), a king of Ireland in the sixth century BC, whose origins were in counties Clare, Sligo and Limerick, with another branch in Donegal. The others were the de Lench family who came with the Normans and settled in Connacht, where they built many castles. As was fitting for prosperous merchants, they were one of the Fourteen Tribes of Galway, and there were eighty-four Lynch Mayors of Galway between 1484 and 1654. A school founded by **Dominic Lynch** attracted thousands of pupils to Galway.

A remarkable number of Lynches were priests and scholars, many of whom had to flee to France and Spain, where they held high positions in the Church. A family which settled in Bordeaux owned the vineyard where the famous **Château-Bages Lynch** wine is made.

Many Lynches went far afield. The **Blosse Lynch** family of County Mayo were courageous nineteenth-century explorers in the Middle East. **Thomas Lynch** signed the American Declaration of Independence. **Dr. John Lynch** was a chaplain during the American Civil War.

They are also to be found in Australia and in South America, especially in the Argentines. **Patricio Lynch** was regarded as "the foremost Chilean naval hero". Francisco Lopez II and **Elizabeth Lynch** reigned over Paraguay for twelve years.

Jack Lynch (b. 1917), winner of six All-Ireland medals—five for hurling and one for Gaelic football—was Taoiseach for two terms during the 1970s.

It is thought the Norman Lynches may have originated in Lintz, Austria. The lynx on their azure blue crest—the most sharp-sighted of animals—commemorates a forebear who, as a governor of the city, defended it bravely against invaders and was awarded the city's symbol, the lynx, for his courage. Their shield, a matching azure blue, has a golden chevron with three gold trefoils.

Lyons

Ó Liatháin Ó Laighin

Lane Lehane (O) Lyne

The Irish Lyons are quite distinct from the English and Scottish families of this name. One of the many variants of the name probably came in the twelfth century with the Normans from the city of Lyons and were known as de Leon or de Lyons. They settled in County Meath.

Lyons is also the anglicized form of Ó Laighin, or Lyne, an ancient family who owned much property in County Galway until the end of the seventeenth century.

In County Kerry, the name can also be found as Lane or Leyne, especially around Dingle, where Leyne is particularly numerous.

In County Cork, the Lyons were originally Ó Liatháin. Near Fermoy there is a village called Castle Lyons. A family of Lyons who were formerly Ó Leighin were physicians to the Roches of Fermoy.

Father Matthew O Leyn (d. 1599) was one of a number of Franciscan martyrs during the sixteenth and seventeenth centuries, when many Lyons also suffered confiscation of their lands.

In the eighteenth century there were several distinguished Lyons antiquarians and physicians.

Matthew Lyon (1746–1822), a poor Wicklow boy, emigrated to become a colonel in the American army in the War of Independence and a member of Congress.

F. S. Leland Lyons (1923–83), born in Londonderry, was a historian and a distinguished provost of Trinity College Dublin.

see also (O) Lehane

M

MacAfee *see* Mahaffy

MacAlary *see* Clarke

MacAleer *see* MacClure

MacAleevy *see* Dunleavy

MacAlinion *see* Leonard

MacAlister

Mac Alastair

Alastair is the Gaelic equivalent for the personal name Alexander. The McAlisters were one of the principal branches of the clan Donald, who were descendants of the thirteenth-century Alexander, brother of Angus Mór. They trace their ancestry back to the three Collas of Oriel in County Monaghan.

These MacAlisters were among the many families who left Ireland to settle in Scotland. Towards the close of the fourteenth century, a branch of the Scottish MacAlister clan returned to Ireland as gallowglasses, or mercenary soldiers. They settled mainly in Ulster, in County Antrim, where the name is very numerous today, although there are also many representatives of the name in and around County Dublin.

In 1799, when the insurgent leader, Michael Dwyer, was trapped by the British troops in his County Wicklow stronghold where he had been hiding for several years, **Samuel MacAlister** gave his own life by drawing the fire, thus enabling Dwyer and his men to escape.

Two Dublin men have brought distinction to the name. **Robert Alexander MacAlister** (1870–1950), an archaeologist, was director of the excavations for the Palestine Exploration Fund from 1900 to 1909. He was the first professor of Celtic archaeology at University College Dublin and was a president of the Royal Irish Academy. He wrote widely on his subject, and *The Secret Language of Ireland*, an account of ogham inscriptions on tombstones, is regarded as his most important work.

Alexander MacAllister (1877–1944) started his career as a librarian in Dublin. After serving in the First World War he settled in England, where he wrote plays and novels under various pseudonyms. He had great success with a long series of detective novels which he published under the name Lynn Brock.

MacAloon

Mac Giolla Eoin

MacGloin MacGlone Monday

MacAloon is one of a variety of anglicizations of the ancient Irish surname, Mac Giolla Eoin, meaning son of the follower of Saint John. It also occurs as MacGlone, MacGloin, MacAloon and Clone. There was an inaccurate translation to Monday, a haphazard anglicization from the similar-sounding Irish word for the first day of the week—*Luan*!

Compared to its more numerous synonym MacGloin, MacAloon is rarely to be found in any part of Ireland. Originally, in its various forms, it was a patronymic of the counties Tyrone, Derry and Leitrim. It was in counties Derry and Fermanagh that it suffered the indignity of becoming Monday!

Today, the name is occasionally found in the United States of America, where **James MacGloin** was a prominent Texan pioneer.

MacAnally *see* MacNally

MacArdle

Mac Árdghail

The not very numerous name, Mac Árdghail, derives from *árdghal*, an Irish word meaning high valour.

The MacArdles are more numerous in the northern counties, where they are believed to be a branch of the MacMahons of Oriel in County Monaghan.

In the mid-eighteenth century, **James MacArdle** of Fews in County Armagh is recorded as being a Gaelic poet. So, too, was **Siobhán nic Ardghail**, or Johanna MacArdle.

In the 1750s, **James McArdle** (*c.*1728–65) was at the height of his popularity as a mezzotint engraver in London.

Dorothy Macardle (1899–1958), historian, novelist, playwright and drama critic, was the daughter of **Sir Thomas Macardle**, the proprietor of a brewery in Dundalk, County Louth. She took an active part in the republican movement—at one time going on hunger-strike. In 1937, her close friend Eamon de Valera encouraged her to write *The Irish Republic*, the definitive history of the struggle for independence. She later wrote novels, two of which were made into films. After the Second World War, she devoted herself to the problems of the refugee children of Europe.

Joseph Ardle McArdle (b. 1934), a Dublin barrister and former international civil servant, founded the Co-op Books. He is also a translator from Polish and French, and a novelist.

MacArthur

Arthur

MacArthur is a Scottish surname and is distinct from the surname Arthur, although they are sometimes confused. MacArthur comes from the old Irish word for bear and is connected with Celtic bear worship.

There were Arthurs of Norse origin in Limerick since the twelfth century who were among its prominent citizens. Some were mayors or sheriffs, some were Members of Parliament, and there were also two Arthur bishops.

Thomas Arthur (1593–1675) was a leading physician who became famous for his diaries. **Major Thomas Arthur** fought in Ireland in the army of James II (1633–1701). There were also Arthurs prominent in France at that time.

For several centuries, the Arthurs were prominent landowners in County Dublin and in the Midlands. In the records of the seventeenth century, there are many accounts of their lands being confiscated, while some members of the family were transplanted to Connacht.

In Scotland, the MacArthurs reached the height of their power in the fourteenth century, when Robert Bruce made them keepers of the Castle of Dunstaffanage in Argyllshire. James I

(1566–1625) beheaded their chieftain, **John MacArthur**, and most of his estates were forfeited. A sept of the name were hereditary pipers to the Macdonalds of the Isles. In Islay there is a Gaelic saying:

Cnoic is uilt is Ailpenich,
Ach cuin' a thanaig Artaraich?
(Hills and streams and Alpinites,
But whence came the Arthurites?)

General Arthur MacArthur (1845–1912) was of Scottish parentage and served in the Philippines, rising in 1902 to be lieutenant-general. He was the twelfth officer in the history of the US army to attain to this rank. His son, **Douglas MacArthur** (1880–1964), is equally famous, especially for his part in the Second World War. He also led the UN forces into the Korean war in 1950.

In Ireland today the MacArthur name is very rare.

MacAtamney *see* Tamney

MacAteer *see* MacIntyre

MacAtilla *see* Tully

MacAuley

Mac Amhlaoibh

MacAwley Cawley Magawley

There are many variations of this name. Some scholars believe that the Viking name Olaf went through a series of mutations—Amlof, Anlaib, Aulaib—until it was eventually simplified to Auley. The Vikings came from Norway to pillage and to carry back their booty. However, some must have remained to marry Irish wives, for they appear in the annals from about AD 851, when two septs are recorded.

The MacAuleys took their name from Auley, a thirteenth-century descendant of Niall of the Nine Hostages. As Lords of Calry, they ruled parts of Offaly and Westmeath, where their stronghold was Ballyloughnoe, referred to as McGawley's Country in the Elizabethan records. Their detailed pedigree is in Dublin's Genealogical Office. The last recognized Chief of the Name was known as **Count Magawley Cerati**. His father was Prime Minister to the Austrian Empress Maria Louisa, Napoleon's second wife, who reigned over parts of northern Italy.

Clanawley commemorates another branch of the family who belonged to Fermanagh, where they were kinsmen of the MacGuires.

The MacAulays of Red Hall in Antrim descend from the Scottish Earls of Lennox and came to Ireland in the seventeenth century, where many of the family are now buried in the old churchyard at Loyd near Cushendall. One of this family, known as **Hugh McAulay Boyd**, went to London to write, and is one of many possible candidates thought to have written the celebrated letters of "Junius".

The most famous of the MacAuleys is **Catherine McAuley** (1778–1842). Her parents died when she was an infant, and she was adopted by the Callahan family of Dublin, who subsequently left her their fortune. This enabled her to found the Sisters of Mercy. She began by helping the poor children of Dublin and their working mothers. The Sisters of Mercy developed into the largest religious order, with convents all over the world.

James J. McAuley is a Dublin journalist, poet and critic.

MacAuliffe

Mac Amhlaoibh

MacAuley

MacAuliffe, son of Amhlaoibh, is the Irish version of the Norse name Olaf. There were three branches of this name, which today remains most deeply entrenched in Munster, particularly in the County Cork area. They were originally a branch of the powerful McCarthy sept and their seat was Castle MacAuliffe in County Cork.

The MacAuliffes of Fermanagh were a branch of the Maguires of Clanawley. There was also a branch of the family in Ardincaple in Dumbartonshire, Scotland.

A **Major Dermot MacAuliffe** was in the army of James II. After his defeat, when many Irish men and women fled to France, they appear in the papers and genealogies of Irish families which are held in the Bibliothèque Nationale in Paris.

Philip II of Spain supported many impoverished Irish in Europe, including **Dona Cecilia Macaulif**. There is also mention of a Demetrius MacCarthy who wrote in French from Barcelona in 1718 to Cardinal Noailles concerning a disagreement he had with his wife, **Helen MacCauliffe**.

The last Chief of the Name is thought to have been **Michael MacAuliffe**, a colonel in the Spanish army who died in Spain in 1720.

Lord Thomas Babington Macaulay (1800–59), the celebrated historian who is best remembered for his five-volume *History of England*, was descended from a County Antrim branch of the family.

The French physician, **Joseph Oliff** (1808–69), was born a MacAuliff in Cork.

MacAvoy *see* MacEvoy

MacAwley *see* MacAuley

MacBirney

Mac Biorna

Birney (Mac)Burney MacBirnie

MacBirney and its many variants evolved from the Norse personal name Bjarni—the Norwegian name for bear is *björn*. It is said to be the Irish equivalent of MacMahon, or Mac Mathghamhan, which means son of a bear. It is essentially a Scottish name. In Dumfriesshire it is usually shortened to Burnie, while in other parts of that country it is to be found as MacBirnie, MacBurnie, and even Macfurney.

It was not until the seventeenth century that it first appeared in the Acts of Parliament in Scotland, although a **David M'Birney** is mentioned as a witness in Kirkcudbright in 1466, while a **Cuthbert McBurnie** was appointed the "Brigmaistre" of Dumfries in 1520—an area where there is a concentration of the surname.

They must have come as mercenary soldiers or planters to Ulster, where MacBurney is still a common name. It is rarely found in other parts of Ireland.

Until recently, one of the big department stores long established on the Dublin quays was owned by the McBirney family, who had also promoted the Belleek porcelain industry in County Fermanagh.

MacBride

Mac Giolla Bhrighde

MacBride is an anglicization of the Gaelic name Mac Giolla Bhríghde, which means a devotee of St. Bridget. It is very much an Ulster name, particularly in County Donegal, where, in medieval times, they were administrators to the Church and its lands around Raymunterdoney and Tory Island. From this family came a number of Bishops of Raphoe, including **John MacGilbride**, who died in 1440.

John was a favourite MacBride first name. There was a **John MacBride** (1650–1718) who was a Presbyterian writer, a **John MacBride** (1730–1800) who was a British admiral and yet another **John MacBride** (1778–1868) who was a scholar and the head of Magdalen College in Oxford University.

David MacBride (1726–78) was a physician and inventor. The miniaturist **Alexander MacBride** (1798–1852) came from County Monaghan.

Major John MacBride (1865–1916) was born in Westport, County Mayo. He fought in the Boer War against the British and, for his part in the 1916 Easter Rising, he was executed.

In 1903, Major MacBride had married Maud Gonne, with whom the poet W. B. Yeats was infatuated for many years. **Madame Maud Gonne MacBride**, a very handsome woman, was one of Ireland's most colourful characters, fighting for many national causes as well as pursuing justice for the oppressed. Her only son, **Sean MacBride** (1904–88), was born in Pietermaritzburg. He was mainly educated in Ireland and played an active part in the War of Independence. As a barrister he defended his republican colleagues. A statesman of international standing, he acted on many United Nations committees and had the distinction of being awarded the Nobel Peace Prize in 1974, the Lenin Peace Prize in 1977 and the American Medal of Justice.

In Connacht, Kilbride can be a synonym for MacBride. This is also a Scottish surname and is still numerous in Ulster.

MacBurney *see* MacBirney

MacCabe

Mac Cába

In medieval times, when fighting was commonplace, the Irish chiefs imported gallowglasses (mercenaries) from Scotland. The MacCabes came to Ireland to join forces with the O Rourkes and the O Reillys of Leitrim and Cavan. Because of their peculiar headgear, they acquired the name *cába*, meaning a hat or a cap.

The MacCabes have been in Ireland ever since. **Cathaoir MacCabe** of Cavan was a musician and poet whose great friend was the blind Turlough O Carolan, the most renowned of Irish harpists. Fooled into believing his friend had died, Turlough wrote a lament for Cathaoir who, when he heard about it, was not pleased. However, it was not long before he was writing a genuine elegy for his dead friend.

Some MacCabes settled in Ulster, where **Thomas MacCabe**, who was in the cotton mill business, campaigned to stop Belfast shipowners from allowing their ships to be used for slave trading. His son, **William Putnam MacCabe** (1776–1821), a United Irishman, escaped execution following the 1798 Rebellion because of his remarkable talent for disguising himself. When his friend Lord Edward FitzGerald died, he fled to Rouen in France, where he established a cotton mill.

Edward Cardinal MacCabe of Dublin (1816–85) studied for the priesthood at Maynooth College, became Archbishop of Dublin in 1879 and was appointed a cardinal three years later.

Alasdair Mac Cába (1886–1972) was born near Ballymote in County Sligo. He was a teacher until 1914, after which he took an active part in the 1916 Easter Rising and was imprisoned several times. He supported the Treaty and sat in the Dáil for several years. He gave up politics and, in 1935, with £500 capital, founded the Educational Building Society, which still flourishes today.

Eugene MacCabe, who farms in County Monaghan, has filled Dublin's Abbey Theatre many times with his popular plays.

The MacCabes have a green heraldic shield with a wavy fess, or band, and three salmon. Their crest is a green demi-griffen and their motto is *Aut vincere aut mori* (Conquer or die).

MacCallum *see* MacColum

MacCann

Mac Cana

Canny MacAnna MacCanna

The MacAnnas, who were an important sept in their territory of Clanbrassil around Lough Neagh in County Antrim, derive their surname from *cano*, meaning a wolfhound—Ireland's most ancient breed of dogs.

The *Annals of the Four Masters* described **Ambhlaith Mac Canna** as being "a pillar of chivalry and vigour of the Cenél Eoghain", signifying his descent from the great O Neills of Ulster.

Until late in the sixteenth century, **Donnell MacCanna** was still styled Chief of his clan. Afterwards, they began to suffer the dispossession common to many of the native Irish, although the name is still numerous in their Lough Neagh homeland.

Patrick MacCanna defended the Irish College in Paris from the mob, during the French Revolution. He accompanied Wolfe Tone's abortive maritime expedition to Ireland, and subsequently retired to France, where he prospered in Boulogne.

Two MacCanns have made significant contributions to Ireland's national theatre, the Abbey Theatre in Dublin. **John McCann**, who wrote popular satirical plays about Irish rural life, was also Lord Mayor of Dublin in 1946 to 1947. **Donal McCann** of the Abbey Players has an international reputation on the stage and television.

In the United States, many MacCanns featured on the roll of officers serving with the Irish brigades during the American Civil War.

MacCarrick

Mac Concharraigh

Carrick

Carrick is a Scottish surname from Ayrshire which is a geographic toponymic referring to a *carraig*, or crag, being Scots-Gaelic for rock. The surname could also be of French or Norman origin. There was, for instance, a **Richard Carrigue** of Tewkesbury *c.*1580.

In Ireland, to which the Carricks may have come as mercenary soldiers, the name was transformed to Mac Concharraigh (*con* means hound, *carrig* means rock). The families of this name settled in the counties of Clare and Limerick and in due course their name was anglicized to MacEncarrigg.

MacCarricks do not feature in the pages of history, although there is mention of a **Thomas Carrick** who was an officer in Cromwell's army.

The name is not numerous in any part of Ireland, although the Carricks now outnumber the MacCarricks.

MacCarthy

Mac cárthaigh

Carty Cotty Macartie MacCartney

MacCarthy is the most common of all the ancient Irish names and the counties of Tipperary, Cork and Kerry have always been their territory. They claim descent from a third-century king of Munster, Oiloill Olum. In the eleventh century, one of their lords was **Cárthach**, meaning the loving one, and it was from him that they took their name. As the clan multiplied and spread abroad, the name developed as many as twenty variations, and they acquired a few titles of nobility.

The MacCarthys were imaginative builders. It was a MacCarthy king and bishop, **Cormac**, who, in about 1130, built the beautiful and still much admired Cormac's Chapel on the Rock of Cashel, once the seat of the high kings. They built all over Munster, including Blarney Castle, with its world-famous Blarney stone, which is supposed to give eloquence to those who, suspended upside down, manage to kiss it!

The MacCarthys were incessant combatants for land and power. They became too powerful for Queen Elizabeth I, who did her utmost to suppress them. Inevitably, they followed the doomed Stuart king and had to flee to Europe, where **Callaghan MacCarthy**, 3rd Duc de Clancarthy, was killed at the Battle of Fontenoy in 1745. His successors served with the French army for generations.

Other MacCarthys were able administrators and were colonial governors of Portugal, West Africa, India and Ceylon (now Sri Lanka). They were always good churchmen and even had the distinction of a beatification in 1896. This was **Thaddeus MacCarthy**, a bishop who died in 1492.

MacCarthy history is littered with poets and writers. A MacCarthy architect was called the Irish Pugin, because of the many excellent churches he designed.

In America, they were prominent in government. **Colonel Daniel E. MacCarthy** was the first American soldier to set foot in France in 1917, where he was greeted with a letter from **Pol MacCarthy**, 7th Duc de Clancarthy.

MacCarthys settled in Australia, too, and have also done well in England. It was a MacCarthy who, in 1797, exposed the inhuman conditions in the British navy to George III.

MacCartney is the Scottish version of the name. The most celebrated bearer of this name is pop star **Paul McCartney**, born in Liverpool in 1942, who achieved world fame as a member of the Beatles.

The magnificent Muckross estate by Killarney's Lakes, once a castle belonging to the senior branch of the family, **MacCarthy Mór**, is now under State care and is open to the public.

Terence MacCarthy, who was born in Belfast in 1957, is recognized by the Irish Genealogical Office as a chieftain of the MacCarthys and uses the designation MacCarthy Mór.

MacCartney *see* MacCarthy

MacCloskey

Mac Bhloscaidh

The O Kanes were one of the leading septs in Ulster up until the plantations began in 1609, when they lost much of their land and power as a Gaelic clan. The MacCloskeys of County Derry were a branch of the O Kanes who had taken their name from **Bloskey O Kane**, the notorious slayer of Murtagh O Loughlin, heir to the high king of Ireland in 1196.

The most distinguished MacCloskey so far was **Archbishop John McCloskey** of New York, an Irish émigré who was to become the first American cardinal when he received the red biretta in Saint Patrick's Cathedral in 1875.

The name is not very common, other than in the northern half of Ireland. Here, two Drogheda men made an outstanding contribution to the life of the community. **Malachy McCloskey** (b. 1939) founded Boyne Valley Foods Limited, and is one of the biggest honey producers in the country. He has also contributed to the local community, establishing parks and encouraging an awareness of local history, including the battle of the Boyne which was fought near Drogheda. **Phelim McCloskey** (b. 1945) trained as a hotelier and, with his invaluable international experience, is a director of holiday camps and a dynamic entrepreneur.

Some McCloskeys dropped the Mac prefix. One such, a Dublin man called **Frank Cluskey**, is a member of the Labour Party and has held a seat in the coalition government.

see also Keane

MacClure

Mac Giolla Laoire

MacAleer MacCallery MacColleary

The MacClures came from Galloway in Scotland to Ulster, where today they are still far more numerous than in any other part of Ireland. Yet it was Wexford which gave them their one claim to fame, **Admiral Sir Robert John le Mesurier MacClure** (1807–73), the world-famous explorer. He was adopted by General le Mesurier, who provided him with an excellent education, sending him to Eton and Sandhurst. Serving in the navy, he went on many Arctic expeditions. When Sir John Franklin and his crew disappeared, in search of the Northwest Passage, MacClure went on several expeditions to look for them. He was eventually successful in discovering both the Bering Strait and the elusive Northwest Passage.

Variants in Ireland of the MacClure name are MacAleer, MacColleary and MacCallery.

MacColleary *see* MacClure

MacColum

Mac Giolla Choluim

Colum MacCallum

There are a variety of spellings of this name which derives from the personal name Colm (*colm* means a dove). Mac Giolla Choluim means a follower of Saint Colmcille.

From earliest times it has been a numerous name in counties Antrim, Tyrone and Donegal. **Mac Gil Colum** is recorded by the Four Masters as being a prior of Ardstraw in County Tyrone in 1179.

A MacColum family whose home was Lisnalary in County Antrim from *c.*1650 to 1940 is well recorded in the Irish archives. The Genealogical Office in Dublin holds a copy of a 1918 confirmation of arms to the descendants of **R. Randal McCollum** of Lisnalary.

Minus the prefix, a similar name, Colum, is also to be found in County Longford, the birthplace of the poet **Pádraig Colum**, who was among the earliest playwrights for Dublin's Abbey Theatre.

In the early days of the Gaelic League, **Fionán Mac Coluim** was an active advocate of the Irish language revival.

MacConaghy

Mac Dhonnchaidh

MacConkey

MacConaghy, which is also sometimes MacConkey, was the name of a branch of the great Robertson clan. **Dhonnchaidh Reamhair** (Stout Duncan), from whom the name comes, was descended from the Earls of Atholl in Scotland and is supposed to have taken part in the battle of Bannockburn in 1314.

In 1317, **Mac Dhonnchaidh** (MacConaghy) came to Ireland to fight for Robert Bruce and his brother Edward. They defeated the Anglo-Irish at Slane. Many of the MacConaghys remained in Ireland and settled mainly around north Armagh. There is a Ballymaconaghy near Newry in County Down.

The name is rarely found in other Irish counties. A very full account is given in a book published in 1946 by the New York Public Library, *The Surnames of Scotland, Their Origin, Meaning and History*, written by George F. Black.

In 1969, a clan Dhonnchaidh museum was opened in the clan's original territory, Bruar Falls, where documents and pictures show the social and martial history of the clan. On display is their traditional *Clach na Brataid*, which has been a charm stone for the clan since the battle of Bannockburn.

(Mac) Concatha *see* Battle

MacConkey *see* MacConaghy

MacConville

Mac Conmhaoil

Conwell

MacConville is the anglicization of the name Mac Conmhaoil. Conwell, another version of the name, is now very rare.

As it is today, the MacConville territory has always been in Ulster, particularly the area historically known as Oriel, consisting of counties Armagh, Down and Louth. Some scholars equate MacConville with another Ulster sept, the MacGonigles, but this may have been due to misspelling on the part of the ancient scribes.

In the eighteenth century, the MacConvilles were on the side of the Jacobites, especially in County Down, where six of the family lost their land, and in some cases their freedom, after the defeat of James II at the battle of the Boyne.

Few of the family, so far, have been either famous or notorious. **Michael McConville** (b. 1925) graduated from Trinity College Dublin, followed a career first in the Royal Marines and then in the Malayan civil service. Afterwards, he joined Her Majesty's diplomatic service. He has written novels and short stories under several pseudonyms, including Anthony McCandless and Miles Noonan.

MacCormack

Mac Cormaic

MacCormick

MacCormack (son of Cormac) is a very numerous and widely distributed name. Cormac was a popular boys' name and many families adopted it as a surname, so there were unrelated MacCormack families all around the country.

In the thirteenth and fourteenth centuries, there were three Bishops of Killaloe using a variant of the name, O Cormican.

The national archives contain many MacCormack records. There is a 1571 grant by the Earl of Ormond (a Butler) to **Thomas MacCormycke** of a town and a castle in County Tipperary. Thomas's wife was a Butler.

In the sixteenth and seventeenth centuries, the MacCormacks were leading gentry in County Cork. One branch of the family had sufficient influence and wealth to raise an army to assist the Earl of Desmond in his hopeless struggle against the Elizabethan conquerors.

MacCormacks were also a prominent family in Ulster, particularly in Fermanagh and Armagh. From this family came two distinguished medical men. **Henry MacCormac** (1800–86) and his son, **Sir William MacCormac** (1836–1901). Tyrone was the birthplace of the Arctic navigator, **Dr. Robert MacCormack** (1800–90).

In 1920, **Wright McCormick** launched a movement to establish an annual day of celebration in Boston commemorating both Saint Patrick's Day and the expulsion of the British from America.

The most illustrious MacCormack was **Count John McCormack** (1884–1945). Born into a modest Athlone family, he studied singing in Italy. He performed in opera worldwide and was recognized as the greatest lyric tenor of his time. He made a huge number of recordings and his contribution to charity was honoured by the Pope, who made him a hereditary papal count.

MacCory *see* Corry

MacCoughlan *see* Coughlan

MacCourt

Mac Cuairt Mac Cuarta

Courtney MacCourtney

The MacCourts were a sept of Oriel, an area which includes the counties of Armagh and Monaghan, plus parts of Down, Fermanagh and Louth. In Irish the name is Mac Cuarta (*cuart* means visit).

Séamus Dall Mac Cuarta (1647–1732) was blind from birth (*dall* means blind). He was unusually erudite and came to be regarded as the leading northern poet of his time. He was a friend of the great harpist and composer, Turlough O Carolan. One of Mac Cuarta's best-known poems has a modern ring to it. It is in the form of a dialogue between himself and a castle which a greedy Pádraic Ó Murchadha was vandalizing just to build himself a cowshed. Mac Cuarta lived in troubled times, and when his many patrons died before him he sank into poverty in his old age. In 1971, his poetry was edited and published in book form.

Courtney is believed to be either a variation of Mac Cuarta or of O Curneen, which was a family of poets and chroniclers to the O Rourkes of Breffny (Cavan and west Leitrim). The Courtneys are still mostly found in north-east Ulster, sometimes with a Mac prefix. It is also possible that they are settlers from England, as Courtney is a well-known Norman name.

The MacCourts have not been much recorded in history. In Dublin and throughout the country they are found in the professions and in agriculture. Many are still to be found in their ancient County Louth territory, but the greatest number are now in Northern Ireland.

Kevin McCourt is an exception. He was born in Tralee in County Kerry in 1915. One of Ireland's leading businessmen, he has been a director-general of Radio Telefís Éireann, the Irish broadcasting company, and has held a great number of other directorships, including that of An Bord Tráchtála (The Irish Trade Board), Irish Distillers and the Federation of Irish Industries.

MacCoy

Mac Aodha

MacHugh MacKay

The Irish name Mac Aodha means son of Hugh. It is possible that the MacCoys may have originally crossed from Ulster to Scotland, although it is more generally believed that they came from Islay and the islands of southern Scotland, accompanying the MacDonnells as gallowglasses (mercenaries). MacKay can be a variant of MacCoy.

Today the MacCoys are most numerous in the northern half of Ireland, although some have also settled in other parts of the country.

In the Genealogical Office in Dublin there is a pedigree of the MacCoys of counties Waterford, Kildare and Derry from *c.*1750 to 1926, of the MacCoys of Dromore in County Down from 1770 to 1880, and those of Cork, Dublin and Armagh between 1754 and 1854.

There was an **Art MacCoy** (*c.*1715–74) who had anglicized his name from Mac Cobhthaigh. The **Reverend Edward MacCoy** (1839–72) was a popular writer in the Irish language. Dublin-born **Sir Frederick MacCoy** (1817–99) made his name in Australia as a naturalist.

The expression "the real MacCoy" is thought by some to come from a corruption of the word Macao, the Portuguese island, off the coast of China near Hong Kong, notorious for its production of heroin. There is also a theory that the expression refers to the dandy boxer **"Kid" MacCoy** (1873–1940), who was not a MacCoy at all, having been born Norman Selby.

The many MacCoys in the USA do not appear to be of Irish origin.

MacCracken

Mac Reachtain

MacNaughton

MacCracken, a name hardly to be found in the Republic of Ireland, is very numerous in the counties of Northern Ireland, where their antecedents arrived, probably from Argyllshire, at the time of the Ulster plantations in the sixteenth and seventeenth centuries. Some scholars suggest that MacCracken is a corruption of Mac Reachtain, which is believed to be Scots-Gaelic for MacNaughton.

In the Genealogical Office in Dublin there are some papers relating to MacCracken families who, at one time, had lands in counties Meath, Dublin and Wicklow.

With one outstanding exception the MacCrackens have not yet made any remarkable contributions, good or not so good, to the island of Ireland. The most distinguished bearer of the name is **Henry Joy MacCracken** (1767–98), who was born in Belfast of Huguenot extraction. In Dublin the Genealogical Office holds his draft pedigree. Henry Joy MacCracken was employed as a young man in the administration of a cotton factory. He was inspired by the ideas of Wolfe Tone and active in the newly founded Society of the United Irishmen in Belfast. The Society's aims were to secure the reform of a corrupt parliament, to abolish all religious discrimination and to unite against the unjust influence of Great Britain in Ireland. Henry Joy MacCracken led an attack on Antrim town which was defeated by numerically superior British troops. He escaped and tried to reach America, but he was captured and hanged in Belfast.

MacCrea *see* Crea

MacCrory *see* Rogers

MacCrossan

Mac an Chrosáin

Crosbie Cross Crossan

There are two distinct septs of Mac an Chrosáin (*cros* means a cross). One belongs to counties Tyrone and Derry, where, in some cases, the Mac has been dropped.

In the fourteenth century this sept provided two Bishops of Raphoe, **Henry Mac an Crossan** and **Richard Mac Crossan**.

The second sept were hereditary bards to the powerful O Mores and O Conors of counties Laois and Offaly. There is a record of 1550 mentioning **Owen Oge Mac Crossan**, "a rhymer" of Ballymacrossan.

Some members of the family anglicized their name to Crosby or Crosbie and joined the English side, thus acquiring much land in County Kerry as well as titles of nobility. Later, some reverted to the Irish side and one, **Sir Thomas Crosby**, served as an officer in the army of James II at the battle of the Boyne.

At the time of the Great Famine, **John Murtagh Macrossan** (1832–91) left his native Donegal for Australia, where the name still flourishes today.

The Genealogical Office in Dublin holds notes and copies of deeds relating to the MacCrossan family dating from 1657 to 1810.

MacCrory *see* Rogers

MacCullen *see* Cullen

MacCurry *see* Corry

MacCurtin

Mac Cuirtín

Curtin

For a thousand years or more, the Mac Cuirtín (originally MacCruitín) have been located on the Atlantic coast around Clare. They are kinsmen of the great High King Brian Boru who died at the battle of Clontarf in 1014. The name is descriptively personal—*cruitín* means hunchback. For generations they were scholars and teachers in the O Brien household. They were also outstanding poets and musicians.

A chief of the Mac Cuirtíns, **Hugh Buídhe** (*buídhe* means fair), who died in 1755, was a famous poet and scholar. He fought with Sarsfield at Limerick and went with him to France to join the Irish brigade. For a time he tutored the French monarch's children.

Jeremiah Curtin was one of the signatories of the National Convention during the French Revolution. A kinsman, **Major General Benjamin Curtin**, fought with the royalists against the revolutionaries.

A **Jeremiah Curtin** in the USA, a distinguished linguist, spent from 1864 to 1870 in St. Petersburg as his government's translator. Afterwards, he collected folk tales, both in America and Ireland. Another American Irishman, **Andrew Gregg Curtin**, a lawyer and politician, was at one time the US Minister to Russia.

The parents of **John Curtin** (d. 1945) emigrated from their farm in County Cork to Australia. A convinced socialist who believed in sovereignty for Australia, he was to become Prime Minister of that country.

Tomás MacCurtain, a Corkman who was a pioneering member of the Gaelic League, was imprisoned during the struggle for independence. Shortly after his release, he was elected Lord Mayor of Cork, while still playing an active role as commandant of the Cork brigade of the IRA. Despite warnings, he was callously shot at home with his family by the Royal Irish Constabulary, who were censured for this brutal act by the British government. His place as Lord Mayor was taken by an even more tragic patriot, Terence MacSwiney.

MacCusker *see* Cosgrave

MacCutcheon *see* Hutchinson

MacDermot

Mac Diarmada

MacDermottroes

The MacDermots are the only family in Ireland to be princes. They also have an authenticated Chief of the Name. They descend from the kingly O Conors of Connacht, from an eighth-century king, Muiredach Mullethan, through to Maelruanaidh Mór (Mulrooney), Prince of Moylurg, when they became known as Mulrooney for several generations. When, in the twelfth century, a descendant called **Dermot** became King of Moylurg, they took his name, Dermot, meaning a free man, as their surname.

For centuries, they possessed thousands of acres in Roscommon and Sligo, which became known as MacDermot's Country. They built their fortress on the rock on the legendary island of Lough Cé. In Douglas Hyde's *Love Songs of Connacht*, he tells the tragic love story of **Una MacDermot** and Thomas Costello. Thomas was heir to the Costellos, who were the MacDermots' enemies. Una's brother imprisoned her on the island and Thomas was drowned trying to swim to her, shortly after which Una also died.

Brian MacDermot, a sixteenth-century Prince of Moylurg, encouraged the writing of the *Annals of Lough Cé* which are now preserved in Trinity College Dublin.

When they were driven from Lough Cé by the English colonizers they settled at Coolavin by Lough Gara in Sligo. They took part in all the battles, including the battle of the Boyne and Aughrim. When they had to go into exile, they served abroad in the Church and in the armies and navies of Europe, including those of England.

There were three MacDermot septs: the MacDermots who descended from the royal O Conors, the MacDermottroes (the suffix roe is an anglicization of *rua*, meaning red) whose seat was at Alderford in County Roscommon, and the MacDermotts who were formerly chiefs of Airteach.

In the nineteenth century, the MacDermots of Coolavin held high office. A Prince of Coolavin, **Hugh Hyacinth O Rourke MacDermot** (1834–1904), was Attorney-General of Ireland and a member of the privy council. His eighth son, **Frank**, was a distinguished political writer. Another chief and Prince of Coolavin, **Sir Dermot MacDermot** (1906–89), was an ambassador with the British diplomatic service when he retired.

Seán Mac Diarmada (1884–1916), a signatory of the Proclamation of the Republic, was executed after the 1916 Easter Rising.

Lough Cé, now known as Lough Key, is a popular Forest Park and Wildlife Centre in County Roscommon.

MacDonagh

Mac Donnchadha

Donaghy

MacDonagh is a very numerous Irish name meaning son of Donagh. In counties Tyrone and Derry, Donaghy is sometimes a variant of the name.

In Connacht, where MacDonagh is very numerous, they were at one time a branch of the MacDermots. In Cork they were kinsmen of the powerful MacCarthys—in fact many assumed that name—and they were known as Lords of Duhallow. **MacDonagh MacCarthy**, Lord of Duhallow in *c.*1609, was building a castle at Kanturk when his English neighbours, feeling threatened, complained that it was like a fortress. He tore it down in a fit of rage, including its glass skylight—an innovation for its time.

Always a very patriotic breed, there are many MacDonagh papers in French archives relating to those who fled there following the defeat at the battle of the Boyne in 1690 when their lands were confiscated. A **Captain Anthony M'Donagh** who distinguished himself at the battle of Fontenoy was afterwards sent to County Clare to find recruits for the French army. There were at least forty MacDonagh officers and men in the various Irish regiments in France. A number of them dropped the Mac.

Andrew MacDonagh, born about 1738 in Sligo, accompanied Wolfe Tone on his unsuccessful French expedition to Bantry Bay.

Thomas MacDonagh (1783–1825) emigrated to America and was a naval officer at the battle of Plattsburg.

John MacDonagh, an American philanthropist of Irish birth, devoted himself to freeing the slaves in his adopted country.

Thomas MacDonagh (1878–1916), a poet from County Tipperary, was one of the executed leaders of the 1916 Easter Rising. His was one of the signatures on the Proclamation of the Republic. His son, **Donagh MacDonagh** (1912–68), a lawyer, was also a poet and dramatist.

see also Duncan

MacDonald

Mac Domhnaill

MacDonnell

It is difficult to be precise regarding the MacDonald surname, which is the name of one of Scotland's leading clans. Not everyone bearing this name is a true MacDonald; some followers of the clan adopted it. It is also often interchangeable with MacDonnell, which can be native Irish as well as Scottish. MacConnell in Ulster is also a deviation.

That the Scottish MacDonalds have had long and ancient connections with Ireland there is no doubt. Their homeland was Argyle, where their chieftain was Lord of the Isles. They first came to Ulster as mercenary soldiers in the thirteenth century. By the fifteenth century they had acquired much land, through grants and marriage alliances. Having displaced the MacQuillans, they settled in the Glens of Antrim, where **Randal MacSorley MacDonnell** was created Earl of Antrim in 1620.

Various offshoots of the family settled in other parts of Ireland, and many were fervent followers of the Jacobite cause. As a result, they were forced to join the exodus of Irish exiles, and many a MacDonald or MacDonnell appears in the lists of Irish soldiers who served in the wars in Europe.

The Belfast Public Records Office holds a pedigree of the MacDonalds of the Isles and the MacDonalds of Ballinamalard in County Fermanagh. In Scotland's National Library at Edinburgh, there are Ossianic poems in Irish attributed to **Alexander MacDonald**, who lived in the eighteenth century.

An interesting light is cast on Irish social history by correspondence between the Earl of Selkirk and **Alexander MacDonald** written in 1813 concerning the emigration of men from the west of Ireland to Hudson Bay in Canada.

The historian G. A. Hayes-McCoy wrote an account of the MacDonalds in Mayo in the *Journal of the Galway Archaeological and Historical Society.*

Walter McDonald (1854–1920) was a distinguished Kilkenny theologian and a professor at Maynooth College. At one time his views were considered to be quite unorthodox.

In Scotland, **Ronald Alexander MacDonald** of Clanranald (b. 1934) is the 24th chief and Captain of Clanranald. There is a MacDonald Museum in the Isles.

see also MacDonnell

MacDonnell

Mac Domhnaill

MacDonald

The MacDonnells, who are still very numerous in Ireland today, have three distinct origins. Firstly, there were the MacDonnells of Fermanagh, whose family is now extinct. Secondly, there were the MacDonnells of Thomond (counties Clare and Limerick), who were bards to the royal O Briens and were, in fact, descended from Domhnaill, son of King Murtagh Mór O Brien. Lastly, there were the MacDonnells, or MacDonalds, who were Lords of the Isles and who came from Scotland in the twelfth century to serve as mercenaries. These settled in Antrim, where they acquired much land and formed a strong military clan, with powerful leaders such as their famous chieftain, **Sorley Boy MacDonnell** (*c.*1505–90), "a foe to the English".

Alastair "Colkitto" MacDonnell was killed fighting the Cromwellians in 1647. Later, some of the MacDonnells followed the army of James II to fight in the wars in Europe. Those who stayed behind became Lords of Antrim. The ancestral fort which they built in the fourteenth century, Dunluce Castle, is now a dramatic ruin clinging to the steep cliffs overhanging the Antrim sea coast, near the Giant's Causeway.

Many MacDonnells have played a prominent role in Ireland. **Seán Clarach MacDomhnaill** (1691–1754) of Cork translated Homer into Irish verse and was chief poet of Munster. **Alexander MacDonnell** (1798–1835) of Belfast, who was for a while a merchant in the West Indies, returned to London to become a world-class chess player.

Anthony MacDonnell (1844–1925) of County Mayo, a member of the Indian civil service, was Lieutenant-Governor of the united provinces, ruling forty million people. Back in Ireland he was influential in promoting Wyndham's Land Act of 1903, which gave tenants the right to land ownership. In 1908 he was created Baron MacDonnell of Swinford.

MacDonald is often used as a variant of MacDonnell.

see also MacDonald

MacDowell

Mac Dubhghaill

MacDugall

In Irish or Scots Gaelic the name MacDowell means son of the dark foreigner (*dubh* means black and *gall* means foreigner). They came originally to Scotland from Scandinavia, possibly Norway.

They were of the MacDugall clan of Scotland and they came to Ireland from the Hebrides during the fourteenth and fifteenth centuries as mercenary soldiers. However, some may have come earlier to Ireland, because their name is mentioned in the *Annals of the Four Masters* (a history of Ireland) between AD 978 and AD 1013, but they are not recorded in the Irish genealogies. They settled in County Roscommon where they gave their name to the town of Lismacdowell. In time many of them migrated to Ulster, where they are now very numerous.

In 1659, **Peter** and **Allen Dowell** are recorded as property owners in the parish of Shankill in County Roscommon.

Before 1649, some are recorded as royalists serving both Charles I and Charles II in Ireland. However, **Colonel Luke MacDowell** followed the ill-fated King James II, who was defeated by William III following the battle of the Boyne in 1690. His son, **Denis MacDowell**, whose name was incorrectly recorded as Donnell, was outlawed by the Williamites.

Patrick MacDowell (1799–1870), born in Belfast and a distinguished sculptor, had his work shown at the Great Exhibition in London in 1851. He sculpted the "Europe Group" for the Albert Memorial in London.

R. B. McDowell, formerly of Belfast, is a leading writer on modern history and government, both Irish and European, and is now professor emeritus of Trinity College Dublin, following a distinguished career there.

Henry McDowell of Celbridge, County Kildare, is a leading Irish genealogist.

see also Doyle

MacDugall *see* MacDowell

MacEgan *see* Egan

MacEnawe *see* Forde

MacEnery

Mac Éinrí   Mac Innéirghe

FitzHenry   Henry   Irvine   Irwin   MacHenry   MacNair   Neary

Some believe that the Mac Innéirghe (from the Irish, meaning easily roused) were descendants of the third-century king of Munster, Olioll Olum, and were, therefore, kinsmen of the O Donovans. County Limerick was, and remains, their territory, and their name is commemorated by the town of Castletown MacEnery.

It is a remarkable name, its origins often obscured by the vast number of forms it has taken because of anglicization, including Henry (q.v.), MacHenry (q.v.), FitzHenry, Irwin, Irvine, MacNair and Neary. The Mac Éinrí who were associates of the Flahertys of Connacht were anglicized to MacHenry.

Many of the MacEnery chieftains were slain in battle and, until Cromwellian times, they owned great estates in the Limerick area. After the Gaelic suppression, they fled to Europe and reached high rank in the armies of France and Spain.

The FitzHenrys came from Normandy to Wexford and, in time, their name was shortened to Henry. **Mrs. FitzHenry** was a popular eighteenth-century actress.

The MacEnris of Ulster, as well as the MacEnerys of Thomastown, County Kilkenny, are recorded in the ancient archives. Compared to MacHenry, McEnery is now a rare name, other than in the Limerick area.

MacEnroe *see* Crowe, Roe

MacEntee

Mac an tSaoi

Translated from the original Irish, Mac an tSaoi means son of the scholar.

The MacEntees, who are not very widely recorded, are a very old Gaelic family of Oriel, an area in Ulster which includes counties Armagh and Monaghan, plus parts of Donegal and Louth. They seem to have moved south over the generations and are far more numerous today in County Dublin and some southern counties.

Jervis MacEntee (1828–91), a highly esteemed American landscape painter, was of Irish origin.

One of the most outstanding politicians in the setting up of the newly formed Irish Free State was **Sean MacEntee** (1899–1984), who was born in Belfast. For his part in the Easter Rising of 1916 he was condemned to death. This was changed to life imprisonment, but he was freed during the 1917 amnesty. In his long and distinguished political career he held many ministerial posts. He was also a poet. His daughter, **Máire Mac an tSaoi**, is one of the leading poets writing in Irish. She is a barrister and worked with the Department of External Affairs. She married the writer, columnist and broadcaster—and former Labour minister—Dr. Conor Cruise O Brien.

MacEoin *see* Owens

MacEvoy

Mac Fhíodhbhuídhe

MacAvoy

This surname is thought to have come from the Irish word *fíodhbhadhach*, which means a woodsman. In ancient times they were one of the Seven Septs of Leix.

The formidable Irish name Mac Fhíodhbhuídhe (pronounced Mac-ee-vee) was more easily anglicized to MacEvoy, now a very numerous name which in Northern Ireland is usually spelled MacAvoy. There are legal papers relating to a **Daniel MacAvoy** of Dungannon who, in the eighteenth century, served "with credit for twelve years in Ireland and France", probably in the army.

The MacEvoys built a mansion, Tobertynan, at Enfield in County Meath. A MacEvoy daughter from Tobertynan married Sir Bernard Burke, the Ulster king of arms and chief of the Irish genealogical office who edited *Burke's Peerage*, a series of volumes on the peerage and landed gentry.

The other version of the name, Mac Giolla Buídhe (*buídhe* means yellow), was simplified to Mac a Buidhe and then to MacAvoy, a name to be found in Sligo, Leitrim and Donegal and thought to have come originally from Scotland.

MacFall *see* Lavelle

MacFee *see* Mahaffy

MacGarry

Mag Fhearadhaigh

Garrihy Garry Hare O) Garriga

This is a very old Gaelic name derived from the word *fearadhach*, which means manly. They were originally kinsmen of the MacHughs and occupied the same territories in counties Leitrim and Roscommon.

Through the centuries the name has been subjected to many variations. When they moved to County Monaghan their name was overcome by the local dialect and became O Garriga. With the imposition of the penal laws when the O and Mac were forbidden and Gaelic names had to be anglicized, it was mistranslated to Hare (and even to O Hehir), as the Irish word for hare (*giorriadh*) sounds something like Garrihy or Garry, which were other variations of the original Mag Fhearadhaigh.

In 1585, **Moygarry** of Sligo is recorded as being Chief of the Name. In 1649, **Gillygroome MacGarry** was on the list of "1,649 Officers" who served in the English army in Ireland.

The MacGarrys must also have fought with the Irish army of James II, possibly also at the battle of the Boyne in 1690, because there are papers of the seventeenth and eighteenth century in the Bibliothèque Nationale in Paris relating to various families of Irish origin in France, including the names MacGarry and Garry.

The name is now very widespread in Ireland, especially in the west.

MacGee *see* Magee

MacGeever *see* MacKeever

MacGennis *see* Magennis

MacGeough

Mag Eochadha

MacGoff MacGough

Dr. Edward MacLysaght says that this name belongs to the Oriel territory (Armagh, Monaghan and Louth), where it is also spelled MacGoff and MacGough. Sometimes MacGeough has been used as a synonym for Gough, from which, however, it must be distinguished, as it is in no way related.

In Sir Richard Griffith's valuations, made halfway through the last century, a number of McGeoughs and McGoughs are recorded in Oneilland, near Armagh, where they were householders.

In 1857, **Reverend Richard McGeough** of Belfast published a very controversial pamphlet addressed to the Catholic clergy at home and abroad.

About 1820, **Walter MacGeough** engaged leading local architects to build a splendid mansion at Charlemont in County Armagh which he named "The Argory". He added the surname Bond to MacGeough. Another member of the family, **Captain Ralph MacGeough-Bond-Shelton**, added yet another surname, Shelton. His home was the seventeenth-century mansion, Drumsil, in County Antrim. He served in the Kaffir and Crimean wars of 1852 to 1856. In 1916, Drumsil was sold and was a hotel from 1957 until 1972, when it fell to the IRA's campaign of destruction.

MacGeough is rarely to be found outside the Ulster counties.

MacGill

Mac an Ghaill

Magill

MacGill can also be of Scottish origin and, in both Irish and Scottish Gaelic, the name Mac an Ghaill means son of the foreigner.

The Magills—one of its variations—came to County Antrim from Scotland as mercenary soldiers. Some also came later, with the plantation of Ulster by Scottish farmers and tradesmen.

Michael Henry Gill (1794–1879), son of a woollen draper, trained as a master printer. He bought a publishing and printing house, which was to print the seven volumes of the prestigious *Annals of the Four Masters.* His work for the Royal Irish Academy and its manuscripts was outstanding. A descendant of his is still in the company which, trading as Gill and Macmillan, is one of Ireland's leading publishers.

Patrick MacGill was the first of eleven children born to a poor farmer in Donegal. His schooling finished at the age of ten and he then worked as a labourer. He found existence on the Scottish potato fields so harsh that he later wrote scathingly about it in poems and novels. He educated himself by means of the circulating libraries and so successful was he that he was given the job of editing the Chapter Library of Windsor Castle. His volumes of poetry, particularly *Songs of a Navvy*, and his novels and play, were extremely popular and are still in print.

In the 1920s, **Donald MacGill** was a popular story-teller.

The MacGill University in Montreal, Canada, was founded with a bequest made by **James McGill** (1744–1813), a Scots-Canadian who made a fortune in the Canadian fur trade.

MacGillapatrick *see* Fitzpatrick

MacGillegea *see* Gildea

MacGillycuddy

Mac Giolla Chuda

Coady

The surname Mac Giolla Chuda means son of the devotee of St. Mochuda, probably referring to St. Cathage of Lismore in County Kerry. Unlike most Gaelic surnames, it only came into use in the sixteenth century, assumed by a branch of the important O Sullivan Mór family of County Kerry. Kerry has always been their territory, with a variety of seats.

In the Genealogical Office in Dublin there is reference to a collection of documents of the seventeenth and eighteenth century mentioning their properties and various activities. There are also letters of 1666 to 1667 written to a **Lieutenant-Colonel Donagh MacGillycuddy** of Carrowmahon and of Dunkerron in County Kerry. In the eighteenth century, **Colonel Denis MacGillycuddy** commanded a regiment in the Irish brigade of France.

In London, in 1867, W. Maziere Brady published *The McGillycuddy Papers* and there is also an account of the MacGillycuddys in a *Kerry Archaeological Journal* of 1915.

Dr. Valentine T. McGillycuddy, who was born in Detroit in 1849, worked as an Indian agent and a physician on the borders between the USA and Canada. He was constantly in contact with the Sioux Indians, and with Buffalo Bill and other famous characters of that time. In 1941 his wife, **Julia B. McGillycuddy**, published his biography.

The MacGillycuddys have an authentic chieftain—The MacGillycuddy of the Reeks. MacGillycuddy's Reeks, which feature as a crest on their armorial bearings, is a range of mountains featuring the highest peak in Ireland, Carrantuohill.

Lieutenant-Colonel Ross Kinloch, The MacGillycuddy of the Reeks (1882–1950), served in the First and Second World Wars. He was a chevalier of the Légion d'Honneur and, from 1928 to 1943, an Irish Senator. His grandson, the present chieftain, **Richard Denis Wyer MacGillycuddy** (b. 1948), has his pedigree recorded in *Burke's Irish Family Records.* In 1986 he sold Beaufort, the family seat, and its six hundred acres and went to live in England.

MacGillycuddy is not a numerous Irish name.

MacGinley

Mag Fhionnghaile

Finlay Ginley Ginnell MacGinnelly

This surname, which is seldom found in Ireland without its Mac prefix, is concentrated in the county of Donegal. The Irish version, Mag Fhionnghaile, means son of the fair hero. There are a number of variants of the name, with consequent confusion. It has been regularly confused with the Scottish name MacKinley, which has a somewhat similar spelling in Scots Gaelic, Mac Fionnghal, meaning fair foreigner, or Norseman. Sometimes, too, it has been anglicized to Finlay. Yet another translation from the Irish could be MacGinnelly. Today, MacGinley is a numerous surname all over Ireland.

There were many MacGinley ecclesiastics, particularly in the diocese of Raphoe.

Dr. John B. MacGinly, who was consecrated in 1922, was the first Roman Catholic Bishop of Monterey in Fresno, California.

Laurence Ginnell (1854–1928), Member of Parliament for Westmeath, took part in the cattle-driving campaigns which preceded the 1916 Easter Rising and was involved in the foundation of *Sinn Féin.*

There are a number of ancient records of the MacGinley families of Drumholm in County Donegal between 1821 and 1841, including extracts from the census returns. Also, in the Genealogical Office in Dublin, as far back as 1636 a grant of lands is recorded to **Andrew Ginley** of Ratoath, County Meath.

Patrick McGinley, who was born in Donegal in 1927, was originally a teacher and is now a journalist and publisher living in England. He has written a number of novels, of which his *Bogmail* is probably the best known.

Peader Mac Fhionnghaile (1857–1940), originally **Peter MacGinley**, was born in Donegal. A writer and protagonist of the Irish language, and known as Cú Uladh (The Hound of the North), he was president of the Gaelic League between 1923 and 1925.

MacGinnis *see* Magennis

MacGinty

Mag Fhinneachta

Ginty MacGinity Maginnity

In the sixteenth century, MacGinty was found mainly in County Donegal in the province of Ulster, but it is now a rare surname in any part of Ireland. In Irish it was Mag Fhinneachta, meaning fair, or blond haired as the snow. There were many variations of the name, of which Maginnity, MacGinity and Ginty are probably the most notable.

The late Dr. Edward MacLysaght, a pioneer of the study of Irish surnames, says that MacEntee has no connection whatever with MacGinty, although the two names certainly do sound alike.

Because of the mass migration of families from County Donegal at the time of the plantation of Ulster, the MacGintys were driven south and settled in Connacht, where they became fairly numerous in the counties of Mayo and Clare.

Remarkably little has been recorded of this ancient family. Percy French, the famous painter, comedian, and songwriter from County Roscommon, immortalized the name in his ballad, "Paddy McGinty's Goat". This catchy song tells of "all the ladies who lived in Killaloe" who went in fear of the depredations of Paddy McGinty's goat, who had a taste for their bustles hanging out on the line to dry!

MacGlavin *see* Hand

MacGloin, **MacGlone** *see* MacAloon

MacGlynn

Mag Fhloinn

Glynn

The original Irish version of this name means son of Flann of the ruddy complexion (*flann* means ruddy). It has had many anglicizations, including Glynn, which is also a Welsh name.

The main Mag Fhloinn sept had their territory in counties Westmeath and Roscommon, from where they spread across the country, especially to counties Clare and Sligo, but they are not now at all numerous.

In 1617 **James Glynn**, a grand juror in Tipperary, was fined and imprisoned because he refused to betray a neighbour who would not attend an obligatory Protestant church service.

Many bearing this name have been active in the Church. **Reverend Bonaventure Maglin** was a Franciscan vicar-provincial of Ireland in 1654. **Reverend Martin Glynn** (1729–94) of Tuam became superior of the Irish College in Bordeaux and was guillotined during the French Revolution in 1794. **Reverend Dr. Edward Glynn** (1837–1900) was suspended from his New York parish because of his radical views but was reinstated by Pope Leo XII.

Martin Henry Glynn (1871–1924) left a humble family in Ireland for America, where he rose to be Governor of New York.

Patrick MacMahon Glynn (1855–1931) of Gort in County Galway left Ireland to practise law in Australia. After a difficult beginning, he rose to become Attorney-General and Minister for External Affairs, visiting the United Kingdom on the invitation of the Empire Parliamentary Association.

Joseph Glynn (1869–1951), a tireless worker for the Society of St. Vincent de Paul and the poor, was knighted in 1915. He wrote a life of the mystic, Matt Talbot of Dublin, who was considered for canonization.

There have been a number of MacGlynn writers and poets and pioneers of the Irish language and culture.

MacGoff *see* MacGeough

MacGoogan *see* MacGuigan

MacGookin *see* MacGuigan

MacGorman *see* (O) Gorman

MacGormley *see* Gormley

MacGough *see* MacGeough

MacGovern

Mag Shamhráin

MacGowran Magauran

This very old Gaelic surname derives from the Irish word *samhradh*, meaning summer. Its most numerous variant is Magauran.

The surname derives from Samhradh, who lived in about AD 1100 and was a descendant of Eochadh, an eighth-century warrior who gave his name to Teallach Eochaidh, now Tullyhas, in County Cavan. Not far from there is also the town of Ballymagauran. Although the MacGoverns were allies of the powerful Maguires and O Rourkes, Ballymagauran was burned by the Maguires in 1481 for an allegedly dishonourable act on the part of a MacGovern.

Edmond Magauran, Archbishop of Armagh from 1588 to 1595, was an early martyr. **Hugh Magauran** (alias MacGovern) was a popular Gaelic poet. **John McGovern** (1850–1917) was an American novelist.

The MacGoverns are remarkably well recorded, including a book called *An Irish Sept* by **J. B.** and **J. H. McGovern**, published in Manchester in 1886, a *General History Notes of the MacGauran or McGovern Clan*, published in Liverpool in 1890, and *The Book of the Magaurens*, which was edited by Lambert McKenna in Dublin in 1947.

The MacGovern name figures prominently in the passenger lists of ships sailing to Argentina. **Michael**, the son of a MacGovern who left Ireland in 1868, was the father of **Lorenzo McGovern** (b. 1906), who was appointed Argentine ambassador to Ireland in the 1950s.

MacGowan *see* Smith

MacGowran *see* MacGovern

MacGrath

Mac Graith Mag Raith

MacGraw Magrath Magraw

In Irish the name is Mag Raith, meaning son of Raith. *Raith* means either grace or prosperity. The MacGraths (also sometimes spelled Magrath) descend from two distinct septs. One originated in counties Donegal and Fermanagh, where they were important chiefs in Ulster, and the other is from the south-west, mostly County Clare, where for many generations they were poets and record-keepers for the powerful O Briens of Thomond.

Through the upheavals of war and conquest, the MacGraths spread throughout the country and the name is still common in much of Ireland.

One of their most notorious characters was an apostate Franciscan who, in the Elizabethan age, was an opportunist who held several archbishoprics, both Catholic and Protestant, was twice married, had seventy sources of income and died at the age of 100!

In the seventeenth century, the MacGraths went to France, and in the nineteenth century they emigrated to the United States of America, where they were prominent in the Confederate wars and, later, in administration and sport. They were also influential newspaper owners in Newfoundland.

In Ireland, the MacGraths were one of the founders of the successful Irish Hospitals' Sweepstakes and of the Waterford Crystal company—the biggest crystal glass manufacturer in the world.

Termon Castle at Pettigoe in County Donegal was built by the MacGraths and bombarded by the Cromwellians. There is another ruined MacGrath castle outside Waterford city.

"Master McGrath" was the name of the great Irish greyhound who was only beaten once in the 37 courses he ran.

The MacGrath coat of arms is an elaborate one, consisting of three lions, an antelope, a hand holding a battleaxe and another holding a cross.

MacGraw *see* MacGrath

MacGrealish

Mag Riallghuis

Grealish MacGrellis MacNelis

According to Dr. Edward MacLysaght, who wrote several valuable scholarly works on Irish names, MacGrealish is a Connacht form of MacNelis. He also said that "In Ulster it sometimes takes the form of MacGrellis or MacGrillin."

Though of ancient Irish origin, it is one of the many obscure names which have not so far featured in the historical records.

It is essentially a Galway name. In the comparatively small town of Oranmore, between Athenry and Galway, and especially around the Cornmore Cross area, there is a concentration of thirteen Grealish names in the telephone directory. There are others of the name in the County Galway area, but none at all in the Dublin or Northern Ireland telephone directories.

MacGregor *see* Greer

MacGrellis, MacGrillin *see* MacGrealish

MacGrory *see* Rogers

MacGuckian *see* MacGuigan

MacGuigan

Mag Uiginn

Geoghegan MacGuckian Wigan

This Ulster surname is one of a number around that part of the country whose origin may well have been Norse. There is a veritable litany of variants of the name, including Gavigan, Geoghegan, Guigan, Maguigan, MacGoogan, MacGookin, MacGuckian, MacWiggan, Meguiggan and Wigan, as well as Fidgeon and Pidgeon! Although the name is now distributed thinly around Ireland, its homeland remains the counties of Armagh and Tyrone.

Members of this family feature very little in the records. **William MacGuckin** (fl. 1837–68), Baron de Slane, who was born in County Antrim, was a distinguished oriental scholar. **Barton MacGuckin** (b. 1853), a Dubliner, was a popular singer. **Dan McGuigin**, the 1904 football champion of the Vanderbilt campus in the USA, was undoubtedly an Irish import. The Archbishop of Toronto was **Cardinal MacGuigan**.

Barry MacGuigan (b. 1961) of Clones in County Monaghan was an outstanding sportsman and featherweight boxing champion. He represented Northern Ireland in the Commonwealth games in Canada in 1978 and, in 1980, he represented Ireland at the Moscow Olympics. In 1985 he became the world champion featherweight boxer.

MacGuinness *see* Magennis

MacGuire *see* Maguire

MacGurk *see* Quirke

MacGurrin

Mag Corraidhín

Curreen MacGurran MacKiverkin

MacGurrin and MacGurran are related to Curreen and MacKiverkin. *Corradh*, from which the name derives, is the Irish word for spear. As far as they can be traced through the genealogies, the Mag Corraidhín family were a sept of the Uí Fiachrach, whose stronghold was in the parish of Skreen in County Sligo.

Unhappily for the genealogists, in some places Curreen and Curren have been transformed to Curran and even Crean, both far more common names.

By the end of the sixteenth century, the Mag Corraidhín sept had moved to County Leitrim, where they were very numerous. MacKiverkin and MacGurran are synonymous in the south County Down area.

MacGurrin is a rare name which has yet to come into prominence. The majority now seem to be in the Belfast area.

MacHaffy *see* Mahaffy

MacHenry

Mac Éinrí

MacHenry is a surname belonging to several distinct families in different parts of Ireland, including the Síol Eoghain Mac Éinrís of Bannside in Ulster, and a Norman Fitzhenry family in Connacht. The enforced removal of the O or Mac prefix during the time of the penal laws has made it difficult to distinguish between the various Henry septs.

The Bibliothèque Nationale in Paris holds papers relating to the history of many families of Irish origin in France, including several MacHenrys in the seventeenth and eighteenth centuries. In the eighteenth century, several M'Henrys served in various Irish regiments in France.

A manuscript in Dublin's Genealogical Office shows a 1908 confirmation of the quartering of arms of MacHenry to the descendants of Colonel Henry Williamson Lugard and **Margaret Anne MacHenry**, his wife, with Colonel Edward John Lugard, their eldest surviving son.

In the nineteenth century, a number of MacHenrys, all with the first name James, became distinguished American citizens. **James MacHenry** (1753–1816) of Ballymena in County Antrim studied medicine in the USA and, in 1778, was Secretary to George Washington. Another **James MacHenry** (1785–1845) was born in Larne in County Antrim and paid his medical school fees in Dublin and Glasgow by writing verse. He emigrated to Philadelphia, where he combined medicine with trade and journalism. He also wrote novels and returned to Ireland as US consul to Derry. His son, yet another **James MacHenry** (1816–91), became a leading American financier.

MacHugh

Mac Aodha

Eason Hewson MacCoy MacKay

Mac Aodha means son of Hugh, and this is a very numerous name in every part of Ireland. There were several septs, including one in west Ulster and two in Connacht who were kinsmen of the powerful O Flaherties, chiefs of the barony of Clare and County Galway.

In the fourteenth century, **Malachy "Molassie" MacHugh** is mentioned in the annals of Clonmacnoise as being Archbishop of Tuam.

In 1556, a MacHugh covenanted to pay Sir Edmund Butler rent due for the parsonage of Rebane in County Kildare. In 1588, some MacHughs were recorded as being in Athlone in County Westmeath. The Lambeth Palace Library in London holds extracts from accounts written by **Brian MacHugh** concerning his grievances and the causes of his entering into rebellion in Ireland in 1595.

The Genealogical Office in Dublin has an application from Malaga in Spain for the pedigree of **Margaret McHugh**, daughter of **Simon McHugh** of County Limerick and Elizabeth Arthur. This Margaret was the second wife of Daniel O Donovan of Rosscarbery *c.*1770.

Following the battle of the Boyne and the penal laws, the MacHughs joined the exodus to Europe of the exiled native Irish. Their name appears among the histories and genealogies of Irish families in France in the Bibliothèque Nationale in Paris.

In the early part of the twentieth century, **Martin J. McHugh** wrote poetry and comic drama. At that time also, **Mary Frances McHugh** was writing novels and a biography called *Thalassa* which was popular at the time.

A distinguished bearer of this name was **Roger McHugh** (1908–87). A professor of English and Anglo-Irish literature at University College Dublin, he was also visiting professor at a number of colleges in the USA. Dramatist, critic and essayist, he was an outstanding teacher who influenced a generation of Irish writers.

There have been a number of versions of the ancient MacHugh name, including MacKay, MacKee, MacCoy, Hughes, Hewson and even Eason. Eason's bookshops lead the Irish bookselling trade.

MacIago *see* Igoe

MacIlhoyle *see* Coyle

MacIlroy

Mac Giolla Ruadh

Gilroy Kilroy MacElroy MacGilleroy

The Irish and Scottish Gaelic are not dissimilar, and it should be no surprise to discover that MacIlroy originated as Mac Giolla Ruadh—meaning son of the red-haired youth—almost simultaneously in both Scotland and Ireland. Since the fourteenth century, it has been a common name in the parish of Ballinatrae in Ayrshire.

In Ireland, the sept appeared first in County Fermanagh, where their settlement was at Ballymackilroy, on the banks of the River Erne. In fact, there are three towns of this name in Ulster. Mac Giolla Ruadhs were also located in County Leitrim, where the name became MacGilleroy, while in Connacht it can be Kilroy or Gilroy. Today, MacElroy seems to be the most common version of the name, especially in Ulster, where they must have come as mercenary soldiers, perhaps with the Cromwellians or, later, as planters.

The still numerous MacElroys were distinguished in the fifteenth century by frequent references in the famous *Annals of the Four Masters.*

In the late eighteenth century, **John MacElroy** was educated in Fermanagh and fought with the United Irishmen in the 1798 Rebellion. He subsequently became a member of the Jesuit order and went on the American missions.

Dr. Robert MacElroy (b. 1872), a former professor of history at Oxford University, filled the same post in Princeton, USA.

Archibald McIlroy (1860–1915), born in County Antrim, worked in insurance and banking and wrote stories about his native county. He lost his life when the *Lusitania* was torpedoed in 1915.

MacInerney

Mac an Airchinnigh

MacNairney

MacInerney is a very numerous name which derives from the Gaelic Mac an Airchinnigh. *Airchinneach* means an erenagh, or steward of church lands, which was originally an ecclesiastical office but later became a hereditary office for laymen. Because it is a name which refers to an office rather than to a person, it was adopted by many families who were unrelated, which makes it difficult to work out exact pedigrees.

There was a MacInerney sept in Thomond (County Clare) in the early fourteenth century, where it was a very numerous name. Today, with the exception of Ulster, it has spread throughout the provinces.

In 1642, a Catholic priest called **Laurence MacInerheny** suffered martyrdom at the hands of the Cromwellians.

A Dominican priest, **M. H. MacInerney**, wrote many ecclesiastical works, including *A History of the Irish Dominicans.*

Today the name is prominent in sport, particularly in hurling, and a MacInerney family is one of the big civil engineering and building families in Ireland.

MacInnes *see* Magennis

MacIntyre

Mac an tSaoir

Carpenter MacAteer

The name Mac an tSaoir originated both in Northern Ireland and Scotland. In Ireland, it has gone through a variety of transformations, of which MacAteer is the most common, especially in counties Antrim, Donegal and Armagh—where there is a townland called Ballymacateer. Mac an tSaoir means son of the tradesman and it is very likely that the Irish name, Carpenter, also derives from MacAteer. Both MacIntyre and MacAteer are more plentiful in the north than in the south of Ireland. In County Mayo there is a Carrickmacintyre (MacIntyre's Rock), but Cahermackateer is a County Clare placename.

St. Kieran, who founded the famous Abbey of Clonmacnoise in AD 541, was known as Mac an tSaoir long before the establishment of surnames, designating his father as a craftsman. **Michael Mac an tSaoir** was Bishop of Clogher in County Tyrone from 1268 to 1287.

In Dublin, Carpenter became the accepted anglicization of Mac an tSaoir. Its outstanding representative was **Dr. John Carpenter**, Archbishop of Dublin from 1770 to 1786. He took an active part in the Catholic emancipation movement.

From County Clare came Enrí Mac an tSaoir, alias **Henry Carpenter** (fl. 1790), a distinguished poet and scribe.

MacIver, **MacIvor** *see* MacKeever

MacJordan *see* Jordan

MacKay, **MacKee** *see* MacCoy, MacHugh

MacKeever

Mac Íomhair

Ivers MacGeever MacIver MacIvor

MacKeever and its many variants, including MacKiever and MacGeever, is mainly to be found in the area which was known in ancient times as Oriel (the counties of Armagh and Monaghan and parts of south Down, Louth and Fermanagh).

Some believe the name to come from the Norse personal name, Ivaar, but others are of the opinion that, at least in Oriel, the name should be spelled Mac Éimhir, from the ancient forename, Éimhear, or Heber, which was greatly favoured by the MacMahons, a great family of County Monaghan to which the MacKeevers claim kinship.

Scholars suggest that Ivers, mostly found in County Louth, is an abbreviation of MacIver, which could also be a synonym of MacKeever. Both these forms of the name are most numerous in the northern counties. It is also possible that these Ivers are related to the illustrious Taaffes, who were a noble family, not only in counties Meath and Louth, but also in Austria.

Some MacKeevers believe themselves to be of Scottish origin, but it is interesting to note that, before the plantations of the seventeenth century, the name was often recorded in the Hearth Money rolls for County Armagh, including a **Neile MacKeever** who, in 1567, was secretary to the great chieftain Shane O Neill.

The MacKeevers, who have blazed no trails in history or the arts, mostly pursue the sober occupations of farming, shopkeeping and the professions.

MacKehoe *see* Keogh

MacKenna

Mac Cionaoith

The Mac Cionaoith homeland was Trough, in the north of Monaghan, where they were a prominent sept. They do not appear in the records until the eighteenth century, when they showed considerable literary talent. **Nial MacKenna**, the poet and harpist, wrote the popular "Little Celia Connellan".

The late eighteenth century was a time of revolution in France as well as Ireland. But, while Wolfe Tone was trying to entice the French to Ireland, **Theobald MacKenna** was writing, tirelessly, advocating peaceful land reform and Catholic emancipation.

In the nineteenth century, there were two **Stephen MacKenna** novelists and a **Stephen MacKenna** journalist and idealist who fought for the Greeks and made translations of their great philosopher, Plotinus. A MacKenna Jesuit priest edited a large collection of bardic poetry and historical works in Irish.

The MacKennas did not escape the ravages of the Cromwellians and the Williamite wars, and many fled to join the Irish brigades in Europe. The most colourful was **John (Juan) MacKenna**, who studied engineering in Barcelona and in the Spanish army, aided by his kinsman, General Alexander O Reilly. He subsequently set sail for South America and worked for the famous Ambrosio O Higgins, Viceroy of Peru and liberator of Chile, in the struggle to drive out the French and the Spanish. Sadly, John MacKenna became caught up in the rivalry between two revolutionary dictators and died following a duel. However, his son **Benjamina Vicuna MacKenna** inherited the MacKenna talent for writing and became a distinguished Chilean writer and historian.

The MacKennas have also been to the fore in North America, particularly in the Church and law.

Acting is yet another MacKenna talent, personified by the internationally famous **Siobhán McKenna** (1923–86) and by **T. P. McKenna**, of stage, screen and television fame.

In Australia, **Martin McKenna** (1832–1907), originally of Kilkenny, raised a large family in Kyneton, Victoria, where he farmed five thousand acres and established the very successful Campaspe Brewery. He was at one time the mayor of Kyneton.

MacKenzie

Mac Coinnigh

MacKinney

This Scottish surname comes from the Gaelic, MacCoinnich, meaning son of the fair. In some cases MacKenzie has become MacKinney. There are a variety of spellings and it is often pronounced Macaingye.

In medieval days they were an important family, owning much land in Western Ross. With very little evidence to support it, there are some who deduce that this family descends from the noble Norman-Irish families of Leinster and Desmond—the FitzGeralds—a number of whose followers had settled in Scotland *c.*1261.

An eleventh-century Irish scholar, Conry, had a dispute, in writing, with a **MacKenzie** about the relative antiquity of Scottish and Irish kings.

The MacKenzie family expanded very rapidly. Before 1600, six younger sons of a chieftain had founded twenty-five separate families. **Kenneth MacKenzie** was created Lord of Kintail in 1609. However, many were to follow the doomed Catholic Stuart cause and lose their estates. The home of the Earls of Cromartie, one of the MacKenzie titles, is today National Trust property.

Some MacKenzies probably came to Ireland as planters in Ulster, where they are most numerous. A branch of the family had a brewery and distillery at Dungannon in County Tyrone.

Because of religious persecution, many MacKenzies fled from Scotland to France. In the National Archives in Paris there are receipts of money paid, and certificates of Catholicity, referring to the support given there to MacKenzie widows between *c.*1737 and 1752.

Around 1700, **George MacKenzie**, Earl of Cromarty, was a soldier serving in Ireland and forty-two letters written by him to his mother are preserved in Dublin archives. Between 1824 and 1835, **Sir John MacKenzie** was having a very good time in Dublin, and many of his short letters acknowledging invitations to fashionable events from noble families have been preserved.

There were MacKenzies who travelled abroad to the USA, and also to Canada, where **Donald MacKenzie** (1783–1851) was a fur trader and governor of the Hudson's Bay Company. He weighed a mighty three hundred pounds and was so active he was known as "Perpetual Motion".

In *Chamber's Biographical Dictionary* (1984), ten MacKenzies are listed, including prominent statesmen, composers, authors, lawyers, physicians and politicians in Canada. R. W. Munro's *Kinsmen and Clansmen* (1971) gives a good account of the MacKenzie clan, including a colour picture of their tartan.

MacKeon

Mac Eoghain Mac Eoin

Hone MacEwen MacKeown Owens

Mac Eoghain means son of John—*Eoghain* is Irish for John. There are at least seventeen variations of this name, including Owens and Hone.

The main sept of this family was in north Connacht, with a branch in County Galway. The MacKeons are very numerous in Northern Ireland. In the Glens of Antrim in County Armagh, they are said to be descendants of the Scottish Bissetts.

Miles Keon, who came from County Leitrim, drew up a new constitution for the Catholic Committee in 1792. **Miles Gerald Keon** (1821–75) was a popular novelist.

There are eighteenth-century papers in the National Library in Dublin relating to a County Antrim MacKeon family and a **John MacKeon** of Albuquerque, New Mexico, USA, a son of **John MacKeon** of New York whose parents came from Ireland. They applied for, and were given, a grant of arms.

The most famous MacKeon or MacEoin was "The Blacksmith of Ballinalee", **General Sean MacEoin** (1893–1973), a blacksmith and farmer who was a leader in north Longford in the War of Independence. With his flying column he held Ballinalee village against superior British forces. He survived capture and the death sentence to serve in the *Dáil.* He accepted the Treaty and held a number of important government posts, including the ministries of Justice and Defence.

Robert MacOwen (1744–1812) was born into poverty in County Mayo. He was handsome and had a good voice. Encouraged by Oliver Goldsmith and other literary friends, he went on the stage in Dublin and London. His daughter, **Sydney Owenson** (1783–1859), later Lady Morgan, wrote the hugely successful *The Wild Irish Girl* and other romantic novels and travel books. She opened the eyes of the English to their mistreatment of the Irish while, through the force of her personality, scaling the heights of the aristocracy.

MacKetian *see* Keating

MacKigo *see* Igoe

MacKillen *see* Killeen

MacKinnawe *see* Forde

MacKinnon

Mac Fionguine

MacKinnon—in Gaelic, MacFionguine, meaning son of the fair child—is the surname of a Scottish clan closely connected with the island of Iona in the Hebrides of north-west Scotland. In *Who's Who*, **MacKinnon of MacKinnon** is described as "36th Chief of the Clan MacKinnon". He descends from a branch of the clan which was exiled to Antigua and returned to the Highlands in the nineteenth century and where they reclaimed the chieftancy.

During the nineteenth century, there were MacKinnons who campaigned in Europe and further afield. **Major Henry MacKinnon** wrote a journal about his campaigns in 1809 and 1812 in Portugal and Spain. **J. P. MacKinnon** was soldiering in South Africa in 1879. **Lauchlan Bellingham MacKinnon** was a Royal Navy commander in *c.*1848. **Captain D. H. McKinnon** has written about his military adventures in the Far East. In 1839 he went on to fight in Afghanistan and the Punjab.

There were other, more peace-loving, MacKinnons. **Donald MacKinnon** (1839–1914) was a Scots-Gaelic scholar and first professor of Celtic in the University of Edinburgh. **Sir Frank Douglas MacKinnon**, a lawyer, published his biography, *On Circuit, 1924–37.* In 1935, **Albert G. MacKinnon** wrote on ecclesiastical matters.

In Ireland the MacKinnon name is very rare.

MacKiverkin *see* MacGurrin

MacKnight *see* Knight

MacLaren *see* MacLarnon

MacLarnon

Mac Giolla Earnáin

MacLaren

MacLaren is another of the many spellings of this name, which is numerous today only in Ulster. They were a sept of Iveagh in County Down known as Mac Giolla Earnáin (devotee of St. Earnán). In the twelfth century they were chiefs of Clann Ailebra.

There is also a Scottish clan who came to Ireland from the Braes of Balquidder near Loch Lomond where they were an important family and so numerous that no one dared enter Balquidder Church until they had all taken their places! In the fourteenth century, when their earldom failed, they dispersed, some going to Canada and possibly some to Ireland. It is almost impossible now to distinguish between the Irish and Scottish MacLarnons or MacLarens.

In the records offices there are various papers dealing with their leases and tenancies, mainly in the counties of Down and Antrim.

In 1699, **Paul and Hugh MacLarrinan** of County Armagh were outlawed as Jacobites.

Daniel MacLarinan of Tullyboy, County Down, left a small sum of money to be divided equally between his (Catholic) parish priest and the local Protestant clergyman—most unusual in 1745!

Who's Who lists MacLaren as being the family name of Baron Aberconway.

MacLavin *see* Hand

MacLean

Mac Giolla Eáin

MacClean

The MacLeans, or MacCleans, originated in Scotland, where the MacLeans of Duart were one of the great seafaring clans of the Hebrides. Later, they scattered to the Island of Mull and other areas of Scotland.

In the fifteenth century, they came to Ulster as mercenary soldiers to the MacDonalds. In Gaelic their name is Mac Giolla Eáin, meaning servant of Saint John; Eán, Eoin and Seán all mean John.

In the late seventeenth century, a Scottish scribe called **Eoghan Macgilleoin** was famous in Argyllshire for his writing in Irish.

James MacLaine, or Lean (1724–50), was born in Monaghan, the second son of a Presbyterian minister. He quickly dissipated his inheritance through riotous living, but, by marrying a wealthy lady, he again achieved a comfortable place in society. However, when she died he was again left penniless, so he took to the road, robbing pedestrians and coaches. He was very successful at this and was able to set himself up as an Irish gentleman and a man of fashion. When he was eventually caught red-handed and his lodgings were searched, they were found to be full of purses, and also wigs and other means of disguise. He was tried and hanged at the age of twenty-six, to the grief of many ladies who shed tears for the fashionable highwayman.

In the archives of the Bastille for 1748, among the names of the many who were imprisoned there, is a **Laughton MacLean**.

The Belfast Public Records Office holds many records of the family, including a will of **M. McLean** of Ballymore, County Derry, and several accounts of **Adam McClean**, who mapped lands and estates around Belfast.

In 1959, the Dublin Genealogical Office granted arms to **Donald Francis Stuart McClean**, descendant of **Donald S. McClean** of Killyville in Athy, County Kildare, and to his son, also **Donald Stuart McClean**, of Cobham in Surrey, England.

Anna Jane MacLean of Killarney was a nineteenth-century poet who wrote many Gaelic songs and folk tales.

Spelled MacLean or MacClean, the name is numerous throughout Ireland, especially in Northern Ireland—with the MacCleans slightly ahead of the MacLeans. They are also numerous all over the United States of America.

MacLoughlin

Mac Lochlainn

MacLaughlin   O Melaghlin

There are two distinct septs bearing this name, as well as a number of variations. The sept who originated in Donegal and spread to Derry were a senior branch of the Ulster O Neills. In Ulster the name is spelled MacLaughlin. Although they were Irish, they seem to have adapted Loftus, a Norse personal name, for their Mac Lochlainn surname. They were chieftains in Tirconnell until they were swept aside by the Normans in the thirteenth century.

The other sept—originally Ó Maoilseachlainn (*Maol* means follower and Seachlainn was Saint Secundinas)—descend from Malachy II, who was king of Ireland from AD 988 to AD 1002, when he lost his throne to the great Brian Boru. They were of the race of Niall of the Nine Hostages. The name slimmed down to O Melaghlin until after the rising of 1691, when it was anglicized to MacLoughlin and other variants.

The two separate septs have long since become almost indistinguishable. Although in medieval times they were mentioned frequently in the annals, they have made little impact on modern history.

John MacLoughlin (1784–1857), who went to North America and joined the great fur-trapping industry in Oregon, was a prominent member of the Hudson Bay Company. He was the chief governor west of the mountains, where he ruled with a firm but kindly hand for twenty-two years and was known affectionately as the "father of Oregan". He built Fort Vancouver, which became the region's port for ocean-going vessels.

A descendant of the MacLoughlins (formerly O Melaghlin) compiled a pedigree of the family which is in the Irish Genealogical Office.

The O Loughlin name is in no way connected with either of these two septs.

MacMahon

Mac Mathúna

Mohan   Vaughan

MacMahon, in Irish, is *Mac Mathúna*, meaning son of the bear. The MacMahons divided into two septs: the Lords of Corcabaskin, mostly in County Clare, and the Lords of Oriel in counties Louth and Monaghan.

The Lordship of Corcabaskin died out in 1601 with the death of **Teige MacMahon** following the battle of Kinsale. **Hugh Oge**, the last of the Lords of Oriel, was executed for treason at Tyburn in London in 1646.

They were a remarkable military and ecclesiastic family, including the famous **Bishop Heber MacMahon** who combined the two, becoming a general and taking part in a few bloodthirsty battles which led to his capture and execution. Three MacMahons were Bishops of Armagh.

Their one outstanding woman was the daughter of **Turlough MacMahon**, the fearsome **Máire Rua** (*rua* means red), is credited with having several husbands! The last one, a Cromwellian soldier, she married in order to protect her eleven children and the fine castle of Lemaneagh which had been built by her and her O Brien husband. Its remains can still be seen in County Clare. Another Clare castle, Carrigaholt, was taken from the last Lord of Corcabaskin by Sir William Penn, whose son founded Pennsylvania.

A noble family of MacMahons fled to France where, in the third generation, they produced the famous Field Marshal and, later, President of France, **Edmonde Patrice MacMahon**. He was also Duke of Magenta, a title awarded to him for capturing a fortress which was in danger of blowing up and refusing to leave, saying "*J'y suis, j'y reste*" (Here I am, here I stay).

When the MacMahon family gave up the hopeless endeavour to drive the English out of Ireland, they crossed to England themselves and had no difficulty in fitting into the establishment, earning a succession of baronetcies.

Many emigrated to Australia and played leading roles in the police and the legislature. **Sir William MacMahon** was Prime Minister of Australia in 1970.

Charles Patrick Mahon, who called himself "The O Gorman Mahon", was one of the great nineteenth-century eccentrics. A compulsive traveller, he made friends and influenced people, including Louis Philippe, Talleyrand and the Czar—who appointed him to his bodyguard. He was an admiral in the Chilean navy and a colonel in the army of Brazil. He fought thirteen duels and was also responsible for introducing Kitty O Shea to Parnell.

In the USA, the MacMahons propagated the plant *Berberis mahonia* and introduced the Atomic Energy Act.

The author of many fine Irish short stories is **Bryan MacMahon** of Listowel in County Kerry.

The name Mahon is not related to the MacMahon family, though Mohan or Vaughan might well be variants.

MacManus

Mac Maghnuis

Although Maghnuis is probably the Norse name, Magnus, Mac Maghnuis is an ancient Irish family. The Magnus from whom they adopted their name could possibly have been an admirer of the ninth-century King Charles the Great (Charlemagne), the Roman emperor.

The Irish Magnus was a descendant of Turlough O Conor, who was high king of Ireland in 1119. This MacManus sept had its territory in Roscommon. The other MacManus sept was a branch of the Maguires of Fermanagh where they had their headquarters on Lough Erne, on the island of Ballymacmanus, now known as Belle Isle. The MacManus name is still numerous in Fermanagh, while the other branch is mostly to be found in Mayo.

Cathal MacManus, who died in 1498, was a scholar and compiler of ancient manuscripts, including the famous *Annals of Ulster*. In the national archives in Paris, there is mention of an **Abbé Constantin MacManus** of 1787.

Provoked by the agitation for land reform and Home Rule in the mid-nineteenth century, **Terence Bellew MacManus**, formerly of Fermanagh, left his prosperous Liverpool shipping business to join the ranks of the revolutionaries. Following the uprising of the young Irelanders, his death sentence was commuted to deportation to Tasmania. He managed to escape from there to the United States of America but was unable to make his living there, eventually dying poverty-stricken.

In the twentieth century there has been a blossoming of literary MacManuses. **Seamas MacManus** (1870–1960) of Donegal was a schoolteacher who later became a writer. Teachers in Ireland were poorly paid, so he emigrated to the United States of America in 1899. There he wrote folk tales, novels, poetry and plays, with great success. He married the Irish poet whose pseudonym was Eithne Carbery. His 1938 autobiography was called *The Rocky Road to Dublin.*

Francis MacManus (1909–65) of Kilkenny, was a schoolteacher for eighteen years before he moved into broadcasting. During his fruitful years with Radio Éireann as Head of Features and Talks, he initiated the inspirational and on-going Thomas Davies Lectures.

In 1944, **M. J. MacManus** wrote a biography of Eamon de Valera.

MacMurrough *see* Kavanagh

MacNairney *see* MacInerney

MacNally

Mac an Fhailghigh

MacAnally Nally

This ancient surname originates from the Irish word *failgheach*, meaning poor man. It has a number of variants in different parts of the country. In County Westmeath, it was recorded in 1659 as Knally, while in Connacht it is generally now Nally, without its Mac prefix. It is also sometimes rendered MacAnally, usually in Ulster. It is thought that some bearers of this name could be of either Welsh or Norman origin.

Some MacNallys served in the Irish brigades in France in the eighteenth century.

The most notorious MacNally was **Leonard MacNally**, who joined the United Irishmen when he was studying law at Trinity College Dublin. When he was supposed to be defending the United Irishmen at their trials for treason, he was instead betraying them to the government, for which he received a handsome pension from the British. He was able to enjoy a successful career as a writer of verse plays and it was he who wrote that popular ditty, "Sweet Lass of Richmond Hill".

Dr. John MacNally (b. 1871), who was of Irish descent, was Archbishop of Halifax in Canada. **Reverend Charles MacNally** was Bishop of Cloyne from 1843 to 1864. **David Rice MacAnally** (1810–95) was a Methodist preacher and sheriff who was famous for his girth—he weighed 360 pounds!

Ray MacAnally (1926–89) was born in Donegal and was an outstanding actor on stage and screen.

MacNamara

Mac Conmara

The MacNamaras are from the sea coast of Connacht. Their name, Mac Conmara (meaning son of the hound of the sea), comes from an ancient lineage going back to Cas, the head of the Dalcassians, which also included the royal sept of the O Briens whose chiefs they had the right to inaugurate. They separated into the chiefs of Clancullen West, known as MacNamara Fionn (fair), and the chiefs of the East,

MacNamara Reagh (swarthy). They occupied themselves with building many fortresses and castles, by no means all of which are ruined, notably the famous castles of Bunratty and Knappogue.

The Cromwellians put an end to the dominance of the MacNamaras, and they departed and made a new life abroad. Essentially a sea-going family, they produced a number of admirals, including a commodore of the French fleet, **Count MacNamara**. He had also played a diplomatic role in the Far East and it was on a voyage there with the French fleet that he met his death at the hands of a garrison of French revolutionaries who disliked his royalist background.

James MacNamara nearly lost his naval career and his head when he killed an opponent in a duel over a dog. However, he was so popular in high places that he was pardoned and went on to become an admiral—one of a number of MacNamara admirals.

Although **"Fireball" MacNamara** enjoyed some popularity, his aggressiveness and fondness for the gun caused his expulsion from France. Back in Ireland he became a highwayman. He met his death on the scaffold and was buried in Quin Abbey, built by the MacNamaras, beside one of the people he had killed.

Donnchadha Ruadh Mac Conmara was another MacNamara renegade but also a fine poet in the Irish language. Expelled from the priesthood in Rome, he became an itinerant teacher in Ireland. He sailed to and from Newfoundland, where many Irish had travelled via Waterford. Although dogged by drunkenness, he wrote some beautiful poetry and lived to be 95.

A more recent poet and eccentric, **Francis MacNamara** of Ennistymon House (now the Falls Hotel), was the father of Caitlin who married Dylan Thomas.

In 1920, a former regimental sergeant-major in the Munster Fusiliers, **Thomas MacNamara**, helped Eamon de Valera to escape to the USA.

In the USA, **Robert MacNamara** was President of the World Bank, General Manager of the Ford Motor Company and Secretary of Defence. The MacNamaras also emigrated to Canada and to Australia.

MacNaughton *see* MacCracken, Naughton

MacNeeley

Mac Conghaile

Conneely MacNeal MacNeela Neely

MacNeely (also MacNeilly) is a very common name in Ulster, though it is scarcely found anywhere else in Ireland. It is of Scottish-Irish derivation, the Irish element mostly to be found in County Antrim. However, MacNeely—or Neely—was originally of Connacht origin, deriving from *cú* (hound) and *Gaola* (a County Galway place-name). Ballyconneely in County Galway possibly commemorates the early origins of this ancient sept.

There is a Connacht tradition that the Conneelys were changed by magic into seals and since then seals have seldom, if ever, been killed on that part of the Atlantic seacoast.

Another version of this versatile name could be Mac an Fhilidh, meaning son of the poet. **Giollachriest Mac Philidh** was a learned and popular poet who died in 1509.

Father Charles MacNeely (1816–70), who was born in Mountcharles, County Donegal, was a distinguished parish priest in the diocese of Raphoe.

Of MacNeal or MacNeela there are but a few examples now in the Republic of Ireland, but the name is very numerous in Ulster.

MacNelis *see* MacGrealish

MacNeill

Mac Néill

MacGreal

The MacNeill name is the same in Irish and English, but in the south it has sometimes been corrupted to MacGreal. They came to Ireland as mercenary soldiers from the Western Isles of Scotland and have been prominent in Antrim and Derry since the fourteenth century—long before the plantations.

A MacNeill was killed in the service of an O Rourke chieftain, but it is in the nineteenth century that the family came into prominence.

Sir John MacNeill (*c.*1793–1880), a civil engineer, pioneered the building of railways and a waterways transport system both in Scotland and Ireland. He was the first professor of engineering in Trinity College Dublin, but eventually lost his sight.

Hugh McNeill (1795–1879), a Dean of Ripon, was notorious for his anti-Catholic preaching in England.

John G. Swift MacNeill (1849–1926), a Member of Parliament and a professor in the National University in Ireland, was the author of many historical and constitutional works.

John Gordon MacNeill (1849–1926), a politician and authority on parliamentary procedure, was born in Dublin and educated at Trinity College Dublin and Oxford University. He campaigned for the abolition of flogging of sailors in the Royal Navy.

James McNeill of Antrim served in the Indian civil service. Retiring early, he joined Sinn Féin. He was Irish high commissioner in London and governor-general of Ireland until de Valera had this British office abolished.

Eoin MacNeill (1867–1945), professor of early Irish history at University College Dublin, was co-founder of the Gaelic League. He tried to prevent the 1916 Easter Rising. For a while he was Minister of Education in the new Irish Free State government. An academic rather than a politician, he resigned to publish a wide range of important books.

Two MacNeill women have made a name with their writing in the twentieth century. **Máire MacNeill**, an archaeologist and folklorist, and **Janet McNeill**, a storyteller.

Today, in Scotland, **MacNeill of Barra** is The Chief of the Clan Mac Neil. MacNeill or O Neill or Neill, they are all descended from Niall of the Nine Hostages, the fifth-century founder of the ancient O Neill dynasty.

MacNelis *see* MacGrealish

MacNicholas

Mac Nioclàis

Clausson

The MacNicholas name is said to have come from a branch of the powerful Norman de Burgos (Burke or Bourke) who arrived in Ireland in the twelfth century. In some instances they assumed the surname Clausson.

County Mayo has remained the stronghold of the MacNicholas families who once held extensive estates around Bohola in the barony of Gallen and in the adjacent barony of Clanmorres.

In the seventeenth century, along with their Irish neighbours with whom they had thoroughly integrated, they suffered the loss of their lands and transplantation during the Cromwellian conquests.

Patrick MacNicholas was bishop of

the important See of Achonry from 1818 to 1852. From Kiltimagh in County Mayo came **Dr. MacNicholas** (1879–1950), a Dominican priest who was Archbishop of Cincinnati in the USA.

In the Royal Irish Academy in Dublin there is a manuscript collection of Ossianic verse in Irish which was compiled about 1815 by **Eoin Mac Niocláis** of Balrath House in Kells, County Meath.

MacNulty

Mac an Ultaigh

Nulty

MacNulty is the anglicized form of Mac an Ultaigh, which means son of Ulster—in this case Donegal. Today, the MacNultys are numerous in every part of the country. In County Meath they have dropped the Mac and are more numerous as Nulty.

In the Middle Ages the MacNultys had much to contend with from their very powerful neighbours, the O Donnells of Tirconnell. In 1281, one of the MacNulty chieftains was slain in the battle of Desertcreagh, and in 1431 the MacNulty fortress at Tirhugh in County Down was raided by the O Donnells.

Bernard MacNulty (d. 1892), a friend of John Boyle O Reilly, founded the first branch of the Fenian Brotherhood in the USA.

Owen McNulty was a lieutenant in the 69th New York Volunteers of the Irish-American brigade serving under General Thomas Francis Meagher in the American Civil War. His eldest son, **Frank McNulty** (1872–1926), was an American labour leader.

Edward McNulty (1856–1943) of Antrim went to school with George Bernard Shaw and remained a great friend of his. He wrote "stage-Irish" novels and plays and was a drama critic. His memoirs of Shaw, published after McNulty's death, are greatly prized by academics in the United States of America.

Daniel McNulty, who was born in 1920, was blinded at the age of four in an accident. A man of outstanding musical talent, he graduated from University College Dublin and became an organist, teacher, composer and arranger, and he also wrote songs in the Irish language.

Michael McNulty (b. 1935) of Dublin has followed a varied career in commerce, including being appointed director-general of the Irish Dunlop Company and the Irish Tourist Board (Bord Fáilte).

MacPaul *see* Lavelle

MacPeake

Mac Péice

The MacPeake surname is still very numerous in Ulster, particularly in their homeland around counties Tyrone and Derry. It has been anglicized from the Old-English *peic* which is synonymous with a thick-set man. Without the Mac prefix, the name could be of English origin, referring to a peak or hilltop, probably in the vicinity of York.

In a head count taken between 1659 and 1660, the MacPeakes were shown to have one of the most numerous surnames in Loughinsholin in County Derry, where there is also a Ballymacpeake.

In the aftermath of the defeat of the Irish and Spanish at Kinsale in 1601, **Dermot and Manus MacPeake** were with the many men of Ulster who followed Rory O Donnell, 1st Earl of Tirconnell, into Connacht. At the same time, **Owen Callowe MacPeake** and

Owyne Peake were among the rebels who were granted "pardons".

In Belfast, the MacPeakes have been renowned for their contribution to Irish traditional music.

MacPhilbin *see* Philbin

MacQuade

Mac Uaid

MacQuaid MacQuoid MacWade

The origin of this ancient surname is obscure, but it is thought to have come from Mac Uaid, meaning son of Wat—pet name for Walter. It has gone through a number of variations, including MacQuaid, MacQuoid and MacWade. It is fairly numerous throughout Ireland, particularly in Ulster, where its original territory was County Monaghan and, later, Fermanagh and Offaly.

The two most distinguished bearers of the name were both bishops, one in the USA and the other, a century later, in Ireland.

Bernard John MacQuaid (1823–1909) was born in New York to Irish emigrant parents. His father, a labourer in a glass factory, was murdered in 1832. Bernard rose to become the first Bishop of Rochester. During his long life he built many schools, convents and churches. An autocratic disciplinarian, he was totally opposed to co-educational schools.

John Charles McQuaid (1895–1973) was born in Cootehill, County Cavan, where his father was a doctor. He joined the Holy Ghost order and was dean of studies at Blackrock College in County Dublin. He was appointed Archbishop of Dublin in 1940. An outstanding administrator, he too was a religious autocrat, but showed great compassion for the poor. He is remembered for his abhorrence of Catholics attending Trinity College Dublin.

Harry McQuade is recorded as being a lieutenant in the 69th New York regiment with the Irish-American brigade, from 1861 to 1865. In the same century, Lady Sarah Cochrane, wife of Alderman Sir Henry Cochrane of Woodbrook in Bray, County Wicklow, was a daughter of **George McQuade** of Dromogoland in County Cavan.

MacQuillan

Mac Uighilín

Mac Uighilín (a diminutive of Hugh) is the Gaelic form of the Welsh-Norman Hugeli de Mandeville. This family came from Wales to Ireland with the Normans in the twelfth century and became rich and powerful chieftains known as Lords of the Route, an area in north County Antrim, where their chief residence was the castle of Dunluce. They fought side by side with the O Neills, the O Donnells and the O Cahanes and were described by the English as "being as Irish as the worst".

They were Princes of Dalriada and high constables of Ulster until they were destroyed by Sorley Boy MacDonnell (*c.*1505–90) who, with support from Scotland, dominated north-east Ulster for many years.

Rory Óg MacQuillan has been quoted as saying in 1541 that "No MacQuillan chieftain ever died in his bed." The last of the known Lords of the Route died in 1649 and then began the exodus of the Irish to France and Spain, where the MacQuillans are well recorded in the European archives.

Father Peter MacQuillan (*c.*1650–1719), a distinguished Dominican priest from County Derry, went to France and became a prior at the Irish College at Louvain.

John Hugh MacQuillan (1826–79), the son of an Irish Quaker family, was a very distinguished dentist in Philadelphia, USA. He helped to organize the American Dental Association and, in 1863, he founded the Philadelphia Dental College.

A number of informative pamphlets written by Irish scholars have been published on the Lords of the Route and can be found in the MacQuillan archives in the National Library of Ireland in Dublin.

MacRannall *see* Reynolds

MacRory *see* Rogers

MacSheehy *see* Sheehy

MacSweeney

Mac Suibhne

MacSwiney Sweeney Sweeny

The MacSweeneys derive their name from a personal name meaning pleasant. Some members of this now widespread clan claim descent from the fourth-century King Heremon who came from Spain.

The MacSweeneys who established themselves in Donegal were descendants of Suibhne Ó Neill, a chieftain of Argyle in Scotland. His grandson, **Murrough MacSweeney**, was the first of a succession of mercenary soldiers who served the O Donnells of Donegal. They branched into three kindred septs: the MacSweeneys of Fanad, the MacSweeneys of Banagh, and MacSweeney na d'Tuath (of the Districts). Doe Castle, near Creeslough, once a MacSweeney headquarters, is one of the more impressive remains of their Donegal fastnesses.

The MacSweeneys of Fanad, who built the priory in Rathmullan in the fifteenth century and compiled the *History of the Clan Suibhne*, were driven south to Muskerry in County Cork, where they are now very numerous.

Always a military family, there were eleven MacSweeneys in James II's Irish army. Following the defeat at the battle of the Boyne, they fled abroad and held high office in the military and diplomatic services of Europe and North America—and of England.

The **Marquis MacSweeney of Mashanaglass** belonged to a Munster family who acquired this papal title. Also from Munster was **Thomas William Sweeney** (1820–92), who led the Fenian raid into Canada.

Terence MacSwiney (1879–1920), Lord Mayor of Cork and a scholar and revolutionary fighter for independence, died in Brixton prison on the 74th day of his hunger-strike.

Chevalier Loughlin Sweeney of Dublin is head of the Irish branch of clan Suibhne.

MacTaigue *see* Montague

MacTansey *see* Tansey

MacTeague *see* Tighe

MacTiernan *see* Kiernan

MacWade *see* MacQuade

MacWiggan *see* MacGuigan

Madden

Ó Madáin

The Ó Madáin, who were a distinguished family in County Galway, were kinsmen of the powerful O Kellys. They descended from **Madadha**, who was slain in 1008. Gadhra Mór was their chieftain from 1014 to 1027. Their name is believed to derive from the Irish word for dog—*madhara* or *gadhar*.

In the twelfth century the Norman de Burgos drove many Maddens from their east Galway strongholds, but they held their chieftainship of Silanchia (approximately Longford and Offaly) in unbroken succession from the eleventh to the seventeenth century.

Madden can also be an English name and, particularly in Ulster, they may have Anglo-Irish roots. The Maddens are very well recorded in the national archives, where there are pedigrees, wills and letters, and a grant of arms of *c.*1800 to a Waterford lady whose son was **Don Luis de Pedrosa y Madan, Conde de San Esteban de Canongo**.

The **Reverend Samuel Madden** (1686–1765) was an outstanding philanthropist. He promoted education, industry and more efficient agriculture, and was one of the founders of the Royal Dublin Society.

Richard Robert Madden (1798–1886), a Dublin surgeon with international connections, worked in Jamaica, Havana and Western Australia for the abolition of slavery. He also campaigned for justice for the peasantry in Ireland. Among his many writings are the seven volumes of *The History of the United Irishmen*.

Two other Maddens were distinguished literary men of their day. They were **Daniel Owen Madden** (1815–59) and **Thomas More Madden** (1844–1902), a son of Richard Robert.

Sir John Madden was chief justice of Victoria in Australia. He was the son of **John Madden** of Melbourne, whose father was **David Madden** of County Cork.

The Maddens who settled in County Kilkenny have contributed a number of admirals to the British navy.

In the 1600s there was a mayor of Waterford, **R. Madan**, who tried to bribe Sir R. Cecil with a pair of bed coverings and a cask of whiskey. Later, he is found appealing over a breach of trust in the sale of merchandise sent from Dublin to Tenerife.

Magauran *see* MacGovern

Magee

Mag Aoidh

MacGee

Mag Aoidh means son of Hugh. It can be of Scottish or Irish origin and today it is numerous in Ulster, particularly spelled Magee, with MacGee coming second in popularity. In the Republic, both Magee and MacGee are equally common.

Their Irish lineage descends from Colla Uais, whose territory bordered Donegal and Tyrone. At Lough Larne, the peninsula of Islandmagee marks their early Ulster territory. Until the arrival of the Normans, there was also a MacGee chief of his sept in County Westmeath.

There were a number of Ulster Protestant Magee archbishops, one of whom accused the Roman Catholic Archbishop of Armagh of placing a calf's head on the altar of a chapel in Ardee!

In Dublin's National Library there are letters written by **James Maighee** describing his activities in 1717 at Dunkirk, where he was spying for King James II.

Early in the nineteenth century, a father and son both called **John Magee** fearlessly exposed political and legal corruption in their newspapers, *Magee's Weekly Packet* and the *Dublin Evening Post*. They suffered frequent court cases and heavy fines. John Magee the elder was so incensed at the harsh treatment meted out to him by the Chief Justice,

Lord Clonmel, that he organized a hugely popular pig hunt around Clonmel's County Dublin home. The pigs caused considerable destruction when they broke into his grounds. Magee was eventually imprisoned in Newgate, but his newspapers did expose many scandals.

Martha Maria Magee (d. 1846), née Stewart, was married to a Presbyterian minister called **William Magee**. Both he and their two sons died prematurely and she moved to Dublin, where her two brothers lived. They left her a fortune which, after much legal wrangling, went to the founding of Magee College in Derry city, later an important part of the new University of Ulster.

Thomas D'Arcy Magee (1825–68) of Carlingford in County Louth emigrated to Boston, where he became editor of the *Boston Pilot*. A fervent Irish nationalist, he believed in constitutional rather than violent methods. However, in Ottawa where he was an MP, he was shot dead by the Fenians, of whom he had written very critically.

Magennis

Mag Aonghusa

Guinness McGenis MacGinnis MacGuinness MacInnes

MacAonghusa comes from the personal name, Aonghus, which means one choice—hardly applicable to their name, as they have at least sixteen different ways of spelling it!

This prominent Irish family is recorded as far back as the fifth century, the time of St. Patrick, and their descendants have been both illustrious and notorious. At one time the Magennis clansmen were the Lords of Iveagh in County Down. In the nineteenth century, this ancient title was adopted by the internationally famous Guinness family of brewers, since which time the head of the firm has been an Earl of Iveagh. Iveagh House in Saint Stephen's Green, Dublin, the fine headquarters of the Department of Foreign Affairs, was just one of the many gifts to the nation made by this philanthropic family. "Uncle Arthur" is Dublin's nickname for the firm of **Arthur Guinness** which, since 1759, has been making the black porter that has made the family millionaires.

There were many Magennis fortresses in Ulster, most of which were destroyed following the Anglo-Norman invasion in the twelfth century. Their castle at Rathfriland, near Newry, was destroyed by the Cromwellians, but there are remains of their twelfth-century fortress at Dundrum.

In the sixteenth century, **Sir Conn Magennis** and his wife ransacked Newry and horribly ill-treated its Protestant inhabitants. Also in the sixteenth century, in complete contrast, there were two worthy bishops, **Arthur Magennis** and **Hugo Magennis** (d. 1640). The family has had a long succession of bishops, both Catholic and Protestant, but Arthur managed to be both at the same time!

In the eighteenth century, following the exodus of many exiled Irish, many Magennis soldiers served with distinction in the armies of France, Austria and Spain.

Charles Donagh Magennis (1867–1955), who was trained as an architect in Dublin, built many fine churches, schools and colleges in the USA, and also designed the bronze doors of St. Patrick's Cathedral in New York City.

Viscount Elveden, a Guinness heir, was killed in the Second World War. The only Northern Ireland man to win a Victoria Cross in the Second World War was Leading Seaman **James Magennis**, who was ceremoniously honoured in Bradford, where he died in 1986. Also in Northern Ireland, **Ken Magennis** is the Ulster Unionist Party spokesman on security.

The Magennis armorial shield shows a yellow lion on a green field with the red hand of Ulster on top.

Mageown *see* Smith

Magill *see* MacGill

Maginnity *see* MacGinty

Magrath, **Magraw** *see* MacGrath

Maguigan *see* MacGuigan

Maguire

mag uidhir

MacGuire

In Irish the Maguire name is Mag Uidhir, meaning pale coloured. It has featured in the records since the tenth century, although it was not until four centuries later that the Maguires appear as Barons of Enniskillen, where they had their fortress (still there) and lorded over the county of Fermanagh. They protected their country against the encroachment of the colonizers, and their great chieftain, **Hugh Maguire**, led the battle in the defeat of the English at Yellow Ford in 1598.

A later kinsman, **Conor**, brought disaster to the Ulster chieftains—who were trying to capture Dublin Castle—by foolishly revealing the plans to a traitor. He was executed at the Tower of London.

A Maguire Baron of Enniskillen commanded an infantry regiment at the battle of the Boyne. There was also a Maguire in the pay of King James's secret service. Following defeat at the Boyne, the Maguires joined the "Wild Geese" who began the exodus of the Irish by sailing to Genoa. They went into the service of the armies of Europe, and those who went to France were well received in the royal court.

The Maguire aristocracy has long since died out. In the nineteenth century, a historian discovered that some sailors on the Irish ferry were direct descendants of the seventeenth-century **Hugh Maguire**.

Maguires have long filled high ecclesiastical posts in the Church. It is believed that the housekeeper of a nineteenth-century parish priest, **Father Tom Maguire** (1792–1847), an awkward and aggressive theologian, was so enraged by him that she poisoned him! Another **Thomas Maguire** (1831–89) was the first Catholic to become a fellow of Trinity College Dublin, where he was also professor of moral philosophy.

Many Maguires emigrated to the USA, mostly as priests. A MacGuire of the Connacht spelling was surgeon to Stonewall Jackson. Many Irish-American MacGuires, mostly of Kentucky and Kansas, are recorded in Dublin's Genealogical Office.

The *Cork Examiner* newspaper (recently re-named *The Examiner)* was founded by **John Francis Maguire**.

Since 1991, **Terence Maguire** has been recognized as the authentic Chief of the Name—The Maguire.

Mahaffy

Mac Dhuibhshithe

MacAfee MacFee MacFie MacHaffy Mahaffery

Mahaffy is a singularly rare name in Ireland, except for in Ulster, where they came via Scotland. Father

Patrick Woulfe gives a number of variations of the name, including MacAffie, MacAffee, MacHaffie, MacHaffy, MacFie, MacFee and Mahaffy. Translated from the Gaelic he says the name means the black-haired man of peace and describes them as being "of a Scottish family who for many centuries held the island of Colonsay. They were a brave and warlike clan and, as followers of the MacDonalds of Islay and the Camerons of Lochiel, showed their prowess on many a field. They suffered severely at Culloden in 1745, when the whole clan was out for Prince Charlie. A branch of the family settled in County Antrim in the sixteenth century, and others probably came over at a later period."

The **Reverend Daniel MacAfee** (1700–73), a Wesleyan minister in Ireland, was a controversial character who was a strong opponent of Daniel O Connell's campaign for Catholic emancipation.

A very distinguished Mahaffy in Ireland was **John Pentland Mahaffy** (1839–1919), who was born in Switzerland where his father was a chaplain. He returned to Ireland to be educated in Donegal and to become one of the great characters of Trinity College Dublin. A brilliant scholar and a fellow of Trinity, he served the college for fifty-five years. His talents were diverse, which was probably not in his favour for he did not achieve the position of provost until his seventy-fifth year! He was a professor of ancient history and wrote many books on life in ancient Greece. He had to take holy orders—essential for his fellowship—and he was also a musician, a first-class shot and one of the most popular conversationalists in Dublin, although his wit could sometimes be wounding. Oscar Wilde was one of his star pupils. He regarded the nationalism of his day as mere provincialism and, in the 1917 Irish Convention hosted by Trinity College, he proposed that Ireland should be a federal constitution on the Swiss model, with Ulster as an autonomous province.

There are very few Mahaffys in Ireland today, except in Ulster, where they also spell the name Mahaffery.

Maher

Ó Meachair

Meagher

This name comes from the Irish word *michair*, meaning hospitable or kindly. The name was anglicized to Maher or Meagher and they were of the same blood as the distinguished O Carrolls of Ely in counties Tipperary and Offaly.

In 1345 there is mention in the archives of a **Henry Maghyr** and "a rental taken by him and others".

Unusually, the Mahers were not driven out by the arrival of the Normans. However, many followed the beaten path to Europe in the seventeenth century, including **Don Theodoro (Thadeo) Meaher**, "a Coronel in the Service of the Prince of Condé" and Mariscal de Campo. A **Don Juan Meagher** was a captain in 1660 in the Spanish Netherlands.

A **Thady Meagher** of Kilkenny was in the Irish parliament of James II.

Today, Meagher is the more usual spelling of this very widespread name whose most celebrated representative was **Thomas Francis Meagher** (1823–67), a nationalist who was dubbed "Meagher of the Sword" by the writer Thackeray. He was sentenced to penal servitude in Australia for his "traitorous" activities but escaped to America, where he took up journalism and organized the Irish brigade to fight for the North.

In archives in Paris there are letters from a Maher who was an attorney for the Irish College in Paris during the

French Revolution. **John Maher**'s account of his tour in Italy, between 1821 and 1822, is in the National Library of Ireland.

Ballinkeale in County Wexford has long been in the Maher family who were high sheriffs and Members of Parliament for that county. **George Maurice Maher**, born there in 1847, was a captain in the 7th Dragoon Guards.

And who was the Maher who gave his name to the Maher Terminal at Port Elizabeth in New Jersey, USA?

Mahon *see* Mohan

(O) Mahony

Ó Mathghamhna Ó Mathúna

Mahoney

The O Mahonys take their name from Mathghamhan, a tenth-century prince who was married to Sadbh, daughter of the High King Brian Boru. They were a powerful clan who claimed ancestry going back to the second-century King of Munster. Munster was, and is still, their territory, where once they were princes and owned vast areas of land. There were so many O Mahonys at one stage that they divided into eight separate septs. They built more than a score of fine castles in West Cork.

When they were driven abroad in the seventeenth century, many followed distinguished careers in Europe in the army and the diplomatic and administrative services, and they were admitted into the European aristocracy.

It was a **John O Mahony** (1815–77) who founded the Fenian brotherhood in the United States of America. **Francis Sylvester Mahony** was a priest and wrote the famous song, "The Bells of Shandon", and other poems in praise of his native Cork.

Proud and knowledgeable about their family history, the O Mahonys have been holding family rallies at one or other of their West Cork castles every August since 1955. This was originally the idea of an **Eoin O Mahony** (1904–70), affectionately known as "The Pope", who was an expert in Irish genealogy.

Although their name derives from the Irish word for a bear, *mathghamhan*, there are no bears, only lions and snakes, on their elaborate armorial bearings.

The majority of the clan now spell their name O Mahony.

Mainey *see* Mooney

Mairs *see* Mayer

O Malley

Ó Máille

Melia

The O Malley name—in Irish Ó Maille—is said to have come from the ancient Celtic word *maglics*, meaning chieftain. For thousands of years they have been settled in Connacht, where they were chieftains of the two baronies of Burrishoole and Murrisk.

The daughter of the chieftain **Owen O Malley** was one of the most notorious women in Irish history. **Grania (Grace) O Malley**—known as Granuaile, meaning Grania the bald, because she cut her hair to look like a boy—was one of the greatest sea captains of her time. She was married first to an O Flaherty, who was killed in war, and then to Richard Burke, by whom she had a son. The child was born at sea in the middle of an attack by pirates and she had to rise from her bed and go on deck to rally her men. She frequently fought the English, one of whom said of her that she was "for forty years the stay of all rebellion in the West". She escaped the gallows several times and described herself as "a Princess and an equal" on a visit to Queen Elizabeth in London in 1593, by which time both women were elderly and got on quite well.

When the Cromwellians finally dispersed the chieftains of Ireland, many O Malleys went to make their living in Europe, in the only profession they knew—the army. However, not all had left Mayo when the French landed at Castlebar. **Austin O Malley** joined them, while his kinsman, **George O Malley**, fought with the victorious English! Afterwards, George joined the Irish regiment of Dillon in France and later took part in the battle of Waterloo and the American War of Independence.

There were a number of O Malley archbishops of Tuam, and there was also an unorthodox O Malley priest who was sent back from America to Dublin, having been considered altogether too progressive!

Ernest O Malley, who fought in the Irish Civil War, was to write a very successful autobiography, *On Another Man's Wound*.

The O Malleys had distinguished careers in the British service abroad. One much-travelled diplomat, **Sir Owen O Malley**, who claimed to be the Chief of the Name, retired to Rockfleet, which was one of his ancestor Granuaile's castles in Connacht.

O Malley is almost never used without its O prefix, although in some parts of Mayo it is occasionally transformed to Melia.

Malone

Ó Maoileoin

The servant of Saint John is the descriptive translation of this old Irish name, which is very numerous in Dublin, Wexford and Clare. In medieval times, their sept was very prominent in the Midlands—Offaly in particular. The O Conor kings of Connacht were close kinsmen. The Malones were attached to the international centre of religion and learning at Clonmacnoise, where they filled the posts of abbot and bishop.

When the old Gaelic order was submerged, in the seventeenth century, those who did not conform to the new religion fled to France, Spain and Italy, where a Malone cleric became president of the Irish College in Rome.

The Malones who had saved their property by conforming had their seat at Baronstown in Westmeath (recently demolished). **Richard Malone** of this family was the 1st and only Baron Sunderlin. His uncle, another **Richard Malone**, was a Chancellor of the Exchequer.

Edmond Malone (1741–1812), born in Dublin, practised as a lawyer and a journalist in Ireland before moving to London, where he moved in high literary circles, with friends such as Samuel Johnson and Horace Walpole. He came to be regarded as the most erudite critic of Shakespeare's works.

The Malones have also been well represented in the USA. A priest called **Sylvester Malone** is remembered for his work with the immigrants from the famine ships. **Walter Malone** wrote the famous epic poem telling the story of the American Indians who were driven from the Mississippi River by the Spaniards.

Many ballads have been written and sung about Dublin, but none more enduringly popular than the sad tale of the real street character, **Molly Malone**, who "wheeled her wheelbarrow through streets broad and narrow, singing cockles and mussels, alive, alive oh". The song ends when "she died of a fever from which no one could save her, and that was the end of sweet Molly Malone". In these more medically enlightened times, it is thought to have been either typhoid or shellfish poison which carried the poor woman off. However, "her ghost still wheels that wheelbarrow through streets broad and narrow".

Maloney

Ó Maoldhomhnaigh

Malony Moloney Molony

The translation of Ó Maoldhomhnaigh is a descendant of a servant of the Church. They were a Dalcassian sept of Kiltanon near Tulla in east Clare. They are now widespread and are very numerous, especially with the Moloney spelling.

An uncle and his nephew, both named **John Moloney**, between them occupied the bishopric of Killaloe in County Clare for more than seventy years. The nephew had to flee to France in 1696 because of his allegiance to James II. There he founded the Irish College in Paris.

In order to escape the Great Famine, **Martin Malony** (1847–1929) and his family left their home in Ballinagarry, County Tipperary, for America, where he successfully combined the roles of financier and philanthropist. He built a palatial mansion modelled on the White House and called it Ballinagarry. It occupied an entire block at Spring Lake, New Jersey. For his generous charitable donations, the Pope created him a papal marquis. In the depression of the 1940s, his daughter had to sell the house, and it was subsequently razed by a building speculator.

A Dubliner called **Helena Molony** (1884–1967), who was an actress at the Abbey Theatre, and a trade unionist, took part in the attack on Dublin Castle in the 1916 Easter Rising, for which she was imprisoned. She was later to be a president of the Irish Congress of Trade Unions.

Paddy Moloney is a musician, a composer and the leader of Ireland's most distinguished and internationally acclaimed folk group, "The Chieftains". He is also actively involved in the Claddagh Record Company.

Brian Molony, who was an assistant bank manager in Canada, was jailed in 1964 for six years for stealing over ten million Canadian dollars (6.7 million Irish pounds) which he had secreted in eleven false bank accounts. While on bail, he got a job managing a computer software company, and succeeded in transforming it from a loss-making to a profitable company.

The family of **Sir Thomas Francis Molony**, a lord chief justice of Ireland, settled in England, and his son, **Sir Joseph Molony**, became an appeal judge in Jersey and Guernsey. Sir Joseph's son, **Thomas Desmond Molony**, has dropped the title.

Burke's Irish Family Records (1976) has five pages on the Molony family, concluding with **Fergus Norman Malony**, who served in the Second World War in the Australian expeditionary force and described himself as "a classifier of sheep's wool".

Maloughney *see* Loughney

Maloy *see* Molloy

Mangan

Ó Mongáin

Mongan

In Irish, *mongach* means hairy, and this is the origin of Ó Mongáin, which was anglicized to Mangan and sometimes to Mongan, especially in north Connacht. There was a separate sept in

County Limerick, where Ballymongane is a place-name, and a third sept belonged to Ulster, where Termongan in County Tyrone perpetuates a name which has almost died out there.

From the Tyrone family came the renowned **Charles Mangan** (1754–1826), who was a blind itinerant harpist. He improved his prospects remarkably when he turned Protestant and, in time, he was appointed Bishop of Limerick and of Cloyne in County Cork. He also changed his name to Warburton and subsequently, between 1810 and 1894, some of his descendants—three Warburton brothers—were distinguished, especially for their travel writing.

For a long period, the Mangans owned much land in County Offaly, where many of the name are still to be found.

Undoubtedly, literature ran in the Mangan blood. The **Reverend Edward Mangan** (1772–1852) was a poet and an essayist, and the most celebrated bearer of this very numerous name was **James Clarence Mangan** (1803–49). He was born into an impoverished Dublin family and a priest gave him a basic education. However, he had to suffer extreme drudgery before he managed to break into the literary world of Dublin with his poetry. From translations of Irish poems he produced the very popular "Dark Rosaleen" and "The Woman of the Three Cows", among many others. But poverty, an unhappy love affair and an innate melancholy led him to over-indulgence in alcohol, and he finally died from cholera.

Mannin, **Manning** *see* Mannion

Mannion

Ó Mainnín

Mannin Manning

A very old family, the Mannions are said to descend from pre-Gaelic Pictish rulers of the Galway and Roscommon area, where a great number of Mannions are still located. There is also a Mannin Bay near Galway Bay, on the Connemara coast. They were also a sept of the population group known as the Uí Maine, which included most of the important septs of Connacht. They were located in the barony of Tiaquin in County Galway and the headquarters of their chieftain was the castle of Clogher.

Ó Mainnín, King of Sodhan, is mentioned in an Irish chronicle of 1135. Up to the time of James I (1566–1625) they were still a clan of some importance and their chieftain's residence was at Menlough Castle, which was later to be taken over by the Blakes who were descendants of the Fourteen Tribes of Galway.

In the seventeenth century the Mannions were besieged by the powerful O Kellys, who confiscated much of their land.

In 1617, **Hugh O Mannin** had to surrender his estates to James I. Later he had them returned to him. However, a few decades later they were confiscated by the marauding Cromwellians.

Manning is a common surname in England, but in Ireland it can also be an anglicization of Ó Mainnín. The Mannings of Dublin and Cork could be of English descent.

In the Irish army of James II (1633–1701), **John Manning** is recorded as being a "cornet" in O Neill's Dragoon.

Frederick Manning (1812–83) of Dublin followed his father to Van Diemen's Land (now Tasmania). He was well received by the Maoris and, in time, became a judge in their courts. He published a number of books on New Zealand and local folk culture.

Henry Edward, Cardinal Manning (1808–92), Archbishop of Westminster, was one of the English Mannings.

Marrally *see* Morley

Martin

Mac Mártain Ó Martáin

Gilmartin Kilmartin Martyn

There are many variations of this name, which is common both in Britain and Ireland. There were Ó Martáins who were bards, lawmakers and bishops in medieval times. There were also Mac Giolla Mártains, whose name changed to Gilmartin, and there were the Mac Mártains of Ulster, kinsfolk of the O Neills of Tyrone.

Most notable of all the Martins were the descendants of the crusader, **Olyver Martin**, who accumulated two hundred thousand acres of land in Connacht which had formerly belonged to the O Flahertys. They were one of the Fourteen Tribes of Galway and they produced many endearing eccentrics.

When duelling and gambling were all the fashion, **Richard Martin** was dubbed "Hair Trigger Martin". Having outgrown this phase, he became active in campaigning for the protection of animals and founded the Royal Society for the Protection of Animals. He became known affectionately as "Humanity Dick", even though he imprisoned people who ill-treated animals on his island at Ballynahinch! However, he spent recklessly and was forced to flee to Boulogne to escape his creditors, eventually dying there.

His granddaughter, who inherited his encumbered estate, was known as **"Princess of Connemara"**. She was as talented as she was beautiful and, instead of living it up in London, she joined her father in Connemara, caring for the famine victims. Afterwards, she went to the USA with her penniless husband, where she died in childbirth.

A later kinswoman, **Violet Martin** of Ross, collaborated with her cousin Edith Somerville in writing *The Experiences of an Irish RM*, which has been made into a successful television series. Violet died young, but Edith continued writing, believing that Violet was still helping her.

Edward Martyn of Tulira Castle also had the Connacht eccentricity, but he made many positive contributions to Ireland, including founding the *Feis Ceoil*, promoting the Irish language and Home Rule, and being active in the literary revival of the early 1900s.

In 1937, **Mother Mary Martin** (d. 1975) founded the international order of nuns known as the Medical Missionaries of Mary.

The Ulster Martins were outstanding for their contribution to the public services, particularly abroad, where one was three times Prime Minister of Australia.

Masterson

Mac an Mháighistir

Scotland and England are both sources for this surname, as well as Ireland, where it is an anglicized version of the old Gaelic Mac an Mháighistir, meaning son of the master. They were a sept of Breffny (counties Cavan and west Leitrim) and were of the same stock as the once mighty MacGuires of Fermanagh.

Masterson is a very numerous name all over Ireland and it would be impossible to distinguish between the Gaelic and English versions. It is also remarkably numerous in New York!

Sir Thomas Masterson of Cheshire was granted vast properties in County Wexford by Queen Elizabeth I. In 1583 he was constable of the castle of Ferns, once the seat of the King of Leinster, Dermot MacMurrough, ancestor of the Murphys of Wexford. In the course of time, these Mastersons of Wexford changed their allegiance to the Catholic cause and for this they forfeited their large estates. Some were transplanted to Offaly. Others may have joined the armies of Europe, for there is mention of **Don Tomaso Masterson** serving in the Spanish Netherlands.

In the nineteenth and twentieth centuries there were a number of writers and poets. The **Reverend Edward Masterson** was a distinguished writer on ecclesiastical ethics. **C. S. Masterson** wrote on agriculture and science. **Annie Masterson** published an important book on early Irish education. **Ronnie Masterson** is an actress.

Patrick Masterson (b. 1937), a former dean of the Faculty of Philosophy in University College Dublin, was president of the university from 1986 until he transferred to Florence, Italy.

The name MacMaster is usually purely Scottish in origin.

Maughan *see* Mohan

Maxwell

Maxwell is a Scottish name belonging to one of the most powerful and wealthy families who, in the thirteenth century, were lords of the castle of Caerlavock in Dumfriesshire. Originally the name was Maccuswell or de Maccesville. They came to Ireland, and in particular to Ulster, with Cromwell's armies and also at the time of the plantations.

The outstanding Maxwell family in Ireland is that of **Lord Farnham** of Cavan whose ancestor, the **Reverend Robert Maxwell** of Calderwood, was sent to Ireland by Queen Elizabeth. He was Bishop of Armagh, as well as holding the bishopric of Kilmore. His eldest son, **John Maxwell** (d. 1713), built the splendid family mansion of Farnham in County Cavan. There were a number of high ecclesiastics and earls in the family. In a tragic disaster involving the Irish Mail at Abergele in Wales in 1868, the **7th Lord Farnham**, a distinguished genealogist, and his wife were burned to death.

In New York, the American Irish Historical Society was enriched by a collection of rare Irish books which had belonged to a **Miss Kate Maxwell**, a great-great-grandmother of Wolfe Tone.

A number of Maxwells followed King James II to fight in the battle of the Boyne, including **Brigadier Thomas Maxwell**. After their defeat, a number went to France to fight with the Irish brigades.

William Hamilton Maxwell (1792–1850) of County Down fought at Waterloo and afterwards became the rector at Balla in County Mayo. A respected Irish historian, his most famous book is *Wild Sports of the West of Ireland*.

Constantia Maxwell (1886–1962) of Dublin was a professor of history at Trinity College Dublin and the first woman to be appointed to a chair there. Her histories of Dublin under the Georges set an example followed by many later historians.

William Henry Maxwell (b. *c.*1879) of County Tyrone went to the United States, where he pioneered in the education system of New York.

The most notorious Maxwell was **General Sir John Maxwell**, who came to Ireland as commander-in-chief of the British army and was very much involved in the executions following the 1916 Easter Rising.

Mayer(s)

Ó Midhir

Mairs Meares Meere Meyer Myers

There are very few representatives of the surname Mayer in Ireland, north or south. This name has a very complex history, claiming many origins and a confusing number of variations, including Mair, Mairs, Mayers, Meares and Meyer. The English version of the surname is derived from the Old English *mere*, meaning a mere or lake, or *maere*, meaning a boundary.

In Ireland, Meere is probably an anglicization of the Irish Ó Midhir, which is almost exclusively a County Clare name. **Rory O Meere** is mentioned in an Inchiquin deed of 1627. In 1693, **Evelin Ní Mire** is mentioned as being of the same family.

Some Irish Meeres changed their name to Myers. The Meares of Mearescourt in County Westmeath are of English, or possibly French, origin. The French name derives from *mire*, which can mean either physician or marsh. In the fourteenth century there were families of de Meer and of de la Mere who are now regarded as being the same family as the Meares.

The Genealogical Office in Dublin holds a pedigree of the Meares of Mearescourt and of Cornamucklough in County Longford dating from 1560 to *c.*1811. Another pedigree of the same Meares, formerly of Devenish and Portlick Castle, dates from 1720 to 1862. In 1901, armorial bearings were granted to the descendants of **Richard Meares** of Mearescourt.

Mayer is a very common name in Europe. *The Annals of European Civilization* (1949) has biographies of Mayers who were writers, artists and musicians in France, Germany and Switzerland.

Mayer is also a common surname in the USA, encompassing noteworthy clergy, authors, physicians, lawyers, artists and some émigrés from France.

Meaney, **Meeney** *see* Mooney

Meares *see* Mayer

Meehan

Ó Miadhacháin

(O) Meighan

The Irish word *miadhach* signifies noble or honourable. The Ó Miadhacháins are an ancient sept, kinsmen of the powerful MacCarthys of south Munster. In the eleventh century they moved to County Leitrim, where they were sufficiently important and numerous to have a town near Rossinver named Ballymeighan. Some branches of the family moved further west to County Clare where, early in the fourteenth century, they joined with the other septs of Thomond led by the lordly O Briens.

In medieval times the Meehans, with a variety of spellings, were recorded as very senior churchmen. Between 1251 and 1285, first **Thomas Ó Miacháin**, then **Denis Ó Miacháin,** were Bishop of Achonry. **Edru O Meighan** was Bishop of Meath for twenty-one years from 1152.

There are many Meehans in the list of those who were transplanted from their properties between 1653 and 1654. Many also fled abroad, where a distinguished member of the family, **Le Comte de Mehegan** (O Meehan), was a brigadier in the French army and, in 1790, was maréchal de camp. His brother, **Chevalier William Alexander Mehegan** (1721–66), was a writer in France. They were both sons of **Chevalier O Mehegan**.

In the USA, **William F. Meehan** was in the 63rd New York Regiment of the Irish brigade.

Two outstanding scholars of the family were **Tomás Ó Miodhcháin** (1754–1806) of County Clare, who wrote political poetry showing an astonishing intellectual grasp of current affairs, and **Reverend Charles Patrick Meehan** (1812–90) of Dublin, who was known as a "patriot historian".

For over a thousand years the O Meehans preserved a sixth-century manuscript of St. Nolaise of Devenish. Today it is housed in the National Museum of Ireland in Dublin.

Meere *see* Mayer

Meguiggan *see* MacGuigan

(O) Melaghlin *see* MacLoughlin

Melia *see* (O) Malley

Meyer *see* Mayer

Miley *see* Molloy

Millea *see* Molloy

Minogue *see* Monaghan

Mohan

Ó Móchάin

Mahon Maughan Vaughan

Ó Móchάin was anglicized to Mohan and, in County Galway, to Mahon, and it is sometimes traced to Maughan. It can also be an abbreviation of MacMahon, with which it has no connection. Vaughan, a Welsh name in Ireland since the sixteenth century, might, in some cases, particularly in Monaghan, have been an anglicization of Ó Móchάin.

There were two Ó Móchάin septs, one at Kilmacduagh in south Galway and the other who were hereditary custodians of the cross of St. Attracta's Church in Killaraght, County Sligo. The Ó Móchάins were patrons of learning and had many distinguished ecclesiastics, including an Archbishop of Tuam, **Gregory O Moghan**, who died in 1392.

Skipping five centuries, when little is known of the family, there was **Alfred Thayer Mahon** (1840–1914), who was a prominent historian in the USA, where his grandparents had emigrated. His father, **Denis Hart Mahon** (1802–71), had been a distinguished soldier and a very learned man.

Charles James Patrick Mahon (1800–91), who styled himself The O Gorman Mahon, was an incredibly adventurous man. He travelled the world, mixing with kings and statesmen in Europe. He achieved high rank in the Czar's international bodyguard, fought under the flags of Turkey and Austria, and, in South America, was an admiral in Chile and a colonel in Brazil. Returning to Europe, he served as a colonel in France, then he fought in the Civil War in the USA. Back in Ireland once more, he joined Parnell's party and it was through him that Parnell met Kitty O Shea.

Sir Bryan Mahon (1862–1930) of Galway, a great military leader, campaigned with the Royal Irish Hussars in the Middle East and helped in the defeat of the Boers at Mafeking. During the First World War, he commanded the 10th Division of the Irish at Gallipoli. He was commander-in-chief in Ireland from 1916 to 1918 and afterwards became a Senator in the newly formed Irish Free State.

Today Mohan is most numerous in County Monaghan, and the name is equally represented in both Dublin and Belfast.

Molloy

Ó Maolmhuaidh

Maloy Miley Millea Mulloy

Ó Maolmhuaidh stems from an Irish word meaning noble or venerable chieftain. Molloy, the more usual spelling, can also be an anglicization of another Connacht family, the Ó Maolaoidh—other translations of this name are Millea, Miley or Mullee. Maloy and Mulloy are yet more variations of the Molloy name.

This is an ancient family claiming descent from the fourth-century King Niall of the Nine Hostages, ancestor of the O Neills of Ulster. The head of the O Molloy sept was a chief or lord of Fercal in County Offaly.

Albin O Molloy (d. 1223), Bishop of Ferns, officiated at the coronation of Richard I at Westminster Abbey. Although the O Molloys fought consistently to drive out the English colonists, this did not deprive them of their hereditary duties as bearer of the standard to the Crown of England, which a Molloy family of Kells in County Meath carried out as recently as 4 June 1856.

Draft pedigrees and confirmations of arms ranging from the sixteenth to the nineteenth century are stored in the National Library of Ireland. Some of these Molloy families came from Pitlochry in Scotland, where Molloy is a common name, as it is also in England.

Francis Molloy, a seventeenth-century Franciscan monk, compiled the first printed Irish grammar.

There were also Molloys in abundance writing in the nineteenth century. **James Lyon Molloy** composed many popular ballads, including "Love's Old Sweet Song" and the "Kerry Dances". **Joseph FitzGerald Molloy**, was a poet and novelist who also wrote historical biographies.

Michael J. Molloy of Galway has had his plays produced successfully at the Abbey Theatre in Dublin.

Today there is a concentration of the Molloy name in counties Roscommon and Offaly.

Moloney *see* Loughney, Maloney

Monaghan

Ó Manacháin

Minogue Monahan Monk

The name Ó Manacháin derives from the Irish word *manach*, meaning monk. The more numerous form of the name is now Monaghan, but it can also be traced to Minogue. Today's Monk or Monks can be the descendants of the famous ninth-century Connacht warrior, Manacháin.

Connacht was the original Ó Manacháin territory and the Four Masters record them as being Lords of Roscommon in 1287 when the O Hanlons drove them away.

In the Dominican church in Athenry in County Galway there is a remarkable Monaghan tomb dated 1686.

James Henry Monaghan (1804–78), a Catholic attorney-general—rare for those times—was unpopularly impartial in his prosecution of the Young Irelanders, who were led by William Smith O Brien, Charles Gavan Duffy and others, and afterwards banished to Australia. As chief justice, he also tried the Fenian prisoners.

James Monaghan, born in Westmeath in 1862, became a popular Irish-American poet. One of his best-loved ballads was "She is far from the land".

Monaghan—with Monahan not far behind—is a very numerous name throughout Ireland, with the exception of Ulster.

Monday *see* MacAloon

Monk *see* Monaghan

Montagu(e)

Mac Taidhg

MacTaigue

The name Montague originally came from Normandy, where, in Latin, it was de Monte Acuto. Following the Norman invasion of England, the Montagues settled in Britain, where they became rich and powerful. Montacute in Somerset is just one of many towns bearing the name.

Montague pedigrees abound in *Burke's Peerage*, including earls, viscounts and barons of Halifax, Manchester and Sandwich.

It was the corrupt politician, **John Montagu**, 4th Earl of Sandwich, who invented the sandwich, in about 1740, to sustain himself at the gaming table.

There are many letters extant from **Edward**, 1st Baron Manchester, concerning the sending of troops to Ireland to quell rebellions. He thought ten thousand Scots should also be sent and, in about 1642, he set up a fund to get "adventurers" to settle in Ireland. He cannot have been too successful because, apart from the six counties of Ulster, the name is rare in Ireland.

Charles Edward Montague (1867–1928), whose parents were from Ireland, made a name as a novelist in England and was on the staff of the *Manchester Guardian.*

John Montague, born in Brooklyn, in 1929, was educated in his native Ulster. An academic who has lectured in American and European universities, he is one of Ireland's leading poets.

MacTaigue, with several spelling variations, is considered to be an Irish synonym for Montague. It is to be found mainly in Ulster and is believed to have come from a Taidgh who was a poet and philosopher. One family of MacTaigue were ancient chiefs in County Westmeath.

Mooney

Ó Maonaigh

Mainey Meaney Meeney Moony

There are two choices for the Irish derivation of the surname Ó Maonaigh: either ***moenach***, meaning dumb, or ***maonach***, meaning wealthy. There was an Ó Maonaigh sept of Ulster who were descendants of King Ailioll Mór. Another sept was of Tireragh in County Sligo where there are four townlands called Ballymeeny and where the surname is usually Meeney. In Munster, yet another sept goes under the name Mainey or Meaney.

The Genealogical Office has a pedigree of Mooney of Treugh in County Monaghan, a family which spread to Canada and to York in England, from where a descendant applied for a grant of heraldic arms in 1929.

A Franciscan friar, **Donatus Mooney**, was a celebrated Latin historian and a principal of the Irish College in Louvain, Belgium, from 1615 to 1618.

There is a record of 1726, when **Elizabeth Mooney** took **Eugene Mooney** to the Irish Court of Common Pleas over a dowry dispute.

In the 1830s **Rose Mooney** was a popular harpist.

The name is very numerous in the Midlands, where a distinctive family, the **Enraght-Moonys**, have always had their roots. They were at Esker Castle from 1556—the esker was the ridge the pilgrims followed to the monastery of

Clonmacnoise—and later they moved to Doon, also near Athlone in County Westmeath. They are always styled Moony—without the e—and the Enraght was added through a marriage in the seventeenth century. A prominent family for centuries, they have the right of burial at Clonmacnoise and, until recently, were custodians of the shrine of St. Monahan, which locals believed quarrelsome people had only to touch to be cured of their bad temper.

Ria Mooney (1904–73) began her acting career at the age of six, which led to her being invited to join the prestigious Abbey Theatre Company in 1924. She played many leading parts, touring in England and the USA. She was the first woman director at the Abbey.

Moore

Ó Mórdha

O More

The Ó Mórdha (O More) lineage goes back to the legendary Knights of the Red Branch, to one of their hero warriors, Conal Cearnach. Laois has always been their territory and, at Abbeyleix, where they founded a Cistercian abbey, there is the tomb of Malachi, believed to be the last of the O More chieftains.

Until the dispersal of the Irish aristocracy following the battle of Kinsale, a succession of **Rory O Mores** led the O Mores against the invaders. **Owney O More** captured the Duke of Ormond and returned him to his Butler family with a millstone around his neck! During the internecine wars of the sixteenth century, the great Garret FitzGerald was killed by an O More. The ruins of their stronghold on the Rock of Dunamase indicate the strength of this important clan.

It would be impossible to disentangle the ancient Irish Moores from the Moores who came from England or Normandy many hundreds of years ago. Mellifont in Louth was the home of the Moores from Kent who were ennobled as viscounts of Drogheda. They moved from there to Kildare, where they built Moore Abbey, one-time home of Count John McCormack, the singer, and now a hospital.

Michael Moore was one of a rare breed—a Catholic provost of Trinity College Dublin. However, he was dismissed by James II when he took his sermon from the text about the blind leading the blind—James's chaplain was blind! Michael found a new life abroad, as rector to the University of Paris, where he died in 1726.

Thomas Moore is celebrated more for the melodious songs he wrote about Ireland than for the plays and operas he wrote when he became popular in London society. Moore's songs were to become an important part of John McCormack's repertoire.

A Moore who fled to France with the "Wild Geese" set up in the wine trade and flourished, later returning to Ireland, where he built Moore Hall in Connacht. His son, **John Moore**, joined the Young Irelanders and was killed in the 1798 Rebellion. His story featured in the television film, *The Year of the French*. A descendant was **George Moore**, the famous wit and novelist.

Today, **Brian Moore**, formerly of Ulster, is a successful novelist who lives mostly in the USA.

Moran

Ó Muireáin

Murrin

The Morans, or Murrins, are an ancient Connacht family of the Uí Fiachrach who were located in north Mayo and Sligo. Another branch settled in south County Galway. In later times, the name became changed to Moran, in Irish Ó Moráin, possibly deriving from the word *mór*, meaning big.

There have been many distinguished Morans. **General James O Moran** (1739–94) served with Dillon's Regiment in the French army and was guillotined during the French Revolution.

Michael Moran (1794–1871), a blind balladeer from Dublin, has been immortalized as "Zozimus".

Patrick Moran (1870–1936), a churchman from Carlow, became a cardinal in Australia.

David Patrick Moran (1870–1936) was a founder of the influential patriotic review, *The Leader*.

In Killybegs in County Donegal, an important Irish fishing port, there is a surprising enclave of Murrin families, their most famous son being **Joseph "Joey" Murrin**, who for many years was a fisherman and, in 1984, became chairman of the Irish Fishery Board. He is a spokesman both at home and abroad for this vital industry.

Moriarty

Ó Muircheartaigh

Murdoch Murtagh

Ó Muircheartaigh (*muircheartach* means navigator) is essentially a Kerry name and it would seem an appropriate one for a family whose ancient lands encircled the seas around Castlemaine Harbour on the Dingle peninsula. They were an offshoot of the O Donoghue and O Mahony families. With the arrival of the Anglo-Normans, they were driven out from the Castlemaine lands by the FitzGeralds.

There was another sept in Meath, whose name was anglicized to Murtagh, a name now mostly found in Ulster and, sometimes, in Scotland, where its synonym is Murdoch.

The Cromwellians also dispossessed many of the Moriarty sept of their Kerry lands, which they left to follow the fatal Stuart cause led by James II. There is a sad record of **Thomas O Moriarty**, aged only eleven, being taken to France to fight with the French king. Thomas later went to America, but many remained in France, including a **Captain Moriarty** of the Regiment of Clare who is recorded as being wounded at the battle of Fontenoy in 1745.

In the eighteenth and nineteenth century there was a naval Moriarty family in New Zealand. A member of this family wrote to Dublin Castle requesting their Moriarty pedigree and armorial bearings.

Patrick Moriarty of Dublin was one of a number of Moriarty priests. He was a member of the Augustinian order and he went to Philadelphia, where he became one of the leading temperance reformers. It was he who, in 1842, founded the famous Villanova College.

David Moriarty of Kerry was educated for the priesthood in France and in Maynooth, County Kildare. A distinguished scholar, he was appointed Bishop of Kerry in 1856. He was ardently opposed to Home Rule and his venomous denunciation of the Fenian revolutionaries has gone down in history: "Hell is not hot enough for them, nor eternity long enough for them."

In the twentieth century, **Joan Denise Moriarty** of Cork studied dance in London and Paris and returned to establish the Cork Ballet Company. Against almost hopeless odds, she finally succeeded in founding the Irish National Ballet Company and was recognized with an honorary doctorate from University College Dublin and a Harvey Special Award.

Morley

Ó Murghaile

Marrally Morrolly Murhila

Morleys are very numerous in England, where there are many distinguished bearers of the name, particularly in the arts, especially the theatre. **John Morley**, the first viscount, was a chief secretary of Ireland towards the end of the last century. He was, of course, from England.

However, Morley is also an anglicization of a Gaelic Irish surname which originates from a first name, Murghal, meaning sea valour—this might explain the preponderance of Morleys in and around County Mayo! Other forms of this old Irish name were Morrolly, Marrally and Murhila. Morley remains the most common form and is mainly found today in the west of Ireland and also in County Cork.

Two of their fine houses are mentioned in the first volume of *Burke's Guide to Country Houses.* They are Islandmore in Croom, County Limerick, which **Derrick Morley** sold in about 1957, and Milfort in Portlaw, County Waterford, which was sold by **Miss Violet Morley** in 1950.

In 1945, Derrick Morley had been given Islandmore and Rockstown Castle in County Limerick by his uncle, Lieutenant-Colonel Basil James Roche Kelly, a high sheriff of County Limerick. In *Burke's Landed Gentry of Ireland* (1958)—the last edition of this valuable publication—Derrick Morley is mentioned as being chairman of, among other companies, the now defunct Limerick Steamship Company and Shannon Travel. He had served on the staff of the intelligence corps in North Africa during the Second World War.

In the ancient records there is mention of four Morley officers who served Charles I and Charles II in the seventeenth-century wars in Ireland.

Moroney

Ó Maolruanaidh

Mulrooney

The ancient surname Ó Maolruanaidh (meaning son of Rooney) was anglicized to Mulrooney. There were three distinct Mulrooney septs. One was in County Fermanagh, where, until they were displaced by the MacGuires in medieval times, they were a powerful people. Another sept were powerful chieftains of Cruffen in County Galway, while a third sept, west of the Shannon, were a branch of the Dalcassians. These Mulrooneys were numerous, and still are, in counties Clare, Limerick and Tipperary, where the name was anglicized to Moroney, which is still the most numerous variation of this old Gaelic patronymic.

In the seventeenth century, many of this family suffered confiscation and transplantation by the invaders.

The grandson of a **Miss Moroney** of Miltown Malbay (by her marriage to a Kent) was in the army of William III. Another descendant of hers was an intimate friend of the ill-fated Lord Edward FitzGerald.

John Moroney, a teacher of mathematics, wrote *Use of the Globes* in 1831. It was published by Charles Dillon and Son of Cork. Moroney described it as "a treatise designed for the use of schools and containing information of many problems not to be found in any other such book". He also had a *Treatise on Mensuration* "ready for the press".

There are some Moroneys found in Dublin, but there are more to be found around the country and hardly any at all in Ulster.

Morris

Ó Muirghis

FitzMaurice Morres Morrissey

When this family arrived in Galway in 1485 their name was written Mares (of the marsh), referring to the part of Normandy from which they had originated. The name went through a bewildering series of changes, including de Maries, de Marisco, Morrissey, Fitz-Maurice and Morres.

There was also an authentic Irish family of Sligo whose name was anglicized from Ó Muirghis to Morris.

The Galway family were a very powerful clan, members of the famous "Fourteen Tribes of Galway". They were also mayors and sheriffs and were active members of the Galway Corporation until the arrival of Cromwell and his usurpers in the seventeenth century.

Various branches of the family spread out to Tipperary, Kilkenny and Mayo. One family who settled in Kilkenny were created Baron and, later, Viscount of Mountmorres. They claim descent from a brother of Hervé de Montmorency, who came to Ireland in 1170 with Strongbow, who had been enticed there by Dermot MacMurrough.

Hervey Montmorency Morres (1767–1839) was born in Tipperary. While still only fifteen, he served in the Austrian army with another Irish exile, Field Marshal Lacy, against the Turks. He returned to Ireland in 1793 and joined the United Irishmen, who were planning an uprising. He was betrayed and extradited to England, but he escaped to France and followed a political career. He wrote prolifically about Ireland and left three sons, all of whom served in the Austrian service.

A kinsman, **Hervey Redmond Morres** (d. 1797), Viscount Mountmorres of Tipperary, was so distressed by the developments in Ireland at that time that he became deranged and shot himself.

The **Reverend Francis Orpen Morris** (1810–93) of Cobh in County Cork became one of the leading naturalists in England and wrote a classic work, *The History of British Birds.*

Michael Morris (1827–1901) of Spiddal in County Galway was a judge who was created a peer, with the title Lord Killanin. His grand-nephew, **Michael Morris** (b. 1914), the 3rd Lord Killanin, has brought world fame to the name for his sensitive handling of many political crises when he was president of the International Olympic Committee, of which he is now life president. He served in the Second World War, was an author, journalist and film producer, and has received innumerable European decorations and Irish directorships.

See also Begley

Morrissey

Ó Muirgheasa

This numerous surname could derive from a number of sources. Firstly, there was the powerful twelfth-century de Marisco family, who came from Normandy and attached themselves to the Butlers, Dukes of Ormond, who gave them great tracts of land, mostly in County Kilkenny. They integrated with their Irish neighbours and styled themselves MacMuiris and, eventually, Morrissey.

Then there was a Gaelic family called Ó Muirgheasa who were a branch of the ancient Uí Fiachrach, whose clan homeland was located in counties Mayo and Sligo. Another family were of south Galway and descended from Muiris, the grandson of the famous Donogh MacDermot, known as "na Mainstreach" because of the number of monasteries he built. This Muiris was a member of the royal family of MacDermot of Coolavin in County Sligo.

The name is usually spelled Morrissey and is to be found in most counties, with the exception of Northern Ireland. It would now be difficult to distinguish the Norman from the English settlers, let alone the early Irish Ó Muirgheasa. A townland near New Ross in County Wexford is called Morrisseyland, demonstrating how the name has spread.

Énri (Feargus Mac Roigh) Ó Muirgheasa (1874–1945), who was born in County Monaghan, was an inspector of primary schools and a tireless campaigner for the revival of the Irish language. He was a poet and compiled many collections of folklore.

Reverend Thomas M. Morrissey was a regular contributor of historical articles to *Studies*, an academic Irish periodical.

Morrolly *see* Morley

Mosley

Moseley

Mosley is the name of what was once a small hamlet in Saddleworth in the West Riding of Yorkshire, England. This surname is exceedingly rare in Ireland.

John Ivan Mosley published an English–Manx dictionary in 1866.

Henry Gwyn Jeffreys Moseley (1887–1915), an English physicist, is famous for his discovery of atomic numbers. He was killed at Gallipoli. **Leonard Mosley** has written a series of popular books on the Second World War and on the last days of the Raj. Earlier this century, there was a distinguished naturalist called **Charles Mosley**.

Ravensdale was the family name of the most notorious Mosley, the 6th Baronet, **Sir Oswald Mosley** (1896–1980). He was first a Conservative, then an Independent and finally a Labour Member of Parliament, before turning to fascism. He became leader of the British Union of Fascists, which led to his internment during the Second World War. He wrote a number of books on European unity and lived in Ireland in the 1960s, first in County Galway and later in Fermoy in County Cork. His second marriage was to the former wife of Lord Moyne of the Guinness family in Ireland. In 1968 he published his memoirs, *My Life*.

There are a few Moseleys in Ireland, who are probably descendants of the armies of the Commonwealth.

Moss

Ó Maolmóna

Mosse

Moss is a translation from Ó Maolmóna, which means chief of the bog. An unusual Ulster surname, it was mostly confined to Fermanagh and Donegal. Moss is also an English surname which probably meant "at the moss", referring to a residence.

Seven hundred years ago, Moss was also a nickname for Moses, a name which can also have Jewish origins. The

Jews who settled in England changed their name from Moses to Moss or Moyses. It is a very numerous name in England, where the most famous representative in recent times was the racing motorist, **Stirling Moss** (b. 1929).

In Ireland the name is rare but greatly respected because of **Bartholomew Mosse** (1712–59), son of a rector of Maryborough in County Laois. Having graduated in surgery, he travelled widely and, on his return to Dublin, revolutionized maternity care by opening the first ever lying-in hospital in the British Isles. With very little money, he engaged the leading architect—Richard Cassels—to build the handsome Rotunda Hospital. The landscaped grounds became a focus for the fashionable Dubliners attending concerts and balls to raise money for the hospital. Unfortunately, Bartholomew Mosse's idealism was ahead of its time and he died penniless, but he left a hospital which continues to be regarded with great esteem and affection by the citizens of Dublin.

At Bennettsbridge, south of Kilkenny, there has long been a settlement of Moss families who are millers, and today the excellent **Nicholas Moss** pottery is also located there.

Mulcahy

Ó Maolchathaigh

This ancient Gaelic surname means a devotee of St. Catach. The O prefix is seldom if ever used today. Originally this sept—of which there is very little recorded, either in medieval times or today—came from counties Tipperary and Limerick. The name is now very numerous in Dublin and throughout the provinces, with the exception of Ulster.

In the nineteenth century there was a minor painter called **Jeremiah Mulcahy**. The **Honourable Edward Mulcahy**, who was born in Munster in 1883, emigrated to New Zealand, where he became a cabinet minister.

Denis Dowling Mulcahy (1833–1920) emigrated to the USA and became a prominent member of the republican organization known as the Fenians which was founded in New York in 1858. He was also an author.

Lovat Mulcahy, who was born in Dublin in 1850, sailed from Liverpool on the *Cordoba*, in 1867, for Argentina.

The most distinguished Mulcahy to date is **General Richard James Mulcahy** (1886–1971), who was born in Waterford. A soldier and politician, he took part in the 1916 Easter Rising and later, in 1922, commanded the Free State armed forces, working closely with Michael Collins. He held several ministerial posts and was a Senator in the first Dáil (parliament). For several years, he led the Fine Gael Party. A forceful personality, he retired in 1961. One of his sons, **Dr. Risteard Mulcahy**, is a leading Dublin heart specialist.

The Genealogical Office in Dublin holds a grant of arms dated 1953 for the **Right Reverend Dom Columbus Mulcahy**, a lord abbot of Sancta Maria Abbey in Nunraw, Scotland.

John Mulcahy (b. 1932), a businessman and publisher, was editor of the prestigious but now defunct magazine, *Hibernia*. He was founding editor of the *Sunday Tribune* newspaper and of *Phoenix*, Ireland's satirical magazine.

Muldowney *see* Downey

Mulhall

Ó Maolchathail

Hally Mulcahill

Mulhall stems from an old Gaelic sept called Ó Maolchathail, signifying a follower of St. Cathal. In an earlier form, it was Mulcahill and it can sometimes be traced to Hally. The sept originated in the counties of Laois and Offaly, where representatives of this not very numerous name may still be found.

Volume 5 of the military magazine, *The Irish Sword*, contains a full account of **Colonel John Dillon Mulhall**, who was probably the John D. Mulhall listed as a first lieutenant in the 69th New York Volunteers who served under General Thomas Francis Meagher in the American Civil War.

Michael George Mulhall (1836–1900), who was born in Dublin and educated in the Irish College in Rome, was one of Ireland's foremost statisticians. In 1858, he went to South America, where he founded *The Standard* in Buenos Aires, the first English-language newspaper in Argentina. Remaining there for many years, he also published the first English-language book printed in Argentina, *Handbook of the River Plate.* On his return to Ireland, he published many books on statistics, including his famous *Dictionary of Statistics.*

Miss Mairin Mulhall, who was undoubtedly related to Michael George, was in South America at the same time and wrote a number of books about her travels around that vast continent.

Mullally

Ó Maolalaidh

Lally

The Connacht name Ó Maolalaidh derives from *aladh*, which means speckled. In medieval times, the Ó Maolalaidh who settled near Tuam in County Galway were constantly at war with their Norman de Burgo (Burke) neighbours.

There were a succession of Mullally archbishops, two in the diocese of Tuam and two more in Clonfert and Elphin.

Following the defeat at the battle of the Boyne in 1690 and the siege of Limerick the following year, many of the Mullallys joined the "Wild Geese" exodus to Europe. This occurred when exiled soldiers and their families fled abroad, mostly to France.

One of the most famous members of the Mullally family was **Thomas Arthur O Mullally** (1702–66). He was the son of **Sir Gerard O Lally**, who was a follower of the defeated James II, thereby forfeiting his land. Thomas, who was also a Jacobite, had to flee abroad and married a French noblewoman. It was from her that he inherited his titles, Comte and Baron Laly de Tollendal. He fought with the French army at the victory of Fontenoy and went with the French expedition to conquer India, where they were driven out by the British. A man of courage but of great ferocity, he was disliked by his men, particularly his officers, who unfairly accused him of treason. Despite many pleas, he was beheaded.

Dublin's Genealogical Office has a number of Mullally and Lally pedigrees and papers, and there are numerous Lally papers and letters in French archives.

A History of the O Mullally and Lally Clan, which was published in Chicago in 1941, has been described by the historians as "fanciful but with much useful information about the sept".

The Mullallys are still fairly common around Dublin, but they are most numerous throughout Connacht. A bearer of the name whose forebears must surely have originated from there is the distinguished art critic (since 1958) of the London *Daily Telegraph*, **Terence Mullally**.

Mullins

Ó Maoláin

Millane Mullane Mullen Mullin

The name Mullins offers a wide choice of origins and spellings, including Mullen, Mullin, Mullon and Mullane. There is also MacMullen, a surname of seventeenth-century settlers in Ulster. The Irish form, O Maoláin, derives from *maol*, meaning bald). It is thought that the Irish lineage stems from a family who in ancient times were kings of Connacht and kinsmen of the neighbouring Concannons.

The O Mullan or O Mullen sept was one of a number of septs in Ulster. From one of these came **Shane Crosagh O Mullan** of Derry who, having been dispossessed of his lands in 1729, turned to a Robin Hood type of highway robbery. He was captured and hanged with his two sons.

In Cork the name became Mullane, which was the maiden name of Daniel O Connell's mother, to whom he bore a close resemblance.

John Mullan (1830–1909), the American explorer, was first-generation Irish.

Dr. James Mullin (1846–1920), was the son of a poor family and worked his way up to become a distinguished medical doctor and writer.

The Barons Ventry of Burnham in Dingle, County Kerry, were a Mullins family who came from Burnham in England in 1666 and became an influential Kerry family. In 1736, **Thomas Mullins** was created Baron Ventry. They married into all the important local families—the O Briens, Boyles and Blakes. In 1841, another **Thomas**, Lord Ventry, reassumed what he described as his ancient Norman surname of **De Moleyns**. A Mullins family who were kinsmen of the Ventrys were flour millers in Kells in County Kilkenny in the nineteenth century.

Mullins are to be found plentifully in the Republic of Ireland, particularly in Munster, with a lesser number in Connacht.

Mulloy *see* Molloy

Mulrooney *see* Moroney

Mulryan *see* (O) Ryan

Murdoch *see* Moriarty

Murhila *see* Morley

Murphy

Ó Murchú

Maccamore MacMurrough
Ó Morchoe Ó Murchadha

Murphy is Ó Murchadha or Ó Murchú in its original Irish, *murchadh* meaning sea warrior. It is the most numerous of all Irish names in Ireland, and is even more common in the USA. In its various forms, Murphy fills over twenty-two pages of the Irish telephone directories. There are Murphys in all four provinces.

They were chiefs in counties Tyrone, Sligo, Wexford and Cork. The Murphys of Wexford descend from **Dermot MacMurrough**, who was King of Leinster at the time of the Anglo-Norman invasion. His brother, **Murrough**, is the direct ancestor of The Ó Morchoe, the present-day holder of one of the authentic Irish chieftaincies.

The Murphys are a versatile clan. In earlier times they were bards and harpists. **Arthur Murphy** (1727–1805) was both an actor and playwright, who went on to study law. They have also been artists, sculptors and patriots. In the nineteenth century they almost dominated the lists of the Irish brigades in Europe. **Marie Louise Murphy,** whose father had been an Irish soldier in France, was a favourite of Louis XV. There have been Murphy archbishops, ministers and scholars, and a remarkable number have had important private libraries.

The body of one Murphy who died suddenly in Italy had to be smuggled home in a piano, because the Italian sailors would not allow a corpse on their ship.

There is a concentration of Murphys in County Cork, where once they boasted around seventeen family seats. Since 1825, the Murphys of Cork have flourished in the distilling business. After several mergers, they joined with Powers and Jameson in 1966 to form Irish Distillers International Limited, the biggest distillers in the country.

A Cork Murphy was one of the tallest men in Europe. Another County Cork Murphy founded the *Irish Independent* group of newspapers in Dublin.

Dr. Terry Murphy (1917–95) worked for more than forty years in Dublin's Zoological Gardens and was director from 1957 until 1984. He championed the use of wildlife parks, rather than cages and paddocks. He also pioneered the rearing of rare specimens such as the endangered cheetah, so that Ireland now has well over one hundred of these beautiful animals—the largest group outside Africa.

Over the years, many Murphys emigrated to Australia and to the USA, where they became prominent in local development, the law, medicine, the construction industry and, as always, the collection of books.

Murray

Ó Muireadhaigh

On the whole, Murray is a Scottish name and is especially numerous in Ulster, where many Scots have long been settled. However, there is also an old Irish name, Ó Muireadhaigh (descendant of a seaman or mariner), which has been anglicized to O Murray or, nowadays, Murray. At one time there were several septs of this family, most of which were dispersed by the arrival of the Anglo-Normans.

It is recorded that, in 1585, the Chief of the Name lived at Ballymurray in County Roscommon.

Donogh O Murray, Archbishop of Tuam in County Galway from 1458 to 1484, established the Wardenship of Galway, its first local authority.

Bartholomew Murray (1695–1767) was a generous benefactor of the Irish College in Paris.

Sir Terence Aubrey Murray (1810–73) of Limerick, a pioneer in crop cultivation in Australia, built a house in Canberra which later became the residence of the governor-general. Two sons were **Sir John Hubert Plunket Murray** (1861–1940), governor of New Guinea, and the celebrated Greek scholar, **Professor Gilbert Murray** (1866–1957).

In the nineteenth century, three of Ireland's leading architects were Murrays. The various homes that have been occupied by the wealthy Murray families have, sadly, been demolished.

The arts in Ireland today have two Murray representatives: **Anne Murray**, the mezzo-soprano who is on the international opera circuit, and **Brian Murray**, an actor of stage and screen who is remembered for his performance in *The Irish RM*, the television series.

Murrin *see* Moran

Murtagh *see* Moriarty

Myers *see* Mayer

N

Nairy *see* Neary

Nally *see* MacNally

Narry *see* Neary

Nash

Ashe

This surname comes from the Norman de Nais family, who are thought to have come to Ireland with Walter Raleigh. In 1679, **Andrew Nash** is recorded as having a lease of land from the Earl of Orrery and a house at Charleville in County Cork. The house was burned down by the rebels known as rapparees.

The Nashes are very well documented, with a number of pedigrees bringing the succession up to 1895. **Edward Nash** has written a small pamphlet on *The Nash Family* which gives a very detailed account of their Irish genealogies, with twenty-one allied families, and includes illustrations and maps.

Munster has been, and still is, their territory, and Farahy and Convamore in Cork in particular have been closely associated with the family.

The name de Nais is said to signify "at the ash tree", and so Nash and Ashe probably come from the same roots. It has also been suggested that some Nashes may have taken their surname from the town of Naas in County Kildare.

In *Irish Family Records* (1976) there is an extensive pedigree of the Nash family which settled in Kanturk in County Cork in about 1690. Their descendants are now mostly to be found in England.

From **John Nash**, George IV's favourite architect, to **Ogden Nash**, the great American humorist, the Nash name has been internationally renowned.

Through the female line, **Piers O Conor Nash** has succeeded to Clonalis House, County Roscommon, the mansion of the great family of the O Conor Dons whose antecedents were kings of Connacht.

Richard Nash (b. 1943) is the managing director of a soft drinks company which has had phenomenal success in challenging the famous Perrier water of France with its bottled Ballygowan Spring Water.

Naughton

Ó Neachtáin

MacNaughton O Naghten

There are a number of versions of this ancient Gaelic name. Ó Neachtáin derives from a personal name meaning bright or pure. They were a Dalcassian sept of the same stock as the O Quinns, formerly of Corofin in County Clare. Until the arrival of the Normans, they were chiefs of a territory near Loughrea in County Galway. Afterwards they settled in the Fews in the Barony of Athlone. As late as the 1880s, a Naughton owned Thomastown Park, an estate of 4,829 acres between Athlone and Ballinasloe—traditional Naughton territory.

An Ó Neachtáin of this sept was elected Bishop of Limerick in 1581. For unknown reasons, **John Ó Neachtáin** (1655–1728) left his wealthy County Roscommon family to work as a farm labourer in County Meath, where he married his master's daughter. He wrote popular poetry and stories in Irish and other languages. His son, **Teig O Naughton**, was a member of the Gaelic literary circle in Dublin in the 1720s.

In the Genealogical Office in Dublin there are accounts of the many fine houses and estates owned by the Naughtons of Connacht and County Tipperary. In the upheaval of the sixteenth and seventeenth centuries, many of the Naughtons were driven from their lands and transplanted to other parts of the country. There are also accounts of grants of arms to Naughtons and a report on the surname MacNaughton, dating between *c.*1600 and 1846.

Bill Naughton was born in County Mayo in 1910 and raised in Lancashire, England. He is the author of many novels and award-winning plays on television and radio.

The name in its many versions is very numerous throughout Ireland, but in the North the surname MacNaughton is usually of Scottish origin.

Neary

Ó Náraigh

Nairy Narry

Neary is a very common name in Ireland, except in Ulster, where it is now comparatively scarce. It comes from the Irish word *nárach*, meaning modest.

The family has not been prominent in Irish history, but it has been well researched by **Michael Neary**, who, in 1968, wrote a long account of his forebears in the County Louth *Archaeological Society's Journal*. He traces them back to the third century, when a Nera was a lawmaker and a druid. He goes on to connect them with the ancient Irish epic of the Táin Bó Cúailnge at the time of Christ, when Queen Maeve of Connacht made war on the king of Ulster and his Red Branch knights, led by the great hero, Cu Chulainn. He also connects them with the Milesians who came from Spain and provided many of the colourful figures of Irish mythology.

In Roscommon and Louth, the name is usually pronounced Nairy, while in Sligo and Mayo it would be Narry. It is also sometimes believed to be connected with McEnery.

It has also been suggested that the Nearys of County Louth were either Normans or Norsemen and that they came to Louth to plunder and loot!

Father Nicholas O Naraigh was provincial of his Franciscan order from 1504 to 1508.

In 1546, two members of a Louth family tangled with the law. **Henry Boy** (*buidhe* means yellow) **O Nare** was accused of murder, but was pardoned by Henry VIII. **Donal Boy O Nare**, described as an "idleman" or kern (soldier), was pardoned for various offences, including the murder of John Vale.

O Hart, the genealogist, writes that Neary, Irwin, Irvine, Irving, MacNair and MacNeary are all derived from Mac Ineirghe, which he believes comes from a word meaning useful.

The most distinguished representative of this name in Ireland today is **Peter J. Neary** (b. 1950), who has an international reputation as an economist.

Needham

Ó Niadh

(O) Nee

Needham is not a very common surname in Ireland. It comes from the Irish *niadh*, which means a hero or champion, and was anglicized to Needham, which is a common name in England.

The Irish Needhams were a very ancient County Kerry family who originally lived in the neighbourhood of Tralee. Later they moved north to Foynes in County Limerick, where they acted as administrators of ecclesiastical property. They are thought to be an ancient branch of the Scottish MacGregor clan.

In England, Needham is the name of a parish in Norfolk, of a town in Suffolk, and is also the name of an estate in Derby. The proprietors of this Derby estate had a son named **Robert** who was given important commands in Ireland by Queen Elizabeth I. In 1625—two years before he died—he was elevated to the peerage of Ireland as **Viscount Kilmorey** of County Clare. Some of his descendants appear to have settled in County Down, where the 12th Viscount, **Francis-Jack**, was created Viscount of Newry and Mourne and Earl of Kilmorey in 1822. They had several big houses, including Lecan, which was the seat of **Thomas Needham** until the last century and is now a retirement home.

In the Public Records Office in Belfast there is a collection of leases, wills, letters and other papers relating to the Needhams of Newry. The Genealogical Office in Dublin has a pedigree of the Needham family of Newry from 1750 to 1864.

At the beginning of this century, **Alicia Adelaide Needham** composed the music for a song cycle, "A Bunch of Shamrocks", to words by the distinguished writer, Katherine Tynan-Hinkson.

Joseph Needham was an editor, an essayist and writer of a wide variety of pamphlets on religion and science, and on travel in China.

There is a representative of the Needham family in the administrative services in Northern Ireland.

(O) Neill

Ó Néill

Creagh Nihill

The O Neills are one of the three most important Gaelic families—the others are the O Briens and the O Connors. They claim descent from the legendary warrior, **Niall of the Nine Hostages**. It was from **King Nial Glúin Dubh** (Black Knee), who was killed fighting the Norsemen in AD 919, that Donnell O Neill adopted the name. The name is the same in both Irish and English—O Neill, meaning champion.

With few interruptions, this mighty Ulster family looms large in Irish history for almost seven hundred years, until the close of the seventeenth century.

There were several minor O Neill septs. It is possible that the Nihills of County Clare were originally from Ulster. Surviving the defeat at the battle of Kinsale, they stayed in County Clare and took the name of their O Neill chieftain. Earlier O Neills were nicknamed Creagh, deriving from *craobh*, meaning a branch, because they camouflaged themselves with greenery when battling against the Norsemen near Limerick. Descendants of the Ulster O Neills have long since settled around Waterford, Tipperary, Cork and Carlow.

In the fourteenth century, the O Neills of Ulster had become so numerous—today there are reckoned to be about twenty-nine thousand in Ireland—that they divided into two. The senior were the Earls of Tyrone, while the other, the O Neills of Antrim and Down, were known as the Clan Aodh Buídhe (Clan of yellow-haired Hugh), or Clanaboy.

For years the great **Hugh O Neill** (1550–1616), 2nd Earl of Tyrone, kept Queen Elizabeth's armies in constant warfare. However, having failed to win the vital battle of Kinsale, many O Neills sailed for Spain and Portugal. In 1983, an O Neill clan gathering in Belfast was attended by O Neills from countries across the world, including **Jorge O Neill**, whose family have been in Portugal for generations. He held the title The O Neill of Clanaboy, followed by his son **Hugh**. The senior O Neill of Tyrone cannot be traced—if he still exists.

Shane's Castle near Belfast, a former O Neill stronghold, is now open to the public, with various attractions including a steam railway. The castle is presided over by a **Lord O Neill** of a nineteenth-century creation.

Acting and writing is a strong attribute of the O Neils of America, typified by the famous **Eugene O Neill**.

Thomas P. (Tip) O Neill (1912–94) was Speaker of the House of Representatives. He advocated the Irish cause internationally.

Nesbitt

Nisbet

Although this surname came to Ireland before the sixteenth century, Nesbitt—sometimes Nisbet—has never acquired an Irish synonym. It is thought by some to have Huguenot origins, but it has very definite roots in Durham, Northumberland and Berwick in England, where it was a very common name.

In 1898, **A. Nesbitt** of Torquay wrote a *History of the Family of Nisbet or Nesbitt in Scotland and Ireland*, and in 1930 in Belfast an R. Nesbitt wrote a *History of the Nesbitt Family*, both of which were printed for private circulation only. In Northern Ireland, Nesbitt is very numerous with only a few Nisbet variants.

They are well recorded in the archives. Among "A List of Papist Proprietors' names in the County of Donegal as they are returned" there is mention of **John Nesbit**, "an abetter of the League of Derry". For this he had his lands confiscated. During the Williamite reign, in 1688, **Albert Nesbitt** was granted forfeited lands.

In 1797, before Ireland lost its parliament, **Thomas Nesbitt** was a Member of Parliament in the House of Commons.

Nesbitt papers going back to 1666 are in Dublin's Genealogical Office, where there is also a draft pedigree of Nesbitt of Rathfriland in County Down between 1740 and 1861. In the Royal Irish Academy in Dublin there are also Nesbitt pedigrees and notes and many papers relating to land in Ulster and abstracts of wills, etc.

Nisbett's Medical Directory was published in 1910. **Professor William Nesbitt** of Queen's College Galway published many learned pamphlets between 1837 and 1875.

Arnott's, the big department store in

Dublin's Henry Street, has been in the Nesbitt family for several generations.

Neville

Ó Niadh

Neville was an aristocratic English name. They arrived with the Anglo-Normans in the twelfth century, settling in Wexford, Carlow and Kilkenny. The Nevilles who settled in Limerick and Cork were of a different ancestry.

The name has had a great number of transformations. The Ó Niadh (meaning descendant of the hero) family who were keepers of St. Patrick's bell at Knockpatrick in County Limerick anglicized their name to Neville.

From 1480 to 1503 **Lawrence Neville** was Bishop of Ferns. In 1511, **Robert Nevyll** is recorded as a notable burgess of New Ross in County Wexford.

David Nevil, last Baron of Rosegarland, was disgraced in 1535 for his part in Silken Thomas FitzGerald's rebellion and lost all his lands. A descendant, **Richard Nevill**, built a stately home called Furness in County Kildare in 1740. His grand-nephew, **Richard Nevill**, enlarged the house and landscaped the gardens. When he died in 1822 the house passed to his daughter and it was later sold.

Borrismore House, near Urlingford in County Kilkenny, was built by **Garrett Nevill** in 1765. When he married Mary Hodson he changed its name to Marymount. It has since reverted to its original name.

Thomas Neville (1755–1802), who lived in London, had a sugar plantation in Jamaica. There is a Neville vault at Rathmore in County Kildare.

Dr. Neville of Blackrock College in County Dublin, who was a priest in the tropics for over thirty years, was vicar-apostolic of Zanzibar in 1913.

Neville is a very numerous name in all the provinces of Ireland except Ulster.

Newell

Ó Tnúthghail

Knowles Neville

Newell—and sometimes Knowles—comes from an Irish word with the strange translation, envy valour.

The Newells are most numerous in Ulster, where the Belfast Public Records Office holds a number of records of their wills and other papers, including extracts from a pay book of **Sergeant John Newell** of the Mourne Yeomanry of *c.*1824.

In the Genealogical Office in Dublin, there is a document of *c.*1792 concerning the descendants of the Newells of Mitchelstown in County Cork. There was also a **James Newell** of County Dublin who added the name of his maternal great-uncle to his family name. There is a very ancient manuscript of *c.*1514 concerning a **Robert Newell** of Clonmeen, and there is a record of John Ropp's marriage to **Kathleen Newell** in Ross Church on 24 June 1525.

In England, Newell and Knowles are common surnames and it is believed that Newell has something to do with New Hall, a town in Chester. Neville can also be a synonym for Newell, both in England and Ireland.

Edward J. Newell of County Down (1771–98) was a sailor before settling in Belfast to become a miniature portrait painter. He joined the United Irishmen, but was enraged at their distrust of him and turned informer, earning thousands of pounds sending innocent people to prison or to their death. He was discovered and was assassinated as he was escaping to America with another man's wife.

Alexander Newell (1824–93) was a distinguished Belfast scientist. **Hugh Newell** (b. 1830) left Belfast to emigrate to the United States of America, where he became a popular painter.

Nihill *see* (O) Neill

Nisbet *see* Nesbitt

(O) Nolan

Ó Nualláin

Nowlan

The root of this ancient Irish personal name is *nuall*, which probably means noble or famous. They were an important sept of Forth in Carlow. There is a strange story of "the intrusion of an O Nolan sept into the barony of Forth in County Wexford which was the property of the Dukes of Norfolk"! Nolans had the hereditary privilege of inaugurating the MacMurrough kings of Leinster, whose nearby ancient seat is now Borris House. With the arrival of the Anglo-Normans in the twelfth century, the Irish kings were abolished, but the Nolans are still very numerous in County Carlow.

The Nolans also had a branch in West Cork, some of whom became known as Ó hUallacháin, meaning proud.

In the sixteenth century the Nolans were pushed west into Connacht, and there is an account of **Thomas Nolan** who was "one of the first owners of an English type inn or tavern hitherto known as *biatach* or houses of hospitality". There followed a line of tavern keepers and merchants.

Three Nolan gentlemen were officers in the army which fought the Cromwellians in 1649. After their defeat they escaped to Europe, where many Nolans are mentioned in the archives of several of the capital cities. A **Don Diego Nolan** was a captain in the Spanish Netherlands in 1660, and several other Nolan officers and colleagues served in various regiments throughout Europe.

Captain Moses Nolan of Carlow smuggled wines from France. He was hanged in Saint Stephen's Green in Dublin for having shipped hundreds of men to France from Bulloch Harbour in Dalkey, County Dublin. He had listed his contraband human cargo as "Wild Geese", the name given to the Irish soldiers who fled to France after the defeat at the battle of the Boyne.

In the 1860s in the USA, many Nolans are listed among the names of soldiers who fought with the Irish-American brigades in the Civil War. **Philip Nolan**, who was born in Ireland in 1771, emigrated to America, where he became a notorious smuggler.

Captain John Philip Nolan of Galway, an aspiring politician and Home Ruler, lost his seat after the Fenian trials when Judge Keogh accused the Roman Catholic clergy of undue influence.

Sir Sidney Nolan, the famous Australian painter, made his name with a series of pictures depicting the lives of two of his compatriot émigrés—the gangster and bushranger, Ned Kelly, and the traveller, Robert O Hara Burke.

Brian O Nolan (alias Flann O Brien and Myles na gCopaleen), was an intellectual satirist in both Irish and English. His enormously popular column in the *Irish Times* ran for over twenty years until his death in 1966.

Norris

Noiréas

Norreys

Norris is a very common name in England and, since the thirteenth century, is also very numerous in Ireland.

It was a **Sir John Norris** who, in 1575, directed the frightful massacre of the populace of Rathlin Island off the Antrim coast. In 1584 he was made president of Munster and, in 1597, was succeeded by his son, **Thomas Norris**. Thomas' brother, **Henry**, who died in 1599, is mentioned favourably in the great history of Ireland written by the Four Masters.

Mallow Castle in County Cork, which was the historic home of the Jephson family for four hundred years, was sold comparatively recently to an American. In 1603 Thomas Jephson, who was a major-general and a privy councillor in Ireland, married **Elizabeth**, the heiress of **Sir Thomas Norreys**, Lord President of Munster. By this marriage the Mallow estate, which had been granted by Queen Elizabeth I to Sir Thomas Norreys, came into the Jephson family, who assumed the Norreys name.

A shoemaker called Norris is recorded as serving in the Cromwellian army in 1689. A **Thomas D. Norris** is mentioned as being in the Irish-American brigade in New York in 1865.

The best-known Norris in Ireland today is **David Norris**, a professor in Trinity College Dublin, a senator in Dáil Éireann and a man of many interests. He has a sparkling wit, is a Joycean scholar, an active conservationist and a fearless campaigner for the rights of homosexuals.

Nowlan *see* (O) Nolan

Nugent

Nuinseann

Gilsenan

The Nugents can trace their ancestry back to *c.*AD 930, when they were counts in the town of Nogent in Normandy. They arrived in Ireland several centuries later and have long since been accepted as indigenous to the population. They acquired lands in Westmeath and were ennobled as barons of Delvin, which was their principal castle.

With few exceptions, the Nugents were a military family, serving wherever and whoever fate decreed. Some who followed the English rulers were rewarded as lord deputies of Ireland, while others joined the various Irish risings and lost much of their lands.

Between the sixteenth and nineteenth centuries the Nugents are recorded in the archives of Europe where, in France, **Christopher Nugent** founded the Nugent Regiment. Nugents also served with the French at Fontenoy. There were many Christopher Nugents, including one who was a general in the Republic of Venice. **Count Michael Nugent** retired as governor of Prague, while his nephew, **Laval**, a field marshal and count, fought the Habsburgs. His uncle, **Major-General Count Oliver Nugent**, was distinguished in both the Austrian and the British services. **George Nugent** was another of this name who served with the British army in America.

There were exceptions to the military rule, including **Robert Nugent** (1702–88), who was a poet. It was for him that the verb "to nugentize" was coined, because of his propensity for marrying wealthy widows who conveniently died, leaving him with the riches to successfully woo George III for a peerage.

When Hugh O Reilly changed his

name to marry a Nugent, thus bringing the splendid Ballinlough estate in Westmeath into his family, the local wits dubbed him "New Gent". These Ballinlough Nugents, who are counts of the Holy Roman Empire, still live there and have many Canadian kinsmen.

All the Nugents in *Burke's Peerage* share a similar crest, the mythical cocatrice, or basilisk, said to have come via a serpent from a cock's egg and to have an evil eye!

Names that begin with the O prefix are listed alphabetically under the main stem of the name (e.g. for O Byrne see Byrne).

Owens

Mac Eoghain

MacEoin Owain Owenson Owin

Owen is the anglicized form of Mac Eoghain, Eoghain being an Irish alternative for John. At one time the Mac Eoghains were an important Dalcassian sept in County Clare.

In Wales, Owen or Owens has long been a prominent name. It is also quite numerous in Ireland, particularly in Ulster, where many Scottish mercenary soldiers came in the thirteenth century and changed their name from Bissett to Owens.

Another common form of the surname is MacEoin. An outstanding representative of this County Longford family was **General Séan MacEoin,** known as "the blacksmith of Ballinalee" for his remarkable bravery during the War of Independence, and afterwards a minister in the new Free State government.

Before the standardization of surnames, there were a number of variations in the spelling, including Oweyn, Owin, Owain and Owenson. The Genealogical Office in Dublin has an account of a **John Oweyn** whose family had been living in County Kilkenny since 1294.

Owen occurs in the military records; some Owens came with the Cromwellian armies; in 1865 there was a **1st Lieutenant, John Owen** in the USA in the Irish American Brigade.

Robert Owenson (1744–1812) of County Mayo, became an actor and changed his name from MacOwen to Owenson. He was highly thought of on the London stage as well as in Dublin. His daughter was **Sydney**, later to become Lady Morgan, celebrated author of Irish romantic novels burning with patriotism.

Earlier in this century the **Reverend Richard Owens** was the Roman Catholic Bishop of Clogher.

see also MacKeon

P

Paul *see* Lavelle

Peables *see* Peoples

Pearse

Mac Piarais

Pierce

This surname is of Anglo-Irish origin and stems from the Norman first name, Piers, meaning Peter. With at least seven different spellings, it is also an old and numerous surname throughout Britain. In Ireland it is also very numerous, in all the provinces except Ulster.

In Kerry, the Pierces (sometimes with the Mac prefix) who fought in the Desmond wars were a branch of the Fitzmaurice family.

A **William Piers** (d. 1602) of Piers Hall in Yorkshire was sent to Ireland in 1566 by Queen Elizabeth, whom, it was said, he had saved from the frenzy of her sister, Mary. She rewarded him with much valuable land, including the abbey of Tristernagh in County Westmeath. He was also granted property in Antrim and a huge reward for delivering the head of the rebellious Shane O Neill.

Dr. Richard Pierce was Bishop of Waterford and Lismore from 1701 to 1735.

Several members of the Pierce family served in the English armies, including **Sir Henry Pierce**, Lord of Slane, whose lands were confiscated in 1657.

The most distinguished Pearce was **Sir Edward Lovet Pearce** (1699–1733) of Meath, whose travels when serving with the army in Italy aroused his interest in architecture. Returning to Ireland he became a Member of Parliament and a surveyor-general, and it was he who designed the Irish Houses of Parliament in Dublin, now the Bank of Ireland. His brother, **Lieutenant-General Thomas Pearce**, a governor of Limerick, served in the army in Spain.

Three children of an English father, a sculptor in Dublin, and a Gaelic-Irish mother were leaders of the 1916 Easter Rising. **Patrick Pearse** (1879–1916) founded Scoil Éanna, a bi-lingual school, at Cullenswood House in Rathmines. He was commander-in-chief of the republican army and, with his brother **William** (1881–1916), was one of the sixteen leaders of the Rising who was executed. Their sister, **Margaret Pearse** (1881–1968), who was a teacher, carried on running Scoil Éanna. She was also a politician and was a member of the Irish Senate until her death.

Colman Pearce (b. 1938) of Dublin is a pianist and a much-travelled conductor of Radio Telefís Éireann's orchestra.

Pebbles, **Peebles** *see* Peoples

Pennington

This is essentially an English name, which appears in the Irish archives as early as 1522, when **Anne Pennington**, daughter of **Baron Muncaster of Pennington**, married Christopher Curwen, who was said to be a descendant of the kings of Scotland.

In 1661, **Isaac Pennington** is recorded as forfeiting his lands to James, Duke of York, later the notorious James II of England. Isaac had been accused of taking part in the plot to behead Charles I of England in 1649 known as the regicide. Isaac's daughter married Captain Robert Lowther (of the now extinct earls of Lonsdale), who became governor-general of Barbados and died in 1745.

Mary Pennington is mentioned in the famous Ballitore papers, which were gathered together by the Quaker community there between the eighteenth and nineteenth century and are now beautifully preserved in their Dublin headquarters.

Pennington is a rare name now in Dublin. There are two people of that name mentioned in the current *Who's Who*, one an actor and writer and the other a university professor, both in England.

Peoples

Ó Duibhne

Peables Pebbles Peebles Pheables

Peoples is an unusual surname and the only place where a concentration of representatives of this name are still to be found is where it originated—in County Donegal and on the other side of the border in counties Antrim and Derry.

Dr. Edward MacLysaght, in his book *More Irish Families* (1982), says that this name "is an example of the more absurd type of pseudo-translation—it arose from the similarity of the sound of the word *daoine* (people) and the *duibhne* of O Duibhne, anglicized Deeny". This happened during the penal times when the Irish were forced to drop the O and Mac prefixes and to anglicize their surnames.

It is recorded that, in 1631, **Hugh Peoples** of Carnetellagh acquired the lands of Ballehabestocke in County Antrim.

In the *Hearth Money Rolls* (1669) for County Antrim there are a variety of spellings, including Peoples, Peables, Pebbles, Pebles, Pheables and, sometimes, Peebles.

In the *Edmondstone Manuscript* in the National Library of Ireland there is a reference to a letter of 1631 from Randal, Earl of Antrim, to A. Edmondstone in connection with a difference between tenants, one of whom was **R. Peoples** at Dunluce.

Phelan *see* Hyland

Philbin

Mac Philbín

Philips

There were several septs of the MacPhilbin family—all originating in Connacht. In Irish *pilibín* means plover, and Philbín is also the Irish equivalent of the forename Philip.

The MacPhilbin family are thought by some scholars to be a branch of the Burkes, the powerful Norman family who dominated Galway for many centuries. Others say they were a branch of the Barrett family. There was a Clanphilbin sept settled at Burrishoole. A head of the sept had his headquarters at Doon Castle, near Westport in County Mayo.

At one time they must have owned much land and property for seventeenth- and eighteenth-century records give accounts of repeated Philbin confiscations, with comparatively few regrants. At least three Philbins fought on the side of James II at the battle of the Boyne.

Today the name is a rare one in Ireland. Their most outstanding representatives have been ecclesiastics. **Philip Phillips** (d. 1787) was Bishop of Achonry and, later, Archbishop of Tuam. There is no doubt that he was originally MacPhilbin. The **Reverend William J. Philbin** (b. 1907) of Ballaghadereen was Bishop of Clonfert and Bishop of Down and Connor from 1962 to 1982. A considerable scholar, he contributed widely to ecclesiastical literature.

Professor Eva Philbin (b. 1914) of Ballina in County Mayo has brought lustre to the name. A professor of organic chemistry with an international reputation, she was head of the department of chemistry at University College Dublin.

Philips *see* Philbin

Pidgeon *see* MacGuigan

Pierce *see* Pearse

Pigott

Pigot

Pigott is derived from *Pic*, an old French personal name. However, another school of thought says it derives from the name Becket.

There were Pigotts among the forty Norman knights who accompanied William the Conqueror when he defeated England at the battle of Hastings in 1066.

A **John Pigott** went to Ireland in 1562, where he was granted a castle and estate known as Disert. Many of this family were in the army, including **Sergeant-Major John Pigott**, a governor of Athy who retired to Disert in Laois where he was murdered by the rebels in 1646.

A **Sir Robert Pigott** wrote a letter to the Lord Deputy of Ireland asking for a word in his favour for a draft warrant for twenty footmen to continue to be bestowed on him in Ireland in return for his services. A **Colonel Thomas Pigott** who was campaigning in Ireland with the Cromwellian army is recorded as shipping seven thousand men to Spain, including many of the Irish nobility.

George Pigot of Patshull in Staffordshire, England, was elevated to the peerage in Ireland as Baron Pigot of Patshull. He died in prison in India leaving no heirs.

The notorious **Richard Pigott** (*c.*1828–89), a journalist and a forger, published a string of newspapers with extreme nationalist views, for which he suffered imprisonment on several occasions. He dissipated his wealth, wrote anonymous libels and accepted bribes. The famous *Pigott Letters* published by the *London Times* were his downfall and he fled to Madrid, where he killed himself.

Music features strongly in the Pigott name. *The Pigott Collection of Irish Music* in sixteen volumes is in the Royal Irish Academy. A shop in Dublin, **McCullough Pigott**, is one of the oldest music emporiums in the country.

The name today is most numerous in the County Dublin area, with but a few others scattered around the rest of the country, north and south.

Plunkett

Pluincéid

Plunket

Plunkett is thought to be a corruption of the French word for white or blonde, *blanc.* **Randall Plunkett**, the 19th Baron Dunsany and custodian of the magnificent Dunsany Castle in Meath, inclines to the view that his antecedents may have come from Denmark.

There is no doubt that they have been settled in Meath for a very long time and have contributed richly to their country, especially their illustrious ancestor, **Oliver Plunkett** (1625–81), who was canonized in 1975. Oliver Plunkett was ordained in Rome and returned to Ireland in very troubled times as Bishop of Armagh. He suffered persecution for his pastoral work and was executed at Tyburn on a trumped-up charge.

The Plunketts who followed the doomed Scottish Stuarts escaped to join the Irish regiments in France and many other countries.

William Conyngham, **1st Baron Plunket** of Enniskillen, received his peerage as chief justice. A succession of this family of Plunkets—with one t—were bishops of the established Church.

Joseph Plunkett, a revolutionary and a poet, was a signatory of the Proclamation of the Irish Republic and was executed in 1916.

Irish farmers owe much to the efforts of **Sir Horace Plunkett,** whose whole life was dedicated to the improvement of Irish agriculture. His brother **Edward Plunkett**, 18th Baron Dunsany, a soldier, sportsman, and writer with an abiding interest in the supernatural, wrote novels, poems and plays and was a popular broadcaster, especially in the USA. His fantasy stories, *The Sword of Welleren*, *The Gods of Pegana* and many other works, anticipated J. R. R. Tolkien's *Lord of the Rings.*

A Plunkett who went to Australia from Roscommon became a statesman and one of the first Catholics to be appointed solicitor-general of New South Wales.

The Plunketts are still a numerous family, particularly in the counties north of Dublin.

Poher *see* Power

Powell

Mac Giolla Phóil

Powell, which can be either Welsh or English in its origins, can also be a synonym for the Irish surname, Gilfoyle—an anglicization of Mac Giolla Phóil (servant of St. Paul). This was an ancient family who were chiefs in County Offaly.

On the whole, the Powell surname, which is very numerous all over Ireland, would seem to have originated during the Elizabethan plantations, followed by more Powells who came with the Cromwellians and were afterwards rewarded with grants of forfeited land. They owned a number of fine houses in various parts of the country.

In Dublin's Genealogical Office there are many Powell pedigrees. An English one dates from 1300 to 1604 while pedigrees of the Powells in Ireland date from 1600 to the eighteenth century.

In 1682, **Giles Powell** was a high sheriff in Limerick while, in 1689, **Edward Powell** was a Member of Parliament for County Limerick.

For generations, Powells were prominent in the Church and the services. **Richard Powell** was an assistant surgeon to the Irish-American brigade in the American Civil War.

Books were also an abiding interest

for many Powells. In the sixteenth century one of the first printers in Dublin was a Powell and he founded a dynasty of printers there. **G. R. Powell**'s guides to the new Irish railways and his tours of the country were very popular in the nineteenth century. In the 1960s, **Roger Powell** of Trinity College Dublin helped in the rebinding of some of Ireland's most treasured books, including the *Book of Kells*.

see also Gilfoyle

Power

le Paor

Poher

The Powers are a very numerous Irish family who might be surprised to discover that they came to Ireland with the Normans. Their name was le Poer, meaning poor, as they had, for a time at least, taken a vow of poverty.

The Powers are the subject of many legends. A young **Countess Poher** is supposed to have been Bluebeard's fifth wife. As was his habit, he had her beheaded. She is recorded as a saint and the mother of St. Tremeur of Brittany. In Ireland, **Sir John de Power** took a big risk by becoming the fourth husband of Alice le Kytler from Kilkenny, who was renowned for killing her husbands.

The Powers settled in Wicklow and Waterford, where the Marquess of Waterford and his family still live in their ancient mansion, Curraghmore. An ancestor, **Catherine Power**, Countess of Tyrone, won an important victory when she fought for the right of Irish heiresses to inherit property through the female line.

The Earl of Blessington married the penniless **Margaret Power** of Knockbrit in Limerick. She was known as "the most beautiful Countess of Blessington" and she wrote books about their extensive travels in Europe. When he died, she hosted regular salons in her London house for the intelligentsia—male only. Debt forced her to sell her house and she spent the rest of her life writing to support not only herself but also her feckless Limerick father, who had married her off in her teens to a drunken officer who had subsequently killed himself.

The Powers held many ecclesiastical positions, both in the Catholic Church and in the Church of Ireland. They also took part in many battles on the European continent.

Frank Power, one of the earliest war correspondents, wrote for the *London Times* but died early as a result of an ambush in Egypt.

Albert Power was an important sculptor. He was commissioned to make many commemorative sculptures, including one of the *Lusitania* which sank off Cork.

The theatre was much in the Power blood. **William Grattan Tyrone Power** of the Marquess of Waterford's family played many leading roles on the London stage. He was drowned on the *President* when sailing home from New York. His great-grandson was the romantic, devil-may-care film star, **Tyrone Power**. Another kinsman was the distinguished film and stage director and producer, **Sir Tyrone Gutherie** of Monaghan.

John Power's whiskey distillery, founded in 1791, which pioneered the miniature liquor bottle, the "Baby Power", merged with Irish Distillers Limited in 1966.

Prior

Mac an Phríora

Friar Friary Pryer

Prior is equally common in England and Ireland and derives from the prior of a religious house. In Ireland, most Priors are of true Gaelic stock. Their name is an anglicization of Mac an Phríora, denoting a connection with an ecclesiastical office.

The Midlands predominates as Prior territory and there, from the seventeenth century, the Priors who later, through marriage, added Wandesforde to their surname owned Ireland's largest coal mine at Castlecomer in County Kilkenny.

In the National Library there are many Prior records, including a letter in French from Lord Galway asking for the king's permission to retire from his royal office following a dispute with **Matthew Prior**, an Irish Member of Parliament who was secretary to the chief justices at Dublin Castle in 1699. There are many letters from this Matthew Prior, including one in which he accuses Irish priests travelling abroad in merchant ships of being spies.

The most illustrious member of the family was **Thomas Priors** (1682–1751), of the County Laois Priors of Rathdowney, who, in about 1731, founded the Royal Dublin Society to promote agriculture, manufacturing, the arts and sciences—which valuable work it continues to do.

The very many townlands in Ireland which incorporate the Prior name—Ballymacprior, Priorstown, etc.—in all probability refer to the office rather than the surname.

In some instances, Prior was transformed to Pryer and even to Friary.

Prunty

Ó Proinntigh

Brontë Pronty

Father Woulfe, the scholarly nineteenth-century writer on the origins of Irish names, hazards a guess that Prunty "is doubtless a corruption of na Proinntighe", meaning of the refectory or dining room. Later scholars think the name could mean a descendant of the bestower (a generous person).

It is a Gaelic name, essentially of Ulster, chiefly in County Armagh, where it was anglicized to O Prounty or O Prunty.

Patrick O Prunty was an Ulster Gaelic poet who was probably an ancestor of **Hugh Prunty**, a small farmer in County Down. His son was **Patrick** (1777–1861), who worked as a blacksmith's labourer and then as a schoolteacher. The local vicar recognized that he was very talented and paid for him to go to Cambridge, where he was eventually ordained as a Church of England clergyman. On leaving Ireland he had changed his name to the more euphonious Brontë. He married the niece of a Cornish parson and was appointed to the parish of Haworth in the wilds of Yorkshire, where he remained for over forty years, the sole survivor of his family. He wrote minor poetry but his real claim to fame was as the father of the most distinguished trio of novelists in English literature: Charlotte, Emily and Anne Brontë.

His four children—there was also a reprobate son, Branwell—had a spartan upbringing and it was their father's eccentricities and moodiness which drove them to escape into writing secretly. Neither Emily nor Anne lived to be more than thirty, while Charlotte died at forty-nine, but they left behind such enduring novels as *Jane Eyre* and *Wuthering Heights.*

Dr. Robert Mathew ('Max') Brontë was the pathologist at Dublin's Meath Hospital in 1914. Born in Armagh, a member of the famous Brontë family of County Down, he was a pharmacist in Enniskillen before he took up medicine. He qualified from the College of Surgeons in 1906 and developed a special interest in forensic pathology. He was appointed 'Crown analyst' for a time before he left Dublin for London in 1922.

Prunty and Brontë are very rare names in Ireland today, although in Northern Ireland there may be a dozen or so Brontës.

Pryer *see* Prior

Purcell

Puirséil

The Purcells first went to England from France and later they went on to Ireland. In its original Norman-French, *pourcel* means little pig.

The Purcells were attached to the powerful Butlers of Ormond in County Kilkenny. It was the Earl of Ormond who gave them the courtesy title of Barons of Loughmoe, their territory between Kilkenny and Tipperary. Their castle at Loughmoe is now a picturesque ruin, classed as a National Monument.

Colonel Nicholas Purcell, a Baron of Loughmoe who fought beside Sarsfield at the battle of the Boyne, followed that defeat by helping to negotiate the 1691 Treaty of Limerick.

The Purcells fought for the Irish cause and when they had to join the exodus to the Continent they joined the Irish regiments in the French army, especially Clare's Dragoons and Purcell's Horse.

Through the ages they have had a number of exalted ecclesiastics, including bishops and abbots and, in the last century, an archbishop of Cincinnati, USA. This last was **John Baptist Purcell** (1800–83) from Mallow. With his brother, **Edward Purcell**, he founded a private bank which, unfortunately, failed and became notorious as "Purcell's Bank".

One of the Loughmoe family, **Sir John Purcell**, was knighted in 1811 for his gallant defence when attacked by a gang of robbers.

Mary Purcell, who was born in Cork in 1906, was a teacher and lecturer and a prolific biographer of religious subjects.

Patrick Purcell (b. 1914) was a sports journalist and has had a number of novels chosen as Book of the Month.

Tall, gangly **Noel Purcell** (1900–85), variety artist of stage, screen and television, was one of Dublin's much-loved entertainers.

Q

Quiddihy *see* Cuddihy

Queally *see* (O) Kiely

Quigley

Ó Coigligh

Cogley Coigley

The Quigleys were a sept of the powerful northern Uí Fiachrach whose territory was in north Mayo and Sligo. The name derives from *coigeal* and is descriptive of an unkempt person, possibly referring to untidy hair.

A record dated 1659 mentions a numerous Quigley sept living around the Inishowen Peninsula between Lough Swilly and Lough Foyle in County Donegal. During that very disturbed century the Quigleys were scattered, mostly to Connacht. Today, they are quite numerous and distributed around all four provinces—Ulster, Munster, Leinster and Connacht.

In a manuscript in Dublin's National Library there is mention of a Quigley family of County Monaghan, and a **D. Quigley** of Australia who was in correspondence with general merchants in Glenavy in County Antrim.

Father James O Coigley of Armagh was caught in France during the French Revolution, where he survived many dangers. On his way home through England he was hanged on false evidence in 1798—the year of the rising in Ireland.

The Quigley name appears a number of times for the year 1865 in the lists of the Irish-American brigades.

Dr. James Quigley (d. 1915) went to the USA, where he became Bishop of Buffalo. He was remarkable for his interest in the trade unions and the facility with which he could help to settle strikes.

Quinlan

Ó Caoinleáin

Kindellan Quinlevan

Quinlan is one of several anglicizations of the Ó Caoinleáin sept, who claim kinship with the senior O Neills whose progenitor was Laoghaire (d. 463), King of Ireland at the time of Saint Patrick. It was this Laoghaire who, from his palace on the Hill of Tara across the plains of Meath, saw the flames of the paschal fire lit defiantly by Patrick. To the pagans of those days, fire was a very sacred thing, reserved for kings, and King Laoghaire at once sent for Patrick to explain himself. Incidentally, the harbour in south county Dublin, Dún Laoghaire, is named after this early ancestor of the Quinlans.

Until the arrival of the Anglo-Normans, the Quinlans were prominent landowners in County Meath. They followed the Stuart cause and so, after the defeat of James II at the battle of the Boyne in 1690, many of them went to

Spain where, as Kindellan or Kindeln, they can be found to this day.

John Ambrose Kindellan (1750–1822) was a general in the Spanish army. **General Alfredo Kindeln** was an important member of General Franco's cabinet.

In the 1659 census, the Quinlans were found to be one of the most numerous families in County Tipperary.

There is a description in *Burke's Guide to Country Houses* of Rynskaheen, a nineteenth-century fishing lodge on the shores of Lough Derg in County Tipperary which was built by a **Reverend W. R. Quinlan**.

The Quinlans are now mostly rooted in Munster, particularly in counties Cork, Limerick and Tipperary. In County Clare, the name has become Quinlevan. There are few Kindellans, Kindelans or Kindelns now in Ireland.

Quinlevan *see* Quinlan

Quinn

Ó Cuinn

Quin

Ceann is the Irish word for head and from it derives the surname of at least five distinct Quinn or Quin families. In general, Catholics spell the name with two "*n*"s while Protestants spell it with one, although this has never been a rigid rule.

The first of these five families were the O Cuinns of Thomond in Limerick, who, like the O Briens, were of the Dál gCais, or Dalcassian sept. Originally, Inchiquin was their headquarters. The second were the O Cuinns of Annaly, who were of the same stock as the O Farrells, the chiefs of Longford who displaced them. There was also a family of O Cuinn chiefs in Antrim, where their great chief, **Conghalach**, was slain in battle in 1218. Fourth were the O Cuinns of Magh Ita in Raphoe in Donegal, and last were the O Cuinns of Clann Cuain who were chiefs near Castlebar, County Mayo.

There have been many distinguished Quinns, including poets, actors and singers and a thirteenth-century bishop of the famed Clonmacnoise. In the seventeenth century, many Quinns were forced to join the exodus to Europe, often to become leading citizens in France, particularly in Bordeaux, where the street rue O Quinn testifies to their prominence and where the Quinns still flourish.

Their most outstanding family descends from **Thady Quin** of the Inchiquin family of County Clare, who built the magnificent manor at Dunraven, in Adare, County Limerick. Styled **Earls of Dunraven**, they are among the few Gaelic titled families. The **3rd Earl of Dunraven**, born 1812, was internationally recognized for his scholarship, particularly in Celtic and medieval learning. The 4th Earl, **Windham Thomas Wyndham** (b. 1841), was a steeplechaser, yachtsman and war correspondent and he also hunted in Texas with Buffalo Bill. He inspired the landlords to accept the Wyndham Land Act of 1903, which at last allowed tenants to own their land. He was made a Senator in the first Irish government in 1922.

Edel Mary Quinn (1907–44) came from a County Cork family which fell upon hard times. Her ambition to join the Poor Clare order of nuns was frustrated by having to earn a living. Declining an offer of marriage, she joined the Legion of Mary and went to work for them in Africa, where she devoted herself, still a lay person, to spreading the Gospel, until her early death from tuberculosis.

The Earls of Dunraven have an unusual motto on their coat of arms: *Quae sursum volo videre* (I wish to see the things that are above).

Quirke

Ó Cuirc

MacGurk

There are a number of variations of the Ó Cuirc name, which derives from the Irish word *corc*, meaning heart. These include Kirke, Quick and even Oats, a mistranslation from *coirce*, the Irish word for oats!

Before the arrival of the Anglo-Normans, the Ó Cuirc sept ruled over many acres in south-west Tipperary. They were numerous around Clonmel, where a bishop, **Murchad O Curk**, was acquitted in 1295 from a charge of harbouring a robber. Muskerry in Cork was at one time referred to as Quirke's Country. During the devastation of the Cromwellian armies, a number of Quirkes were transplanted to Connacht. There are also many Quirkes in England, and some of Cromwell's soldiers serving in Ireland were of that name.

In 1642, a Dominican priest, **Thomas O Quirke**, was an eminent preacher and chaplain to the Confederation of Kilkenny.

There were Quirkes in the army of James Butler, 1st Duke of Ormond in Kilkenny in 1649. They were also in the Irish army in the 1670s and in the service of James II of the ill-fated Stuart family.

In Ulster, where MacGurk is the more usual rendering of the name, there are various townlands incorporating the name, including Ballygurk near Magherafelt in County Derry, Termonmahuirk in County Tyrone and Carrickmaguirk near Granard in County Longford.

Father Brian MacGuirk died at the age of ninety when he was captured and imprisoned by the notorious priest hunter, Dawson.

This sept is said to be descended from Nial Naoighiallach (Niall of the Nine Hostages), who was the joint hereditary keeper of St. Colmcille's bell, which is now in the Edinburgh Museum.

Quirovan *see* Kirwan

Radcliffe

Ratcliffe Ratliss

It is probable that the name Radcliffe comes from the Lancastrian town of that name in England. There are few Ratcliffes and Radcliffes in Ireland, except in Ulster, where they are remarkably numerous.

The Radcliffes featured prominently in colonial times. In 1599, **Sir A. Ratcliffe** wrote concerning his defeat by the Irish, led by O Donnell: "The troops are weakened by sickness. Those sent from England were of poor quality."

Sir George Ratcliffe wrote in 1633 to Lord Deputy Wentworth, telling him that there was a pirate in the mouth of Dublin Bay. He also wrote concerning "the yield from the customs and licences for the export of butter etc." The following year Sir George was accused of high treason and sent to the Tower of London. As recently as 1877, there was a case brought by a family trying to claim back money taken by Sir George from their confiscated estates.

In 1601, **J. Ratclyff**, Mayor of Chester, was shipping horses to Ireland and complaining that the troops could not leave in either August or September because of unfavourable winds.

There have been many distinguished English Radcliffes and the name is commemorated in Oxford by a number of institutions of learning and the famous Radcliffe Infirmary.

(O) Rafferty

Ó Raithbheartaigh

This surname, when spelled Ó Raithbheartaigh, is thought to mean prosperity wielder, but an alternative spelling, Ó Robhartaigh, derives from the word *robharta*, which means a flood tide. It is significant in light of the latter meaning that there are fish on the Rafferty arms. In records of 1663 the name is spelled O Raverty.

In County Donegal the O Raffertys were co-arbs (administrators) to the monastery founded on Tory Island by one of the three patron saints of Ireland, Saint Columcille (AD 521–97). The Sligo branch of the Raffertys have been described as the "seven pillars of Skreen", one of the areas where they had their lands. Their descendants have long since scattered throughout the thirty-two counties and they are now numerous, especially in the province of Ulster.

Apart from an abbot of Durrow in 1090, the Raffertys have not yet come to prominence.

The name is not to be confused with Raftery, a different name, the origins of which are in Connacht.

(O) Rahilly *see* (O) Reilly

Ramsey

Ramsay

Ramsey was first mentioned in Scotland as a surname in 1153. In time, the Ramsays were to become earls of Dalhousie in Scotland and were to give this name to a town in Ontario, Canada. They are not very numerous in Ireland, except in Northern Ireland, where they probably arrived as immigrants from Scotland.

The Belfast Public Records Office holds a collection of leases, deeds and other legal papers relating to property mostly in Belfast and Ballyhenry, County Down. There is also a letter from a **Sir James Ramsay** to the Earl of Salisbury, in which he writes, "auditors in Ireland have refused to let his agent examine some accounts" and asking for a warrant to be signed giving him the power to do this.

In records dating from 1755 to 1857 there are papers relating to the Mahon family of County Roscommon regarding **Maureen Mahon Ramsay**'s title to Crohane and Ballykein in County Tipperary. This obviously related to a dispute over property between the Mahon and Ramsay families.

There were also many military Ramsays, including **Ensign David Ramsay**, who served in the English army in Ireland in 1649. There was a **Colonel Ramsay** who fought with King James's army in every seventeenth-century battle of note, including those at the Boyne, Limerick and Aughrim and the siege of Derry.

In the nineteenth century the Ramsays produced a significant number of clergymen, physicians, lawyers, writers, antiquarians and mineralogists. **David Ramsay** published a *History of the American Revolution* in 1793 and **Sir George Ramsay** wrote *A Proposal for the Restoration of the Irish Parliament* in 1845. Quite a number of Ramsays were land surveyors, a very important job in Ireland in the nineteenth century when there was so much conflict over land.

Ratcliffe *see* Radcliffe

Ratliss *see* Radcliffe

Ray *see* Crea

(O) Reagan *see* (O) Regan

Reardon *see* (O) Riordan

Redmond

Réamonn

This numerous surname of Norman origin is said to have come via Raymond le Gros, one of the leaders of the Normans who landed in Ireland in *c.*1169. For centuries they have been big landowners in County Wexford. In 1598, "**Redmond of the Hooke** was one of the principal gentlemen in County Wexford, as was in 1608, **Redmond of the Hall**". They owned many fine houses, but lost much of their property when they sided with the rebels in 1691.

The Redmonds are well recorded as soldiers and distinguished politicians. **Chevalier Gabriel Redmond** (1713–89) was one of the several Redmonds who, having left Ireland because of political oppression, reached high rank on the Continent, especially in the Irish brigades in France. **Sir Peter Redmond**, a Jacobite agent in Madrid in 1718, was appointed by James II as consul-general to Portugal.

In 1798, **John Redmond** and **Michael Redmond**, both priests, took part in the Wexford rebellion. In 1864, another **Michael Redmond** was killed in action with the Irish-American brigade.

The Genealogical Office in Dublin has a pedigree dating from 1170 to 1817, encompassing the Redmonds of Wexford, Dublin, Spain and Portugal.

The Redmonds were lawyers and very active politicians. **John Redmond** (1856–1918), the son of a County Wexford Member of Parliament, was a leader of the Irish Party in the British House of Commons, where he championed Home Rule. With his younger brother **William Redmond** (1861–1917) he toured the United States and Australia raising funds. John Redmond was shattered by the 1916 Easter Rising and its aftermath of executions. William, who was also a politician, joined the army and was killed in France in the First World War. He wrote several books about his travels in Australia.

Reeves

Ó Rimheadha

Reeve Ryves

The Ó Rimheadha were an ancient family of the Ards peninsula in County Down. The name comes from a first name, Rimead, which is said to mean a calculator. In 1004 the death is recorded of **Maelbrighde Uí Riméada**, the abbot of Iona. The Irish name is now extinct.

The English name Reeves, or Reeve, is now rare in Ireland, where they arrived in the seventeenth century. It is an occupational name for a bailiff or steward.

A number of Reeves served in the army in Ireland in 1649, including a **Lieutenant-Colonel Richard Reeves**.

Charles Reeves was Bishop of Limerick, Ardfert and Aghadoe early in the nineteenth century.

William Reeves (1815–92) was the most outstanding of the name. Born in Cork and educated at Trinity College Dublin, he graduated in medicine and then took holy orders with the Church of Ireland at Derry. He lived in County Antrim, where he became Bishop of Down, Connor and Dromore. He was a tireless antiquarian, and author of many learned essays. He is best remembered for his edition of the *Life of St. Columba* by Adamnan.

In the nineteenth and twentieth centuries, many Reeves contributed to specialist Irish journals on subjects as diverse as travel and medical science, politics and peat fuel, zoology and conchology.

Clara Reeve wrote historical romances and **Annette Reeves** was the subject of a poem by Desmond O Grady. **Alan Reeve** was a very popular cartoonist in Dublin in the 1940s.

(O) Regan

Ó Riagain Ó Réagain

(O) Reagan

The Ó Riagain clan can trace its origins back almost a thousand years to Riagain, a nephew of the High King, Brian Boru. From this great king descend many of the Irish nobility and the British royal family, into which they married. As surnames came into use, the name became a popular one, especially in the counties of Cork, Clare and Tipperary. The Dunnes are a sept of this big clan.

In the twelfth century, **Maurice Ó Riagain**, who was scribe to Dermot MacMurrough, King of Leinster, wrote a history of the Anglo-Norman invasion.

In the seventeenth century, many Regans served in the armies of France, where their families can be researched in the archives. They also established themselves in America well before the Great Famine in Ireland.

Direct ancestors of **Ronald Reagan**, former President of the USA, have been traced back four generations to **Thomas Regan** of Ballyporeen in County Tipperary. It was his son, Michael (1829–80), who first emigrated to London and, in the mid 1850s, to Fairhaven, Illinois, where he became a prosperous landowner. His grandson, Ronald Reagan, was born into this family in Tampico, Illinois. When he was president of the Screen Actors' Guild, Ronald fought valiantly for the underpaid in his profession. During the Second World War he was in the armed forces, but poor eyesight kept him from active service. He was Governor of California from 1967 to 1974.

In Munster, home of the Ó Raogains from which sept his ancestors came, Regan was pronounced Reagan, so in California they continue to pronounce their name as did their Gaelic forebears. In Ireland today "Reegan" is the usual pronunciation.

(O) Reilly

Ó Raghailligh

(O) Rahilly

The O Reillys are thought to be descendants of the O Conor kings of Connacht. They took their name from a **Ragheallach** (*rag* means a race, and *ceallach* means gregarious) who was killed with King Brian Boru at the battle of Clontarf in 1014. At one time they ruled the network of lakes around Lough Erne, where their chieftains were inaugurated and they had their fortress at Lough Oughter. As they multiplied, they spread out to County Longford, Meath and Cork.

Their chief was styled "Breffny O Reilly". When they were driven from their lands in the seventeenth century, their aristocratic genealogies assured them of seniority in the armies of Europe, and their name took on a variety of spellings including Orely in Spain and Oreille in France. At one time there were no less than thirty-three O Reilly officers under the command of an O Reilly.

They commanded armies in Spain and South America, where they also governed. There are still streets bearing their name in several Spanish cities, and also in Havana. In fact, descendants of theirs can still be found in Cuba.

The O Reillys were clever financiers. In the fifteenth century they devised their own coinage, which probably gave rise to the saying, "living the life of Reilly". Conversely, there were those who "hadn't a Reilly to their name".

The O Reillys in the Middle Ages were good churchmen and built abbeys and held many bishoprics. They also boasted relationship to Saint Oliver Plunkett.

In the nineteenth century some were poets and many were politicians, often punished for their patriotism by transportation to Australia, where, they contributed to local administration and to politics.

In Ireland, they became successfully involved in the native whiskey distilling business. A former rugby hero, **Tony O Reilly**, is one of Ireland's leading financiers and is chief executive officer of the Heinz Corporation in the USA. He is also involved in many other consortiums, including newspapers.

One County Cavan town in the heart of O Reilly country was immortalized in Percy French's ballad, "Come back Paddy Reilly to Ballyjamesduff".

Reynolds

Mac Raghnaill

MacRannall

The old Irish name Mac Raghnaill (son of Randal or Reginald) has been long anglicized to Reynolds, a name also very common in England and Scotland.

The MacRannalls were a sept of Muintir Eolais in County Leitrim who sometimes feuded against, and sometimes fought with, their powerful O Rourke neighbours. The Chief of the Name was known as Magranill of Moynigh.

An interesting account of the family in the seventeenth century is given in volume five of the *Journal of the Royal Society of Antiquaries*, of 1905. **James Reynolds** of Lough Scur Castle was one of a number of Reynolds who were Members of Parliament. At one time the MacRannalls who changed their name to Reynolds owned 6,600 acres in Leitrim and 1,000 acres in Roscommon.

More than a dozen Reynolds fought on the side of James II at the battle of the Boyne and, after his defeat, lost much of their land.

Thomas Reynolds (1771–1836), son of a wealthy Dublin poplin manufacturer, was a brother-in-law of Wolfe Tone. Low living and bankruptcy lost him his fortune and led to his accepting a bribe to betray his colleagues in the revolutionary society of United Irishmen. He fled the country after they were captured.

The **Reverend Christopher Reynolds** (1834–93) was the first Catholic bishop of South Australia.

Dr. Osborne Reynolds (d. 1866) was a novelist and playwright, while his son, **James Emerson Reynolds** (1844–1920), was a distinguished and innovative professor of chemistry at Trinity College Dublin.

Patrick Reynolds (b. 1920), a former *Fine Gael* deputy for Sligo, was chairman of the Seanad in Dáil Éireann. **Albert Reynolds** (b. 1935) is a member of the Fianna Fáil Party and has held a number of ministerial posts. Originally a businessman, he became very wealthy through his pet food company, and also through publishing and running dance halls. Albert Reynolds was Taoiseach for a short time until the fall of the Fianna Fáil government in 1994. He will be remembered best for his work promoting the peace process in Ireland.

(O) Riordan

Ó Riordáin

Reardon

Ó Riordáin derives from the Irish *ríogh bhard*, which means royal bard. Father Woulfe believes them to have been kinsmen of the Ely O Carrolls of Offaly, descendants of a Lord of Ely who fell in 1058 at the battle of the Glen of Aherlow. In 1576, **Gaven O Rewardene** was one of Sir William O Carroll's most important followers. In 1597, **Maurice O Riordan** was accused of treason and lost his lands, as did many others of the O Riordan sept. They subsequently moved to Cork, where they are still most numerous today.

Some O Riordans went abroad, and a **Don Jacques Alferez Rirden** is recorded as serving in the Spanish Netherlands in 1660. An O Riordan family of Derryroe in County Cork settled in Nantes and were created Peers of France in 1755. Riordans also served in the Irish-American brigades.

Conal Holmes O Connell O Riordan (1874–1948) of Dublin was injured in a riding accident, which turned his ambitions from the army to the stage.

He wrote novels and plays which were produced at Dublin's Abbey Theatre, of which he was a manager. Norroys Connell was the pseudonym he used for his early novels.

Professor **Sean O Riordan** (1905–57) of Cork earned an international reputation as an archaeologist, especially for his excavations at Tara, the ancient seat of the high kings.

Sean O Riordáin (1916–77) of Ballyvourney in County Cork is regarded as one of the finest poets writing in Irish.

Antoine Breandan O Riordan (b.1927) from Galway was the archaeologist who pioneered the famous Viking excavations in Dublin (now entombed beneath a modern office block). In 1979 he became director of the National Museum.

With the exception of Northern Ireland, the name is very numerous in Ireland, more so with its O prefix than without.

Roark *see* (O) Rourke

Robertson

Mac Roibeáird

In Scotland, the lands of Clann Donnachaidh (Duncan) were said to stretch from the Moor of Rannoch to the gates of Perth. They were kinsmen of the Earl of Atholl and may have acquired the Robertson name as reward for fighting with King Robert at Bannockburn.

Many Robertsons left their native Scotland over the centuries to settle in Ireland, especially in nearby Ulster, where they are now most numerous. They must have been late arrivals in Ireland for there is little reference to them in the Gaelic annals. In County Kildare there is a Robertstown, marked by the ancient Robertstown Canal Hotel, a reminder of the traffic which once plied on the inland waterways.

Huntington Castle in County Carlow came to the **Durdin-Robertsons** through marriage into the family of its original owner, the 1st Lord Esmonde, in *c.*1625. **Olivia Manning Robertson** (b. 1917) of this family started a successful literary career with *St. Malachy's Court*, an account of her work in a Dublin Corporation playground. She has since specialized in books about the goddess Isis for the Fellowship of Isis which is centred on Huntington Castle.

Architecture has been a strong trait in the Robertson family in southern Ireland. **James G. Robertson**, a nineteenth-century architect, published many papers on the archaeology of Kilkenny. **William Robertson** was asked to rebuild Kilkenny Castle, home of the Butlers, in the mid-nineteenth century. He designed many of the big country houses of that time. **Manning Robertson** of the Huntington Castle family was also an architect. In the 1940s he contributed articles on this subject to a number of Irish journals.

Roche

de Róiste

de la Roch

The Roches, who were of Norman stock, became remarkably prosperous Irishmen. They took the name from their Pembrokeshire stronghold, Roch Castle. They soon separated into five main branches, almost all in Munster, commemorated by sixteen Rochestowns!

They joined with the natives in their many struggles to keep out the English. The Roche who was created 1st Viscount Fermoy, an ancestor of Princess Diana of the British royal family, lived at Castletownroche.

The 8th Viscount Fermoy fought in the 1641 rebellion. His wife, who was born a Power, desperately defended their castle, for which she was hanged by the Cromwellians. With all his possessions gone, **David Roche** departed, like so many of his colleagues, to join the armies of Europe. Another Roche, on returning from the wars in Europe, set up one of the earliest glass furnaces.

The Limerick Roches, although remaining Catholic, still managed to become comfortable merchants. One of their wealthy sons, in his will, threatened to cut off his two daughters if they married either an Irishman or a Spaniard. They married English army officers!

Some of the Roche children who were sent to France for their education remained there, many becoming scholars or wine merchants. However, they were ruined during the French Revolution.

During the Napoleonic Wars, the Roches opened a bank in Cork which was famous for its hanging gardens. The bank was gravely affected by the recession, following the victory at Waterloo.

"Tiger" Roche (b. 1729), so-called because of his ferocious temper, also had a sly charm, which he used to dispossess heiresses of their fortunes. His brother, **Boyle Roche** (1743–1807), a soldier and politician, achieved notoriety for his Irish "bulls", the most quoted being his assertion "Why should we do anything for posterity. What has posterity ever done for us?"

In the twentieth century, the distinguished Irish scholar, **Liam de Róiste**, who fought in the War of Independence, afterwards represented Cork in the newly formed Dáil Éireann. The Roches can also boast the first woman to be appointed a judge in Ireland, **Maura Roche** of Mayo.

From the 1960s until recently, they have held an annual clan rally in one of their surviving castles. It is to be hoped that they will not let this happy and popular custom lapse.

Rodgers *see* Rogers

Roe

Ó Ruaidh

MacEnroe Ormond

There are several theories concerning the origin of this name, which is also common in England. Some Roes came to Ireland with the Norman conquest. However, it can also be an abbreviation of MacEnroe, or it may have had a connection by mistranslation with Ormond. Roe is numerous in all parts of Ireland except the north-east and, in most cases, it probably now comes from the anglicized version of Ó Ruaidh (meaning descendant of the red-haired one).

For understandable reasons, the Roes who came to the fore in Irish history were mainly colonizers. A Roe who was comptroller in the Isle of Man wrote in 1615 to General Ginkel that a Dublin-bound ship which sought refuge there had been seized, and he demanded its release.

In 1612, **Sir Thomas Roe** made the first Irish settlement in North America. This, however, did not last for very long.

In 1654, **Colonel Owen Roe** was granted property in Ireland by Cromwell in settlement of a debt of £5,065. During the penal times a number of Gaelic Roes are recorded as being transplanted to various parts of the country.

In about 1717, **George Roe** was nominated Mayor of Dublin, and in the eighteenth century two Roe brothers, **John** and **Peter**, were busy surveying and mapping properties.

Many Roes graduated from Trinity

College Dublin with distinction. **Reverend Peter Roe** (1778–1842) was a famous preacher, **Reverend Richard Roe** (1765–1853) pioneered stenography, and **George Hamilton Roe** (1795–1873) became a leading London physician.

Samuel Black Roe (1830–1913), an army surgeon, was twice sheriff of his native Cavan.

Dr. William Roe (1841–92) of Galway was a member of the great distiller families of Dublin—Power, Jameson and Roe, who used their great fortune to restore Christ Church Cathedral in Dublin, as the Guinnesses did for St. Patrick's Cathedral.

Rogers

Mac Ruaidhrí

Rodgers MacCrory MacRory

This name goes back to the Vikings, to the Norse Hrothrekr, Roric of the Domesday Book, anglicized to Rory, Roderick and Roger.

In Ireland, Rogers is the name of two different septs, one of which were the Mac Ruaidhrí, who were chiefs in County Tyrone and hereditary administrators of Church property at Ballynascreen in County Derry. The other sept came to Ireland from Scotland in the fourteenth century as mercenary soldiers. There were also several Rogers among the Cromwellian soldiers who disbanded to settle in Ulster. Today, Rogers, Rodgers and MacRory are far more numerous in Ulster than elsewhere in Ireland.

Cardinal MacRory (1861–1945) was of the Ballynascreen sept in County Derry.

William Robert Rodgers (1910–69) of Belfast was a poet and, for a while, a Presbyterian minister in Armagh, until 1946, when he left to join the BBC as a producer and scriptwriter. He became immensely popular as presenter of Irish literary programmes and was elected to the Irish Academy of Letters.

"Bill" Rodgers was poet-in-residence in a California college and his sparkling wit made him into a well-known television personality. When he died he was greatly mourned.

Terry Rogers, who was born in Dublin in 1928, is a flamboyant character who has developed his turf accountancy business into a large enterprise. He is also a poker player of international renown.

MacCrory and MacGrory are other variations of this Northern Ireland name.

Rohan

Ó Robhacháin

In earliest days there were several ecclesiastics of this name. They were attached to the monasteries at Swords in County Dublin and Lismore in County Waterford. In the sixteenth and seventeenth centuries, the Ó Robhacháins were stewards to the O Gradys in County Clare.

In archival correspondence from **Sir Denis O Roughan**—who must have accepted the established Church to acquire his title—he insisted that the various governors Queen Elizabeth had appointed to Ireland were traitors, while others were not active enough in prosecuting Sir John Perrot, the lord deputy for Ireland. Sir Denis O Roughan's information was found to be untrue, but Sir John Perrot still lost his head in the Tower of London.

In the seventeenth century, the Rohans owned a number of fine houses in Munster, including Thomastown Castle in Golden, County Tipperary. In this grand house (now a ruin) Father Theobald Mathew, who was to become a priest and the "Apostle of Temperance", was reared. He was a relative of the famous Huguenot de Rohan family of Brittany, one of whom, **Louis William de Rohan Chabot**, had an estate at Thurles in County Tipperary.

The Genealogical Office has a copy attested by the British envoy at St. Petersburg of the Bull by **Frater Emmanuel de Rohan** admitting Anthony O Hara to the order of Malta in 1790.

In Dublin and throughout Munster, a large family of Rohans are involved in the construction and development industry.

Rooke *see* (O) Rourke

Rooney

Ó Ruanaidh

This numerous Irish surname originates from the name Ó Ruanaidh, which in English means descendant of the hero. They were a sept of Dromane in County Down. Despite tribal warfare and colonial conquest, they increased and spread throughout the whole of Ireland.

Felix Ó Ruanaidh, an archbishop of Tuam, quarrelled with the O Conor ruler of Connacht who put him into prison. He resigned from his bishopric and retreated to a monastery, where he died in 1079.

There has been a continuing line of Rooney poets. **Ceallach Ó Ruanaidh** (d. 1079) was known as the chief poet of Ireland, while **Eoin Ó Ruanaidh** (d. 1376) was chief poet to the MacGuinnesses of Iveagh. Several centuries later, across the Atlantic, **John Jerome Rooney** was regarded as an Irish-American Catholic poet.

William Rooney (1872–1901), who was born in Dublin, was a poet and Gaelic revivalist. With Arthur Griffith, he was one of the founders of the *United Irishman Journal.*

Philip Rooney (1907–1962) of Sligo began a career in banking but had to abandon it because of ill health. He worked the rest of his life as a journalist, novelist and radio and television scriptwriter. His most renowned novel, published in 1944, was *Captain Boycott*, which was made into a film.

Rooney's Island in County Donegal is a reminder of the family's Ulster origins.

(O) Rourke

Ó Ruairc

Roark Rooke Rorke

The O Rourkes came with the Norsemen from Scandinavia, and they probably descend from one of the Norse leaders, Hrothrekr, whose name was gaelicized to Ruairc. They dominated counties Cavan and Leitrim, where Dromahair, close to Lough Gill, was their headquarters. They were styled Lords of Breffny. Of nineteen chieftains all named Tiernan the most memorable was the twelfth-century **Tiernan O Rourke** (d. 1172) who followed the family tradition of territorial warfare.

While he was away fighting, his wife Dervorgilla was abducted by Dermot MacMurrough (*see* Kavanagh), King of Leinster. They were both in their forties and, two years later, when their passion had cooled, she returned to her father and built a church at Clonmacnoise. The vengeful Tiernan allied himself with the O Conor King of Connacht to prevent Dermot from achieving his ambition of becoming high king of Ireland. Dermot went to England to enlist the aid of the king, and this sparked off the Anglo-Norman invasion.

In Elizabethan times, **Sir Brian O Rourke** accepted a title in 1578 but soon lost faith in the English and changed his allegiance. For his courage and humanity in looking after the sailors who came ashore from the wreck of the Spanish Armada he was executed at Tyburn in 1591.

Several O Rourkes were bishops of Killala, including one who had been chaplain at the Austrian court, where many O Rourkes had achieved high positions when they were forced to leave Ireland after the confiscation of their lands. They served in the Irish brigades in many European armies. In the eighteenth century, **Count Iosif Kornilievich O Rourke** helped to drive Napoleon out of Russia. He was one of a number of high-ranking officers in the service of the Tsars. Countess Tarnovska, who was an O Rourke born in Kiev, was the central figure in a notorious trial held in Venice in 1910 when she was accused of murdering her husband.

Many O Rourkes are still in Russia and Poland. One was known as the "Irish Bishop of Danzig" because of his great interest in his family origins.

The O Rourkes are not only numerous in Ireland but also in the USA and Australia.

Ruderry *see* Knight

Russell

Russell, which was originally a French name meaning red-haired, is numerous in England as well as Ireland, where it is also thought to have originated with the Huguenots. Earlier, the Russells who came with the Anglo-Normans settled in Downpatrick in Northern Ireland, where the name is most numerous.

For centuries, the Russells were sheriffs of Limerick. At one time this family owned Bunratty Castle, famous today for its medieval banquets.

The **Reverend Patrick Russell** (1629–92) of Swords in County Dublin was the Roman Catholic Archbishop of Dublin. **Thomas Russell** of Mallow in County Cork was a prominent Ulster Protestant who joined the United Irishmen.

In the sixteenth century, **Sir William Russell** was lord deputy of Ireland and his journals, preserved in the National Library, give a vivid account of his travels throughout the country.

During the French Revolution in Paris **William Russell** saved the Countess Letellier from the guillotine by marrying her. Their descendants still live in Toulouse. Since the eighteenth century many representatives of this Russell family, once of Bunratty, have emigrated to South Africa, Argentina, Brazil and New Zealand.

Reverend Charles Russell (1812–80) was president of Maynooth College. His sister, **Katherine Russell**, was a member of the Sisters of Mercy in America. His nephew, the famous **Charles, Lord Russell** of Killowen, was principle defence counsel for the Irish nationalist leader, Charles Stewart Parnell.

George "AE" Russell (1867–1935) was a man of many parts—poet, painter and economist. He came from Armagh and died in London. His wife, **Violet Russell**, published stories of the legendary Finn cycle.

William Howard Russell (1821–1907), born in Dublin, was a highly respected war correspondent. His vivid and objective reporting of Britain's many colonial wars brought about much-needed reforms in the armed forces.

Several Russells fought in the Irish War of Independence. Prominent among them was **Seán Russell** (1893–1940), the republican chief-of-staff of the IRA who instigated the bombing in England in 1939. He travelled in the USA and in Europe during the Second World War and was being repatriated by a German U-boat when he died at sea.

(O) Ryan

Ó Riain

Mulryan

There could be at least 30,000 Ryans in Ireland alone. Originally their name was Ó Maolriain, which derived from an ancestor called Maolriain (meaning follower of Riain). The name is also believed to mean illustrious. In the thirteenth century they were a powerful sept in counties Tipperary and Limerick, where they were chiefs of Owney.

They have always held high rank in the Church at home and abroad. Two Ryan abbés were guillotined during the French Revolution and a Ryan was chaplain to the American Confederate army. There were Ryan bishops in the United States of America, Canada and Australia. A Ryan priest at the Vatican helped allied prisoners to escape during the Second World War.

They also excelled abroad in other capacities. They had a vice-admiral in the Chilean navy and they also served in the Austrian and Napoleonic armies with distinction. In the eighteenth century they were advisers to the Spanish monarchy, and their descendants remain in Spain to the present day.

In the twentieth century, the Ryans of Wexford have been prominent in government service as well as politics and there have been a succession of best-selling Ryan writers.

For generations, the family of **Thady Ryan** and his Scarteen Hounds have been putting County Limerick on the international fox-hunting map.

Strangely, the animals represented on their crest and coat of arms are griffins. Their motto is "Death before dishonour".

O Mulryan and O Ryan are rarely found today.

S

Sandys *see* (O) Shaughnessy

Sarsfield

Sáirséil

There was a **Thomas de Sarsefeld** who was chief standard-bearer to King Henry II when he was in Ireland in 1172, but **Willielmus de Sharisfeld** is the first representative of this surname to be mentioned in the Irish records, in 1252.

There were two branches of the family, one of which has been settled in counties Cork and Limerick since the twelfth century. Another branch were at Lucan in County Dublin and from this family came the eminent **Patrick Sarsfield**, an outstanding figure who came from a remarkably military family. He served in England with King James II and followed him to Ireland, where James was to create him Earl of Lucan. His most famous deed was to destroy King William of Orange's siege train at Ballyneety, County Limerick, in 1690. Following the defeat of the Irish army at the battle of the Boyne, Patrick Sarsfield joined the Irish brigade in France and was killed in Flanders in 1693.

Many members of the Sarsfield family of Killmallock in County Limerick served in the French army. **Chevalier Colonel Sarsfield** (b. 1736) followed the most unusual course by transferring his allegiance to the French revolutionaries. **Claude Comte de Sarsfield** (1718–89) was a field marshal. A Sarsfield family from Doolin in County Clare had five of their six sons serving in the French army.

Sarsfields from Killmallock settled in Nantes in 1653, where they went into commerce. Sarsfields also served in Spain.

Many records in France, and in Ireland, including books, pamphlets and histories, record the dynamic Sarsfields. Sarsfield's Rock near Ballyneety commemorates Patrick Sarsfield's famous defeat of the English armies and there is a Sarsfieldstown in County Meath. It was not Saint Patrick, but Patrick Sarsfield, who set the fashion for so many Irish parents to give their sons the name Patrick.

Scanlan

Ó Scannláin Mac Scannláin

In earlier times there were two distinct Scanlan septs: Ó Scannláin of Munster and Mac Scannláin of Louth. The name comes from Scanlan, a diminutive of Scannal, which was a first name. In due course the O and the Mac were lost and the Scanlans dispersed all over Ireland, leaving their mark on Ballymascanlan near Dundalk and a host of other townlands throughout the country, not forgetting Scanlansland and Scanlan's Island.

There were branches of this family in Sligo, Galway, Cork and Fermanagh.

However, by the end of the sixteenth century they were further scattered by the political upheavals of the time.

In the nineteenth century, the name was made famous by the trial of **John Scanlan** who, with Stephen Sullivan, was charged with the murder of Ellen Hanly, the "Colleen Bawn", who was thought to have been pushed into a lake near Limerick. The murder became the theme of several popular novels, plays and an opera by Dion Boucicault.

There were a number of distinguished Scanlan clergy, including **Patrick O Scanlan**, who was Bishop of Armagh from 1262 to 1272. **James Donald Scanlan** was Bishop of Cyme and coadjutor Bishop of Dunkeld in Scotland. Another Bishop of Dunkeld, **James Donald Scanlan** (b. 1899), was a vicar delegate to the US forces in Britain. **Dr. Lawrence Scanlan** (1843–1915) was Bishop of Salt Lake City.

Also in America, there were many Scanlans serving with the Irish-American brigades between 1861 and 1865, and there were also a number of minor authors, poets and songwriters.

Scott

There is no Irish equivalent of this British name, which is very numerous in Ireland today, concentrated mainly in Ulster and County Dublin.

According to the Salisbury manuscripts, an "**E. Scott** was recommended for service under Essex in Ireland in 1598". Less than a hundred years later, there is an order for a "**W. Scott** to be arrested for taking undue fees at the Custom House".

The Scotts are well recorded for their military and academic prowess, some even serving on the side of the Jacobite King James II and following him to exile in France. For this they had their lands confiscated, while other Scotts who were faithful to the English Crown were awarded lands which had been confiscated.

Until the title fell into abeyance in 1935, the earls of Clonmel whose seat was Bishop's Court in Straffan, County Kildare, were probably the most distinguished of the Scott families. **Captain Thomas Scott**, according to *Burke's Peerage*, "Having been bred to the Bar graduated from solicitor to attorney-general, prime serjeant of Ireland and chief justice". In 1784 he was created Baron Clonmel. In the National Library of Ireland there is an unsorted collection of the Clonmel (Scott) papers.

The Belfast Public Records Office holds a pedigree of the Scotts of Enniskillen dating from 1731 to 1880. The Genealogical Office in Dublin has a confirmation of arms to John Scott of Donegal and his great-grandson, **George Cole Scott** of Richmond, Virginia, USA.

In the twentieth century, **Michael Scott** of Kerry and Dublin was one of the leading architects in Ireland.

Senior

Seanor Saynor Syner

Senior is essentially an English name. It came originally from the French *seigneur* (lord) and the Latin *senior* (older, or greater). In France, Seigneur is often found as a surname. In English the variants Senier, Seanor, Saynor and Syner all mean the older of two or more persons with the same first name.

Various forms of the name Senior have been in Yorkshire since the thirteenth century, when John became such a popular name, even among brothers, that this name was used to distinguish either the father or the eldest son.

There is such meagre reference to

Senior in the Irish records it would seem they did not settle in Ireland until the last century. Representatives of the name are mostly to be found in Belfast, Dublin and the Midlands.

Shanahan

Ó Seanacháin

Shanahan, which in Munster has sometimes been anglicized to Shannon, has nothing to do with the mighty river. The Shanahans, who were an ancient sept of the Dalcassians of Clare, were descendants of Seanacháin, which derives from the diminutive of the Irish word *sean*, meaning old or wise. Until the fourteenth century they were chieftains in east Clare, until the O Briens and the MacNamaras drove them south to Waterford. Shanahan is a very numerous name, especially in the south of Ireland.

In the nineteenth century, **J. F. Shanahan** was Bishop of Harrisburg in Philadelphia.

Joseph Shanahan (1871–1943) of Tipperary was with the Holy Ghost order and volunteered for the missions, spending thirty years in southern Nigeria, where he built many schools and hospitals and was a most energetic promoter of education. For many years he was on the Education Advisory Council set up in 1906 by the British colonial authorities. He also helped to found an order of missionary sisters of the Holy Rosary in Killeshandra, County Cavan.

In the medical world, a number of Shanahan physicians have advanced the horizons of medical science and the treatment of disease.

Shanley

Mac Seanlaoich

The common surname Shanley was originally Mac Seanlaoich, meaning the old hero. In the Middle Ages they were prominent in their territories of County Leitrim and Roscommon.

In 1404, **Donnachy MacShanley** is described as "a wealthy farmer of Corcoachlann", his father, **Murray MacShanley**, being "a servant of the tribute to the King of Connacht". All too often they were at war with their more powerful neighbours, the MacRannells, who "destroyed their dwellings by fire and slew several of their leading men". Following the imposition of the penal laws in the seventeenth century, many went abroad.

In the Genealogical Office in Dublin there is a genealogy and a copy of the coat of arms of the Shanley family of Dromod in County Leitrim dating from *c.*1800 to 1900.

There were three Shanley officers fighting with O Gara's Regiment in the army of King James II at the battle of the Boyne. They were later outlawed as Jacobites. Around this time, in 1689, **William Shanly** was a Member of Parliament for Jamestown in County Roscommon. Following the defeat at the Boyne the Shanleys followed the general exodus of Irish exiles to Europe. **Michel Shanly** was a captain in the Irish brigade in France in 1750.

Timothy Shanly was a captain in the Irish-American brigade during the American Civil War.

Early in the nineteenth century, the Shanleys of The Abbey in Stradbally, County Laois, sailed for Canada with their young family. One son, **Walter Shanley** (1817–79), a civil engineer, became a general manager of the Grand Trunk Railway and sat in the Canadian Legislative Assembly and the House of Commons. His brother **Francis** (1820–

82), also an engineer, published his memoirs. Another brother, **Charles Dawson Shanley**, was a Canadian poet.

Also in the famine-stricken mid-1800s, members of another Shanley family left County Longford for Australia and the USA, many settling eventually in Argentina, where they are still numerous, particularly in Buenos Aires.

Shannon

Ó Seanáin

Shannon has been described as "a scattered surname with many variations". It derives from a diminutive of *sean*, meaning old or wise. The Gaelic Ó Seanáin means son of the follower of St. Senan. There was a Dalcassian Ó Seanáin sept whose territory lay between Bodyke and Feakle in County Clare. In 1318 they were dispossessed by the MacNamaras.

The surname is numerous in all the provinces, most particularly in Ulster. It has no connection with the River Shannon, nor has it anything to do with the earls of Shannon, who are of the family of Boyle in County Cork. Shannon could also be a variation of Shanahan, the middle "*h*" being suppressed owing to the English tendency to drop their aitches!

Edward Shannon (*c.*1790–1860) of Galway was a poet whose verse was so similar to that of Byron they were often confused by the critics.

Wilson Shannon (1802–77), a lawyer and diplomat, was a governor of Ohio.

Charles Shannon (1863–1937), a London portrait painter, is thought to have had Irish origins.

In the Public Records Office in Belfast there is a record dated 1698 of the leasing of a tenement in Antrim town by Lord Masserene to **S. Shannon**. In the Genealogical Office in Dublin there is a confirmation of arms, dated 1957, to the descendants of **Thomas Shannon** of Craggaknock House in County Clare and to his grandson of Bolton, Lancashire. There are also Shannon papers in the care of a firm of Dublin solicitors of the same name.

Cathal O Shannon (1889–1969) of County Antrim was a leading trade unionist and a very active nationalist and journalist. He spent several periods in English gaols because of his writings and activities during the struggle for Home Rule.

Sharkey

Ó Searcaigh

Starkie

This surname, which was originally from County Tyrone, derives from the Irish word *searcach*, meaning loving or darling.

In the 1720s, **Seamus O Sharkey**, a Gaelic poet of the old Irish school of poets, wrote a love poem based on his name (darling)!

In the Genealogical Office in Dublin there is a copy of a confirmation of arms dated 1837 granted to **Richard Fortescue Sharkey** (alias Starkey), who was a barrister and a Member of Parliament in the city of Dublin.

During the typhus fever epidemic in Cork in 1816 to 1817, a local physician, **Dr. Patrick Sharkey**, wrote very knowledgably about the disease, its cause and treatment.

Reverend Patrick A. Sharkey wrote a travel book, *The Heart of Ireland*, and also a life of Saint Brigid, *The Lily of Erin*, which was published in New York in 1921. In the 1950s **Nora M. Sharkey** wrote sheet music for popular folk songs.

Sheamus Ó Searcaigh (1887–1965), who was born in Donegal and educated at Queen's University in Belfast, was a lecturer in the department of Celtic studies at University College Dublin and also at Maynooth College. He wrote many stories and biographies in the Irish language.

In County Tyrone the name has sometimes been transformed to Starkie.

Sharman *see* Sherman

Sharpe

Ó Géaráin

Guerin Sharp

Sharpe, a fairly common name in England, is comparatively rare in Ireland, except in Ulster, where the greatest concentration of Sharpes will be found. It is thought to be an anglicization of Ó Géaráin, a sept of the population group known as the Uí Fiachrach, whose homeland was around Erris in County Mayo.

In the mid-eighteenth century the Sharpes were officers in the English army in Ireland and overseas. A **Captain Christopher Sharpe** is mentioned as being killed "in the Maroon war", which was probably in Jamaica.

The most outstanding representatives of the Sharpe name were a family of ecclesiastical sculptors who, in the nineteenth century, carved numerous monuments in churches all over Ireland. **A. P. Sharpe** made the Celtic cross at Bonn in West Germany which commemorates the unfortunate Judge William Keogh, formerly of Galway and Dublin, who died there by his own hand in 1878.

Evidently some of the Sharpes belonged to the Society of Friends, for there are records of an **Anthony Sharp** who was a Quaker merchant in the Liberties in Dublin, probably in the nineteenth century.

David Sharp was a prolific naturalist writer.

(O) Shaughnessy

Ó Seachnasaigh

Sandys

The O Shaughnessys descend from Daithí, who was the son of Fiachra and who, in *c.* AD 500, was the last pagan king of Ireland. A strong and prosperous sept, their headquarters were at Kiltartan, Kilmacduagh and Gort in south Galway. From the eleventh to the seventeenth century they were recognized chieftains.

The church at Kilmacduagh was founded by St. Colman, and the O Shaughnessy bishop of Kilmacduagh held the saint's crozier. A family heirloom, it was said to have the miraculous property of influencing suspected thieves to surrender stolen property.

Dermot O Shaughnessy (d. 1559) betrayed the Irish cause in favour of Henry VIII, who bestowed a knighthood on him. His son violently opposed the Gaelic order, to the extent that he even slaughtered his own brother. The O Shaughnessy castle at Gort was taken by the O Briens and de Burgos and there were also continuous family feuds, but a later **Sir Dermot O Shaughnessy** (d. 1606) managed to leave 12,600 Irish acres to his son, **Sir Roger**.

Following the battle of the Boyne, **William O Shaughnessy** (d. 1744) joined the Irish brigades in France. He was a lifelong soldier and died a marshal after fifty years service. About 1755, a kinsman, **Roebuck O Shaughnessy**, had to part with the family's Lough Cutra Castle when it was confiscated and given to the Prendergasts, for which, after much legal wrangling, he was given some compensation.

Sir William Brook O Shaughnessy (d. 1889) of Limerick was a surgeon in India, where he also pioneered telegraphy.

An O Shaughnessy poet, **Arthur**, born in London in 1844, is best remembered for his "Ode" ("We are the music makers").

In Australia, **"Big John" O Shanassy** was knighted and became an eminent statesman.

In the USA in the 1920s there must have been an energetic O Shaughnessy engineer in Columbus, Ohio, as the name is remembered in the O Shaughnessy Dam on the River Scioto.

The name is still very plentiful around Galway and Limerick, to which they had later migrated. There, at one time, some changed their name to Sandys.

(O) Shea

Ó Séaghdha

Shee

The name O Shea derives from a personal name which meant dauntless. Originally, the O Sheas were from Kerry where, until the twelfth century, they were lords of Iveragh. In the tenth century they branched out to Tipperary, where **Odanus O Shee** became a great landowner. Another **Odanus**, ten generations later, in the fourteenth century, was styled Lord of Sheesland.

By the fifteenth century they had become important citizens of Kilkenny, the only ancient Irish members of the "Ten Tribes of Kilkenny". **Robert Shee** filled the exalted office of sovereign in 1499. They acquired the prefix Archer through marriage into that important Kilkenny family.

Despite the inroads of twentieth-century developers, Kilkenny has managed to hold on to some remnants of the handsome stone buildings erected by this cultivated family. Though many are now in ruins or have different owners, their tombs and family manors are still adorned with their armorial bearings.

Although the O Sheas survived Cromwell and William of Orange, they were impoverished and many fled to the Continent to become high-ranking officers in the Irish regiments. One became a peer of France, one a grandee of Spain, another a count of Rome. An O Shea fought with Prince Charles at the battle of Culloden.

Sir Martin Archer Shee, born in Dublin in 1769, a portrait painter and writer, was, for twenty years, president of London's Royal Academy.

Daniel Shea, a promising student at Trinity College Dublin, was expelled for refusing to inform on colleagues who were suspected of being members of the United Irishmen. He travelled extensively in the Middle East, becoming an eminent professor of languages and orientalism.

The first Catholic judge since the uprising of 1692 was **Sir William Shee** (1804–68), Member of Parliament for Kilkenny.

Most notorious of the O Sheas was the adventurer **Captain William O Shea**. O Shea's wealthy father had bought him a commission in a fashionable regiment, but balked at paying his bills. O Shea became involved in a number of dubious Spanish business ventures, then went unsuccessfully into Irish politics, with the assistance of Parnell, who by this time was involved with William's wife, **Kitty O Shea**. The O Sheas divorced in 1890, and Kitty married Parnell the following year.

The Dublin-born actor, **Milo O Shea**, who is now based in London, is a well-known face on stage, film and television worldwide.

Jack O Shea, a Cahirciveen plumber and an outstanding sportsman, has won scores of medals and the Kerry Footballer of the Year award.

Shearman *see* Sherman

Shee *see* (O) Shea

Sheehan

Ó Síodhacháin

Sheahan

The Sheehans were an old Dalcassian family, one of a number of leading septs in that part of the country known as Thomond, west of the Shannon. The original Irish name derives from *síodhach*, meaning peaceful.

The branch whose headquarters were centred in Limerick held the office of trumpeters to the powerful O Kellys. The Sheehans today are very numerous, most particularly in Munster and around the West Cork area, with which their name has long been associated.

The name is scarcely found in the records until the nineteenth century, when **John Sheehan** of County Wexford was deputy surveyor of lands. Another **John Sheehan** (1831–53), a journalist, was joint founder of *The Comet*, a nationalist newspaper which campaigned for much-needed land reform. **Richard Sheehan** (1845–1915) was Bishop of Waterford and a contributor to many local journals.

The most outstanding Sheehan was **Canon Patrick Sheehan** (1852–1913), who was born in Mallow. He served as curate in England for a time before returning as parish priest of Doneraile in his native County Cork. He began to note down episodes in the daily life of an Irish priest and this soon expanded into novel writing. His universally popular books, *My New Curate*, *The Blindness of Dr. Gray* and *Glenaar*, are treasured on the bookshelves of many an Irish family at home and abroad.

Dr. Michael Sheehan (1870–1945), who was to become Archbishop of Sydney, Australia, campaigned for the revival of the Irish language. He was instrumental in establishing Ring College in County Waterford, where all teaching is through the medium of the Irish language.

Ronan Sheehan (b. 1953) has made a name as a short story writer and novelist. In 1974 he won the prestigious Hennessy Award for promising young writers.

Sheehy

Mac Síthigh

MacSheehy

This ancient surname comes from the Gaelic word *sítheach*, meaning eerie. Descendants of the Scottish clan MacDonald, the Sheehys came as gallowglasses (mercenary soldiers) to Ireland in the fourteenth century and settled in Limerick, where they served the earls of Desmond near Rathkeale.

With FitzMaurice and the MacSweeneys they were at the sack of Kilmallock in 1570, when it took three days and nights to remove the treasures from the town. During the 1642 uprising they were remembered in Limerick for the savagery with which they treated their prisoners. Later, a **Manus ne Cleggan MacShehe**, a captain of gallowglasses, received £7 15s 6½d "for the head of Mallachy MacClancy, chief of his name, one of O Rourke's allies".

The Sheehys had more illustrious careers in France, where **Dr. John MacSheehy** (1745–1815) was a physician to the French court before the revolution.

His uncle, **Patrick MacSheehy**, who was distinguished in the French army, was killed at the battle of Grenada in 1779. **Chevalier John Desmond Louis MacSheehy** (1783–1867) also held high rank in the French army. **Bernard MacSheehy** (1774–1807) helped to plan Wolfe Tone's French expedition to Ireland. He was aide-de-camp to Napoleon and was killed at the battle of Eylau.

Father Nicholas Sheehy (1728–66), parish priest of Clogheen in County Tipperary, championed much-needed land reform. However, a terrible punishment was exacted for this when he was sentenced to hanging by a perjured court for a murder he could not have committed.

Hanna Sheehy (d. 1946) was co-founder, with her husband, of the Irish Women's Franchise League. Her enlightened husband was Francis Sheehy Skeffington, whose belief in women's rights convinced him to add her name as a prefix to his own. Although he was a pacifist during the 1916 Easter Rising, he was executed by an officer who was later found to be deranged. Hanna Sheehy Skeffington refused the £10,000 offered as compensation for his death by the British government and instead went to the USA to campaign for the Irish cause.

The Sheehy family has been distinguished in recent years by **Judge David Sheehy**, who was a judge of the circuit court for some years from 1974.

Sheridan

Ó Sirideáin

The Sheridan territory was originally in County Cavan, although now they have spread all over Ireland. Their name comes from their only recorded ancient ancestor, Sirideán.

From the seventeenth century, there have been a great number of Sheridans in the Church, both at home and abroad. They were also very partial to the name Thomas, and through every generation they have been a remarkably literary family.

Thomas Sheridan (1687–1738), a friend of the great Dean Swift and a chaplain in Trinity College Dublin, was very absent-minded. Following the death of Queen Anne of England, he preached the sermon, "sufficient unto the day is the evil thereof". For this mighty indiscretion he was accused of Jacobinism and removed from office. His son, also **Thomas**, was an actor-manager in Dublin and London.

His second son was the famous playwright, **Richard Brinsley Sheridan** (1751–1816). Although he lampooned London society with witty plays such as *The School for Scandal* and *The Rivals*, he became a great favourite with audiences, and the Prince Regent was also very fond of him. However, Sheridan was to abandon the world of drama and became a statesman and a Member of Parliament for the next thirty years. Towards the end of his life, he was beset by many disasters. He is buried in Westminster Abbey.

His son, yet another **Thomas** (1775–1817), was the father of **Helen Selena Sheridan**, later Lady Dufferin, who wrote the popular ballad "The Irish Emigrant", which begins with the poignant lines:

I am sitting on the stile Mary,
Where we sat side by side,
On a bright May morning long ago,
When first you were my bride.

Lady Dufferin's daughter, **Caroline**, married George Norton when she was only 19. He was a philanderer and a waster, and she had to write to support herself and her children. She later published a book arguing for the rights of women to hold their own property.

In earlier days there were, of course, military Sheridans. A **Thomas Sheridan** who tutored Prince Charles Stuart also fought by his side at the battle of Culloden. His nephew was a major-general of cavalry with Dillon's Regiment in France. **General Philip Sheridan**'s twenty-mile ride to rally his troops at the decisive battle in the Shenadoah valley has become part of American folklore.

Margaret Burke Sheridan (1889–1958) left Mayo to study singing in Italy. She became one of the leading opera singers in Milan, under the baton of Toscanini.

Sherman

Sharman Shearman

This surname—which can also be spelled Sharman or Shearman—appears in Dublin as early as the thirteenth century. It was an English occupational name: a shearman was a cutter of cloth.

In 1827, **William Sherman** of Stalleen in County Meath was granted a royal licence from the Genealogical Office to bear the name Crawford in addition to his own, in conformity with the will of John Crawford of County Down whose daughter he had married and who had inherited Crawfordsburn, the family estate in County Down.

William Sharman Crawford (1781–1861) was an outstanding politician of his day. He campaigned for Catholic emancipation and for tenants' rights—he had a vast estate himself. He even proposed a federal scheme for the Irish parliament. He and his wife had ten children.

The **Reverend John F. Shearman**, a late nineteenth-century historian, collected the Shearman family papers and deposited them at Maynooth College, County Kildare.

John Sharman was one of the leading teachers of astronomy and geography in the early nineteenth century in Ireland. **Hugh Shearman** was an Ulster historian. At the beginning of this century, **Montague Shearman**, a sports journalist, wrote a history of football.

The name is very much more numerous in England, where it has been adopted by some members of the Jewish faith. **Sir Alfred Sherman**, a journalist, is a member of London's West End Synagogue and of the Council of the Anglo-Jewish Association.

William Tecumseh Sherman (1820–91) was a general during the American Civil War in the USA. He was born in Ohio of a family who had emigrated there in 1634 from England.

Shields

Ó Siadhail

O Sheil

There are a variety of spellings of this distinguished name, which derives from an ancestor called Siadhail. Reputed to be descendants of the famed King Niall of the Nine Hostages, their homelands were originally in Donegal, Derry, Antrim and Down. A branch also settled in Offaly.

Medicine, rather than territorial aggrandisement, was their chosen vocation and, through the generations, they were physicians to many important chieftains.

In the sixteenth century, **Murtagh O Sheil**, their most outstanding physician, looked after the health of the MacCoughlans. Murtagh's was the branch of the family which settled in Offaly, at Ballysheil.

Henry VIII elevated **Connach O Shiel**, who was the abbot of Ballisodare, to the bishopric of Elphin.

An O Sheil family who escaped to the haven of France following the Jacobite defeats in Ireland settled in Nantes, where they integrated with the French aristocracy.

In the eighteenth century there were two distinguished Sheil brothers: **Richard Lalor Sheil**, who was very active in the cause of Catholic emancipation, and **Sir Justin Sheil**, a soldier and diplomat.

James Shields (1800–79) left Tyrone for the USA, where he became a supreme court judge. He was a brigadier-general in the Mexican War, a Senator for Illinois, and he fought on the Unionist side in the American Civil War.

George Shiels (1886–1949) left Antrim for Canada, where he was crippled as a result of a railway accident. Returning to Ireland, confined to his home, he wrote a series of plays, several of which were successfully produced at the Abbey Theatre in Dublin.

Arthur Shields (1896–1970) of Dublin took part in the 1916 Easter Rising and afterwards acted at the Abbey Theatre. Because of poor health he went to California, where he continued acting in films and television. His brother, **William Shields**, was a civil servant when he took up amateur theatricals. He adopted the name Barry Fitzgerald—and became an Oscar-winning star in the USA!

Several biographies and pedigrees have been compiled of the Shields who emigrated to the USA.

Skerett

Huscared Scared

The Huscareds were an aristocratic English family and **Roger Huscared**, a judge, accompanied the Anglo-Normans to Ireland. In 1242, **Robert Huscared** is recorded as holding lands in Connacht.

Walter Huscared and his wife, **Johanna**, were among the founders of the Dominican monastery at Athenry in County Galway.

Gradually the name was reduced to Scared or Skeret. **Richard Scared**, who was the provost of Galway in 1378, owned the Ardboy estates as well as much land in Clare, where he gave the friars some land to build a monastery. Another **Richard Scared** was provost of Galway between 1414 and 1417. From 1476 to 1478, a **John Skeret** filled this important post, while a little earlier, **Nicholas Skeret** had been the collector of customs in Galway and Sligo. The Skerets held the office of mayor of Galway four times and were nine times bailiffs or sheriffs of Galway. They were also members of the Fourteen Tribes of Galway.

Edmund Skerrett, head of the clan, was living in Headfort Castle, Galway, when, in 1652, he was expelled by Cromwell. He was driven out to Foxford in County Mayo and his estates were given to the Hartley St. Georges. In 1688, the family returned to Galway and settled at Ballinduff on Lough Corrib, where they remained until about one hundred and fifty years ago. Other branches of the family were scattered throughout the counties of Galway and Clare.

Nicholas Skerrett was Bishop of Tuam in 1580 and **Mark Skerrett** was its bishop from 1749 until his death in 1782. Several Skerett graves can be found in Loughrea Abbey near Galway.

A deed of 14 November 1808 records the sale of an estate known as Skerrett's in the island of Antigua, West Indies, which included slaves and a list of their names.

There are very few representatives of this once wealthy and essentially Galway family to be found in Ireland today.

Slattery

Ó Slatraigh

O Slattera

Slattery—in Irish, Ó Slatara or Ó Slatraigh—signifies son of Slatara (*slatra* means strong or bold). They were a sept of the ancient Dalcassians of Thomond, an area which included counties Clare and Limerick and the mighty River Shannon. They were supporters of the MacNamaras, who ranked second to the royal O Briens in the Dalcassian hierarchy. The Slatterys played a prominent part at the famous battle of the Abbey in 1317.

In time the sept began to disperse throughout Munster and they must, at one time, have been property owners, for there is a record of **Ellen, John** and **Margaret Slattery** being transplanted to Connacht in the seventeenth century following the Cromwellian wars, probably because they were "papists". The name is very numerous in every county and province, with the exception of Ulster, where there are very few.

Obviously they were a quiet-living people for they have been neither distinguished nor notorious enough to make the headlines.

The most illustrious representative of the name was **Dr. Michael Slattery** (1782–1857), a graduate of Trinity College Dublin. He was president of Maynooth College in County Kildare, where young men were trained for the priesthood. However, he left the college to become Archbishop of Cashel, a post he held for twenty-one years.

Who's Who (1985) records a **Rear-Admiral Sir Matthew Slattery** (b. 1902) of England, whose name suggests Irish origins.

Smith

Mac an Gabhann

MacGowan Smithson Smyth(e)

Smith is the most numerous name in Britain, while in Ireland it holds fifth place. It is easy to understand its prevalence, as for centuries the only means of transport by land was the horse, so there had to be plenty of blacksmiths everywhere! The Irish word gabha means a smith, and Mac an Ghabhann, when anglicized, means son of the smith, whence Smith or Smithson.

From the sixteenth century onwards, hundreds of Smiths from England settled in Ireland. When the laws compelling the Irish to anglicize their names were passed, it became increasingly difficult to disentangle the English Smiths from the Irish Smiths.

The MacGowans (formerly Mac an Ghabhann) were one of the principal septs of County Leitrim. They also populated the borders of counties Donegal and Sligo.

There was also an O Gowan sept of East Ulster, where Ballygowan in County Down commemorates their name, which is now very rare.

Foremost among the families who emigrated and retained their original Irish name were **Samuel MacGowan** (1819–97), a Presbyterian jurist and a USA Confederate soldier, and **James MacGowan** (1841–1912), an outstanding New Zealand statesman.

James Smith (1720–1806), who went to America with his father in 1729, was one of the signatories of the American Declaration of Independence.

Dublin-born **Henry John Stephen Smith** (1826–83), a brilliant mathematician who completed his education at Oxford University, was the foremost authority of his day on the theory of numbers.

Brigadier-General Thomas Smyth

served under Major-General Thomas Francis Meagher in the American Civil War.

Harriet Smithson (1800–54) of Ennis, a promising actress, had a brief success in Paris, where the French composer, Berlioz, fell in love with her and married her. It was for her that he wrote his "Symphonie Fantastique". The marriage, however, only lasted seven years.

Annie P. Smithson (1873–1948) of Dublin was a midwife who covered every district in Ireland. She founded the Irish Nurses' Organisation and retired to become a bestselling novelist.

The Smiths, or Smyths, built many grand houses around Ireland in the eighteenth century, some of which are now in ruins.

To aid identification, some Smiths have added a name to their own, often through marriage: Cusack-Smith, Holroyd-Smith, Nuttall-Smith, Hammond-Smith, Dorman-Smith (O Gowan) and Shaw-Smith are some.

Stagg

Stagg is usually spelled with a double g. It comes originally from England, where it was a favourite nickname for a huntsman, i.e. Nick the Stag, Deer, Roe, Buck, Hart, etc. A very rare surname in Ireland, it has never been translated into Irish.

In the seventeenth century, several officers named Stagg came to Ireland with the armies of the Commonwealth and were granted lands in various parts of the country.

In the middle of the last century, **George Stagg** came over from Sussex to act as butler for the Rutledge family in County Mayo. **Joe Stagg** of County Kildare, the eldest of thirteen, is his eldest grandson, and his brother is **Emmet Stagg**, a politician, county councillor and member of the Labour Party in Dáil Éireann. The Staggs who are now scattered around Ireland are all of this family.

Stapleton

de Stapleton

This is a Norman surname which came to Ireland via England, where there is a village in Yorkshire known as Stapleton. When they came to Ireland, mainly to the area of Kilkenny and Tipperary, some adopted the Irish surname Mac an Ghaill (son of the foreigner).

In 1361, **Thomas Stapiltus**, Lord of Ferten, was allowed by the abbot of Holy Cross "to pass through it with their Ferten horses, carts, carriages, etc.".

James Barry, Viscount Buttevant, granted lands in Munster to **John Stapleton** *c.*1419.

Sir William Stapleton's sixteenth-century ancestors were granted confiscated lands and married into the powerful Butler family of the House of Dunboyne. These Stapletons followed the Catholic Stuarts into exile in France, where they are well recorded in the archives.

Theobald Stapleton (1585–1650) of Kilkenny was a priest in Brussels, where he published the first catechism in Irish to be printed in Roman typeface. In the Vatican archives there are letters written *c.*1682 by **Reverend Doctor Thomas Stapleton** of Louvain University concerning the imprisonment in Ireland of Oliver Plunkett, who was canonized in 1975.

The Stapleton family who live today in County Dublin are included in *Burke's Irish Family Records*, with a special mention of their distinguished son, **Michael Stapleton** (*c.*1747–1839), "the celebrated master builder, architect and stuccoer, called 'the Irish Adam', who was responsible for some of the finest plasterwork in Dublin. Closely associated with Lord Mountjoy in his development of the north side of the city, he built 1 Mountjoy Place for his own residence." His son, **George Stapleton**, was the architect responsible for the decoration of several well-known buildings in Dublin.

Frank Stapleton, born in 1956, currently holds the record for the most goals scored for the Irish international soccer team.

Starkie *see* Sharkey

Stewart

Stiobhard

Stuart

The Stewarts, who came from Scotland, are the most numerous of the non-indigenous names in Ireland, with by far the greatest number in Ulster. The name is descriptive of their one-time office of lord high stewards to the kings of Scotland. Before they arrived as planters in Ulster, there were no Stewarts there.

The Stuart spelling almost always signifies a member of the Catholic religion, and was the spelling used by the doomed Jacobite kings to whom the Gaels were tragically so loyal.

The Stewarts (or Stuarts) are mentioned in all the records or archives. They had many fine castles in Ulster, epitomized by Mount Stewart in County Down, built *c.*1803 by the 1st Marquess of Londonderry. His son, **Robert Stewart** (1769–1822), Viscount Castlereagh, was born in Dublin and sat in the Irish parliament. He introduced a bill for union, which lost Ireland its parliament. He resigned when the king refused the promised Catholic emancipation. Castlereagh was Foreign Secretary at the Congress of Vienna, which ensured the defeat of Napoleon and gave Europe peace for forty years. Overburdened with affairs of state, Castlereagh's mind gave way and he committed suicide.

The magnificent house and garden at Mount Stewart were given recently to the Northern Ireland National Trust, who keep them in excellent condition for the enjoyment and recreation of the public.

James Stuart (1764–1842) of Armagh was the first editor of the *Newry Telegraph* and a very distinguished historical writer.

Francis Stuart, born in Australia in 1902 of Ulster parents, is one of Ireland's most distinguished writers. In 1996, his lifetime achievements were honoured in Ireland by Aosdána.

(O) Sullivan

Ó Súilleabháin

O Sullivan (*súil amháin* means one eye, or possibly hawk-eye) is the third most numerous Irish name. Descending from the third-century King of Munster, Oilioll Olum, the Eoghanacht clan embraced many of the leading families, including the O Sullivans. Originally settled in County Tipperary, they spread into counties Kerry and Cork, where they are now most numerous.

O Sullivan Mór, chieftain of the senior branch of the family, had his stronghold at Kenmare Bay. **Donal O Sullivan Beare** (1560–1618), the next in importance, occupied Dunboy Castle, which guarded Bantry Bay. After the disastrous battle of Kinsale, with hardly a stone of his castle left standing, O Sullivan Beare and his family and retainers made a 200-mile trek north to the safety of O Rourke's hospitality in County Leitrim. Of the original 1,000 who started out, only 35 reached their destination.

Inevitably the O Sullivans joined the exodus to Spain in 1604, where they distinguished themselves in the army and the navy and as scholars. Many O Sullivans contributed richly to literature, beginning with the early Kerry poets and, later, patriot journalists and editors.

An O Sullivan father and son followed the misfortunes of Bonnie Prince Charlie from Scotland to exile in France. Others found careers in the British empire, in the services or as colonial administrators and governors.

The O Sullivans flourished in all their undertakings, whether on building sites and railroads or in the boxing ring. They can boast an honest millionaire and politician, a leading architect and scores of civic leaders who made their homes in the USA. A **General John O Sullivan** (1744–1808) fought in the American War of Independence.

In August 1995, **Sonia O Sullivan** from Cobh in County Cork became the first woman 5000 metres champion of the world when she won a gold medal at Gothenburg in Sweden.

Sutton

de Sutún

Sutton is a toponymic for a Norman family who probably acquired it from one of the several towns of this name in England.

Herbert de Sutton is recorded as coming to Ireland in 1331 during the reign of Edward III. From that time the Suttons were prominent in Wexford and Kildare, where they were attached to the household of the FitzGeralds, the great earls of Kildare.

Until the seventeenth century they were wealthy landowners. At one time, a member of the Sutton family in County Kildare was deputy of Ireland. For their adherence to the Irish cause during the many rebellions in the seventeenth century, they forfeited much of their land and many went abroad.

In about 1770, a **Redmond Sutton** was a lieutenant on a Spanish man-of-war. Suttons were also prominent as officers in the Irish brigades in France, such as the Regiment de Walsh where **Patrice Sutton**, Baron de Clonard (Wexford), was a *colonel d'infanterie* in 1789.

In the library of the Queen's University of Belfast there are forty-six letters written by the famous Donegal poet, William Allingham, to **Henry Sutton** between 1848 and 1862.

Sutton is a numerous name today, especially around Cork, where they feature prominently in the business community. Suttons Coal Merchants Limited are a long-established firm with many local branches.

T

Taaffe

Táth

The Taaffes came from Wales—Taaffe is Welsh for David—and they settled in Louth where, in about 1320, they built Smarmore Castle.

Among the many distinguished Taaffe ecclesiastics, there were two eccentrics. One, **Father James Taaffe**, forged a Papal Bull giving him absolute power as vicar apostolic of all Ireland, but this deception was soon discovered. The other, **Reverend Denis Taaffe** (1753–1813), behaved in such a disorderly fashion that he was defrocked, whereupon he joined the Protestant faith. He fought with the rebels in the 1798 Rebellion and died a Catholic.

As soldiers and European administrators, the Taaffes have been outstanding. Apart from the **1st Viscount Taaffe**, Baron Ballymote, they were always on the side of the rebel Irish. The **2nd Viscount Taaffe**, an army commander in Cromwellian times, had his land forfeited, but had it returned to him with the restoration of the monarchy.

Nicholas, 3rd Viscount Taaffe, and his thirteen sons, all died at the battle of the Boyne mounted on white horses, according to a family tradition. After that tragic battle, the Taaffes migrated to Austria, where they rose rapidly in the army and the Austrian court.

Nicholas, 6th Viscount Taaffe, was a lieutenant-general in the army and a chancellor to the king. He introduced the Irish potato to Silesia. His grandson, **Rudolphus**, was created Count of the Holy Roman Empire by the Empress Maria Theresa.

Eduard, the **11th Viscount Taaffe, Baron Ballymote** and 6th Count of the Holy Roman Empire, was imperial Prime Minister of Austria for fourteen years. The Emperor's son and heir, Prince Rudolph, and his mistress, Marie Vetsera, were found shot dead in what appeared to be a suicide pact in the hunting lodge at Mayerling. The mystery of what had actually taken place has never been solved. All the documents concerning the police investigation were given by the Emperor to Eduard Taaffe, who imposed total secrecy on all succeeding generations of Taaffes.

In the 1930s, his grandson, **Count Edward Taaffe**, came to settle in Ireland. All the Taaffe possessions in Austria and Bohemia were plundered by the Nazis and later the Communists. Count Taaffe was offered huge sums by the press to reveal the secret. However, he died in poverty, having first placed the Austrian papers in the Vatican archives.

The most outstanding Taaffes today are the Taaffe family of County Kildare, who are very successful riders and trainers of thoroughbred horses.

Tamney

Mac an Tiompánaigh

MacAtamney Timoney Timpany

Mac an Tiompánaigh has been anglicized into a great number of variant surnames, including Tamney, Timoney, Timpany, Tenpenny, MacAtamney and Tumpane. Timoney is undoubtedly the most common version of the name to be found today in Ireland. Translated, Mac an Tiompánaigh means son of the timpanist, a player of percussion instruments, probably the kettle drum.

The name in its many variations originated in counties Tyrone, Leitrim and Donegal, where, in about the sixteenth century, **Tadgh Ó Tiománaidhe** was a famous poet. There is a townland called Tamney near Letterkenny in County Donegal.

Seamus Timoney, who was born in Galway in 1926, is the most outstanding member of this widespread family. A professor of engineering at University College Galway, he is an industrial innovator and holds many patents for his inventions, including the Timoney Armoured Personnel Carrier and the Timoney Airport Fire Tender.

Tansey

Mac an Tánaiste

MacTansey

The translation of this ancient Irish surname, Mac an Tánaiste, is son of the tánist, meaning heir presumptive. (The word Tánaiste is used in Irish politics today to denote Deputy Prime Minister.) There would not have been all that many heirs presumptive, which is probably the reason why Tansey—sometimes MacTansey—is comparatively rare.

In the late seventeenth century Mac an Tánaiste was recorded as being one of a number of Irish names in the barony of Corren in County Sligo.

In 1939, **Bernard Tansey**, a minor poet, published a collection of his poems, *A Garden of My Youth.*

Teague *see* Tighe

Teevan

Ó Téimheáin

Teevan is a very rare name. The original Irish version of the name is thought to mean dark grey. It is known to be an Ulster name, though few Teevans are to be found there today. In 1663 they are mentioned in the parish records of County Cavan as being of Errigal Trough.

An O Tewan (an early anglicization of the name) was mentioned as being a tenant of the powerful Maguires in County Fermanagh in 1594.

In the nineteenth century, the Teevans of Enniskillen were owners of large estates in counties Donegal and Fermanagh.

The Genealogical Office in Dublin holds a grant of arms to the descendants of **James Teevan**, son of **John Teevan**, both of Drummullig, County Cavan, and to his eldest son, **John Teevan**, of Croyden in Surrey in 1864.

Tenpenny *see* Tamney

Terry *see* Curley

Tevnane *see* Tynan

(O) Teynane *see* Tynan

Thompson

Mac Tomáis

Thomson

Thompson is comparatively new to Ireland, but it has rapidly become established as the second most numerous non-Irish name, especially in Ulster. When it is spelled Thomson, the name is of Scottish origin.

In the nineteenth century many Thompsons came to the fore as naturalists, scientists, physicians, ecclesiastics and scholars of many kinds.

William Thompson (*c.*1785–1833) was a wealthy landowner in Rosscarbery in County Cork who was distressed by the contrast between his own wealth and the poverty of the people. He became a leading political economist and had a great influence on European socialism, writing many influential books on the subject. He also campaigned for equality between the sexes. His attempt to leave his fortune for the progress of the co-operative movement was thwarted by his heirs-in-law, following twenty-five years of litigation.

William Thompson (1805–52), who was born in Belfast, wrote widely on natural history. One of his most important books was *The Natural History of Ireland.*

William Marcus Thompson (1857–1907) of Derry was a journalist and editor who defended the burgeoning trade union movement.

Sam Thompson (1916-1965) was a shipyard worker in Belfast. From his own working-class experience, he began writing powerful plays which were at first rejected because they were considered dangerously controversial. Eventually, *Over the Bridge* was produced and was a great success. Belfast had never been written about in such a way before, but sadly Sam Thompson died quite unexpectedly.

Alexander Thompson (b. 1936) is assistant professor of the cosmic ray section of the Dublin Institute for Advanced Studies. He has written many academic papers and has earned an international reputation in his field of nuclear science.

Tiernan *see* Kiernan, Tierney

Tierney

Ó Tighearnaigh

Tiernan

The Tierney name means lord (tighearna) and they would probably have been powerful chieftains of their respective territories. In fact there were three Tierney septs, one in Donegal, one in Mayo and another in the Waterford area. In Mayo, the name is synonymous with Tiernan, a far less numerous name.

In the thirteenth and fourteenth centuries, there were two estimable Tierney bishops: **Florence Tierney** of Kilfenora in Galway, and **Cornelius Tierney** of Kerry. In the now Anglican church of St. Nicholas in Galway, there is a Tierney monument dated 1580.

George Tierney, a nineteenth-century Whig politician who was born in Gibraltar, had a reputation for his sarcastic wit. A Member of Parliament in London for many lively years, he was the son of a Limerick Tierney.

Two Limerick brothers of humble origins, **Mathew** (b. 1776) and **Edward Tierney** (b. 1780), educated themselves by their own efforts and attained the highest ranks in medicine and the law. Mathew became physician-in-ordinary to the King, whose life, when he was still Prince Regent, he had saved. Mathew was created a baronet for this and had a lucrative practice in London.

His brother Edward became crown solicitor for Ulster. The brothers married wealthy sisters. Through Mathew's connection with court circles in Brighton, Edward and his family became very friendly with the 4th Earl of Egmont and his family. Egmont appointed him agent for the 101,000 acres of forfeited lands his ancestor, Richard Perceval, had been granted in Munster in 1550. Edward managed them extremely "well", to the point of cruelly expelling the small tenants. The childless Earl of Egmont left his estate to Edward, who left it to his son-in-law when he died.

In 1863, the 5th Earl of Egmont sued for the return of the estates, just eleven months short of the statutory period when they would have passed irrevocably to the Tierney descendants. Egmont consoled them with compensation of £120,000.

Michael Tierney, born in County Galway in 1894, was a professor of classics at Dublin University and a politician. He was vice-chairman of Seanad Éireann until its dissolution in 1944. From 1947 until 1964 he was president of University College Dublin. During this time he campaigned for its removal from the confines of Dublin city to the spacious campus at Belfield, County Dublin, where it is now situated.

Tighe

Ó Taidhg

(Mac)Teague Tigue

Tighe is one of several anglicized forms of the ancient Irish surname Ó Taidhg (*taidhg* means poet). Originally there were four unrelated septs, in Ulster, Leinster (County Meath), Connacht and Munster (counties Limerick and Clare).

Donal MacTaigh of the Ulster sept was Archbishop of Armagh between 1560 and 1562.

Before the Anglo-Norman invasion in the twelfth century, an Ó Taidhg was a chieftain in County Wicklow, prior to being usurped by the mighty O Tooles.

A sept in Connacht was connected to the royal O Conors. In 1228, an Ó Teige is described as chief of the household of the kings of Connacht.

From the Munster sept came **Tadhg Ó Taidhg**, Bishop of Killaloe, who died in 1083. In this area also, in 1307, it is recorded that 30 sheep valued at 8d each were stolen from **John O Tayg**.

In more recent times, the most prominent Tighes have been of a family who came from Market Deeping in England with the Cromwellian armies. **Richard Tighe**, the first to arrive, was the sheriff of Dublin and three times lord mayor. He had many sons who founded a long line of administrators, including sheriffs and politicians.

They were granted much property in Wicklow and Kilkenny. **William Tighe** of Rossana in Wicklow was keeper of records in the Bermingham Tower (the former Genealogical Office) in Dublin and keeper of the Phoenix Park. In 1789, John Wesley made Rossana his base during his tour preaching in Ireland.

The Tighe ladies of Woodstock, County Kilkenny, have left a wealth of interesting letters. They helped the famous "Ladies of Llangollen" to elope to Wales. **Mary Tighe**, a daughter of this house, was a much-admired poet.

William Tighe was one of the most influential men in Ireland in the late eighteenth century and he campaigned strenuously against the Union with Britain.

The Tighes are very numerous throughout the country, except for in Ulster.

Timoney, **Timpany** *see* Tamney

Tinan *see* Tynan

Toal *see* (O) Toole

Toner

Ó Tomhrair

Tonry

Toner—sometimes Tonry—comes from the Norse personal name Tomar, who was a Scandinavian king of Dublin in the tenth century. It was customary when Irish men married women of Norse stock to baptise some of the children with Norse names. Ó Tomhrair (son of Tomar), a most numerous surname throughout Ireland, can be attributed to Irish-Norse origins.

When writing their history of Ireland in the sixteenth century, the monk scribes known as the Four Masters mentioned an Ó Tomhrain priest who was at the abbey of Clonmacnoise in County Offaly when it flourished in the eleventh century.

Patrick Othomyr is described as "an obdurate priest who is reported in 1435 as having for seven years defied a sentence of excommunication"—for what is not mentioned!

John Thomar (or Thomry) was Bishop of Lismore in County Waterford from 1554 to 1565.

In County Donegal there is a church known as Killodonnel which, in fact, was named after a Toner and should be called Killotoner (*kill* means church).

The Ó Tomhrair who were of the Cenél Eoghain—the clan name of the O Neills of Ulster—descend from Niall of the Nine Hostages and are still very numerous in counties Tyrone and Derry.

Toohill *see* (O) Toole

(O) Toole

Ó Tuathail

Toal Tool Toohill Twohill

It was from a tenth-century king of Leinster that the O Tooles (*tuathal* means prosperous) took their name and grew to be one of the dominant septs of Leinster. They were at first settled in Kildare, but fled to Wicklow to avoid the Normans.

Saint Laurence O Toole was their most important representative. When he was only twelve he was captured by Dermot MacMurrough, the king of Leinster, and treated as a slave for several years. When he was finally freed, he joined the monks at Glendalough in County Wicklow and rose to be abbot, aged only 25. He was an energetic administrator and diplomat, and mediated between the Anglo-Normans and the Irish during the next turbulent years. He was canonized in 1220 by Pope Honorius III, and is the patron saint of Dublin.

Castle Kevin was one of the O Toole strongholds in Wicklow. Here, in 1591, **Phelim O Toole** sheltered the young Red Hugh O Donnell on his escape from Dublin Castle.

Rose O Toole was respected both for her beauty and her intelligence. The daughter of a chieftain, she was married to the notorious Fiach MacHugh O Byrne and, while he was away fighting in the wars, she was unanimously appointed his deputy in affairs of state.

Many O Tooles fought at the battle of the Boyne and, later, joined the exodus to France. **Laurence O Toole** (d. 1823) and his eight sons were all in the French army. His eldest son, **Colonel John O Toole**, was the ancestor of the present Count of Limoges. Another son, **Bryan Burrough O Toole**, fought in every war in Europe, the Middle East, the West Indies and Ireland. He returned home to die in his native Wexford.

It was an O Toole who helped Princess Clementina to escape from her disapproving parents in Innsbruck to marry James Stuart, afterwards known as the Old Pretender, in 1719. For this romantic abduction, **Luke O Toole** was decorated by Pope Clement XI. Several O Tooles were later guillotined in Paris during the French Revolution.

There were other O Toole septs, including one in Ulster and another in Connacht, which is probably the one from which **Peter O Toole** of screen and stage fame came.

Toal and Tool are northern variations of the name. Toohill and Twohill are Munster variations.

The O Toole of Fer Tire, the last chieftain of the name, died in 1965.

Toomey *see* Twomey

Townsend

Townshend

The Townsends claim descent from Lodovic, a noble Norman during the reign of Henry I (1068–1135). They originally settled in Norfolk, where they assumed the Townsend surname.

There are no less than ten pages in *Burke's Irish Family Records* concerning the pedigree of a branch of this family who came to Ireland led by **Richard Townsend**, Townsende or Townshend. He was an officer in Cromwell's army and, in 1646, when under the command of Lord Inchiquin (O Brien), he handed over the keys of Cork to Oliver Cromwell. Afterwards the Townsends acquired much land and property, including Castle Townsend. The town of Castletownsend in County Cork remains their main seat to the present day.

Townshend papers from 1735 and deeds relating to the Cork family are with **Mrs. E. Townshend** of Tankardstown in Slane, County Meath. Through the generations, this English family achieved nobility as viscounts and marquesses.

George Townsend, 4th Viscount and 1st Marquess (1724–1807), an experienced brigadier with the English army abroad, was appointed lord lieutenant of Ireland from 1767 until 1772. At first he tried to break the corrupt practices of the government which were carried on by the gentry known as "the undertakers", but unfortunately Townsend's own dissolute habits led to his recall. Among his papers are a collection of letters from guests excusing themselves from dining with him! Townsend Street in Dublin is named after him.

Horatio Townshend (1750–1837) of Ross in County Cork, who was in holy orders, wrote an important book, *A Statistical Survey of County Cork.*

John Sealy Townsend (1868–1957), who was born in Galway, became a professor of physics at Oxford University. He was the first scientist to determine the theory of the ionization of gases.

Derry, a mansion in Rosscarbery in County Cork, was inherited by **Charlotte Frances Payne-Townshend**. She became the wealthy wife of George Bernard Shaw, who promptly sold the mansion.

This surname is not very common in Ireland.

Tully

Mac an Tuile

Flood MacAtilla

MacAtilla, Ó Maoltuile and Mac an Tuile are a few of the variants of this ancient Irish surname. Tuile is the Irish word for flood, and when all things Gaelic were suppressed the name was anglicized to Flood.

The Mac an Tuile or Tullys were originally a medical family and were hereditary physicians to the O Reillys and the O Connors. Tullystown, near Granard in County Longford, commemorates their association with the Breffny O Reillys. They were among the leading families in County Galway in the seventeenth century, when many of them lost their estates and were outlawed.

In the archives there is a letter dated 1684 from the Jacobite Earl of Clanricarde (a Burke of Galway) to Lord Dartmouth (who died in the Tower of London in 1691), asking for employment on behalf of **J. Tully** of Portumna, County Galway.

In the National Archives in Paris there is a copy of a plea from **Marc Tully** who, in 1707, seems to have been arrested in command of a boat from Ireland.

The Tullys must have joined in the flight to Europe following the disastrous battle of the Boyne in 1690. There is a copy of a request from **Mathew Flood** (alias Tully) for a pension from the king of Spain and for his retainer, the Earl of Tirconnell (O Donell).

A nineteenth-century traveller, **Richard Tully**, published a social history of Tripoli, North Africa, written during his ten years' residence there.

George Tully was a dean of Ripon in England from 1820 to 1840.

The Tullys are numerous throughout Ireland, and so are their kindred, the Floods, who have produced a number of distinguished people, including **Henry Flood** (1732–91), statesman, orator and fiery nationalist, and **William Henry Grattan Flood** (1859–1928), a musician and historian of Lismore in County Waterford who published *The History of Irish Music* in 1905.

Tumpane *see* Tamney

Turley *see* Curley

Turner

Turner, which is an occupational name (a locksmith), is a very common name in Great Britain and in Ireland. It is amongst the oldest surnames in Dublin, Wexford and other parts of Munster.

In 1598, a Turner whose family must have risen to landowning status is reported as being one of the principal gentlemen of Ballyhassin.

Samuel Turner (1765–1810), born at Turner's Glen near Newry in County Down, was educated at Trinity College Dublin and joined the United Irishmen. He avoided the 1798 Rebellion by fleeing abroad, but returned afterwards to practise at the Bar and to pose as a patriot. It was only after his death in a duel in the Isle of Man that it was discovered that he had betrayed his associates, for which the government had awarded him a fat pension.

In the mid-nineteenth century, Thomas F. Turner, an architect, was building houses in the Scottish baronial style which was then popular with the gentry. He designed Stormont Castle, the official residence of the Prime Minister of Northern Ireland. The parliament buildings were subsequently built on its estate. He also submitted a design for the O Connell monument in O Connell Street, Dublin. Turner and Gibson designed a "new patent balance rolling bridge", perhaps a forerunner of the Baily bridge?

Many Turners feature in the various army lists. In 1649, at least nine officers served with the Commonwealth army in Ireland.

Captain George L. Turner, who was killed in action, and **Captain James Turner** both served in the Irish-American brigade of the 88th New York Volunteers between 1861 and 1865. Before the First World War, **Sir Alfred Turner** wrote *Sixty Years of a Soldier's Life*, which included many references to the Fenians.

At the beginning of this century, **Charles C. Turner** was writing about aerial navigation.

There are over 50 Turners listed in Who's Who—all living in the UK. Among the more famous is **Dame Eva Turner** (b. 1892), the prima donna. Not listed is the audacious and highly successful pop singer, Tina Turner.

It would be neglectful to omit the most illustrious of all Turners, **Joseph Mallard Turner** (1775–1851). The illiterate son of a London barber, he is recognized today as one of the greatest painters of landscapes and watercolours.

Twohill *see* (O) Toole

Twomey

Ó Tuama

Toomey

Twomey in County Cork or Toomey in County Limerick, this surname means descendant of Tuaim, who was probably an important person in the Dalcassian sept, whose ancient territory covered most of counties Clare, Limerick and Tipperary.

In the seventeenth and eighteenth centuries, a number of Twomeys fought in the armies of King James II.

A pedigree in the Genealogical Office of the Twomeys of Croom in County Limerick relates to a member of the family who was in St. Louis, USA *c.*1677. In 1920 a confirmation of arms was requested for the descendants of **Daniel Thomas Toomey** (d. 1811), son of **Thomas Toomey**, both of Limerick, and great-great-grandsons of **Daniel**, by **Thomas Noxen Toomey**, only son of **Patrick Joseph Toomey** of Bruree, and both of St. Louis, USA.

Sean Ó Tuama (1706–75) of Limerick remains the most outstanding representative of this name. First a school-teacher and then an innkeeper, he was an ardent Gaelic poet. Seeing that the Irish language was fast disappearing, he called a meeting of all the poets of the Maigue valley in County Limerick to see if they could work out a way to keep it alive. Meanwhile, while his wife struggled to keep the inn going, he was so welcoming to all the thirsty poets that, although his head was full of poems, his pockets were soon empty. He ended up having to look after the hens for a Mrs. Quinn to earn his keep—and he wrote some pretty barbed verses about her!

A contemporary namesake of Cork, **Professor Sean Ó Tuama** of University College Cork, is a poet, essayist and distinguished dramatist.

The Twomey/Toomey name is most numerous around Cork and Limerick.

Tynan

Ó Teimhneáin

(O) Teynane Tevnane Tinan

Ó Teimhneáin is a very rare Irish surname which was formerly found mainly in County Laois and also in County Sligo. It derives from teimhneán, meaning dark grey. Through the generations it has taken many variations, including O Teynane, O Tyvnane, O Tinan, Tevnane and Tevna.

An obscure sept, their name would be hard to find, if at all, in any of the usual ancient Gaelic manuscripts and genealogical records. It was not until the late nineteenth century that the name came to the fore with the arrival of **Katharine Tynan** (1861–1931), the poet and novelist. She was born at Clondalkin in County Dublin and, influenced by her father's politics, joined the Ladies' Land League. Even after his fall from grace, she remained a friend of Parnell. One of the leading authors at the time of the Celtic literary revival, her first volume of poetry, published in 1885, was the start of her international reputation. Her output included over 160 books of prose and poetry. Her four volumes of memoirs cover the lives of the major figures in the Ireland of her time. She married another writer, H. A. Hinkson, and their daughter, Pamela Hinkson (1900–82), was a traveller and novelist. One of her books, *The Ladies' Road*, sold 100,000 copies in Penguin paperback.

It is also possible that **Kenneth Tynan**'s family originated from Ireland. He was one of the most influential and controversial British theatre critics, who died in 1980 at the comparatively early age of 53.

Tyrrell

Ciriol

Terrell Tirrell

The Tyrrells came from Normandy to England with William the Conqueror. It has long been presumed, though it was never proved, that one of these English Tyrrells, **Sir James Tyrrell** (d. 1502), murdered the Princes in the Tower of London.

The Terrells or Tirrells came with the Anglo-Normans to Ireland after the eleventh century and were given grants of land in County Westmeath. Hugh Tyrrell was Lord of Castleknock in County Dublin. Castleknock (cnoc means hill) had once been a Danish royal residence. These Tyrrells were styled Barons of Castleknock until that line died out in 1385.

Down the centuries Tyrrells have been prominent in every walk of life. In medieval times, **Hugh Tirrell** filled the post of seneschal of Ulster. However, they did not integrate as much as other Norman families and were regarded as members of the "Old English" Catholic families, taking part in the Catholic Confederation of Kilkenny. They fought against the Cromwellian army and were followers of the doomed Stuart cause. At the battle of the Boyne in 1690 there were at least nine Tyrrell officers in King James II's Irish army.

The town of Tyrrell's Pass in County Westmeath got its name from **Captain Richard Tyrrell**, one of O Neill's commanders in 1597, who won a decisive victory there. **Edward Tyrrell** (1597–1671) was a superior of the Irish College in Paris.

Dr. Patrick Tyrrell, Bishop of Clogher from 1676 to 1688, was a compatriot of Saint Oliver Plunkett.

Professor Robert Yelverton Tyrrell (1844–1914) was a poet and a classical scholar and **Henry J. Tyrrell** was one of the leading surgeons of the nineteenth century.

The Tyrrells have been well recorded in historical journals and they owned many fine houses at one time.

V

Vaughan

Ó Mócháin

Originally from Wales, this surname is derived from fychan, a Welsh word meaning little or small of stature. These Vaughans have been in Ireland since early in the sixteenth century. However, it is also thought that Vaughan can be an anglicization of the Gaelic surname Ó Mócháin or Mahon, meaning that the many Vaughans in Ireland today are predominantly of Irish stock.

There were a number of Vaughans in Cromwell's armies, many of whom were given grants of forfeited land. However, many had the land taken from them again later. A letter dated 1642 from **Bridget Vaughan** complains of her husband, who was "a commander of Lord Cromwell's troops in Northern Ireland and lost all his estates and has received no pay for a long time".

Evan Vaughan, in about 1656, was deputy postmaster of Ireland.

Captain Perkins Vaughan fought for King James at the battle of the Boyne. In 1695, another **Captain Vaughan** and twenty-four other prisoners, both Irish and French, who were captured at sea and brought to Dover, narrowly escaped execution because of threats of reprisal by the king of France.

Lucy Vaughan divorced her husband, **Arthur Vaughan**, in a diocesan court in 1787.

In Dublin's Genealogical Office there are pedigrees relating to the various Vaughans who owned fine mansions in Donegal, Mayo and Offaly, most of which are now in ruins.

The national archives in Madrid record a "**Guilermo Vaughan** de Courtfield y James, a Caballero de Santiago" in 1772.

The Vaughans who built Golden Grove in Brosna, County Offaly, assumed Lloyd as part of their surname.

Waldron

Mac Bhaildrin

Ualdran or Walerand, which originated as a Teutonic name, is recorded in the Domesday Book as a very old English forename. In Irish the name is Mac Bhaildrin, meaning son of little Walter. Another form of the name is De Bhaldraithe.

In Connacht, where the Waldrons are to be found in counties Mayo, Roscommon and Leitrim, they are thought to be a branch of the Costellos, who were once powerful chieftains there.

Many of the English Waldrons came to Ireland at the time of the plantations of Ulster, and they became prominent in County Fermanagh. In the seventeenth century there was a **Sir Richard Waldron**, who was possibly an officer of the English army. In about 1757, **Michael Waldron** had a dispute with the Crown concerning a bond of £1,000 for the high sheriff of County Fermanagh.

They acquired many houses and estates and all are well recorded. Papers dating from 1699 relate to their lands in County Fermanagh, including an estate inherited through a Gilbert Chester, whose wife was an heir of **William Waldron**.

In the Dublin Public Records Office there are many papers relating to the rents on estates which were the property of **Laurence Waldron** between 1854 and 1882. He was of Killenaule, Ballydonough and Templemore, where he had many tenants.

In the National Library in Dublin, there is a manuscript dated 1863 containing religious poetry written in Irish which was copied for a **Father Whaldron**—yet another spelling of the Irish surname.

Strangely enough, although Waldron is a numerous name today in Ireland, there are very few to be found in County Fermanagh.

Walker

tSiúbhail

This Old-English name is of occupational origin. A walker was an old word for a fuller, whose job it was to tread on woollen cloth to cleanse and thicken it. Since the sixteenth century, when they arrived with the armies of the Commonwealth and acquired forfeited land in Ireland, they have become very numerous, especially in Ulster.

In 1601, **Thomas Walker** wrote letters home to England about his adventures in Ireland, where he visited the camp of the Earl of Tyrone. **Abraham, Daniel, Edward, John** and **Josia Walker** are but a few of the Walker officers who served in the army in Ireland in 1649.

Some must later have settled in Ireland and changed their allegiance, for they are recorded as serving with the Irish brigades in France, where a Walker died at the battle of Malplaquet in 1745.

John Walker (1768–1833) was born

in County Roscommon and educated at Trinity College Dublin, where he was ordained in the Church of Ireland. However, he subsequently broke away and founded the "Church of God", first in Dublin and then in London.

William Walker (1870–1918), who was born in Belfast, was a trade unionist. At one time he was acknowledged as an important labour leader, until he fell foul of James Connolly.

The magnificent former FitzGerald castle, The Island in County Waterford, which later became a hotel, was redesigned by the nineteenth-century architect, **Romayne Walker**.

J. C. Walker (1747–1810) was an antiquarian and wrote *Historical Memoires of the Irish Bards*. He also wrote about his visits to the British Ambassador, Sir William Hamilton, and the celebrated Lady Hamilton.

There are many papers in the archives concerning Walker families, including the baronets of Finae, and the Walkers of County Westmeath. There were also **George Walker**, a governor of Derry, **H. Hamilton Walker**, a nineteenth-century land surveyor, **Thomas Walker**, an attorney-general, and a Walker lord mayor of Dublin at the time of Dean Swift.

Wall

de Bhál

The Wall name was originally de Valle (of the valley) when they came to Ireland in the twelfth century with the Anglo-Normans. The Walls have long been a distinguished family, particularly in Munster, where they can boast a variety of achievements, including a trio of medieval bishops and a lord high treasurer of Ireland.

Edmund Wale (1670–1755) was a Gaelic poet.

Lieutenant-General Ricardo Wall (b. 1674), formerly of Kilmallock in County Limerick, filled the important post of minister of war in Spain.

Patrice Viscount Wall, formerly of Carlow, was a noble at the court of King Louis XVI who was murdered in 1787. Many of his kinsmen fought valiantly in the Irish brigades up to the time of the French Revolution. Many Walls are also mentioned at the courts of Russia.

Joseph Wall (1737–1802) was a black sheep who managed to wangle a governorship for himself in Senegal, West Africa. In a drunken brawl he had one of his men flogged to death, but justice caught up with him and he was tried in London and executed.

The outstanding Wall of the twentieth century is **Mervyn Wall**, who was born in Dublin in 1908. A playwright, and short story writer, he is widely acclaimed for his series of humorous novels about an obstreperous monk living in medieval Ireland.

The Walls are very well documented. Hubert Gallwey wrote their history in *The Wall Family in Ireland, 1170–1970*, which was published in Waterford in 1970.

Wallis

Wallace Walsh

Wallis, and its variant, Wallace, comes from the Norman name le Waleis, meaning the Welshman. It is also a synonym for another surname, Walsh. However, Wallace is also the name of a Scottish clan.

Sir Raymond Wallys is recorded as being an attorney in County Kilkenny as early as 1361. In 1644 a grant of arms was made to **Ralph Wallis**, deputy master of the rolls in the city of Dublin. There is also a pedigree of the Wallis (Walsh) family of Castle Walshe in

County Kerry from *c.*1650 to 1769.

In the national archives there are papers belonging to **Jane Wallis** concerning her Dublin property in 1693 and 1694.

In 1695, **Reverend John Wallis** was deciphering letters concerning "Irish spies". He was probably working for the security forces of the day.

The most spectacular Wallace was **William Vincent Wallace** (1812–65), who was born at Waterford, the son of a Scottish regimental bandmaster. Aged only sixteen he became the organist in the cathedral of Thurles. He left that job to play the violin in Dublin, after which began a long saga of worldwide travel, concert performances and unsuccessful business deals. Returning to London, he wrote his first opera, *Maritana*, followed by *Lurline*, both of which were highly successful. He wrote several more operas before he retired to the Pyranees in France, where he ended his days. Wallace was also a composer for the pianoforte.

Walsh

Breathnach

Walshe Welsh

The Walshs have no common ancestor. The name came into use to describe the many people who came to Ireland from Wales with the Anglo-Normans. Naturally they were very numerous, and there are now 24 Walshtowns, as well as the range of Walsh Mountains in Kilkenny. Apart from Kilkenny, they also settled in parts of Laois, Waterford, Wicklow and Dublin. Some became so Irish they changed their name to Breathnach, which is the Irish word for Welsh.

They were a lively people who have been well recorded, earning no less than six entries in *Burke's Landed Gentry of Ireland*. Despite the diversity of their origins, they were remarkably consistent in having a number of ecclesiastics of the Walsh name. From the sixteenth century there has been a long line of Walsh bishops, both Catholic and Protestant.

Nicholas Walsh, Bishop of Ossory, son of the Bishop of Waterford, was killed by a man he had publicly accused of adultery. **Peter Walsh**, a Franciscan friar in the sixteenth century, turned against his fellow Irishmen, and the Church, and was excommunicated.

When Clonmel in County Tipperary was taken by the Cromwellians, the only Walsh left in it was **John Walsh**, legal adviser to Cromwell!

Thomas Walsh, inspired by John Wesley, the founder of Methodism, became one of his most powerful followers and preachers. **John Walsh** was the first Catholic archbishop of Toronto, Canada. **William Walsh** was archbishop of Dublin and the first chancellor of the National University of Ireland.

Antoine Vincent Walsh came from a seafaring Waterford family which had settled in France. He commanded the ship which brought Charles Stuart, the Young Pretender, to Scotland in 1745. He was later chamberlain to the Empress Maria Theresa of Austria. His descendants, the **Counts Walsh de Serrant**, are still in France.

Oliver Walsh, the tenth son of a Kilkenny family, was one of Admiral Nelson's youngest captains at the battles of the Nile and Trafalgar.

There have been a number of distinguished Walsh physicians and writers. **Maurice Walsh** of Kerry wrote a string of bestsellers, one of which, *The Quiet Man*, was turned into a successful film, starring John Wayne.

In the nineteenth century, a number of Walshs emigrated to the USA, where they came to the fore in the law, journalism, commerce and, of course, politics. **Blanche Walsh**, was an actress who played many leading roles in the theatre in America.

Walter *see* Waters

Ward

Mac an Bháird

Ward is a very numerous name both in England and in Ireland, where it is an anglicization of Mac an Bháird, meaing son of the bard. They were a family of hereditary bards, who, in Donegal, served the O Donnells of Tirconnell, where they are commemorated by their headquarters, Lettermacaward near Glenties. In County Galway they served the O Kellys, and Ballymacward near Ballinasloe was named after them.

In the twelfth century, **Maelisa MacAward** was Bishop of Clonfert in County Galway. The first professor of theology at the Irish College of Louvain was the historian, **Hugh Boy Macanuward** (1580–1635) of Lettermacaward. During the seventeenth century, no less than eight of his kinsmen were popular poets.

General Thomas Ward (1749–94) of Dublin went with the Wild Geese to serve in the French army. Despite remaining with the army during and after the revolution, he was, nonetheless, guillotined.

Bernard Ward came from England to settle in Ulster in 1570. A distinguished Ulster family, they had a provost of Trinity College Dublin who later became Bishop of Derry. In 1781, a Ward was created **1st Viscount Bangor**. With his wife, the **Lady Anne**, he built the great mansion, Castleward, in County Down. However, they disagreed over its design, which is why his side of the house is classical while hers is in the Gothic style. A daughter of the family, while visiting the Earl of Ross at Birr Castle, was run over by a steam engine. When the Earl asked the Viscount about collecting her remains, he was told, "You killed her, you keep her." The poor girl was buried at Birr.

On the death of the **6th Viscount** in 1950, Castleward was sold to pay some of the death duties to the Northern Ireland government. It is now extremely well run by the National Trust. The **7th Viscount Bangor** (b. 1905) was a writer who lived in London and was married four times.

Gunnock's in County Meath is the ancestral home of **Laurence James Ward** (b. 1943), the canoeist who represented Ireland in Spain between 1965 and 1967.

Waters

Mac Uaitéir

Walter

The English name Waters has been common in Ireland for at least five hundred years. It has many variations, such as Watter and MacWatters. It is thought that the earlier Waters derived from the first name, Walter, which would have come to Ireland with the Normans in about 1169. Another onslaught of Waters came with the Cromwellian soldiers in the seventeenth century. In fact, there are records of half a dozen Waters who served as officers in Ireland at that time.

Many Waters, no less than the local Irish, suffered in the confiscations and transportations of the seventeenth century.

There was a prosperous family in County Cork whose many branches owned manors and lands. There is a record of a town called Waterstown, in *c.*1583, as well as a Walterstown Castle.

Charles F. Waters was a prolific contributor to the *Irish Monthly* during the 1900s. *A Dash Across Europe* and *Round the World: Letters from a Globe Trotter* are two of his intriguing titles.

In the 1930s, **Eaton W. Waters** of Cork compiled a detailed and illustrated account of his family which runs through seven volumes of the *Cork Historical and Archaeological Society Journal* from 1926 to 1932. There were Waters mayors of Cork and Waters aplenty in the Royal Navy.

The **Reverend John Waters** was president of Holycross College in Clonliffe in 1915. He wrote an article, "The Morality of the Hunger Strike", which drew such a copious correspondence that he followed it later with "The Lawfulness of the Hunger Strike", a topic which has repeatedly been relevant in Ireland.

George F. Waters (b. 1932) was appointed director-general of Radio Telefís Éireann in 1978. He had been an engineer with RTÉ when colour television first appeared in Ireland and he has also been a vice-president of the European Broadcasting Union.

Welsh *see* Walsh

Wheat

Wheat is an English patronymic with obvious agricultural origins. There were Wheats in Walsall in Staffordshire and also in Warwickshire who were of sufficient social standing to be entitled to armorial bearings. There were also Whates or Wheats of Glympton in Oxfordshire who were baronets, but that family finally died out in 1816.

Thomas Wheate of Glympton, who was created a baronet in May 1696, was a grandson of a **William Wheate** who lived during the reign of Charles I (1625–49).

William Wheat of Coventry was a grandson of **Henry Wheat** of Walsall in Gloucestershire. He was the 6th and last baronet of this family and he died unmarried.

Wheat is a very rare name and there have been very few in Ireland.

Wheeler

Wheeler is not a very common surname in Ireland. It is an English occupational name—manufacturing wheels was a very important occupation during the long centuries of horse transport.

One of the first recorded Wheelers in Ireland was **Jonas Wheeler**, who came to Ireland from Oxford in the seventeenth century. On his elevation to Bishop of Ossory in County Kilkenny, he was presented by Queen Elizabeth I with a chalice to mark the occasion.

There were a number of Wheeler officers in the Commonwealth armies during Cromwell's time who were granted confiscated estates in various parts of the country—mostly in the Midlands.

In the Genealogical Office in Dublin there is a pedigree "of Wheelers of Grenan in Queen's County, of Leyrath, Mount Brilliant and Stuncarty in County Kilkenny and of the City of Dublin", dated from *c.*1580 to 1819.

In the eighteenth and nineteenth centuries, a succession of Wheelers were churchmen, high sheriffs and freemen of the city of Dublin.

The most outstanding representative of the Wheeler name was **William Ireland de Courcy Wheeler** (1879–1943), who assumed the name de Courcy from an ancestral heiress. Undeterred by the loss of an eye in his youth, he graduated in medicine from Trinity College Dublin. During the First World War he served as a lieutenant-colonel in Great

Britain and America, and subsequently received a knighthood. From 1923 to 1925 he was president of the Royal College of Surgeons in Ireland. During the Second World War he was a surgeon rear-admiral with the Royal Navy in Scotland.

In *Burke's Irish Family Records* (1976), there is an extensive pedigree of the de Courcy Wheelers of County Kildare.

In the eighteenth century, a descendant of Jonas Wheeler, Richard Wheeler of Leyrath in County Kilkenny, assumed the surname Cuffe on inheriting the Cuffe estates. However, the baronetcy of Wheeler-Cuffe which was created in 1799 is now extinct.

Whelan *see* Hyland

White

de Faoite Mac Faoitigh

MacQuitty MacWhitty Whyte

White, or Whyte, is a very common name in many parts of the world. In Ireland it stems mainly from the "le Whytes" who came to Ireland with the Anglo-Normans. There were also Whites who came from England with the various settlements.

Areas of counties Down and Sligo have been populated by this widespread family, whose name has been converted to MacWhite—or Mac Faoitigh or de Faoite in Irish—and hence to MacQuitty and MacWhitty.

From the thirteenth century, there was a succession of mayors of Limerick of the White family. Many had fine houses in various parts of the country. The Whites are very well recorded in the historical archives and in books written by various branches of the family.

Father James White of County Clare in 1738 compiled a history of Limerick, where there were many distinguished Whites.

Luke White was a Member of Parliament for Longford. A self-made millionaire, he acquired the mansion of Luttrelstown in County Dublin. His son was created **1st Lord Annaly** in 1863.

Field Marshall Sir George Stuart White (1835–1912) of Whitehall, County Antrim, won the Victoria Cross in the Afghan Wars and was at the relief of Ladysmith.

Terence de Vere White (d. 1994), who came from an old family of Limerick and Tipperary, was a novelist and short story writer.

James White, a Dublin art critic, was director of the National Gallery of Ireland from 1964 to 1980. He transformed it from a dull picture museum to a vital and popular centre for art and exhibitions, greatly assisted by Bernard Shaw's legacy.

Variations on the White name include **Grove White** and **Shelswell White**, the family who own the magnificent Bantry House, inherited from the Earl of Bantry, which is open to the public.

see also Kilbane

Whoolahan *see* Houlihan

Whooley *see* Howley

Wigan *see* MacGuigan

Williams

Williams, one of the most common English surnames, means "son of William", which, with John, has competed for first place as the most popular first name for the past eight centuries. The Williams came to Ireland, probably from Wales, and some with Cromwell's armies. They were soon settled throughout Ireland, having received grants of land in lieu of pay.

They are well recorded in Irish national archives, with pedigrees in Belfast and Dublin from 1600 to 1830. A warrant from the Duke of Ormond in 1676 requested that Richard, Earl of Arran, pardon the sheriff of Tipperary for the escape of a criminal called Williams. **Griffith Williams** was Bishop of Ossory in Kilkenny, *c.*1670. In 1691, information was received that **John Williams**, alias Father Welden, was an Irish papist priest.

In the French national archives, **J. Williams** recorded detailed plans for the invasion of Ireland in 1797 by General Hoche and Wolfe Tone.

There were a number of Williams serving in the New York Volunteers during the American Civil War with Meagher's Irish brigade.

Richard D'Alton Williams (1822–62) of Dublin was a natural son of Count d'Alton and Mary Williams, a farmer's daughter. He was a medical doctor, a poet and a Young Irelander and was subsequently acquitted of a treason and felony charge, after which he emigrated to the United States of America.

Charles Williams (1838–1904) of Coleraine, County Derry, wrote one novel and founded the London Press Club.

Williamstown in Carbery, County Kildare, has been a Williams family seat since the eighteenth century.

Daniel Williams was managing director of the old family wine and spirit company of Tullamore in County Offaly. Another family firm, Williams Bakery of Wexford, was founded in 1878 and is now run by **Thomas Williams** (b. 1941).

Winston

Winston is an old English name, both as a surname and as a first name, as with Winston Churchill. It comes from two main sources: a hamlet near Cirencester in Gloucestershire and another hamlet near Barnard Castle in Durham.

The Winstons have been in Ireland since the sixteenth century, but never in great numbers.

There were Winstons in County Waterford from 1573, one of whom was a sheriff in the city of Waterford. A number of them were attainted for being Jacobites and Catholics, thus losing their lands.

The name has also been connected with County Roscommon.

In 1598, **Sir H. Winston** wrote to Sir R. Cecil seeking a regiment for his son, "who has served in Ireland under Lord Burrowes".

A number of retail stores in and around County Dublin and a hotel in Bangor, County Down, display this rare name.

Winters

Mac Giolla Gheimhridh

Winters is a fairly common name, especially in Ulster, where it is more commonly Winter. In County Tyrone, it is a synonym for MacAlivery, a rough approximation of the Irish Mac Giolla Gheimhridh (*geimhreadh* means winter).

However, the name is usually English and came with the Cromwellian army. In lieu of pay, many Winters were rewarded with forfeited lands and property.

The Genealogical Office in Dublin holds a number of Winter pedigrees and deeds relating to various Winter families. There would seem to have been a number of Winters in the naval service. A manuscript of 1577 contains an account written by **G. Wynter** of "a naval matter off Kinsale". In 1580, **Admiral Sir William Winter** described "a siege of Smerwick in County Kerry". There is also a mention of a **Vice-Admiral John Winter**.

O Carroll's castle at Kinnitty in King's County (now Offaly) was granted in 1641 to a **Mr. Winter**, by whom it was held for Charles I.

Dr. Winter, provost of Trinity College Dublin in *c.*1650, wrote to Cromwell asking him "to prevent Bryan Maguire from being transplanted".

In 1825, writing in French, **Lucy Winter** of County Meath wrote a journal of her travels in France. An account of the social history of County Meath between 1795 and 1805 is to be found in the diaries and household accounts kept by **Samuel Winter** of Agher, County Meath.

Wiseman

Although there have been Wisemans in Ireland since the sixteenth century, it is a rare surname and is to be found mostly in the County Cork area.

An English surname, it is interesting to note that thirteenth-century records relating to the Wisemans show that they were all living in the Cambridgeshire and Oxfordshire, seats of the two great English universities!

In Irish archives there is a collection of letters from an **N. Wiseman** "denying that he wrote Lord Shrewsbury's pamphlet on Ireland". This probably refers to Charles, 12th Earl and only Duke of Shrewsbury (1660–1718), who was a lord lieutenant of Ireland. His family name was Talbot and they were hereditary lord stewards of Ireland. These Lords Talbot de Malahide settled in Ireland in 1167. The family is now extinct and their magnificent castle and gardens at Malahide in County Dublin are open to the public.

The most outstanding of the Wisemans was **Nicholas Patrick Stephen Wiseman** (1802–65). He was the son of an Irish family who had settled in Spain, and he was born in Seville and brought up in Waterford. He studied for the priesthood in Rome, where he was, for a while, rector of the college there. In 1850, when the Roman Catholic hierarchy was restored in England, Nicholas Wiseman was appointed a cardinal and was the first Archbishop of Westminster. In 1830, he founded the *Dublin Review*. He also wrote *Fabiola*, a very popular novel about the catacombs of Rome.

Wolfe *see* Woulfe

Woods

Woods is one of the commonest English, Scots or Welsh surnames in Ireland and there are possibly six thousand of the name now living there. It can also derive from a number of Gaelic names, such as O Cuill, a sept of counties Cork and Kerry whose surname was mistranslated from the Irish for wood, *coill.*

Father Patrick Woulfe, one of the experts on surnames, gives a number of ancient variants, such as the Norman de Wode or Void, and admits it is now impossible to distinguish from the many Irish surnames which have been anglicized to Wood or Woods. Many of this name came to Ireland with the Cromwellian soldiers and the name is particularly prominent in Ulster.

The Wood or Woods family is well recorded in the national archives, with records of their properties in Ulster as well as Meath and Dublin. There is mention of **Catherine Woods** of Ballygonly who, at the turn of the century, was prosecuted for a breach of the licensing laws.

Henry Wood was one of the three hundred representatives of the people who sat in the Irish House of Commons in 1797. **Charles Wood** (1866–1926) of Armagh was an outstanding musician. A professor of music at Cambridge, he wrote songs and music for stringed instruments and for the organ. His church music is still played.

Stanley Woods (b. 1903) of Dublin had many successes at home and abroad in Grand Prix motor cycle racing before the Second World War.

Dr. Michael Woods (b. 1935) was Minister of Health and Social Welfare and a Minister of State in a recent Fianna Fáil government in Ireland.

Woulfe

De Bhulbh

Wolfe Wooley Woolfe

Father Patrick Woulfe (d. 1930), a Gaelic scholar, wrote that "Ulf, Wulf, Woulfe, Wofe son of Ulf, is a common personal name among all the Teutonic races . . . and is descriptive of a rapacious disposition."

The name came to Ireland in the twelfth century with the Normans. A branch of the family who settled near Monasterevan in County Kildare were so numerous that a district, Críoch Bhulbhach (Woulfe's Region), was named after them.

There was another Woulfe family in Limerick, and from them came many heroes, including **Father David Woulfe** (1523–78), a Jesuit who, after ordination in Rome, was sent as apostolic delegate to Ireland. Religious persecution was at its height at this time and he was imprisoned and died of malnutrition. A Dominican priest, **James Woulfe**, was hanged following the siege of Limerick in 1651.

General James Wolfe (1727–59), hero of the taking of Quebec, was a godson of **Captain George Woulfe**, whose lands had been confiscated by the Cromwellians. It is interesting to note that they spelled their name differently.

The patriot Theobald Wolfe Tone got his name from **Theobald Wolfe** of Blackhall, County Kildare, with whom he stayed as a child.

Arthur Wolfe (1739–1803) of Kildare was raised to the peerage as Viscount Kilwarden. A vice-chancellor of Trinity College Dublin and a lawyer, he tried to defend the 1798 revolutionaries. However, he was killed by pikemen near Dublin Castle. A kinsman, **Reverend Charles Wolfe** (1791–1823), wrote the famous ode, "The Burial of Sir John Moore".

Stephen Woulfe (1787–1840) from Ennis in County Clare, one of the first Catholic students admitted to Trinity College Dublin, became a judge and a chief baron of the Irish Exchequer.

Forenaughts was for centuries the home of the Wolfes, but has now been sold out of the family.

Wray *see* Crea

By the Same Author

Irish Family Histories

With the study of family history and the search for origins burgeoning in the United States and elsewhere, *Irish Family Histories* will be of interest to all people of Irish descent as well as those interested in Irish history. By organizing over 200 names into 80 groups under one main modern spelling, Ida Grehan both consolidates and expands on the volumes of materials produced by the late Chief Herald of the Genealogical Office in Ireland, Edward MacLysaght.

All the known spellings, past and current, are presented for each group, followed by in-depth material concerning each name's origin, geographical distribution, and information on emigration to America and elsewhere. A kaleidoscope of notable figures having each surname is then documented, from the earliest records to the present. With over two hundred illustrations from sources such as Trinity College and national libraries, *Irish Family Histories* is a picturesque and exciting voyage through Ireland's long history.

Also included is information on how to trace ancestors in Ireland, a short history and chronology of Ireland, an explanation of heraldry by the Chief Herald of the Irish Genealogical Office, and a comprehensive bibliography and surname variations index.

"...indispensable to anyone who is of Irish descent or simply is interested in Irish history. This useful, fascinating book takes readers on an exciting journey through Irish history, through the unique stories of its families." – *The Irish Echo*

1-879373-70-X cloth, $24.95

1-57098-041-1 paper, $16.95